Embrace Chaos, Find Purpose: Series Overview

"Embrace Chaos, Find Purpose" stands as a bold departure from the conventional narratives often found in personal growth literature, such as those presented in "The Secret" and "The Purpose Driven Life." While these books have their unique strengths and have positively impacted many, our book carves out a distinct path in the realm of self-improvement and personal development. Here's how:

Rebellious and Unfiltered Approach: Unlike "The Secret," which focuses on the Law of Attraction and positive thinking, "Embrace Chaos, Find Purpose" adopts a more irreverent and unfiltered tone. It challenges readers to confront life's messiness head-on, embracing chaos as a catalyst for growth rather than seeking to control or simply manifest a different reality.

Active Engagement with Life's Complexities: In contrast to the faith-based and somewhat prescriptive approach of "The Purpose Driven Life," our book emphasizes active engagement with life's complexities. It encourages readers to carve their paths through the chaos of life, fostering a sense of purpose that is deeply personal and evolving.

Celebration of Individuality and Authenticity: "Embrace Chaos, Find Purpose" places a strong emphasis on individuality and authenticity. It diverges from the more general guidelines of "The Purpose Driven Life" and the universal principles of "The Secret" by encouraging readers to find their unique voice and path, even if it means going against societal norms or expectations.

Integration of Resilience and Realism: The book integrates resilience and realism into the journey of personal growth. Unlike "The Secret," which focuses largely on the power of positive thinking and visualization, "Embrace Chaos, Find Purpose" advocates for a balance between optimism and realism, acknowledging the rollercoaster of life's challenges and triumphs.

Holistic and Dynamic Approach to Purpose: Our book offers a more dynamic approach to finding purpose compared to "The Purpose Driven Life." It recognizes that purpose is not a one-size-fits-all concept but a fluid and evolving journey unique to each individual, shaped by their experiences, chaos, and personal revelations.

Confrontation of Difficult Truths: "Embrace Chaos, Find Purpose" doesn't shy away from confronting difficult truths and life's inherent uncertainties, setting it apart from the more comforting and reassuring tones of "The Secret" and "The Purpose Driven Life." It encourages readers to find strength and purpose within life's inherent unpredictability.

Focus on Impactful Actions: The book places a significant emphasis on impactful actions and making a difference in the world. This pragmatic approach contrasts with the more introspective and spiritual journey outlined in "The Purpose Driven Life" and the emphasis on attraction and manifestation in "The Secret."

"Embrace Chaos, Find Purpose" is a unique addition to the realm of personal development literature, offering an audacious, realistic, and deeply personal approach to finding purpose and living authentically amidst life's inevitable chaos, and we hope you'll join us on our journey into the heart of life's complexities.

The "Embrace Chaos, Find Purpose" series, divided into three compelling books, offers a multi-dimensional exploration of personal growth, authenticity, and resilience. Each book, while a standalone work, interconnects to offer a comprehensive guide through the complexities of life. Here's a closer look at each:

Chisel Your Path: Carving Authenticity and Purpose in the Chaos of Life (Book 1):
- **Focus** This book dives into the art of shaping your life amidst chaos. It teaches you how to wield the metaphorical chisel,

carving away distractions and non-essentials to reveal your authentic self.
- **Key Themes**   Prioritizing what matters, embracing authenticity, and navigating life's chaos with intention.
- **Unique Value**   Offers practical tools to actively shape your life's journey, differentiating from the more contemplative approach often found in personal growth books.

Harmony in the Chaos: Cultivating Depth, Balance, and Resonance in Life's Symphony (Book 2):
- **Focus**   This book emphasizes finding harmony in life's complexities. It guides readers on balancing various life aspects, from personal relationships to professional endeavors.
- **Key Themes**   Achieving balance, embracing life's diversity, and cultivating deep and meaningful connections.
- **Unique Value**   Explores the intricate dance of managing life's different facets, offering a nuanced perspective on achieving a harmonious existence.

Orchestrating Impact: Conducting Life's Symphony with Purpose and Resilience (Book 3):
- **Focus**   Centers on making a meaningful impact in the world. This book encourages readers to lead with purpose and build resilience against life's challenges.
- **Key Themes**   Leadership, impact, resilience, and the pursuit of purpose.
- **Unique Value**   Provides a blend of inspirational guidance and practical strategies for creating a lasting impact, both personally and in the wider world.

Single Volume - Embrace Chaos, Find Purpose:
- **Comprehensive Collection**   Combines all three books, offering a complete journey from self-discovery to making an impact.

- **Added Feature**   Includes The Resilient Growth Self-Assessment, a $65 value. This unique tool, accessible via a dynamic app, offers a personalized exploration of resilience. The assessment provides actionable insights for personal development, setting this collection apart from typical self-help books.

The "Embrace Chaos, Find Purpose" series is designed for those who seek a deeper understanding of themselves and their place in the world. It challenges conventional wisdom, encouraging readers to forge their paths and make a meaningful impact. Whether you're navigating personal transformation, striving for balance, or aspiring to influence change, these books provide the tools and insights needed for a journey filled with purpose and authenticity.

Letter from the Author: Dear Rebels, Mavericks, and Seekers of the Unconventional...

In the tumultuous sea of personal growth, there exists a dynamic tapestry woven from the threads of experience, irreverence, and an unyielding commitment to living a life that truly matters. This tapestry, crafted through a journey filled with chaos, challenges, and a healthy dose of rebellion, is not just a collection of ideas; it's an offering, a guide, and an invitation to embark on a journey toward an authentically lived existence.

As we delve into the nuances of giving a fck that matters, navigating the chaos of priorities, and sculpting our lives with purpose, remember that these concepts are not solitary. They're intertwined in a dance, forming the foundation upon which a life well-lived is built. This book is not just a roadmap to personal growth; it's a distillation of a lifetime's worth of fcks given, lessons learned, and moments of unapologetic joy.

This isn't a conventional self-help book. It's a rebellion against the status quo, a celebration of the beautifully messy journey of embracing authenticity, and a guide to navigating the complexities of our ever-changing world with flair, resilience, and an unwavering commitment to personal evolution.

In the crucible of personal growth, one discovers not only the power to shape their narrative but also the profound responsibility that comes with it. It's a journey marked by moments of triumph, as well as moments of introspection and growth. For decades, I've stood at the crossroads of chaos, authenticity, and growth, gleaning insights that have shaped my approach to living a life that matters.

Throughout my own journey, I've been fortunate to witness and participate in pivotal moments of personal history, from the rebellious act of saying no to unnecessary burdens to the liberating embrace of unapologetic joy. These experiences have illuminated the invaluable role of personal growth in times of adversity, reinforcing my belief that genuine growth transcends trends and hinges on the capacity to authentically explore, challenge norms, and adeptly navigate the complexities of our existence.

As we embark on this journey together, I invite you to challenge the expectations, to explore the uncharted territories of your authentic self, and to embrace the chaos and creativity inherent in living authentically. May these pages serve as a compass on your own rebel's journey, guiding you towards a life filled with purpose, passion, and irreverent joy.

With unapologetic rebellion and warm regards,
William R. Stanek

Give a F*ck, Live Well, Embrace Chaos, Find Purpose, Make an Impact

A Liberation Blueprint for Authentic Living

William R. Stanek
Author & Series Creator

Give a F*ck, Live Well, Embrace Chaos, Find Purpose, Make an Impact

A Liberation Blueprint for Authentic Living

Published by Stanek & Associates
in conjunction with
Big Blue Sky Press for Business
www.williamrstanek.com.

Copyright © 2024 William R. Stanek. Seattle, Washington. All rights reserved. Photographs of the author are © HC Stanek. Fine-art photographs and illustrations are © William R. Stanek and were created by the author.

No part of this book may be reproduced, stored in a retrieval system or transmitted in any form or by any means, electronic, mechanical, photocopying, recording, scanning or otherwise, except as permitted by Sections 107 or 108 of the 1976 United States Copyright Act, without the prior written permission of the publisher Requests to the publisher for permission should be sent to the address listed previously.

Stanek & Associates is a trademark of Stanek & Associates and/or its affiliates. All other marks are the property of their respective owners. No association with any real company, organization, person or other named element is intended or should be inferred through use of company names, web site addresses or screens.

This book expresses the views and opinions of the author. The information contained in this book is provided without any express, statutory or implied warranties.

LIMIT OF LIABILITY/DISCLAIMER OF WARRANTY: THE PUBLISHER AND THE AUTHOR MAKE NO REPRESENTATIONS OR WARRANTIES WITH RESPECT TO THE ACCURACY OR COMPLETENESS OF THE CONTENTS OF THIS WORK AND SPECIFICALLY DISCLAIM ALL WARRANTIES, INCLUDING WITHOUT LIMITATION WARRANTIES OF FITNESS FOR A PARTICULAR PURPOSE. NO WARRANTY MAY BE CREATED OR EXTENDD BY SALES OR PROMOTIONAL MATERIALS. THE ADVICE AND DISCUSSION IN THIS BOOK MAY NOT BE SUITABLE FOR EVERY SITUATION. THIS WORK IS SOLD WITH THE UNDERSTANDING THTAT THE PUBLISHER IS NOT ENGAGED IN RENDERING PROFESSIONAL SERVICES AND THAT SHOULD PROFESSIONAL ASSISTANCE BE REQUIRED THE SERVICES OF A COMPETENT PROFESSIONAL SHOULD BE SOUGHT. NEITHER THE PUBLISHERS, AUTHORS, RESELLERS NOR DISTRIBUTORS SHALL BE HELD LIABLE FOR ANY DAMAGES CAUSED OR ALLEGED TO BE CAUSE EITHER DIRECTLY OR INDIRECTLY HEREFROM. THE REFERENCE OF AN ORGANIZATION OR WEBSITE AS A SOURCE

OF FURTHER INFORMATION DOES NOT MEAN THAT THE PUBLISHER OR THE AUTHOR ENDORSES THE INFORMATION THE ORGANIZATION OR WEBSITE MAY PROVIDE OR THE RECOMMENDATIONS IT MAY MAKE. FURTHER, READERS SHOULD BE AWARE THAT WEBSITES LISTED IN THIS BOOK MAY NOT BE AVAILABLE OR MAY HAVE CHANGED SINCE THIS WORK WAS WRITTEN.

Stanek & Associates publishes in a variety of formats, including print, electronic and by print-on-demand. Some materials included with standard print editions may not be included in electronic or print-on-demand editions or vice versa.

Country of First Publication: United States of America.

Cover Design: Creative Designs Ltd.
Editorial Development: Andover Publishing Solutions
Content & Technical Review: L & L Technical Content Services

You can provide feedback related to this book by emailing the author at williamstanek @ aol.com. Please use the <u>name of the book</u> as the subject line.

1st Edition. Version: 1.1.0.0c

Stanek, William.

   Give a F*ck, Live Well, Embrace Chaos, Find Purpose, Make an Impact – A Liberation Blueprint for Authentic Living / William Stanek. — 1st ed.

> **Note**   I may periodically update this text and the edition and version number shown previously will let you know which version you are working with. If there's a specific feature you'd like me to write about, message me on Facebook (http://facebook.com/williamstanekauthor). Please keep in mind readership of this book determines how much time I can dedicate to it.

Table of Contents

Embrace Chaos, Find Purpose: Series Overview 1
Letter from the Author: Dear Rebels, Mavericks, and Seekers of the Unconventional… 7
Table of Contents 15
Acknowledgements: To My Fellow Rebels, Mavericks, and Seekers of Irreverent Wisdom….. 21
Book 1, Chisel Your Path: Carving Authenticity and Purpose in the Chaos of Life... 25
Unmasking the Illusion... 27
The Myth of Giving a F*ck.. 31
F*ck the Status Quo 41
The Realities of F*ck-Giving 47
The Anti-Sugar-Coated-Self-Help Manifesto 53
Life's Dance Floor.. 59
Don't Chase Positivity, Chase Purpose 65
Fck the Noise, Find Your Symphony 71
Raise Your F*cking Banner 77
Navigating the Cosmic Garage Sale..................................... 83
Giving a F*ck That Matters... 93
The Art of Discernment 101
The Lighthouse of Core Values 109
Mastering the F*cking Compass... 115

The Currency of Feels	121
Triaging Life's Challenges	129
The Echo Chamber of Significance	139
Beyond Superficial Echoes	149
The Sculpture of Priorities	157
The Canvas of Time	163
The Symphony of Impact	169
The Legacy of F*ck-Giving	175
The Art of Saying No	181
The Sculptor's Chisel	189
4-Week Action Plan to Chisel Your Path, Embrace Chaos, & Find Purpose	195
Week 1 Action Plan: Unmasking and Embracing Your Authentic Self	197
Week 2 Action Plan: Sculpting Your Path with Core Values and Boundaries	199
Week 3 Action Plan: Amplifying Impact and Legacy	203
Week 4 Action Plan: Living Authentically Every Day	207
Book 2, Harmony in the Chaos: Cultivating Depth, Balance, and Resonance in Life's Symphony	211
The Garden of Priorities	213
The Tapestry of Relationships	221
The Catalyst for Change	225
Beyond the Shallows	229
The Map of Purpose	233
Calibrating Your Moral Compass	237
Avoiding the Temptation of Drift	241
Storms of Distractions	245
Rogue Waves	249

Beyond the Known	255
The Art of Reflection	261
Tools of Wisdom	267
Where Mavericks Reign	271
Weathering Emotional Storms	277
Your Inner Scholar	283
Embrace Your Inner Rebel	287
Liberate Your Choices	291
The Dance of Integrity	297
The F*ck Jar	301
Your Most Potent Sorcery	305
The Comfort Zone	313
The Canvas Isn't Infinite	317
The Procrastination Dragon	325
Purpose is not a Unicorn	331
March Headlong into the Chaos	335
The Busyness Epidemic	339
The Theatre of Judgement	345
The Photoshop Rebellion	349
The Validation Revelation	355
The Eternal Now	359
4-Week Action Plan for Harmony in the Chaos: Cultivating Depth, Balance, and Resonance in Life's Symphony	365
Week 1 Action Plan: Laying Foundations for Harmony	367
Week 2 Action Plan: Deepening Connections and Embracing Change	371
Week 3 Action Plan: Embracing Integrity and Liberating Choices	375

Week 4 Action Plan: Conquering Procrastination and Embracing the Moment 379
Book 3, Orchestrating Impact: Conducting Life's Symphony with Purpose and Resilience 383
6-Week Action Plan for Orchestrating Impact: Conducting Life's Symphony with Purpose and Resilience 385
The Symphony Within 387
The Circus Tent 395
The Messy Threads That Weave Our Lives 399
The Echo Chamber 405
Not Your Grandma's Etiquette Class 409
The Cookie-Cutter Catastrophe 413
Week 1 Action Plan: Diving Deep into Your Symphony 419
The Art of Creative Chaos 423
The Jungle of Human Connection 431
The Unhealthy Connections 437
The Emotional Stock Exchange 445
Forging Your Own Path 451
The Drumbeat You Can't Ignore 457
Week 2 Action Plan: Cultivating Connections and Creative Chaos 463
Where Every Voice is Heard 467
That Dissonant Note 473
Investing in Vintage Experiences 479
Life Without Rose-Tinted Glasses 485
Blind to the Gems 491
No Rehearsed Speeches 495
Week 3 Action Plan: Deepening Authenticity and Embracing the Uncharted 499

The Humble Reminder	503
It Glitters Like the Sun	507
Courageous Self-Expression	513
The Wild, Unrestrained Extravaganza of Life	519
Not Your Grandma's Library	525
The Oracle Within	531
Week 4 Action Plan: Embracing Your Unique Journey and Mastering Balance	535
The Red Button Syndrome	539
The Unsung Hero of Life	543
The Intent Matters	549
The Symphony of Serendipity	555
It's Not About Likes and Emojis	559
Storms Don't Weaken Your Lighthouse	563
Week 5 Action Plan: Deepening Resonance and Strengthening Your Compass	567
Master that Compass Already!	571
The Occasional Cosmic Curveball	577
The Map to Liberation	583
Back to the Garden	587
Unlike Jellyfish Take Aim	593
Life's Balancing Act	599
Reflections for the Journey	603
Building the Relational Tapestry	605
Nurturing Your True Self	606
Week 6 Action Plan: Navigating Uncharted Waters	613
The Resilient Growth Self-Assessment	617
The Unapologetic Revolution of Self-Reflection: Unveiling Paths to Growth	619

    Navigating Life's Complexities 621
    Welcome to the Unapologetic Self-Assessment Blitz! 624
    Instructions for Taking the Assessment 624
    Scoring the Assessments Like a Maestro 627

Unmasking the Scores 629
    Interpreting Your Resilience Scores: The Rebels' Prelude 629
    Very Low: Novice Stage - A Canvas Awaits 631
    Low: Foundational Fierceness Cultivation 634
    Moderate: Crafting a Rebel Fortress 638
    Average: Rocketing Resilience Elevation 643
    Above Average: Resilience Excellence Unleashed 647
    High: Peak Resilience Mastery Strategies 652
    Exceptional: Epic Mastery of Resilience Unveiled 656

Knowing When to Reassess 663
    Achieving a New, Higher Level of Irreverent Resilience 665
    Navigating Diminished Audacity 667

Epilogue: Unleashing the Rebel Within 671

Afterword for the Book: Dear Rebels, Seekers, and Fellow Architects of a Life Well-Lived 675

About the Author: William R. Stanek 677
    Biography 677
    Show Some Irreverent Love 679
    Stay in Touch, Rebel to Rebel: 680
    Artistic Rebellion Unleashed: 680

Acknowledgements: To My Fellow Rebels, Mavericks, and Seekers of Irreverent Wisdom…

Embarking on this wild journey of exploring personal growth and the art of giving a f*ck that matters has been a mind-bending experience, shaped by the chaos and insights gained from a lifetime of navigating the unpredictable landscapes of existence. I want to raise a glass (or a metaphorical rebellious fist) to those who've been a part of this journey with me—you're the only ones who know how truly difficult it was to write this book, and how many years it took to get here.

First off, massive gratitude to those who've dared to challenge the status quo, from the renegades in coffee shops to the audacious souls plotting world domination in their basements. Your trust in my ability to unravel the complexities of life's challenges has been both humbling and empowering. You are the unsung heroes of the revolution, and this book is a nod to your relentless spirit.

To the countless co-conspirators I've had the privilege to share the chaotic dance floor of life with, thank you. Each high-five, each shared glance of "What the f*ck are we doing?" has contributed to the irreverent insights spilled across these pages. Your dedication to embracing the chaos, your refusal to conform, and your wild willingness to dance with innovation have been a raucous source of inspiration.

To my partners in crime, past, and present, thanks for being the co-authors in this saga. Your wisdom, shared over late-night conversations and caffeinated brainstorming sessions, has been the secret sauce that spices up the rebellion. Together, we've birthed ideas, challenged norms, and given life to concepts that refuse to be tamed.

A special shoutout to those rebels who provided feedback, stirred the pot of unconventional thinking, and threw curveballs during the development of this book. Your irreverent perspectives and willingness to dive into the chaos of discussions have been the heartbeat of this rebellious manifesto. This is your book as much as it is mine.

This book is a wild ride through the collective wisdom of rebels, past and present, who have left their mark on the world. It's a tribute to those who've shown that leadership is not about titles but about audacious actions and the impact we leave on the world. It's a celebration of the untamed potential within each of us to lead with purpose, with compassion, and with a commitment to the kind of change that disrupts the ordinary.

Lastly, to my family—thanks for tolerating the madness and standing steadfast in your support. Your belief in me and in the importance of this wild endeavor has been the fuel for the fire. This book bears the imprint of your encouragement as much as it does my own irreverent journey.

With a rebellious salute and deepest gratitude,
Your Irreverent Author,

William R. Stanek

Book 1, Chisel Your Path: Carving Authenticity and Purpose in the Chaos of Life

While the chapters are designed for swift consumption, resist the urge to devour the entire book in a single sitting or even across a fleeting week. Allocate a full day to immerse in each chapter, engaging deeply with the ideas and musings presented. Embrace them closely, get profoundly acquainted, and allow the seeds of rebellion to germinate and flourish within you. This isn't just reading; it's an invitation to a dance with your inner renegade, a step-by-step guide to unlocking the symphony of your potential.

Unmasking the Illusion

Step right up, because you're not just about to read; you're about to unravel the tapestry of your own existence. Our book isn't just a bunch of chapters; it's the opening act of a riveting show where the spotlight is on you. Don't try to gulp down this book in a day or even a week. Ideally, spend a day on each chapter. Dive deep into the concepts and reflections, get fcking intimate with them, and let the rebellion unfold.

Imagine this as the overture to the concert of your life—a pulsating prelude to the symphony of your journey. You're not a mere spectator; you're the headliner, the star attraction in the theater of your own narrative.

So, buckle up for a double feature—because we're not just here to skim the surface; we're diving into the depths of your soul's music. Our book is the chaos and the revelation, the yin and yang that makes the melody of your life so damn irresistible.

As the curtain rises on this adventure, expect the unexpected. It's not a mere introduction; it's an immersion into the extraordinary, where chaos becomes the canvas, revelations are the strokes, and you're the artist creating your unique masterpiece. Thus, a journey that's more fire and brimstone than cotton candy clouds begins. Forget those self-help books peddling rainbows; this is your ticket out of candy land. And guess what? We won't be wading through my life story here—because let's be real, who needs another autobiography disguised as a self-help book? Not you.

Now, don't get it twisted. We won't be mending your deep-seated traumas here; this isn't a magical fix-all clinic. If I had the answers to the colossal struggles some of us carry, I'd probably be chilling on my trillion-dollar yacht right now. Life's a bit like the island of misfit toys, but hey, some of us are carrying gorillas, and others are lugging around the entire freaking Empire State Building.

Me? I'm the one with the Empire State Building on my back, and I get it—the colossal stuff that makes you feel like you're drowning in a sea of... well, you know. If you're here for advice from an emotional twelve-year-old, or someone pretending they live in a perpetual Instagram filter, you might wanna jump ship now. But if you want guidance from someone who's wrestled through the muck and emerged gasping for air—guess what? You just hit the jackpot.

Now, let's set some expectations straight. This book won't magically gift-wrap 24 hours of unending happiness for you. If any book promises that, it's a grade-A bullsh*t peddler. Life is chaos—beautiful, messy chaos. What we're offering here is a compass, a guide, a middle finger to the idea that everything can be perfect all the time.

For some of you, the advice served up here might sprinkle a few hours of joy, satisfaction, or laughter into your day. That's cool—I can live with that, and I hope you can too (I genuinely mean it, by the way). For others, the impact might be grander, stretching into hours on end. Fantastic—we can live with that too, and yeah, I genuinely mean that too.

But remember, this isn't just a book. It's a rebellion, a celebration of keeping it real, and a roadmap to a life that leaves a dent. So fasten your seatbelts, because here at Give a Fck, Live Well, we dive headfirst into the chaos, two-step with authenticity, and throw our fcks where they truly matter.

Throughout this book, we present a rich tapestry of strategies, each woven with care and intent to enrich your life. However, it's essential to recognize that these strategies, numbering in the hundreds, are not all meant to be adopted simultaneously or even by every individual. Our lives are as unique as our fingerprints, and so too should be the application of the advice contained within these pages.

As you explore various practices, reflections, and activities, listen closely to the inner responses they evoke. Does a particular exercise stir a sense of excitement, curiosity, or profound peace within you? Does another feel discordant, uncomfortable in a way that doesn't lead to growth but to unease? These are the cues—your internal applause or silence—that guide you toward what truly resonates.

Choosing what works for you is not a one-time decision but a continuous process of engagement, reflection, and adjustment. It's a dance with life's ever-changing music, requiring you to tune in closely to the shifts in your own inner melody. Some days, you might find solace in the quietude of introspection; on others, you may be drawn to the vibrant energy of connection and learning.

The goal is not to follow a prescribed path to an imagined perfection but to carve out a route that honors your individuality, challenges, aspirations, and joys. It's about creating a life that feels authentically yours, one that celebrates the nuances and textures of your unique existence.

So, as you turn each page and contemplate each practice, do so with an open heart and a curious mind. Embrace what lights you up, what calls to the deepest parts of you, and feel empowered to step past what doesn't. In this journey of self-discovery and growth, your personal resonance is your most reliable guide.

We are merely guides, offering a constellation of possibilities. Let this be your invitation to explore, experiment, and ultimately, embrace the practices that bring harmony to your inner symphony. The world is rich with melodies waiting to be discovered and played. Choose the ones that make your soul sing, and let them guide you toward a life of purpose, resilience, and unending growth. Let the show begin.

The Myth of Giving a F*ck

It's time to pull back the curtain and reveal the smoke and mirrors that have entrapped us. Contrary to popular belief, giving a f*ck doesn't require a heart bleeding with endless emotions. It's not about turning into a saccharine sentimentalist. Instead, it's a surgical precision of emotional investment, choosing what deserves the full orchestra of your feelings.

Imagine your fcks as heavy stones you carry, each engraved with trivial concerns and societal pressures. The myth says you should collect these stones like badges of honor, but the truth is, they burden your journey. Shed them, one by one, and feel the liberation of a lighter load.

Becoming an over-feeler, like a character in a B-grade sci-fi disaster, won't earn you an Oscar for authenticity. It's more likely to lead you to the land of melodrama. Giving a f*ck isn't about drowning in a sea of unchecked emotions; it's about navigating with intention.

Picture this: you're on a hike to nowhere, carrying a backpack filled with rocks of unnecessary concerns. The myth tells you it's necessary baggage. The reality is, it's dead weight, holding you back from the peaks of genuine experiences. Unload that backpack and ascend with purpose.

Society loves to set up smoke and mirrors, creating illusions about what you should give a f*ck about. The myth weaves a narrative that you must care about everything. But, my friend, life isn't a magic show; it's time to see through the illusions and decide where your focus truly belongs.

The myth misses a crucial point—the art of giving a fck is in being selective. It's not a shotgun blast; it's a sniper shot. Precision is the key. Treat your fcks like a limited-edition currency, and spend them on the experiences, relationships, and endeavors that genuinely matter.

Unnecessary fcks act like gravity, pulling you into orbits of insignificance. The myth teaches us that attachment to every passing concern is virtuous. In reality, it's a gravitational pull towards a life cluttered with inconsequentials. Break free from these orbits and let your spirit soar.

The myth often ties giving a f*ck to the relentless pursuit of social validation. It's as if we're riding a never-ending carousel of others' opinions. Break free from this dizzying ride. Your authenticity isn't a ticket you need to validate; it's a journey you undertake for yourself.

One of the myths surrounding giving a f*ck is the fear of being perceived as indifferent. The truth is, indifference is a hollow façade, often worn by those who, deep down, give way too many unnecessary fcks. Embrace the discomfort of being different; it's a sign you're walking your own path.

The myth thrives in the echo chamber of societal fck-giving expectations. It tells you that you should echo the concerns of everyone around you. But here's the revelation: your echo doesn't have to mirror the chorus. Break free, let your voice be heard, and let your fcks be your own.

The myth paints a picture of an emotional whirlpool where giving a fck drags you into endless spirals of concern. In reality, giving a fck is about maintaining your emotional equilibrium. It's the skill of surfing the waves without drowning in the whirlpool.

Navigating the fck-giving quagmire is an art. The myth suggests that getting stuck in the quagmire is inevitable, but the truth is, you can dance on its surface. It's about knowing where to step, choosing your battles, and finding the path with fewer unnecessary fcks.

Giving a f*ck is an exercise in emotional sobriety, not an overindulgence in feelings. The myth glamorizes drowning in emotional excess, but the reality is, emotional clarity comes from knowing when to sip and when to abstain. It's about being sober in a world intoxicated with trivialities.

Contrary to the myth, giving a f*ck isn't a journey of detached indifference. It's about mastering the art of detached attachment. Hold on fiercely to what matters, yet know when to release the grip on what doesn't. It's the dance of holding on and letting go.

The myth might suggest that giving a f*ck is a heavy burden. In truth, it's an empowerment of nonchalant authenticity. It's about wearing your values like a badge, not a burden. When you embrace your authenticity, the weight of unnecessary concerns dissipates.

The myth often lures us into the pitfalls of over-identification, making us believe that every concern is a mirror reflecting our identity. Break free from this hall of mirrors. Your identity isn't a puzzle assembled from every passing concern; it's a mosaic of intentional choices.

One of the grand illusions perpetuated by the myth is the constant need for social comparison. It's as if we're tethered to a never-ending race. Unshackle yourself from these chains. Your journey is unique, and the pace is your own. Comparison is the myth's currency, not yours.

Imagine creating a zone in your life—a sanctuary where unnecessary fcks dare not tread. This is the f*ck-free zone, a haven you curate for what truly matters. The myth might say that such a zone is unattainable, but the truth is, it's a space you craft with intentional choices.

The myth would have you believe that fck-giving is an inescapable destiny. But the reality is, you can transcend the chains of obligatory fcks. It's a journey from fck-giving to fck-liberation, where your choices are dictated by authenticity, not societal expectations.

In the grand finale of unmasking the myth, remember this—the liberation of choice is the true essence of giving a f*ck. It's not an obligation; it's a conscious decision. Break free from the myths that shackle you, and embrace the rebellious art of choosing where your fcks belong.

The myth shattered, the illusions exposed. Now, armed with the truth, let's dive deeper into the realm of selective f*ckery. We're about to turn the tables on everything you thought you knew about giving a f*ck. Before we continue our journey, marinate your thoughts on this reflective rundown:

1. Reflect on the stones of unnecessary worries you're lugging around. Each one is a choice. Which ones are worth your energy? Imagine setting down those that aren't and feeling the freedom of unburdened steps.
2. Consider your emotional investments. Are you scattering your feelings like buckshot or aiming them like a sniper? It's time to get selective, investing deeply in what truly resonates with you.
3. How often are you riding the dizzying ride of social validation? Ponder the strength it takes to step off and walk your own path, unswayed by the opinions of others.
4. Examine your facade of indifference. Is it a shield guarding a trove of misdirected concerns? True indifference isn't about not giving a fck; it's about selectively giving a fck.
5. Your voice doesn't need to echo the chorus around you. Where can you break free from societal expectations and let your unique voice and choices be heard?

6. Think about your emotional balance. Giving a f*ck shouldn't pull you under; it's about surfing the waves of life, maintaining balance amidst the tides of concern.
7. The dance of life involves knowing when to hold on and when to let go. Where in your life do you need to loosen your grip? And what deserves your fierce commitment?
8. Embrace the lightness that comes with authenticity. Reflect on how wearing your values proudly, rather than as a burden, can transform your perspective.
9. Your identity isn't a reflection of every passing concern. Contemplate the pieces of your life's mosaic – which ones truly define you?
10. Imagine a life where you're not constantly measuring up against others. Where can you unshackle yourself from the race of comparison and embrace your unique journey?
11. Envision a sanctuary in your life, free from trivial concerns. How can you create and guard this space for what truly matters?

As we break free from the myths and start to embrace the art of selective fckery, we're not just surviving the chaos; we're crafting a purposeful, authentic life. Let these reflections be your guide as we dive deeper into this rebellious journey. Welcome aboard, it's time to redefine giving a fck on your own terms.

Throughout this journey, we'll dive into the realm of mindfulness. But hey, whether you decide to embrace mindfulness or toss it out the window, that's your call. You're the maestro of your own symphony. So, either tune in and give a f*ck about mindfulness or simply don't; the choice is squarely in your hands.

A daily mindfulness practice involves setting aside a minimum of ten minutes each day to engage in mindfulness or meditation activities. This commitment is a foundational step towards cultivating a deeper sense of presence and awareness in your daily life. Mindfulness practice is about anchoring yourself in the present moment, observing your thoughts, feelings, and sensations without judgment or distraction.

The beautiful thing about mindfulness is its adaptability; it's not a one-size-fits-all kind of deal. You've got options galore. Think of it as your personal mindfulness buffet. You can sit down and dive deep into a classic seated meditation, where the world slows down, and it's just you and your breath, finding peace in the stillness. Or maybe you're the type who finds zen on the move; if so, walking meditation might just be your rhythm. It's all about being fully present with each step, feeling the earth beneath your feet, and turning a simple walk into a tranquil journey.

But hey, mindfulness isn't just about sitting still or walking; it's woven into the fabric of our daily lives. Ever tried mindful eating? It's about savoring each bite, truly tasting your food, and appreciating where it came from—a celebration of the senses and a gratitude practice rolled into one.

And then there's the simplicity of observing your breath—no frills, no special setting needed. It's about tuning in to the rise and fall of your chest, the air moving through your nostrils, and the gentle rhythm that's been with you since the moment you were born. This practice is like coming home to yourself, finding calm in the simplicity of being.

Choose a method that not only resonates with you but also feels like something you can stick with. The key is consistency, not intensity. It's better to spend a few minutes each day in mindful practice than to aim for an hour and end up not doing it at all.

Experiment, explore, and find that sweet spot that makes mindfulness not just a practice but a cherished part of your day.

In a world where our attention is constantly divided between past worries and future anxieties, dedicating time to mindfulness brings us back to the now — the only moment where life truly unfolds. This practice helps in reducing stress, enhancing emotional balance, and improving cognitive focus. By regularly engaging in mindfulness, you train your mind to remain present, thereby enhancing your capacity to appreciate the richness of your immediate experience.

Embarking on the path to mindfulness isn't about overhauling your life overnight or achieving instant Zen. It's about laying down the stepping stones that lead you gently towards a more present, aware, and peaceful existence. Here's how to pave your way, one mindful step at a time:

1. **Choose Your Practice**   Mindfulness can be practiced in various ways, including seated meditation, walking meditation, mindful eating, or simply observing your breath. Choose a method that resonates with you and feels sustainable.
2. **Create a Routine**   Integrating mindfulness into your daily routine ensures consistency. It could be first thing in the morning, during a midday break, or before bedtime. The key is to find a time that works best for you and stick to it.
3. **Set a Timer**   Use a timer to allocate a minimum of ten minutes for your practice. Knowing there's a defined start and end time can help ease the mind into the practice without worrying about duration.
4. **Find a Quiet Space**   Choose a quiet, comfortable space where you're unlikely to be interrupted. This physical

environment supports a mental space conducive to mindfulness.

5. **Adopt a Non-Judgmental Stance**   Approach your thoughts and feelings with curiosity and openness, rather than judgment. Mindfulness is about observing the present state of being without trying to change it.

6. **Use Guided Practices if Needed**   For beginners, guided meditations or mindfulness apps can provide structure and guidance, helping to navigate the initial stages of the practice.

7. **Reflect on Your Experience**   After each session, spend a few moments reflecting on your experience. Notice any shifts in your mood, thoughts, or bodily sensations. This reflection deepens your mindfulness practice and its impact on your life.

Engaging in daily mindfulness practice cultivates a profound shift in how you relate to the world around you. Over time, you may notice:

- **Increased Emotional Resilience**   Enhanced ability to navigate life's ups and downs with grace and equanimity.

- **Improved Concentration**   Better focus and attention in work and personal activities.

- **Greater Self-Awareness**   A deeper understanding of your thought patterns, habits, and behaviors.

- **Enhanced Well-being**   A sense of inner peace and contentment in your daily life.

Mindfulness is not a destination but a journey — a continuous process of coming back to the present moment. By dedicating at least ten minutes a day to this practice, you're not just pausing to catch your breath; you're reorienting your entire being towards a more conscious, present, and fulfilled way of living.

Remember, this isn't just about mindfulness or bust. There are a plethora of paths to finding your zen or cranking up your focus. Think meditation, deep-breathing exercises, journaling, or even the art of doing absolutely nothing in a world that never hits pause. Each one offers a unique route to the same destination: a clearer, more grounded you. Choose your weapon, or don't. After all, in the grand scheme of things, it's all about what resonates with you, what makes you tick, and ultimately, what helps you navigate the beautifully chaotic dance of life.

F*ck the Status Quo

"F*ck the Status Quo" is the rebel's battle cry against the inertia of the ordinary. History is punctuated with the echoes of those who dared to challenge the status quo, igniting revolutions that reshaped the world.

Galileo's f*ck was cosmic. He defied the prevailing belief in a geocentric universe, insisting instead on heliocentrism. In doing so, he challenged not just scientific dogma but the very foundations of societal understanding.

Rosa Parks refused to yield her seat, and in that act of defiance, she gave a monumental f*ck about the basic human right to sit where one pleases. Her quiet rebellion echoed loudly, challenging racial segregation and laying the groundwork for the civil rights movement.

Elon Musk's fck is interplanetary. His vision extends beyond Earth, challenging the accepted limits of human exploration. By giving a fck about making life multi-planetary, he pushes humanity to think beyond its immediate boundaries.

"F*ck the Status Quo" is an anthem for those who dare to be different. It's a call to break free from the shackles of conformity and venture into the uncharted territory of original thought and bold action.

Every echo of nonconformity resonates with a disruptive energy. It's the refusal to accept things as they are, coupled with the audacity to imagine a different reality.

Rebellion against the status quo sends ripples through time. It's not just an act; it's a statement that challenges the comfortable norms and propels society toward progress.

The status quo thrives on complacency. "F*ck the Status Quo" is a declaration against settling for the mediocre, an insistence that innovation and improvement demand a rejection of complacency.

Disrupting the status quo is uncomfortable. It unsettles established norms, questions traditional wisdom, and forces a reevaluation of what is considered 'normal.'

Discontent with the status quo is a potent force for change. It's the inner rebellion that refuses to accept a flawed system and seeks a better, more just, and more equitable alternative.

Challenging the status quo requires courage. It's stepping into the unknown, braving the criticism of the conformists, and standing firm in the belief that a better reality is possible.

Innovation often springs from dissent. Those who give a f*ck about disrupting the status quo are the catalysts for creative revolutions, reshaping industries, societies, and the future itself.

The revolutionaries of history were often unconventional thinkers. They gave a f*ck about ideas that seemed outlandish at the time but paved the way for profound shifts in human understanding.

"F*ck the Status Quo" is a rejection of the chains of conformity. It's an acknowledgment that progress lies outside the comfortable confines of tradition and routine.

Tradition, if unquestioned, can become a force of inertia. Giving a rebellious f*ck means questioning whether the way things have always been done is the way they should continue to be done.

The legacy of nonconformists is etched in the annals of history. It's a testament to the enduring impact of those who were willing to say, "F*ck the Status Quo" and challenge the prevailing norms.

To pioneer change, you must first be willing to challenge what is accepted. "F*ck the Status Quo" is the rallying cry for those who aim not to follow the path but to forge a new one.

The fearless few who give a f*ck about disrupting the status quo become the architects of transformation. They reshape the narrative, redefine possibilities, and leave an indelible mark on the world.

"F*ck the Status Quo" is an invitation to unleash human potential. It's a call for each individual to question, challenge, and contribute to a collective evolution that transcends the limitations of the present.

"F*ck the Status Quo" isn't just about changing the external world; it's also about the revolution within. It's a call to rebel against the self-imposed limitations that hinder personal growth and development.

The call to "F*ck the Status Quo" is ever-present because progress is relentless. It demands a continuous examination of what exists and a courageous willingness to envision what could be.

"F*ck the Status Quo" is an invitation to disrupt, innovate, and challenge the norms that confine growth and progress. It's a declaration that the world can be a better place, and each individual has the power to contribute to that change. Here's a breakdown and action plan to fuel your inner rebel:

- **Recognize the Power of Defiance**   Think of figures like Galileo, Rosa Parks, and Elon Musk. Their defiance reshaped the world. Ask yourself, what prevailing beliefs or norms do you see as ripe for challenge?
- **Embrace Disruptive Energy**   Every act of nonconformity is a step toward progress. Reflect on areas in your life or in society where the status quo needs shaking up. What's your disruptive energy pointing towards?
- **Refuse Complacency**   Complacency is the enemy of innovation. Identify where you've become too comfortable and challenge yourself to seek improvement and growth.
- **Accept Discomfort**   Disrupting norms is uncomfortable. Prepare to question traditional wisdom and be ready for

resistance. Embrace this discomfort as a sign of meaningful change.
- **Cultivate Courage**   Standing against the tide requires bravery. Pinpoint areas where you can show courage in challenging the accepted, even in the face of criticism.
- **Unleash Creativity through Dissent**   Remember, innovation often springs from disagreement. In what areas of your life or work can you bring creative solutions to longstanding problems?
- **Question Tradition**   Take a hard look at traditions in your life. Ask yourself, do they still serve a purpose, or are they just relics of the past? Be ready to forge new paths.
- **Honor the Legacy of Nonconformists**   Draw inspiration from history's revolutionaries. Their legacies remind us that profound shifts often begin with a single, bold idea.
- **Be a Pioneer of Change**   To create a new path, you must first dare to step off the beaten one. Identify one area where you can pioneer change, no matter how small it may seem.
- **Embrace Inner and Outer Revolutions**   Remember, this isn't just about societal change; it's also about personal transformation. Challenge your self-imposed limitations and grow beyond them.
- **Stay Relentless in Progress**   The fight against the status quo is ongoing. Commit to a continuous examination and re-imagination of the world around you.

Action Plan: Unleashing Your Inner Rebel

1. **Identify a Norm to Challenge**   Pick an aspect of your life or a societal norm you believe needs changing. It could be anything from workplace culture to a personal habit.
2. **Educate and Strategize**   Learn about the issue. Understand why the status quo exists and formulate a plan to challenge it effectively.

3. **Consider Building a Coalition:** If you add this step to your plan, find like-minded individuals. Change is more powerful when it's collective. Connect with others who share your vision.
4. **Take Bold Action**   Implement your plan. This could be as simple as starting a new personal routine or as complex as initiating a community project.
5. **Reflect and Adapt**   Observe the impact of your actions. Be ready to adapt your approach based on feedback and results.
6. **Share Your Story**   Inspire others by sharing your journey. Your story can motivate others to question and challenge the status quo in their own lives.
7. **Commit to Continuous Rebellion**   Make challenging the status quo a regular part of your life. Always be on the lookout for areas that need innovation and improvement.

"F*ck the Status Quo" isn't just a section in a book; it's a way of life. It's about being fearless in the face of conformity, daring to dream of a better world, and taking tangible steps to make it a reality. Embrace this call to action, and watch as you transform both the world around you and the world within you. Let's rebel, let's innovate, let's make a damn difference.

The Realities of F*ck-Giving

In the realm of giving a f*ck that matters, unfiltered realities take center stage. It's not a journey paved with constant positivity; it's a rollercoaster ride through the peaks of triumphs and the valleys of challenges.

To give a f*ck that matters is to confront the shadows. It's acknowledging that the pursuit of significance often involves navigating through the dark corners of self-doubt, uncertainty, and fear.

Courage leaves scars. Giving a f*ck that matters means accumulating battle scars—testaments to the struggles faced, challenges overcome, and the relentless pursuit of what truly counts.

In the face of adversity, giving a f*ck becomes an audacious laughter. It's the defiant chuckle that echoes through hardships, declaring resilience in the face of life's unpredictable storms.

Criticism becomes background noise. When you give a f*ck that matters, you develop a resilience that transforms criticism into a mere hum in the symphony of your purpose.

To give a f*ck that matters is to navigate the storm, not avoid it. It's recognizing that life's tempests are inevitable, but in their chaos lies the opportunity for growth and transformation.

Persistence becomes a triumph. Every setback, every moment of doubt, is an opportunity to showcase the tenacity of your f*ck-giving spirit.

Doubt is a gravitational force. Giving a f*ck that matters means defying this force, rising above the doubts that seek to pull you down, and soaring towards your aspirations.

Life's struggles become a symphony. Each note of difficulty contributes to the complex and beautiful composition of a life lived with purpose and resilience.

Resilience is the masterpiece. Giving a f*ck that matters is an art form, and resilience is the brushstroke that turns challenges into opportunities and setbacks into stepping stones.

Imperfections are embraced, not hidden. In the journey of giving a f*ck that matters, the flaws and imperfections become part of the authenticity that defines your unique narrative. Setbacks are reality checks. They punctuate the journey of significance, prompting introspection, redirection, and the recalibration of efforts towards what truly matters.

Laughter becomes a companion in adversity. It's the irreverent response to life's challenges—a declaration that joy can coexist with struggle. Defeat is met with a defiant gesture. Giving a f*ck that matters means flipping the bird at defeat, refusing to be defined by failures, and rising again with renewed vigor.

Triumph echoes louder in the face of adversity. When you give a f*ck that matters, triumph isn't just about personal victories; it's a collective anthem that resonates with the struggles and triumphs of humanity.

To give a f*ck that matters is to be a conqueror. It's facing life's challenges head-on, navigating through the messy, and emerging victorious despite the chaos.

Acceptance becomes a form of wisdom. It's understanding that the path of giving a f*ck that matters is paved with both victories and defeats, and each contributes to the wisdom gained along the way.

Challenges become catalysts for evolution. Giving a f*ck that matters means embracing challenges not as obstacles but as opportunities for growth and transformation.

Authenticity becomes a battle cry. In the realities of f*ck-giving, authenticity is the weapon that pierces through the illusions and establishes a genuine connection with oneself and the world.

Purpose resonates through every trial. It's the unwavering force that sustains and guides, making the journey of giving a f*ck truly meaningful.

In the realities of f*ck-giving, you confront the raw, unfiltered experiences of life, embracing them as integral parts of a journey filled with purpose, resilience, and triumph.

Now that we've plunged into the unvarnished truths of giving a f*ck that truly matters, let's reflect on those realities:

- **Embrace the Rollercoaster**   Recognize that giving a f*ck isn't about unwavering positivity. It's a journey through highs and lows, triumphs and challenges. Reflect on how you navigate these peaks and valleys.
- **Confront the Shadows**   Understand that pursuing significance often means walking through darkness. Self-doubt, uncertainty, and fear are part of the path. Ask yourself, how do I face my shadows?
- **Battle Scars as Testaments**   Your scars are evidence of your struggles and victories. Each one tells a story of resilience. How have your scars shaped your journey?
- **Laugh in the Face of Adversity**   Find strength in audacious laughter amidst hardships. It's a declaration of resilience. How does laughter feature in your coping mechanism?
- **Transform Criticism**   Let criticism become background noise, not a deterrent. How can you better filter criticism to serve your purpose, not hinder it?
- **Navigate, Not Avoid the Storm**   Life's tempests are inevitable. Embrace them as opportunities for growth. How do you find strength in chaos?
- **Persistence as Triumph**   View setbacks as chances to demonstrate tenacity. How do your moments of persistence reflect your commitment to what matters?

- **Rise Above Doubt**   Doubt can pull you down. Resolve to rise above it. What strategies help you overcome doubts?
- **Symphony of Struggles**   Life's difficulties contribute to its richness. How have your struggles harmonized to create the unique melody of your life?
- **Masterpiece of Resilience**   Resilience transforms challenges into opportunities. How do you use resilience to paint a brighter future?
- **Embrace Imperfections**   Your flaws are part of your authenticity. How have you learned to embrace and celebrate your imperfections?
- **Setbacks as Reality Checks**   Use setbacks for introspection and recalibration. What lessons have your setbacks taught you?
- **Authenticity as Your Weapon**   Use authenticity to cut through illusions. How does being authentic change how you confront life's realities?
- **Purpose as a Guiding Force**   Let purpose be your constant guide through trials. How does your purpose resonate in your actions and decisions?

As you reflect on these points, consider how they resonate with your experiences. How do you give a fck in a way that confronts life's raw realities, yet leads to growth, resilience, and authentic fulfillment? Embrace the unfiltered, messy, and triumphant aspects of living a purpose-driven life. Let's face it head-on, laugh in the storm, and rise through it all.

The Anti-Sugar-Coated-Self-Help Manifesto

We kick off our manifesto by championing spiritual wisdom without the sugar-coated nonsense. Life's profound lessons are not found in oversimplified platitudes but in the raw, unfiltered experiences that challenge and shape us.

Say goodbye to the illusion of a life adorned with constant rainbows and unicorns. Our manifesto is a reality check, acknowledging that life is a tumultuous journey, filled with storms and shadows, laughter and tears—a canvas painted with diverse hues.

Rebel against the status quo of self-help with the anti-sugar-coated-self-help manifesto. It's not about chasing fleeting positivity; it's about navigating the complexities of life, embracing discomfort, and finding strength in vulnerability.

The manifesto declares war on rose-tinted glasses. Life is vibrant, messy, and sometimes downright chaotic. Embracing the messiness without the distortion of unreal optimism is the true path to growth and authenticity.

Life is an intricate canvas, and our manifesto celebrates its messiness. Each stroke of chaos adds depth and character, creating a masterpiece that tells a story of resilience, adaptability, and the beauty inherent in imperfection.

The manifesto is a guide to navigating life's contradictions. It acknowledges that happiness and sadness coexist, success and failure dance together, and the dichotomy of our human experience is what makes it profound.

Choose authenticity over forced positivity. The manifesto encourages you to be real, embracing your true emotions and recognizing that it's okay not to be okay. Authenticity, not false cheer, leads to genuine growth.

Our manifesto sees flaws not as blemishes to be hidden but as integral brushstrokes in the artwork of life. Embrace imperfections, for they contribute to the richness and uniqueness of your personal narrative.

Vulnerability is not weakness—it's courage in its purest form. The manifesto champions the strength found in vulnerability, encouraging you to share your unfiltered self with the world without fear of judgment.

Strip away the illusions propagated by traditional self-help. The manifesto unmasks the unrealistic promises and expectations, presenting a pragmatic guide that acknowledges life's uncertainties and challenges.

Life is inherently uncertain, and the manifesto is your companion in embracing this uncertainty. Rather than fearing the unknown, find empowerment in navigating the uncharted territories of existence.

Toxic positivity has no place in our manifesto. It's not about pasting on a smile in the face of adversity but about acknowledging the full spectrum of emotions, from elation to despair, with grace and authenticity.

The anti-sugar-coated-self-help manifesto is a guide for the realists, not the eternal optimists. It's for those who understand that acknowledging life's challenges is the first step toward overcoming them with resilience and wisdom.

Scars are not wounds to be concealed but badges of wisdom earned through life's battles. The manifesto honors these scars, recognizing them as symbols of resilience, strength, and the capacity to heal.

Life's symphony is composed of both chaos and harmony. Our manifesto invites you to dance to the rhythm of this intricate composition, finding beauty in the dissonance and serenity in the moments of alignment.

Existential dilemmas are not brushed aside; they are confronted head-on in the manifesto. It's a companion for those wrestling with questions of purpose, meaning, and the existential intricacies of the human experience.

Growth is messy, and the manifesto is your guide through this tumultuous journey. It celebrates the discomfort of shedding old layers, pushing boundaries, and evolving into the person you're meant to become.

Our manifesto is a lantern for those navigating dark corners. It acknowledges that life's shadows exist but assures you that even in the darkest moments, there's a flicker of light waiting to guide you forward.

Predictability is an illusion, and our manifesto dispels this myth. It encourages you to embrace the unpredictable nature of life, finding liberation in the acceptance of constant change.

In a world saturated with filters, the manifesto stands as a sanctuary for the unfiltered soul. It beckons you to remove the masks, embrace vulnerability, and live authentically in a reality where messiness is not only accepted but celebrated. Thus, your journey begins. To deepen the experience and embrace the raw, real essence of life, here are activities that align with the manifesto's principles.

- **Storm Chasing Journal** Start a journal where you document life's storms – challenges, doubts, fears. Reflect on how these experiences shape and strengthen you. Recognize the beauty in these tumultuous times.
- **The Unicorns and Rainbows Reality Check** Create a two-column list. In one, jot down 'Unicorns and Rainbows' – instances where you've clung to unrealistic optimism. In the other, 'Realistic Reflections' – rewrite these instances with a grounded, authentic perspective.
- **Vulnerability Circle** Organize or join a group where people share their vulnerabilities openly. This exercise embraces the

strength found in sharing real, raw emotions without the fear of judgment.
- **Imperfection Art Project**   Create an artwork that celebrates imperfection. It could be a painting, a poem, or a piece of music. Let this project be a reminder that beauty and depth often lie in imperfections.
- **Authenticity Day Challenge**   Dedicate a day to live authentically. Express your true feelings, wear what feels comfortable, and do activities that genuinely resonate with you. Reflect on this experience in your journal.
- **Ditch the Rose-Tinted Glasses**   For a week, consciously avoid sugar-coating situations. Face challenges and uncomfortable situations head-on, and note your feelings and outcomes.
- **Scars as Stories Activity**   Share a personal story of resilience with a friend or in a group. Focus on how this challenge has shaped you. Encourage others to share their stories of resilience.
- **Embracing the Chaos Meditation**   Practice a meditation that focuses on accepting life's chaos. Visualize the chaos as a storm, and yourself finding calmness within it.
- **The Existential Exploration**   Write down your existential questions and ponder over them regularly. Research, discuss with others, or reflect in solitude. It's about confronting these questions, not avoiding them.
- **Growth Discomfort Diary**   Keep a diary where you note down instances of discomfort due to growth or change. Recognize these moments as signs of evolving and becoming a stronger version of yourself.
- **Unfiltered Social Media Day**   Spend a day on social media being completely authentic. Post what truly reflects your current state or thoughts, not what's 'Instagrammable'.
- **Shedding the Predictability Illusion**   Engage in an activity that's completely new or unpredictable for you. Reflect on how this unpredictability makes you feel and what it teaches you about embracing change.

- **Dance in the Rain Exercise** Literally or metaphorically, dance in the rain. Let this act symbolize finding joy and beauty in what many consider uncomfortable or undesirable.
- **The Lantern in the Dark** In moments of hardship, identify something or someone that acts as your lantern, guiding you through darkness. Acknowledge and express gratitude for this source of light.
- **Mask-Off Moment** Identify a situation where you usually wear a 'mask'. Consciously remove this mask and be your authentic self. Note the reactions of others and how it makes you feel.
- **The Authenticity Mirror** Each morning, stand in front of the mirror and affirm your commitment to living an authentic life. Acknowledge your flaws and strengths equally.

By engaging in one or more of these activities and revisiting this list from time to time, you can practice the principles of the Anti-Sugar-Coated-Self-Help Manifesto, fostering a life of authenticity, resilience, and genuine growth. Remember, it's about embracing life's real journey – the chaos, the messiness, the growth, and the beauty in all its unfiltered glory.

Life's Dance Floor

Life unfolds on a vast dance floor, and the conscious fck-giving dance is your rhythm. Instead of stumbling through the steps, learn to lead confidently, embracing the unpredictable tempo of existence.

In this dance, you're not a passive follower; you're the bold lead in your life tango. Seize the initiative, guiding the steps that resonate with your core values, aspirations, and the authentic beat of your heart.

Imagine life as a symphony, and your fcks as the instruments. The conscious fck-giving dance is about orchestrating a symphony that harmonizes with your soul, where each fck is a deliberate note contributing to the melody of your existence.

Selectivity is the art of the dance. Choose your fcks with intentionality, allowing only those that align with your true desires and goals to take center stage. Weed out the cacophony of unnecessary concerns.

The unnecessary noise, like a distant melody, fades into the background in the conscious fck-giving dance. What was once a distracting clamor becomes a subtle hum as you focus on the fcks that truly matter.

This isn't a refined waltz; it's a wild, rebellious tango. The conscious fck-giving dance invites you to throw away the formalities and immerse yourself in the raw, untamed movements of a dance that celebrates authenticity.

Authenticity is your dance partner. In the conscious fck-giving dance, let your authenticity lead the way. Express yourself boldly, unburdened by the need to conform to society's expectations or the opinions of others.

The dance is in the moment, and so should be your fck-giving. Embrace the present with full presence, allowing each conscious fck to be a deliberate step, creating a dance that reflects your mindful engagement with life.

Achieve inner harmony through the conscious fck-giving dance. Sync your values, actions, and aspirations into a seamless dance, where each fck is not a discordant note but a step toward the melody of your purpose.

Life has its rhythm, and the conscious fck-giving dance encourages you to flow with it. Adaptability is your dance partner, enabling you to navigate the unpredictable twists and turns of existence.

Excess fcks are like clumsy dance partners. The conscious fck-giving dance prompts you to gracefully let go of unnecessary fcks that hinder the fluidity of your movements, allowing you to dance with ease.

Confidence is your dance attire. Wear it with pride in the conscious fck-giving dance. Trust your steps, even when the dance floor gets challenging, and let your confidence radiate through intentional fck-giving.

Each fck is a step, and the conscious fck-giving dance is all about mindful footwork. Be aware of where you place your fcks, ensuring that each step contributes to the overall dance of your life.

External noise is the offbeat drummer trying to disrupt your dance. The conscious fck-giving dance teaches you to silence this drummer, allowing the inner melodies of your true desires to guide your movements.

Break free from rigidity; embrace improvisation and creativity in the dance of conscious fck-giving. Your life is not choreographed—it's an ever-evolving improvisation where you get to create and recreate your dance.

The tango is known for its sensuality, and so is the conscious fck-giving dance. Cultivate a sensual intimacy with life, allowing each fck to be a caress, a connection, and an expression of your profound relationship with existence.

Dare to add bold flourishes of fcks in your dance. The conscious fck-giving dance isn't about restraint; it's about confidently expressing your values, convictions, and passions through deliberate and impactful fck-giving.

Just as a dance has pauses, the conscious fck-giving dance encourages mindful pauses. In these moments, reassess your steps, ensuring that your fcks align with your evolving self and the changing rhythm of your life.

Consider the dance as a journey of self-discovery. The conscious fck-giving dance unveils new facets of yourself with each deliberate step, allowing you to explore the depths of your being through intentional fck-giving.

Celebrate the dance. The conscious fck-giving dance is not a performance for an audience; it's a celebration of your own personal journey. Revel in the freedom of dancing authentically, with each fck a testament to your unique and vibrant existence. This isn't just about navigating life; it's about:

- **Choreographing Life with Intention**   Life's dance floor invites us to lead, not follow. Reflect on how you're actively choreographing your life. Are your choices and actions in sync with the core values and aspirations that define your authentic rhythm?
- **Harmonizing Your Symphony of Priorities**   Imagine each f*ck you give as a note in your life's symphony. Which notes create harmony, and which create discord? Reflect on how to orchestrate your priorities so each one resonates with your soul's melody.
- **Embracing the Dance of Authenticity and Adaptability**   Authenticity is your dance partner, guiding each step you take. How can you more fully embrace your true self in life's dance?

Additionally, think about adaptability. Life often changes tempo and style unexpectedly. How well do you adapt your steps to these changes while maintaining your rhythm?

- **Navigating Life's Rhythms Mindfully**   The dance of life is lived in the present. How can you ensure that each step, each f*ck given, is mindful and deliberate, truly contributing to the dance you wish to perform?
- **Silencing Life's Offbeat Distractions**   External noise and distractions can throw off our rhythm. Reflect on the distractions or external pressures that disrupt your dance. How can you learn to maintain your rhythm amidst this noise?
- **Celebrating the Uniqueness of Your Dance**   Your dance on life's floor is uniquely yours – a celebration of your journey. How do you embrace and celebrate the uniqueness of your dance, with all its twists, turns, highs, and lows?

"Life's Dance Floor" encourages us to view life not as a series of random steps but as a conscious, beautifully choreographed dance. It's about making each step count, tuning into our authentic rhythm, and embracing the dance's dynamic nature. So, let's dance through life with purpose, passion, and a deep sense of self, turning our journey into an art form that reflects the very essence of who we are.

Don't Chase Positivity, Chase Purpose

Positivity, when chased for its own sake, can become a trap. The relentless pursuit of positivity can lead to a denial of reality and an avoidance of necessary challenges.

Constant positivity is a fallacy. Life is a tapestry of experiences, and expecting every thread to be brightly colored is unrealistic. Embracing the full spectrum of emotions, including the so-called negative ones, is crucial for a holistic and authentic existence.

Purpose is a guiding star that transcends the fleeting nature of positivity. It provides a compass, directing your efforts toward something meaningful and enduring, rather than a momentary burst of feel-good emotions.

Positivity can sometimes be misconstrued as maintaining a picture-perfect facade. This facade, however, often masks the rich tapestry of real and meaningful experiences that come from embracing the complexities of life.

While positivity may offer temporary satisfaction, purpose provides a deep and enduring fulfillment. It's the difference between a fleeting smile and a profound sense of contentment that comes from living a life aligned with what truly matters.

The pursuit of constant positivity can become burdensome. It's like carrying an unrealistic expectation that every moment should be sunny, which can weigh heavily on your shoulders and create unnecessary stress.

Ironically, chasing purpose is often the most effective antidote to negativity. When you are engaged in something meaningful, the challenges and setbacks become integral parts of a larger narrative, rather than mere stumbling blocks.

Purposeful living is inherently authentic. It involves acknowledging the ups and downs, the highs and lows, and navigating them with authenticity. This authenticity brings a richness to life that constant positivity might miss.

Chasing purpose is breaking free from the positivity trap. It's a declaration that your life is not defined by a superficial gloss but by the depth and significance of the causes you champion and the meaning you create.

A purpose-driven life embraces complexity. It acknowledges that challenges are not detours but integral parts of the journey. This complexity brings a richness and depth that a superficial pursuit of positivity might lack.

Positivity often relies on external circumstances, which are fleeting. Purpose, on the other hand, is an internal wellspring of motivation. It's a force that propels you forward even when external conditions are not ideal.

Purpose weaves a narrative that goes beyond the binary of positive and negative. It's a story that unfolds with every choice you make, shaping a legacy that is not confined to fleeting moments of joy but encompasses the entirety of your journey.

Perpetual happiness is an illusion. Life is a mosaic of emotions, and each has its place in creating a meaningful and purposeful existence. Chasing constant positivity denies the depth that comes from embracing the full spectrum of human experience. In the darkest moments, it's purpose that acts as a beacon. When positivity seems elusive, purpose remains a steady light, guiding you through challenges with resilience and determination.

Purpose embraces messiness. It's not a neat and tidy pursuit but a messy, chaotic, and beautiful journey. This messiness is where the real substance of life resides, beyond the simplistic duality of positive and negative.

Positivity might seek comfort, but purpose invites growth. It challenges you to evolve, learn, and adapt. The discomfort that comes with growth is an essential part of a purpose-driven life.

Interestingly, positivity often becomes a natural byproduct of living with purpose. It's not chased; it emerges organically as a response to a life that is deeply aligned with what matters.

Positivity can be fleeting, but purpose is a lifelong companion. It stays with you through the highs and lows, offering a consistent sense of direction and meaning. Chasing purpose is choosing meaning over the transient concept of happiness. It's an acknowledgment that a life well-lived is one that is purposeful, even if it doesn't always conform to society's narrow definition of positivity.

The joy that comes from purpose is profound. It's not a surface-level cheerfulness but a deep-seated contentment that arises from knowing that your existence is contributing to something greater than yourself.

Chasing purpose over positivity is an invitation to live a life of depth, authenticity, and enduring fulfillment. It's a commitment to a journey that transcends the superficial and embraces the profound richness of a purpose-driven existence. To transform this philosophy into action, here's a comprehensive plan with activities designed to help you chase purpose:

- **Identify Your Purpose**   Reflect on what genuinely matters to you. What are your passions, values, and the causes that stir your soul? Write these down to form a clear picture of your purpose.
- **Realistic Emotion Acceptance**   Dedicate time each day to acknowledge and accept your emotions, both positive and negative. Journaling can be a helpful tool for this, allowing you to process your feelings without judgment.
- **Purpose-Driven Daily Actions**   Integrate small actions aligned with your purpose into your daily routine. Whether it's

reading about a topic you're passionate about, volunteering, or working on a personal project, make sure your days reflect your purpose.
- **Build Resilience through Challenges** Embrace challenges as opportunities for growth. When faced with difficulties, ask yourself, "What can I learn from this?" and "How does this align with my purpose?"
- **Authenticity Check-Ins** Regularly check in with yourself to ensure you're living authentically. Are your actions and choices reflective of your true self and purpose? Adjust as needed.
- **Complexity Embracing Activity** Engage in activities that require you to navigate complex situations. This could involve problem-solving tasks, engaging in debates, or taking on challenging projects.
- **Set Purposeful Goals** Set short-term and long-term goals that are aligned with your purpose. Ensure they are realistic and measurable, and track your progress.
- **Celebrate Purposeful Achievements** Celebrate your achievements, big and small, that contribute to your purpose. Recognize these moments as milestones in your purposeful journey.
- **Reflective End-of-Day Ritual** End each day with a reflective ritual, pondering how your daily actions contributed to your purpose. Celebrate the wins and learn from the challenges.

By engaging in activities that fit your needs and revisiting this plan from time to time, you can shift your focus from chasing momentary happiness to pursuing a deeper, more meaningful existence. Remember, it's about embracing the full spectrum of life's experiences and finding fulfillment in aligning with your true purpose.

Other activities to consider:
- **Purpose Visualization Exercise** Create a vision board that represents your purpose. Use images, quotes, and symbols that

resonate with your goals and aspirations. This board will serve as a daily reminder of what you're striving for.
- **Mindfulness Practice** Incorporate mindfulness into your daily life to stay present and focused on your purpose. This can involve meditation, mindful walking, or simply practicing present-moment awareness.
- **Cultivate Growth Mindset** Adopt a growth mindset that embraces learning and development. When you encounter setbacks, view them as chances to evolve and align more closely with your purpose.
- **Purpose over Positivity Journaling** Maintain a journal where you document instances when you chose purpose over fleeting positivity. Reflect on how these choices impacted your life and sense of fulfillment.

Fck the Noise, Find Your Symphony

Within the chaos of life, there exists a symphony waiting to be discovered. Fck the noise—turn inward, and you'll find the orchestral brilliance of your authentic self, a melody uniquely yours.

Society plays dissonant notes, attempting to drown your individual melody. Fck the noise of societal expectations; instead, compose your own harmonies and let them resonate with the rhythm of your heart.

Life's symphony is often drowned in superficial noise—opinions, trends, and expectations. Fck the noise that doesn't contribute to your melody. Tune out the superficial, and let the genuine chords of your essence shine through.

Each life is a unique symphony. Fck the noise that urges conformity, and embrace the cacophony of individuality. Find harmony in your uniqueness, and let it echo through the grand auditorium of existence.

You're the composer of your symphony. Fck the noise that stifles your creativity. Unleash the inner composer within, experimenting with notes and rhythms that express the depth and breadth of your being.

Authenticity has its rhythm. Fck the noise of pretense and facades. Let the rhythm of authenticity guide your composition, creating a symphony that resonates not only with you but with the world around you.

Life provides instruments for self-discovery. Fck the noise that distracts you from exploring these instruments. Play each note of self-discovery, and let the instruments guide you to the core of your symphonic identity.

Life presents melodic choices amid discordant noise. Fck the noise of indecision and fear. Make melodic choices that align with your values, weaving a symphony of purpose that conquers the dissonance.

Societal expectations play a symphony of their own. Fck that symphony. Instead, compose your own, defying expectations with the bold strokes of authenticity. Let your symphony be the rebellion against conformity.

You are the conductor of your destiny's symphony. Fck the noise that tries to hand you someone else's baton. Conduct your own symphony, directing each movement with the confidence that comes from authentic self-expression.

Resilience is the echo of inner strength. Fck the noise that undermines your resilience. Let the symphony of your inner strength play loudly, drowning out doubts and reverberating with the unyielding melody of self-belief.

External judgments form a judgmental chorus. Fck that chorus. Your symphony isn't composed for their critiques. Play your symphony with pride, regardless of whether it aligns with the expectations of the external world.

Life is a journey of personal evolution, a symphony in constant flux. Fck the noise that resists change. Embrace the evolving notes of your symphony, recognizing that each new experience adds depth to the melody.

Doubt has its symphony, often loud and distracting. Fck that symphony of doubt. Silence it with the confident chords of self-assurance, and let your symphony resonate with the unwavering belief in your capabilities.

Limitations build a limiting crescendo. Fck that crescendo. Break free from the constraints, and let your symphony reach a crescendo of boundless possibilities, where each note defies the confines of societal norms.

Comparison creates a discordant undertone. Fck the noise of comparison. Find the harmonious notes of self-acceptance and self-love, crafting a symphony that celebrates your uniqueness without seeking validation from external sources.

Inner peace has its melody. Fck the noise that disturbs your peace. Allow your symphony to play the calming notes of serenity, creating an oasis of tranquility amidst the chaotic cadence of life.

The status quo has its sonata, predictable and uninspiring. Fck that sonata. Compose your own, infused with the unpredictable and the extraordinary. Let your symphony be the rebel that disrupts the mundane status quo.

Passion resonates in the heart of every symphony. Fck the noise that dulls your passion. Play the passionate chords of your desires and dreams, letting your symphony become a testament to the fire that burns within.

Regret echoes in a somber tune. Fck the noise of regret. Instead, infuse your symphony with the lessons learned from each experience, transforming regret into a nuanced note that adds richness to the melody of your life.

Embracing individuality and authenticity amidst life's cacophony isn't just about finding your unique sound; it's a deeper exploration of self-discovery, resilience, and authentic self-expression. Let's reflect on the central themes and their implications:

- Society often plays a discordant tune, expecting conformity and adherence to its rhythm. We challenge you to compose your own life's melody, one that resonates with your personal values and beliefs. Reflect on how societal expectations have influenced your life choices and consider how you can more authentically express your individuality.
- Authenticity is the core of your personal symphony. The encouragement here is to discard pretenses and societal

facades, allowing the genuine rhythm of your being to guide your life's composition. Consider the areas in your life where you feel you're not being true to yourself and explore ways to bring more authenticity into these aspects.

- Life presents numerous distractions, challenges, and pressures. We invite you to tune out the noise that doesn't contribute positively to your life and focus on what truly matters. Reflect on the 'noises' in your life that distract you from your goals and contemplate strategies to minimize their impact.
- Your journey is about exploring and embracing the different instruments of self-discovery. Each experience, whether positive or negative, contributes to understanding yourself better. Reflect on your past experiences and consider how they have shaped the melody of your life.
- The echoes of resilience play a significant part in your life's symphony. Facing challenges and overcoming obstacles adds depth and strength to your melody. Think about the times you've shown resilience and how these moments have strengthened your character.
- Doubt and comparison often play loud, distracting tunes. We encourage you to silence these disruptive elements with confidence and self-belief. Reflect on how you can reinforce your self-confidence to overcome doubts and the urge to compare yourself to others.
- Embrace the notion that your life's symphony is ever-evolving. Each new experience, change, and phase of life adds a different note to your melody. Consider how your symphony has evolved over time and how you can continue to adapt it as you grow.
- Inner peace and passion are crucial components of your symphony. It's about finding balance – creating a tune that reflects both the calming serenity of inner peace and the fiery notes of your passions and dreams. Reflect on how you can nurture both these aspects in your life.

- Instead of allowing regret to play a somber tune, we suggest transforming it into a nuanced note that enriches your life's melody. Think about how you can learn from past regrets and use these lessons to enhance your future choices.

Conduct the orchestra of your life with boldness and authenticity. It's a call to break free from the limiting crescendos of societal expectations and compose a symphony that's uniquely yours – one that celebrates your individuality, embraces your journey of self-discovery, and resonates with the authentic rhythm of your existence.

Raise Your F*cking Banner

As you raise your fcking banner, let it echo the battle cry of authenticity. This is not a flag of conformity but a standard that proudly waves in the chaotic winds of individuality.

Unfurl your fcking banner as the flag of purpose. Let it flap vigorously, a reminder that every step in this chaotic arena is guided by a sense of meaning and intention.

The raised banner signifies your triumph over trivialities. In this arena, you're not ensnared by the insignificant. You've chosen to give a f*ck where it truly matters, leaving the rest to wither in insignificance.

Consider your fcking banner a symbol of discernment—a line drawn between the monumental and the minuscule. In its shadow, the grand takes precedence, and the petty fades into obscurity.

Your banner is a compass, guiding your journey through the conscious fck-giving dance. With each flutter, it directs you to give a fck where it counts, orchestrating a dance that resonates with purpose and authenticity.

Chaos may surround you, but your banner is your shield. It's a declaration that you navigate this tumultuous arena with resilience, facing adversity with the unwavering belief that your fcks are reserved for the significant.

Let your raised banner be a symbol of rebellious optimism. In a world often clouded by negativity, your fcking banner is a beacon that cuts through the gloom, radiating the light of positivity and resilience. This fcking banner is your defiance against the Negative Spiral of Overthinking, also known as the Inner Critic's Echo Chamber from Hell. It's a refusal to succumb to the belief that everything must be perfect, a recognition that imperfections and struggles are woven into the tapestry of life.

> **Author's Note** What lies on the other side of the Inner Critic's Echo Chamber from Hell? It's the empowering realm of the Echo Chamber of Significance. This transformative concept is explored comprehensively in a later chapter, aptly titled with the same name, offering a journey from self-doubt to self-affirmation.

As the banner flutters, consider it an oath against overcompensation. No more buying forty pairs of shoes or drowning Xanax with vodka. Your banner signifies a commitment to a genuine and unapologetic existence.

Raise your fcking banner as a call to acceptance. It signals an acceptance of life's inevitable messiness and imperfections. In its shadow, you embrace the art of giving a f*ck with a clarity that transcends the pursuit of an unattainable ideal.

Your fcking banner aligns you with a league of rebels. Rebels who refuse to conform to the societal sonata. It's a standard that signifies you're not alone—a collective movement towards authenticity and individuality.

Let your raised banner be a bridge between the notes of your life's symphony. It connects the highs and lows, the fortissimos and pianissimos, creating a harmonious passage through the diverse movements of your personal narrative.

Chaos doesn't intimidate you; it inspires purpose. Your fcking banner is a declaration that amidst the chaos, you stand tall, guided by the compass of conscious f*ck-giving, and propelled by the rebellion of authenticity.

As your banner flaps in the wind, let it drown out the trivial noise. It's a symbolic gesture, conveying that you're not swayed by the cacophony of meaningless distractions but are attuned to the melodies of what truly matters.

This raised banner is a symbol of defiance against societal expectations. It's a refusal to adhere to a script handed down from cradle to grave. Instead, it signifies your determination to forge a path through the cosmic garage sale of life.

Your fcking banner is a pledge to the symphony of unapologetic living. It's a commitment to play each note boldly, embracing the crescendos and diminuendos, and allowing your unique melody to resonate without fear or inhibition.

As your banner flutters high, you're not just standing in the arena; you're ready to embark on an adventure. The chaos is your playground, and with your banner as a guide, the journey promises discoveries, challenges, and, above all, a life lived authentically.

Every glance at your raised banner is a reminder of selective fckery. It prompts a conscious choice to give a f*ck where it truly matters and to let go of the burdensome baggage of unnecessary concerns.

Think of your fcking banner as the artistic rebellion of the self. It's a declaration that your life is a canvas, painted with the bold strokes of authenticity and individuality. Each flap of the banner adds another layer to this rebellious masterpiece.

Your fcking banner is the symbol of a conscious odyssey. It's not just a piece of fabric; it's a manifesto, a guide, and a celebration. So, in the arena of life, raise your banner high and let the adventure unfold with every courageous step.

Embracing your authenticity and individuality boldly is not just about making a statement; it's about living a life that is fiercely and unapologetically yours. Let's delve into the deeper meanings and implications of this rallying cry:

- Your banner symbolizes the unique melody of your authentic self. Amidst life's chaos, it's a reminder to stay true to who you are, rejecting conformity and societal expectations. Reflect on how you can more vividly express your true self in everyday life.
- The banner represents purposeful living, guiding your decisions and actions. It encourages you to differentiate between what's truly important and what's trivial. Consider how you can make

more purpose-driven choices, focusing on what genuinely matters to you.
- Raising your banner is an act of resilience and optimistic rebellion. It's about navigating life's complexities with a positive and resilient mindset. How can you develop a more resilient outlook that helps you face challenges head-on?
- Your banner is a defiance against the pursuit of perfection and societal pressures. It's about acknowledging that life is imperfect and embracing these imperfections. Think about areas in your life where you can let go of the pursuit of perfection and embrace the beauty of imperfection.
- Raising your banner is a commitment to live genuinely and unapologetically. It's about rejecting superficial remedies and embracing genuine experiences. How can you live more authentically, shedding the superficial layers that don't represent your true self?
- Your banner aligns you with others who share your pursuit of authenticity and individuality. It's a symbol of a collective movement towards living genuinely. Reflect on how you can connect with others who share your values and support each other in this journey.
- The banner bridges the diverse experiences of your life, from triumphs to setbacks. It's about embracing the full range of life's experiences and finding harmony in them. How can you better integrate and accept the highs and lows of your life?
- Your banner is a declaration that chaos inspires purpose. It signifies standing tall amidst chaos, guided by your values and authenticity. Reflect on how chaos has inspired or clarified your purpose.
- Raising your banner is a refusal to live by a script written by society. It's about forging your path, embracing life's unpredictability. Think about ways you can break free from societal scripts and chart your unique course.
- Your banner is a pledge to live each moment boldly, embracing both the crescendos and diminuendos of life. Consider how

you can live more boldly, letting your unique melody resonate freely.
- The banner reminds you to engage in selective fckery—giving a fck about what's truly important and discarding unnecessary burdens. Reflect on how you can practice selective f*ckery more consciously in your life.
- Artistic Rebellion of Self: Think of your banner as an expression of your artistic rebellion, a declaration that your life is a canvas for your authenticity and individuality. How can you add more bold strokes of authenticity to the canvas of your life?

Raise Your F*cking Banner is a powerful metaphor for living a life that is not only authentic and purposeful but also resilient and rebellious. It's a call to hold your head high, embrace your individuality, and navigate life's journey with confidence and authenticity. So, raise your banner high and let it be a testament to a life lived with passion, purpose, and unapologetic authenticity.

Navigating the Cosmic Garage Sale

Picture yourself in the vast cosmic expanse of a garage sale, where the universe lays out its wares, and you stand with a backpack full of fcks. This is no ordinary garage sale; it's a celestial bazaar of life experiences, and it's time for a radical decluttering. Let's navigate this cosmic garage sale, tossing out the meaningless trinkets of anxiety and overthinking while investing your precious fcks in experiences that are vintage, rare, and unequivocally worth the investment.

You start this cosmic journey with a backpack—a vessel carrying the weight of countless f*cks you've gathered. It's a backpack that, unbeknownst to you, has been slowing you down on the adventure of life. The time has come to unzip, unload, and reassess the contents.

The cosmic garage sale is a metaphor for the vast array of experiences life presents. It's a kaleidoscope of opportunities, relationships, and moments, each waiting for a discerning eye to recognize its value. Your f*cks are the currency here, and it's time to spend them wisely.

Amidst the cosmic wares, you find trinkets of anxiety—tiny, seemingly insignificant objects that, when accumulated, clutter the backpack of your mind. It's time to toss them aside. Anxiety trinkets hold no real value in the grand bazaar of life.

Overthinking artifacts, intricate and delicate, have found their way into the backpack. These are the things you've pondered upon for too long, draining your mental energy. At the cosmic garage sale, they are swiftly discarded to make room for clarity.

As you declutter, you realize the true value lies in experiences. These are the vintage pieces at the cosmic garage sale—moments that carry the patina of authenticity, stories that become treasures, and connections that transcend the ephemeral nature of material possessions.

Amidst the cosmic clutter, relationships gleam like rare gems. It's time to invest your f*cks in forging and nurturing connections that withstand the tests of time. Unlike material possessions, relationships appreciate in value, becoming timeless artifacts.

In the cosmic garage sale, time is the antique currency. You've been hoarding it, and now is the moment to spend it wisely. Allocate your time to experiences that resonate with your soul, for time spent on meaningful pursuits is an investment that pays dividends.

Adventures beckon as limited-edition collectibles. They are the rare finds at the cosmic garage sale, waiting to be seized by those who dare to venture beyond the ordinary. Spend your f*cks on adventures that etch indelible memories into the canvas of your life.

In the vast array of experiences, learning stands as priceless artwork. Invest your f*cks in the pursuit of knowledge, wisdom, and personal growth. These are acquisitions that appreciate over time, adding depth and richness to the gallery of your existence.

At the cosmic garage sale, self-discovery is a masterpiece waiting to be unveiled. Allocate your f*cks to the journey within, unraveling the layers of your identity, and painting the canvas of your soul with the hues of authenticity.

Among the cosmic treasures, laughter emerges as a musical harmony. Spend your f*cks generously on experiences that bring joy, humor, and lightness to your journey. Laughter is the tune that makes the cosmic dance of life truly enchanting.

Kindness, a universal language, shines brightly in the cosmic garage sale. Invest your f*cks in acts of compassion, empathy, and generosity. These are treasures that create ripples, echoing across the vastness of existence.

Gratitude sparkles as the elixir of contentment. Allocate your f*cks to moments of thankfulness, appreciating the beauty in the ordinary and finding joy in the simplest of cosmic offerings.

Authenticity stands out as a rare find in the cosmic bazaar. Spend your f*cks on being true to yourself, embracing your quirks, and celebrating the uniqueness that sets you apart in the grand tapestry of life.

Love, a timeless artifact, radiates its brilliance in the cosmic garage sale. Invest your f*cks in cultivating love—for yourself, for others, and for the wondrous journey that unfolds in the cosmic expanse.

Nature unfolds as living artwork in the cosmic gallery. Spend your f*cks on moments immersed in the beauty of the natural world, for nature is a masterpiece that invites contemplation and awe.

Mindfulness acts as a cosmic lens, allowing you to focus your f*cks on the present moment. Clear the clutter of past anxieties and future uncertainties, and invest your attention in the exquisite details of now.

The act of letting go becomes a liberation ritual in the cosmic garage sale. Release the attachments that no longer serve you, freeing up space for new and transformative experiences.

Establishing boundaries emerges as the creation of cosmic containers. Spend your f*cks on delineating spaces that protect your well-being, allowing only the energies that align with your authenticity to enter.

Curiosity serves as the explorer's torch in the cosmic expanse. Allocate your f*cks to the pursuit of the unknown, for curiosity is the flame that guides you through uncharted territories.

Creativity unfolds as the artisan's workshop in the cosmic garage sale. Invest your f*cks in the act of creation, whether it be through art, ideas, or innovative solutions. Creativity is the brush that adds strokes of uniqueness to the canvas of your life.

Resilience stands as the cosmic armor in the garage sale of experiences. Spend your f*cks on building inner strength, facing challenges, and bouncing back from adversities. Resilience is the shield that protects your authenticity.

Forgiveness emerges as the cosmic cleanser in the garage sale of emotions. Allocate your f*cks to the act of forgiving—freeing yourself from the burdens of resentment and making space for emotional liberation.

Amidst the cosmic hustle, rest becomes the cosmic recharge. Spend your f*cks on moments of rejuvenation, recognizing that taking breaks is not a sign of weakness but a vital component of the journey.

Reflection acts as the cosmic pause in the grand garage sale. Spend your f*cks on moments of introspection, contemplating the cosmic gallery you've curated, and ensuring that each experience adds value to the evolving masterpiece of your life.

In the "Cosmic Garage Sale", life is likened to an expansive marketplace filled with varied experiences, where our choices and focuses determine our journey's quality. This isn't merely about making choices; it's a profound exploration of self-awareness, discernment, and intentional living. Let's delve deeper and build an actionable framework based on this powerful concept.

The Cosmic Clarity Framework

1. **Conduct a Life Inventory** Start by assessing the 'wares' in your life. List out your commitments, relationships,

habits, and even material possessions. This is your chance to take stock of what fills your life.

2. **Identify Your 'Anxiety Trinkets'** Recognize the small, seemingly insignificant worries that clutter your mind. Make a conscious effort to discard these, understanding they add no real value to your life. Be sure to examine the emotions behind your worries and fears so you can understand their roots.

3. **Discard Overthinking Artifacts** Identify areas where you've been overthinking without making progress. Decide to let these go to clear mental space for more meaningful contemplations.

4. **Invest in Valuable Experiences** Shift your focus to experiences that enrich your life and align with your long-term goals. Consider experiences that offer growth, learning, and alignment with your core values. These could be moments of connection, learning new skills, or engaging in activities that align with your passions.

5. **Cultivate and Nurture Relationships** Recognize the relationships that add value to your life. Invest time and energy in nurturing these connections, understanding they are more precious than material possessions. Regularly evaluate which relationships are mutually enriching and be open to evolving or moving away from those that aren't.

6. **Allocate Time Wisely** Time is your most valuable currency. Spend it on activities that resonate with your core values and bring you joy, rather than wasting it on unfulfilling tasks.

7. **Let Go of What No Longer Serves You** Consciously release attachments, habits, or beliefs that no longer contribute positively to your life.

8. **Set Boundaries** Clearly define your boundaries. This is crucial for maintaining your well-being and ensuring that you're investing your energy in the right places.
9. **Live Authentically** Make choices that align with your true self. Embrace your uniqueness and let your authentic self shine in all aspects of your life.
10. **Reflect Regularly** Make time for regular reflection. Assess how your choices align with your goals and what adjustments might be necessary.

Zeroing in on what truly adds value to your existence is about decluttering the unnecessary and cherishing the experiences and relationships that make life meaningful. When you are regularly practicing these concepts and finding value in doing so, you may be ready for the extended framework that follows.

The Authenticity and Resilience Blueprint:
1. **Life's Inventory and Mindful Decluttering** Your life is a collection of experiences, relationships, habits, and beliefs. It's essential to periodically review this collection, mindfully decluttering what no longer serves you. This process involves deep self-reflection to identify what truly enriches your life versus what clutters it with worry and redundancy.
2. **Discernment in Life's Choices** The metaphor of the garage sale invites you to be discerning with where you 'spend' your energies and commitments. It's about differentiating between what genuinely adds value to your life and what merely takes up space. Consider the long-term impact of your choices to ensure they align with your life's purpose and goals.
3. **Prioritize Authentic Experiences and Relationships** In the cosmic garage sale, the most valuable 'items' are often authentic experiences and meaningful relationships.

Prioritize these over material gains or superficial achievements. Seek experiences that challenge, grow, and fulfill you, and cultivate relationships that offer depth and genuine connection.

4. **Invest in Growth and Learning**   View personal growth and continuous learning as invaluable treasures in this cosmic marketplace. Dedicate time and resources to expand your knowledge, skills, and self-awareness. This investment often yields the highest returns in terms of personal fulfillment and self-improvement. Expand on this to include emotional intelligence and spiritual understanding.

5. **Embrace Joy and Positivity**   Amidst life's chaos, find and invest in moments of joy, humor, and positivity. These elements are like rare collectibles in the cosmic garage sale, offering respite and balance in your journey.

6. **Acts of Kindness and Compassion**   Allocate your resources towards acts of kindness and compassion. These actions enrich not only your life but also the lives of others, creating a ripple effect of positivity in the cosmic bazaar.

7. **Cultivate Gratitude and Mindfulness**   Practice gratitude and mindfulness as means to appreciate the present moment and the simple yet profound offerings of life. This practice helps you focus on what truly matters, reducing the noise of unnecessary worries or comparisons.

8. **Set Boundaries and Embrace Rest**   Understand the importance of setting boundaries and allowing time for rest and rejuvenation. Just as in a real garage sale, not every item needs your attention. Choose where to invest your energy wisely, and don't hesitate to step back and recharge when needed.

9. **Nurture Creativity and Resilience**   In the cosmic garage sale, creativity and resilience are like rare artifacts. Foster these qualities within yourself as they help you navigate life's challenges with agility and originality. Creativity isn't just a skill; it's a medium for expressing emotions, processing experiences, and exploring the self. Build resilience through rest. Rest is not just a break; it's a crucial part of strengthening one's ability to face life's challenges.

10. **Forgiveness and Emotional Liberation**   Embrace forgiveness, both towards yourself and others, as a means of emotional liberation. Letting go of grudges and past hurt frees up emotional space for more enriching experiences.

11. **Regular Reflection and Course Correction**   Finally, make regular reflection a habit. Assess your 'purchases' and choices in the cosmic garage sale of life. Are they leading you towards the life you envision? If not, don't hesitate to course-correct.

By deeply engaging with these concepts, you transform the idea of the cosmic garage sale from a metaphor into a practical guide for living. It becomes a tool for intentional living, helping you navigate the vast expanse of choices and experiences life offers with wisdom, purpose, and fulfillment.

Giving a F*ck That Matters

So, we've established that giving a fck doesn't mean being overcaring; it means being comfortable with being different. But here's the twist: giving a fck is also about giving a monumental f*ck about the things that genuinely matter. In the vast sea of fcks, it's crucial to become a skilled navigator. It's not about aimlessly tossing your fcks into the waves; it's about setting sail with purpose, steering towards the monumental and steering clear of the trivial.

Giving a f*ck that matters is an art of discernment. It's about distinguishing between the waves that demand your attention and the ripples that can be allowed to fade away. Like a captain on a stormy sea, you decide which currents are worth riding and which are better left unexplored.

Imagine your core values as a lighthouse guiding your ship. Giving a f*ck that matters means steering towards these values with unwavering determination. When the storms of life hit, your values become the anchor that holds you steady in the tumultuous waves.

Consider your moral compass your most valuable tool. Giving a f*ck that matters requires mastering this compass, ensuring it points true north to your principles. With every decision, check your compass, and let it guide you toward the destinations that align with your deepest convictions.

Emotional energy is a currency, and you only have so much to spend. Giving a monumental f*ck means investing this emotional currency wisely. Instead of squandering it on every passing wave, save it for the tsunamis—those moments and causes that truly deserve the force of your emotional tidal wave.

Life throws challenges like cannonballs, and you're the keeper of the triage. Giving a f*ck that matters involves skillfully assessing the wounds—knowing which battles are worth fighting and which skirmishes can be left to the echoes of the sea.

Picture your life as an echo chamber, amplifying the resonance of your choices. Giving a f*ck that matters means creating significant echoes—ones that reverberate with the sound of purpose and authenticity. Let your life's symphony be a composition of meaningful reverberations.

In a world that often values superficial echoes, giving a f*ck that matters is a rebellion. It's a declaration that your life won't be defined by the shallow ripples but by the profound echoes that emanate from the depths of your being.

Life is a sculpture, and your fcks mold its form. To give a fck that matters is to sculpt your priorities with intention. Carve out the unnecessary, leaving a masterpiece that reflects the true essence of your values and aspirations.

Time is the canvas upon which your life is painted. Giving a fck that matters is a stroke of vivid color on this canvas. It's recognizing that time is a limited palette, and each fck you give adds to the masterpiece or detracts from its brilliance.

Your life is not a solo; it's a symphony. Giving a f*ck that matters orchestrates a powerful movement in this symphony of existence. It's a commitment to play your notes in a way that resonates not only with your individual melody but also with the harmonies of those around you.

Consider your fcks as the legacy you leave behind. Giving a fck that matters ensures that your legacy isn't a cacophony of trivial concerns but a harmonious melody that echoes in the hearts of those who follow in your wake.

Sometimes, giving a fck that matters means mastering the art of saying no. It's a shield against the onslaught of requests and expectations, a declaration that your fcks are reserved for endeavors that align with your purpose.

Giving a f*ck that matters is wielding the sculptor's chisel with finesse. It's about chiseling away the excess, leaving only the essential contours of a life well-lived. With every strike, you refine the sculpture into a masterpiece of significance.

Your priorities are the flowers in the garden of your life. Giving a f*ck that matters involves nurturing these flowers, ensuring they bloom with vibrancy. It's recognizing that some flowers need more attention, and your emotional water is best spent on those that truly matter.

In the tapestry of relationships, giving a f*ck that matters is threading the needle with care. It's recognizing the delicate balance between giving too much or too little, and ensuring that each thread contributes to a tapestry of connection and mutual growth.

Passion is an alchemical force, and your fcks are the catalyst. Giving a fck that matters is understanding this alchemy. It's recognizing the transformative power of passion and directing it towards pursuits that elevate your existence and the world around you.

In the shallows, the waves are chaotic and purposeless. Giving a fck that matters means venturing into the depths. It's where the currents of purpose are strong, and every fck you give contributes to the profound ocean of significance.

Imagine a map with coordinates of purpose. Giving a fck that matters is navigating your life with this map. It's an intentional journey towards the destinations that align with your purpose, leaving a trail of purposeful fcks in your wake.

Giving a f*ck that matters is a dance of integrity. It's moving to the rhythm of your values and principles, refusing to be swayed by external pressures or fleeting trends. In this dance, every step is a conscious choice to honor what truly matters.

These principles form the compass for navigating the intricate terrain of giving a f*ck that matters. As we delve deeper, we'll explore how to apply these guiding stars to real-life scenarios and challenges. So, tighten your mental sails, for the journey has just begun.

Giving a f*ck that matters" is about crafting a life of intention, guided by your core values and principles. This isn't just advice on selective care; it's a blueprint for meaningful existence. Let's build on these lessons with a comprehensive reflection and action plan:

1. Your emotional energy is a finite resource. Reflect on how you're currently spending this energy. Are you investing it in areas that align with your values and goals? Start shifting your focus towards issues and causes that resonate deeply with you.
2. Life's challenges can be overwhelming. Develop the skill of distinguishing between what deserves your full attention and what can be let go. This involves assessing challenges based on their alignment with your values and the impact they have on your life goals.
3. Identify your core values and use them as a guiding light. Regularly check if your actions and decisions are aligned with these values. They should serve as a constant reference point, helping you navigate through life's varied circumstances.
4. Master the essential art of saying 'no,' a skill we delve into in the aptly titled chapter of this book. Embracing this skill is vital for safeguarding your time and energy for what truly counts. By confidently declining lesser priorities, you

open the door to wholeheartedly saying 'yes' to the pursuits that enrich your life with meaning and purpose.

5. In the tapestry of relationships, be intentional about where you invest. Foster connections that are reciprocal and growth-oriented. Sometimes, this means prioritizing depth over breadth in your relationships.

6. Channel your energies towards your passions and personal growth. This might involve dedicating time to hobbies, educational pursuits, or self-improvement activities that align with your personal and professional aspirations.

7. When faced with crises, practice emotional triaging. This means quickly assessing situations and determining where your involvement is most needed and effective, thus avoiding unnecessary emotional drain.

8. Ensure that your mental health and overall well-being are at the forefront of your priorities. This might involve setting aside time for self-care, seeking professional help when needed, or engaging in activities that promote mental and emotional balance.

9. Contemplate the legacy you aspire to create, a theme so pivotal that it's the cornerstone of our upcoming book, 'Discover Meaning, Live Empowered: A Liberation Blueprint for Authentic Living, Unleashing Your Potential, and Making a Difference.' Channel your energies into actions and initiatives that shape this legacy, making sure that your impact resonates positively and harmonizes with your core values and deepest beliefs.

10. Engage in regular reflection to assess how effectively you're giving a f*ck about the things that matter. Be prepared to adjust your focus as your life evolves and as new priorities emerge.

By embracing these principles, "Giving a F*ck That Matters" becomes more than just a concept; it transforms into a practical guide for living a life filled with purpose, intention, and authentic engagement. This approach ensures that every bit of energy you invest contributes to building a life that is not only fulfilling for you but also beneficial to those around you and to the greater good.

The Art of Discernment

Discernment is your compass in navigating the murky waters of life. Just as a skilled captain knows how to read the subtle changes in the sea, you must develop the art of discernment to understand the nuances of your journey.

Not every wave is significant. Discernment is the art of gauging the weight of each wave. What truly matters should carry the most weight in your considerations. By discerning the significance, you prevent yourself from being overwhelmed by the inconsequential.

Life's seas are often accompanied by storms of drama. Discernment is your shield against the undertow of unnecessary theatrics. Recognize when drama seeks to pull you under, and, with discerning eyes, stay afloat, refusing to be dragged into turbulent waters.

Distractions are the sirens of the sea, calling you away from your true course. The art of discernment lies in recognizing these seductive calls. Be vigilant against the lure of distractions, staying committed to the journey that truly matters.

Consider the ripple effect of your actions. Discernment involves understanding that your choices send out ripples, impacting not only your voyage but the journeys of those around you. Invest in actions that create positive ripples, contributing to the collective well-being.

Not every wave demands an immediate response. Discernment is your timekeeper. The urgency of a situation may be a mirage. Take a step back, assess the true nature of the wave, and discern whether it requires an immediate, urgent response or a measured, thoughtful one.

Life's waters can be tangled with competing priorities. The art of discernment involves untangling this web. What takes precedence? What aligns with your true north? Discernment allows you to navigate the web with clarity, ensuring you invest your energy in what truly matters.

External influences can create a fog, obscuring your vision. Discernment is your fog light, cutting through the mist of external pressures and opinions. See through the fog of influence, making decisions that resonate with your authentic self.

Authenticity echoes across the sea of f*cks. Discernment is your tuning fork, resonating with authenticity. When faced with choices, listen to the echoes of your true self. Discernment ensures that your decisions align with the melody of authenticity.

Emotions can be like tsunamis, threatening to engulf you. Discernment is your seawall. It helps you fend off emotional tsunamis, allowing you to respond with wisdom rather than reacting impulsively. With discernment, you build a resilient barrier against emotional storms.

In the digital age, information is like sand on the shore—abundant but often overwhelming. The art of discernment involves sifting through this information. What is valuable and what is mere noise? Discernment guides you to absorb what contributes to your journey.

Values are the constellations in your navigational sky. Discernment allows you to identify these constellations clearly. Your values should guide your decisions, and discernment ensures that you navigate by the light of these guiding stars.

Resentment can be heavy anchors, dragging you down. Discernment is your anchor release. Recognize when resentment threatens to weigh you down, and, with discernment, release these anchors. Navigate with a lighter heart and a freer spirit.

Balancing conflicting interests is a tightrope walk. Discernment is your balancing pole. It helps you traverse this tightrope, ensuring that you don't sway too far to one side. The art of discernment is mastering the delicate dance of balance.

Every decision has its terrain of consequences. Discernment is your surveyor's tool. Before making choices, survey the potential terrain. What lies ahead? What impact will your decisions have? Discernment ensures that you navigate with foresight.

Time is your most precious resource. Discernment is the alchemy of time. Use your time judiciously. Discern what activities contribute to the meaningful narrative of your life. Mastering the alchemy of time ensures that you invest it where it matters most.

Negativity is the pirate that seeks to plunder your joy. Discernment is your cutlass. Fend off the pirates of negativity with discernment, refusing to let their toxic influence infiltrate your ship. Navigate with the wind of positivity filling your sails.

Intuition is the beacon that illuminates the path ahead. Discernment is your guide in following this beacon. Trust your intuition, and let discernment be the compass that ensures you navigate true to its guiding light.

Fear is a formidable wave. Discernment is your surfboard. Instead of being engulfed by fear, discernment allows you to ride its waves. It enables you to transcend the paralyzing grip of fear and make decisions from a place of courage and wisdom.

Not every battle is yours to fight. Discernment is your strategist. Choose your battles wisely. The wisdom of selective involvement ensures that you invest your energy where it can make the most significant impact.

In the cacophony of choices, discernment conducts the symphony of clarity. It helps you distinguish between the dissonant notes and the harmonious melodies of life. The art of discernment is the conductor's wand, ensuring that your life's composition resonates with purpose and meaning.

The Art of Discernment is not just about making choices; it's about navigating life with a profound understanding of what truly matters. Let's explore the overarching themes and develop a reflective action plan:

- Discernment involves not just intellectual judgment but also emotional intelligence. Reflect on how you can balance your cognitive assessments with emotional understanding to navigate life's complexities more effectively.

- Learn to gauge the weight of life's challenges and opportunities. This requires a keen sense of what's truly significant in the grand scheme of your life's goals and values. Regularly ask yourself: Is this worth my time, energy, and attention?

- Life's dramas often resemble storms. Use discernment as your shield, recognizing when to engage and when to maintain distance for your emotional well-being.

- In a world rife with distractions, discernment helps you stay focused on your goals. Be vigilant against the seductive calls of distractions that stray you from your path.

- Understand the ripple effect of your actions. Use discernment to ensure your decisions and actions positively impact your life and those around you.

- Develop the ability to discern the real urgency of situations. Not every issue demands an immediate response. Sometimes, a measured, thoughtful approach is more effective.

- Use discernment to untangle competing priorities. Align your actions with your core values and principles, ensuring that you're spending your energy on what aligns with your 'true north.'

- In a world of constant opinions and pressures, use discernment as your tool to cut through the noise. Make decisions that resonate with your authentic self, free from external influences.

- Use discernment as a tool to manage overwhelming emotions. Build emotional resilience by responding to situations with wisdom rather than reacting impulsively.

- In the age of information overload, use discernment to filter what's relevant and valuable. Focus on information that contributes positively to your personal and professional growth.

- Recognize when resentment is weighing you down. Use discernment to release these burdens, allowing for a journey marked by a lighter heart and a freer spirit.

- Life often presents conflicting interests. Use discernment as your balancing tool, ensuring that you're considering all aspects fairly without swaying excessively towards any side.

- Before making decisions, survey the potential consequences. Use discernment to predict and evaluate the outcomes of your choices.

- View time as a valuable resource. Apply discernment to spend your time on activities that enrich your life story and align with your long-term aspirations.

- Use discernment as your defense against negativity. Refuse to let negative influences dictate your mood or decisions, and steer your journey towards positivity.

- Trust your intuition, but pair it with discernment. Ensure that your intuition is leading you towards decisions that are beneficial and aligned with your values.

- Allow discernment to help you navigate through fear. Use it to make courageous decisions, not dictated by fear, but informed by wisdom and bravery.

- Realize that not every battle is worth fighting. Apply discernment to choose your battles wisely, focusing your energies where they can have the most significant positive impact.

- Use discernment to distinguish what's harmonious and what's dissonant. Let it guide you to make choices that contribute to a life of purpose and fulfillment.

In essence, "The Art of Discernment" is about navigating life's journey with grace, wisdom, and purpose. It's about making choices that are not only right for you but also contribute positively to the world around you. As you continue to explore giving a f*ck that matters, let discernment be your compass, guiding you through the intricate dance of life's decisions.

The Lighthouse of Core Values

In the vast expanse of life's sea, your core values are the guiding light, illuminating the path ahead. Giving a f*ck that matters is not a blind journey; it's a deliberate navigation, with your core values shining like a lighthouse, ensuring you stay true to your course.

Core values are the constants in an ever-changing sea. Giving a f*ck that matters requires an anchor, something unyielding amidst the waves of change. Your core values provide that constancy, a North Star that remains unwavering, regardless of the storms.

In life's tumultuous waters, it's easy to be tempted by the currents that pull you away from your true direction. Giving a f*ck that matters involves a resistance to this temptation. Your core values act as anchors, preventing you from drifting into the seas of compromise.

Picture your core values as a North Star in the night sky. Giving a f*ck that matters means aligning your journey with this celestial guide. No matter how cloudy the sky may become, your unwavering commitment to your core values ensures you stay on course.

When the storms of life unleash their fury, your core values become the solid ground amidst the crashing waves. Giving a f*ck that matters means finding stability in the chaos, holding firm to your values even when the sea rages around you.

Life is a sea of constant change, but your core values are the bedrock that withstands the shifting tides. Giving a f*ck that matters involves weathering the waves of change with resilience. Your values keep you grounded when everything else is in flux.

In times of uncertainty, your core values act as a lighthouse piercing through the fog. Giving a f*ck that matters requires navigating through the unknown, and your values provide clarity in moments of confusion, guiding you safely through the uncertain waters.

Imagine your life as a symphony, and your core values as the harmonious notes that give it melody. Giving a f*ck that matters means orchestrating your decisions in harmony with your core values. The result is a life composition that resonates with authenticity and purpose.

Morality can be murky waters, but your core values anchor your moral compass. Giving a f*ck that matters involves navigating the choppy seas of ethical dilemmas with a clear sense of right and wrong. Your values ensure your moral compass remains steadfast.

During life's darkest nights, your core values shine brightest. Giving a f*ck that matters involves holding onto your values as a beacon of hope. When the night is darkest, your unwavering commitment to your core values becomes the light that guides you forward. Shallow waters represent a compromise of depth. Giving a f*ck that matters involves avoiding the drift into these shallows. Your core values act as depth indicators, ensuring you navigate towards the profound and meaningful rather than the superficial.

Compromise is a tempest that can sweep you off course. Giving a f*ck that matters involves guarding against this tempest. Your core values are the watchtowers, alerting you when compromise threatens to pull you into its whirlwind.

Life's sea is rife with hidden reefs that can wreck your journey. Giving a f*ck that matters involves illuminating these hidden reefs with the light of your core values. Your values reveal the obstacles in your path, ensuring a safe passage through treacherous waters.

Integrity is your ship's hull in the swells of life. Giving a f*ck that matters involves maintaining this integrity even when the waves are high. Your core values are the strong structure that prevents your ship from capsizing in the tumultuous seas.

Like echoes across the sea, your core values reverberate in your choices. Giving a f*ck that matters involves listening to these echoes. Your values speak in the decisions you make, creating a resonance that echoes through the vastness of your existence.

Storms will come, but your core values are the shelter. Giving a f*ck that matters involves finding solace in the storm, knowing that your values provide a refuge. Amidst the chaos, your unwavering commitment becomes a sanctuary.

The siren's song calls for deviation, but your core values keep you on course. Giving a f*ck that matters involves steering clear of the seductive calls that could lead you astray. Your values drown out the sirens, ensuring you remain true to your purpose.

Build your life on an unshakable foundation—the bedrock of your core values. Giving a f*ck that matters involves creating a structure that can withstand the tests of time. Your values form this foundation, ensuring the stability of your life's architecture.

In times of uncertainty, your core values act as a lighthouse piercing through the fog. Giving a f*ck that matters requires navigating through the unknown, and your values provide clarity in moments of confusion, guiding you safely through the uncertain waters.

Building upon our Lighthouse of Core Values, let's delve deeper into the nuances of living a life guided by core values. This exploration goes beyond the surface, examining how core values intricately weave into the fabric of our daily existence, influencing our behavior, choices, and interactions.

- Core values aren't just lofty ideals; they should be reflected in our daily habits and routines. Reflect on how your everyday actions can be more closely aligned with your core values. This could mean making small but significant changes in how you interact with others, spend your time, or even consume resources.

- Our relationships offer a prime arena for expressing and living our core values. This involves not only choosing relationships that resonate with our values but also actively fostering those values within existing relationships. Whether it's through empathy, honesty, or support, ensure your interactions embody the principles you hold dear.
- In the realm of work, core values should guide your career path and professional decisions. This might mean choosing roles that align with your values, advocating for ethical practices in your workplace, or even making difficult choices like leaving a job that conflicts with your fundamental beliefs.
- It's during challenges and conflicts that our core values are truly tested. Reflect on how these values can guide you in resolving conflicts, whether personal or professional, and how they can provide resilience in adversity.
- Extend your core values to the broader community and societal issues. This could involve volunteer work, activism, or simply being an informed and engaged citizen. Reflect on how you can contribute to societal change in ways that align with your core values.
- Consider how your spending, saving, and investing reflect your core values. This might involve supporting businesses that align with your beliefs, investing in socially responsible funds, or using your financial resources to support causes you care about.
- Your approach to health and well-being should also be influenced by your core values. This includes not just physical health but also mental and emotional well-being. Reflect on how your lifestyle choices, from diet and exercise to stress management and self-care practices, can be more aligned with your values.
- Pursue personal and professional development opportunities that resonate with your values. This commitment to lifelong learning isn't just about acquiring new skills but also about

deepening your understanding of the values you hold and how they apply to the changing world.
- Even your leisure activities offer a chance to express your core values. This might mean engaging in hobbies that reflect your beliefs, participating in cultural activities that resonate with your values, or even choosing entertainment that aligns with your principles.
- Consider how your core values influence the legacy you wish to leave behind. This includes not just material legacies but also the impact and memories you leave with others. Reflect on how you can live today to create a legacy that truly reflects your deepest values.

By delving into these aspects, the concept of core values transcends from being abstract principles to becoming a tangible, living part of our everyday existence. It becomes clear that core values are not just guiding lights for major life decisions but also for the myriad small choices we make each day, cumulatively shaping the course of our lives.

Mastering the F*cking Compass

Your moral compass is your guiding North Star in the vast expanse of life. To give a f*ck that matters, consider this compass your most valuable tool. It is the unwavering point of reference that directs you towards the principles and values that define your true north.

Mastering the compass involves aligning with your deepest convictions. Each decision becomes a moment to check this compass, ensuring that you are on a course that resonates with the core of who you are. It's not just about going in a direction; it's about going in a direction that feels right to your soul.

In the journey of giving a f*ck that matters, regularly check your bearings. Your moral compass is not a set-and-forget tool; it requires constant calibration. With each decision, pause and consult your internal compass. Is this in alignment with your values? Does it point toward the person you aspire to be?

Life is a landscape of decisions, and your moral compass is the map. Mastering the compass means becoming adept at navigating this decision landscape. Let your principles guide you through the twists and turns, ensuring that every step is a step towards authenticity and purpose.

Consider the calibration of your moral compass a sacred ritual. It's not just a mechanical adjustment; it's a moment of reflection and introspection. Regularly take time to assess whether your compass is still pointing towards your principles, and if not, recalibrate it with the intention of staying true to your course.

In the sea of choices, your moral compass points towards true north—your unwavering principles. Mastering the compass involves embracing the responsibility of choice. Let your compass guide you through the waves of options, ensuring that each decision aligns with the values that matter most to you.

Giving a fck that matters is not a passive journey; it's intentional navigation. Mastering the compass means steering your ship with purpose. Be deliberate in your choices, and let your moral compass be the captain that guides you through the sometimes tumultuous waters of life.

External influences can act like magnetic forces, trying to pull your compass needle away from true north. Mastering the compass involves resisting these pulls. Develop a resilience that ensures your compass remains aligned with your internal principles, even in the face of external pressures.

Your decisions are reflections of your values. Mastering the compass involves recognizing that each decision is a brushstroke on the canvas of your life. Let every choice be a conscious expression of your values, painting a picture that is authentic and true.

The needle of your moral compass is a symbol of integrity. To give a f*ck that matters, master the art of keeping this needle true. Guard against deviations, ensuring that your compass maintains its integrity even in challenging circumstances.

Life's journey can sometimes be shrouded in the fog of moral ambiguity. Mastering the compass involves wielding it as a powerful tool to ward off this fog. Let your compass cut through the uncertainty, providing clarity in moments when the right path might be obscured.

Consistency is the discipline of a master navigator. Mastering the compass requires consistent checking. Make it a habit to consult your moral compass, not just in major decisions, but in the small, seemingly inconsequential choices that collectively shape the narrative of your life.

Compromise is the magnetic declination that can throw off your compass. Mastering the compass involves guarding against compromise. Be vigilant about deviations from your true north, recognizing that even small compromises can accumulate and lead you astray.

Mistakes are inevitable, and they can throw your compass off course. Mastering the compass involves the humility to recalibrate after mistakes. Learn from errors, assess where you deviated, and recalibrate your compass with the newfound wisdom to navigate more effectively.

Mastering the compass requires attuning your ears to the subtle whispers of your true north. Your moral compass communicates in the quiet moments, in the stillness when you listen to the inner voice that nudges you towards the decisions that align with your deepest convictions.

Life's landscape is ever-changing, but your principles can remain consistent. Mastering the compass involves recognizing the difference between the ephemeral scenery and the enduring principles that guide your journey. Let your compass navigate through change, always pointing towards the bedrock of your values.

Storms will come, challenging the stability of your journey. Mastering the compass involves relying on it in the storm. When the seas are rough, and decisions are difficult, let your compass be the steady hand that guides you through turbulence with the assurance of staying true to your principles.

Your moral compass creates a personal cartography of values. Mastering the compass involves being an active cartographer of your moral landscape. Survey the territories of your values, map the contours of your principles, and navigate with the confidence that comes from understanding the topography of your authentic self.

Your moral compass is not just a tool; it's a source of empowerment. Mastering the compass involves recognizing the agency it provides. Your decisions are not dictated by external forces; they are guided by your internal compass, empowering you to shape your journey with purpose and authenticity.

Mastering the F*cking Compass is the essence of living a life aligned with one's deepest values and convictions. This encourages a journey that is both introspective and outwardly aligned, where decisions are consistently reflective of one's true north. Let's delve deeper and expand on these ideas:

- Emphasize the integration of your core values into every decision. This involves a conscious effort to ensure that each choice, no matter how small, resonates with these core principles. Reflect on how your daily decisions can be more aligned with your core values.
- Understand that your moral compass is dynamic, requiring regular calibration. Life experiences, new information, and personal growth all necessitate periodic reassessment and realignment of your compass.
- Develop navigational skills to use your moral compass effectively amidst life's complexities. This means not only knowing your direction but also understanding how to maneuver through the challenges and obstacles that life presents.
- Cultivate resilience against external influences that can sway your moral compass. This involves building a strong sense of self and a firm commitment to your values, ensuring that you remain unswayed by peer pressure, societal norms, or fleeting trends.

- In challenging times, your moral compass is tested the most. Strengthen your moral integrity by standing firm in your beliefs, even when it's difficult or unpopular. Use your moral compass to navigate through ethical gray areas. This requires a deep understanding of your values and the ability to apply them in complex, real-world scenarios.
- Aim for consistency in living according to your values. This doesn't mean inflexibility but rather a steady commitment to act in ways that reflect your true north, even when it's inconvenient or challenging. Acknowledge that mistakes are part of the journey. When you veer off course, approach the situation with humility and a willingness to recalibrate your compass based on what you've learned.
- Cultivate the ability to listen to the inner voice that aligns with your core values. Often, the right decision resonates with a sense of inner peace or integrity, even if it's not the easiest choice. Recognize that while life's scenarios may change, your core principles can remain constant. Use your moral compass to navigate these changes, ensuring that your responses and actions stay true to your enduring values.
- Realize the empowerment that comes from self-guidance. Owning your journey and making decisions based on your moral compass instills a sense of agency and purpose, shaping your life path in a way that is authentic and fulfilling. Learn to rely on your moral compass, especially in life's storms – those moments of crisis or difficult decision-making. In such times, your compass is not just a guide but a source of strength and stability.

By diving deep into these aspects, "Mastering the F*cking Compass" becomes a comprehensive guide for a values-driven life. It encourages not just an understanding of one's moral compass but a mastery of using it as a tool for ethical living, decision-making, and personal empowerment.

The Currency of Feels

Recognize the finite nature of emotional energy—it's a currency you can't print more of. Giving a f*ck that matters involves acknowledging the limits of this currency. Instead of dispersing it recklessly, treat it as a valuable resource, to be allocated with care and intention.

Practice the selective allocation principle with your emotional energy. Just as you wouldn't frivolously spend your hard-earned money, be discerning about where your emotional energy goes. Direct it towards endeavors and relationships that align with your values, and watch as the return on investment becomes profound.

Relationships are emotional investments. Giving a f*ck that matters means investing your emotional energy in meaningful connections. Cultivate relationships that nurture your well-being and reciprocate the energy you invest. Emotional investments in genuine connections yield dividends of joy, support, and fulfillment.

Spending emotional currency without consideration leads to emotional bankruptcy. Giving a monumental f*ck involves avoiding this bankruptcy. Prioritize the emotional investments that will replenish rather than deplete your resources. Guard against emotional expenditures that offer little in return, leaving you drained and emotionally impoverished.

Maintain strategic emotional reserves. Giving a f*ck that matters requires having emotional energy in reserve for the moments when it's truly needed. Like a well-prepared traveler, ensure you have emotional reserves to weather the unexpected storms of life, investing them where they'll make the most significant impact.

Emotional investment involves calculated risks. Understand that not every investment will yield the expected return. Some relationships or causes may not reciprocate your emotional energy, and that's okay. Learn from these experiences and adjust your investment strategy accordingly.

Diversify your emotional investments. Just as financial advisors recommend diversifying investments, apply the same principle to your emotional energy. Spread your investments across various aspects of life, including relationships, personal growth, and meaningful pursuits. This diversification enhances emotional resilience and adaptability.

Emotional energy operates on a compound interest model. Giving a monumental f*ck means understanding the power of consistent, thoughtful investments. Small, meaningful gestures and emotional deposits accumulate interest over time, creating a rich reservoir of positivity and fulfillment.

Develop conscious spending habits with your emotional currency. Mindless spending leads to regret and emotional debt. Giving a f*ck that matters involves being intentional about where your emotional energy goes. Pause and assess the potential return on investment before making emotional expenditures.

Emotional inflation occurs when the value of your emotional currency diminishes. Giving a f*ck that matters involves recognizing signs of emotional inflation. If you find yourself feeling emotionally drained or desensitized, it's time to reassess your spending habits and recalibrate your emotional investment strategy.

Maintain a balance between emotional withdrawals and deposits. Every meaningful relationship or pursuit involves withdrawals and deposits. Be aware of the emotional balance sheet in your life. Strive for relationships and endeavors that contribute positively to your emotional well-being rather than consistently depleting your reserves.

Superficial waves demand cautious spending. Giving a f*ck that matters involves discerning between superficial, fleeting concerns and those that hold deeper significance. Avoid squandering emotional energy on inconsequential matters, reserving it for the profound moments and causes that truly deserve your investment.

Establish emergency emotional reserves. Life's unexpected challenges can deplete your emotional energy. Giving a monumental f*ck involves having reserves set aside for emergencies. This ensures that you can navigate unforeseen emotional storms with resilience and adaptability.

Identify and prioritize inflation-resistant emotional investments. Some relationships and endeavors withstand the test of time and external pressures, maintaining or even increasing their emotional value. Seek out connections and pursuits that demonstrate resilience in the face of life's inevitable challenges.

Strategic withdrawals contribute to personal growth. Giving a f*ck that matters involves making calculated withdrawals for the sake of self-discovery and development. These intentional withdrawals can serve as investments in your personal evolution, leading to a richer emotional landscape.

Beware of emotional pyramid schemes. Just as financial pyramid schemes lead to losses, emotional pyramid schemes can drain your energy with little return. Choose emotional investments that offer genuine value and growth rather than falling prey to short-term, unsustainable promises.

Apply financial literacy principles to your emotions. Understand the concept of emotional budgets, investments, and returns. Develop emotional financial literacy that empowers you to make sound decisions, ensuring that your emotional currency is spent wisely on the things that truly matter.

View the world as an emotional marketplace. Giving a monumental f*ck involves being a conscious participant in this marketplace. Be selective about the emotional commodities you invest in, seeking those that align with your values and contribute positively to your overall emotional portfolio.

Cultivate emotional wealth over time. Giving a f*ck that matters is a long-term strategy. Cultivate emotional wealth by consistently making intentional and meaningful investments. This wealth becomes a source of resilience, joy, and fulfillment that sustains you through life's inevitable highs and lows.

Explore the potential of your emotional energy as a positive influence. Understand that even small gestures of kindness and understanding can have a significant impact. Consider how you can use your emotional resources to enhance your immediate environment, whether it's through empathy, active listening, or simply being present for those around you. This approach to sharing your emotional wealth doesn't necessarily mean grand gestures but focuses on everyday acts that contribute to a more compassionate and understanding world.

"The Currency of Feels," presents a profound exploration of managing emotional energy as a finite and valuable resource. It's not just about being selective with emotional investments; it's about understanding the dynamics of emotional economics in every aspect of life. Let's explore deeper insights and activities to help navigate this currency effectively:

- **Develop Emotional Budgeting Skills**   Just like financial budgeting, learn to allocate your emotional energy wisely. Create an 'emotional budget' that outlines where you want to invest your energy each day or week. This could include time for relationships, work, personal growth, and self-care.
- **Invest in Emotional Assets**   Identify the 'assets' in your life—relationships and activities that consistently replenish your emotional energy. Make a conscious effort to invest more in

these areas. Recognize that like financial assets, these emotional investments compound over time, leading to greater emotional wealth. Identify opportunities for strategic emotional withdrawals that can lead to personal growth. This might include stepping out of your comfort zone, taking on new challenges, or ending unfulfilling relationships.

- **Recognize and Avoid Emotional Debts:** Just as financial debts can be burdensome, emotional debts—situations or relationships that consistently drain you—need to be managed. Identify these areas and develop strategies to minimize their impact on your emotional wellbeing.
- **Practice Emotional Diversification** Diversify your emotional investments. Engage in a variety of activities and relationships that fulfill different aspects of your emotional needs. This diversification helps mitigate the risk of emotional burnout in any one area.
- **Conduct Regular Emotional Audits:** Periodically assess your emotional investments. Are they yielding the desired return in terms of happiness, fulfillment, and growth? If not, it might be time to reallocate your emotional energy.
- **Learn from Failed Emotional Investments:** Reflect on past emotional investments that didn't pan out as expected. What lessons can you learn? How can these insights inform your future emotional spending?
- **Build an Emotional Emergency Fund** Cultivate a reserve of emotional energy for unexpected life events. This could involve practices like mindfulness, meditation, or simply ensuring regular periods of relaxation and disconnection.
- **Conduct Emotional Risk Assessment** Before investing significant emotional energy in a new relationship, project, or endeavor, conduct a 'risk assessment.' Consider the potential emotional costs and benefits, and decide whether the investment aligns with your overall emotional goals. Stay alert to situations or relationships that promise high emotional

returns but are unsustainable in the long run. Learn to identify and steer clear of these emotional traps.

By engaging actively, "The Currency of Feels" becomes more than a metaphor; it transforms into a practical framework for managing one's emotional energy. It's about making each emotional investment count, leading to a life that is not only emotionally sustainable but also rich in fulfillment, joy, and meaningful connections.

Triaging Life's Challenges

Consider life as a battlefield, each challenge a potential skirmish. Giving a f*ck that matters requires understanding the topography of this battlefield. Some challenges are strategic high grounds, while others are mere distractions. Navigate with purpose, recognizing where your energy is most effectively deployed.

In the triage of life, prioritize the wounded warriors. Some challenges are wounded soldiers deserving of your attention and care. Identify the battles that, when won, contribute to your well-being and the well-being of those around you. Direct your efforts towards these worthy causes.

Recognize the deceptive mirage of every battle. Not every challenge is a worthy cause. Some are illusions, mirages designed to divert your attention. Giving a f*ck that matters involves piercing through these illusions, focusing on battles that align with your values and lead to genuine growth.

Strategic retreats are not signs of weakness; they are tactical decisions. Giving a monumental f*ck means understanding when to strategically retreat. Not every battle is worth the toll it takes. Preserve your emotional and physical resources for the wars that truly matter, accepting that some skirmishes are best left behind.

Illusions of significance can cloud judgment. In the triage of life's challenges, beware of illusions that magnify the importance of certain battles. Some challenges may seem grandiose but are ultimately inconsequential. Train your discernment to identify illusions, focusing on the battles that genuinely shape your narrative.

Emotional first aid is a critical triage skill. Just as a medic tends to physical wounds, recognize the importance of emotional first aid in life's challenges. Provide comfort, understanding, and self-compassion as you navigate through difficulties, healing emotional wounds before they fester.

Triaging life's challenges involves discerning between urgency and importance. Not every urgent matter is important, and vice versa. Prioritize challenges based on their genuine importance rather than succumbing to the pressure of urgency. This strategic discernment ensures that your efforts align with meaningful outcomes.

Strategic silence is a powerful triage tool. Not every challenge requires a vocal response. Giving a f*ck that matters involves understanding when to remain silent. This wisdom allows you to conserve your energy for battles that demand a vocal and impactful presence, amplifying the resonance of your voice.

Consider the collateral damage of each battle. Life's challenges often have ripple effects, impacting not only you but also those around you. In the triage process, assess the potential collateral damage and decide whether the battle is worth the broader cost. Strive for solutions that minimize harm while achieving meaningful victories.

Triage necessitates the art of non-attachment. Giving a f*ck that matters involves acknowledging that not every battle will end in victory. Embrace non-attachment, understanding that the journey is as important as the destination. This perspective allows you to move through challenges with grace and resilience.

Calibrate your moral compass in the triage of life's challenges. Your values serve as the guiding force in the triage process. Ensure that your compass points true north, steering you towards battles that resonate with your principles. The calibration of your compass ensures ethical decision-making amid life's chaos.

Listen to the heartbeat of moral imperatives. Some challenges align with moral principles, pulsating with a sense of ethical urgency. In the triage of life, give a f*ck to challenges that resonate with the rhythm of moral imperatives, recognizing the power of your actions to contribute to positive change.

Radical acceptance is a form of surgery in life's triage. Acceptance doesn't imply defeat; rather, it is a strategic decision to acknowledge the reality of certain challenges. Embrace radical acceptance where needed, recognizing that not every aspect of life is within your control.

Maintain strategic reserves of resilience in life's triage. Challenges can be relentless, and resilience is your strategic reserve. Cultivate resilience through self-care, meaningful connections, and practices that fortify your emotional and mental well-being. These reserves empower you to face life's challenges with endurance and adaptability.

Triage demands avoiding the rabbit hole of endless analysis. Not every challenge requires exhaustive scrutiny. Giving a monumental f*ck involves knowing when to pause the analysis and take action. Strive for a balanced approach that considers the significance of the challenge without succumbing to analysis paralysis.

Tactical withdrawal of ego is a powerful triage tactic. Life's challenges can stir the ego, clouding judgment. In the triage process, withdraw the ego strategically. This allows for objective assessment and decision-making, ensuring that battles are chosen based on their intrinsic value rather than ego-driven desires.

Gentle redirection is an art in the triage of life. Not every challenge requires a head-on collision. Master the art of gentle redirection, guiding challenges toward resolutions that align with your values. This skillful navigation ensures that your efforts contribute to positive outcomes without unnecessary conflict.

Unhealthy attachments can poison the triage process. Identify and detoxify unhealthy attachments to specific challenges. Giving a f*ck that matters involves recognizing when attachments are detrimental and choosing to release them. This detoxification allows for a clearer, more objective approach to life's challenges.

Inner turmoil requires its own form of triage. Life's challenges often echo within, creating inner turmoil. Prioritize self-awareness and emotional self-care as you triage inner struggles. Giving a monumental f*ck involves tending to the wounds within, fostering emotional resilience for the battles that lie ahead.

Forge strategic alliances in the triage of life. Not every battle needs to be faced alone. Identify allies—trusted friends, mentors, or family members—who can provide support and perspective. Triage becomes more effective when shared, as the collective wisdom of allies enhances decision-making.

Uncertainty is the fog that shrouds life's challenges. In triage, navigate the fog with a clear sense of purpose. Trust your instincts and values as you move through uncertainty, allowing them to serve as a compass that cuts through the fog and guides you to meaningful resolutions.

Humility is crucial in the triage of life's challenges. Recognize your limits—both in influence and control. Not every challenge can be conquered, and not every outcome can be dictated. The humility to accept these limits ensures that your efforts are channeled into battles where your impact can be truly transformative.

"Triaging Life's Challenges" presents a strategic approach to dealing with life's obstacles. It's about more than just tackling problems; it's a comprehensive method for determining where to allocate your time, energy, and focus. As life often presents us with an array of challenges, each demanding our attention and energy, it's crucial to have a strategic approach. Drawing from the insights of this chapter, we've developed two tailored action plans:

Top 5 Action Plan for Triaging Life's Challenges

- Designed for those who want to prioritize and tackle life's challenges with precision and effectiveness. It provides a streamlined method for managing your resources, making mindful decisions, and maintaining emotional resilience. Ideal for quick reference, it offers essential strategies for immediate application.

    1. **Effective Prioritization of Challenges** Begin by methodically sorting life's challenges into three categories: 'critical and immediate,' 'important but not urgent,' and 'lower priority.' Address the most urgent and impactful issues first, optimizing your resource management and ensuring that your efforts are concentrated where they matter most.

    2. **Mindful Allocation of Energy** Actively evaluate and adjust the distribution of your emotional and mental resources. Channel greater energy towards challenges that not only resonate with your core values but also promise substantial benefits for your personal development and well-being.

    3. **Reflective Decision-Making Process** Adopt a pause-and-consider approach to each challenge. Deliberately assess whether engaging with the challenge will align with your fundamental values and contribute meaningfully to your overarching life objectives. This reflective process helps in making more intentional and impactful choices.

    4. **Strategic Withdrawal as a Strength** Embrace the wisdom of knowing when to strategically disengage. Recognizing the need to retreat in certain situations is a sign of tactical intelligence, not defeat. This approach

allows you to conserve your energy and focus on battles that are truly significant and align with your life's mission.

5. **Master Emotional First Aid Techniques**   Develop a toolkit of quick, effective emotional self-care strategies, such as mindfulness practices, deep breathing exercises, or positive affirmations. Equip yourself to immediately address stress or emotional challenges, enhancing your resilience and capability to navigate life's trials effectively.

Top 10 Action Plan for Triaging Life's Challenges

- Designed for those who seek a deeper and more holistic approach to life's trials. It covers everything from prioritizing challenges to building resilience and practicing tactical silence, offering a robust framework for navigating complex scenarios.

    1. **Effective Prioritization of Challenges**   Classify challenges into 'immediate and critical,' 'important but not urgent,' and 'lower priority'. Address the most pressing issues first, focusing your resources where they have the most impact.
    2. **Strategic Allocation of Emotional and Mental Energy** Assess and allocate your emotional and mental energy consciously. Prioritize challenges that not only align with your values but also significantly impact your personal growth and well-being.
    3. **Reflective and Value-Aligned Decision-Making** Implement a thoughtful approach to decision-making. Evaluate each challenge for its alignment with your core values and potential contribution to your long-term goals.
    4. **Strategic Withdrawal**   Recognize when disengagement is a strategic move. Withdrawing from less significant battles preserves energy for more meaningful conflicts.
    5. **Develop Emotional First Aid Skills**   Cultivate quick, effective techniques for emotional self-care, such as

mindfulness, deep breathing, or positive affirmations to manage stress and emotional disturbances promptly.

6. **Discernment in Urgency and Importance**   Distinguish between what is urgent and what is truly important. Focus on challenges that have significant long-term effects rather than those that appear pressing but are less consequential.

7. **Embrace Tactical Silence**   Understand the power of strategic silence. Choose when to speak up and when to conserve your energy, focusing on battles where your voice and actions have the most impact.

8. **Assess Potential Collateral Impact**   Evaluate the broader effects of your actions, considering how your decisions in facing challenges might affect others. Aim for solutions that minimize harm while achieving meaningful results.

9. **Practice Non-Attachment and Acceptance**   Cultivate a mindset of non-attachment to outcomes, focusing on the effort rather than the result. Embrace acceptance in situations beyond your control to navigate challenges with grace.

10. **Build Resilience Through Self-Care and Support Systems**   Invest in activities and relationships that build resilience. Engage in self-care practices and nurture supportive networks to strengthen your ability to handle life's challenges.

Both action plans are grounded in the principles of thoughtful engagement and emotional intelligence. Whether you opt for the concise guidance of the Top 5 or the comprehensive strategies of the Top 10, these plans are crafted to equip you with the essential tools and perspectives needed to adeptly manage life's challenges. By embracing these strategies, you'll be well-prepared to traverse life's intricate pathways with assured confidence and resilience, always mindful of the broader insights and lessons we've explored.

The Echo Chamber of Significance

Life, akin to an echo chamber, shapes its sonic landscape based on the sounds you choose to emit. Giving a f*ck that matters is about contributing to a harmonious and purposeful composition within this vast sonic landscape. Imagine each choice as a note, creating echoes that define the melody of your existence.

Amplify authentic frequencies within your echo chamber. Authenticity is the purest resonance of self, a frequency that, when amplified, creates echoes that resonate with meaning and purpose. Giving a f*ck that matters involves tuning into your authentic frequencies and ensuring they are the dominant notes in your life's symphony.

Inauthentic echoes create dissonance in the chamber of significance. When you give a f*ck to things that don't align with your values or true self, the echoes become discordant. It's like playing off-key notes in an otherwise harmonious symphony. Navigate away from inauthentic frequencies to maintain the resonance of significance.

Recognize the ripples of influence your echoes create. Every fck given sends out waves of impact, shaping the experiences of those within earshot. Giving a fck that matters involves understanding the potential influence of your echoes and choosing to contribute positively to the shared sonic environment.

Relationships form an intricate tapestry within the echo chamber of life. The echoes of your f*cks resonate within these relationships, creating patterns that either strengthen the fabric or introduce dissonance. Consider the reverberations of your choices on the relational tapestry, ensuring that your echoes contribute to a harmonious connection.

Your life's soundtrack is composed of purposeful choices, each note resonating within the echo chamber of significance. Giving a f*ck that matters means curating a soundtrack that reflects your values, aspirations, and the impact you wish to have on the world. Let your choices create a symphony that uplifts and inspires.

The echo chamber is susceptible to white noise—trivial pursuits that add no meaningful resonance. Giving a f*ck that matters involves filtering out this white noise, avoiding the cacophony of insignificant echoes. Focus on the substantial notes that contribute to the richness and depth of your life's symphony.

Maintain symphonic integrity in your choices. Each decision contributes to the overall composition of your life's symphony. Giving a f*ck that matters means ensuring that every note aligns with the melody of your core values. Strive for coherence and integrity in the echoes you create.

Consciously orchestrate the impact of your echoes. Recognize that your f*cks are powerful notes in the symphony of life, and orchestrate them with intention. Consider how each echo contributes to the overall composition, aiming for a melody that leaves a positive and lasting impression on the hearts of those who hear it.

Altruistic echoes carry a unique resonance. When you give a f*ck to causes beyond yourself, the echoes carry a harmonious and altruistic tone. Contribute to the resonance of altruism within the chamber of significance. Let your echoes be not only self-affirming but also harmoniously attuned to the needs of others.

Live with intention, understanding the choreography of your choices. The echoes of intentional living create a dance within the chamber of significance. Each step is purposeful, contributing to the overall elegance of your life's choreography. Be mindful of the dance you create through your actions.

Identify and soundproof the detrimental echoes. Not every f*ck given contributes positively to the resonance of significance. Some echoes may introduce negativity or discord. Exercise discernment, acknowledging when certain echoes are detrimental, and take measures to soundproof against their impact on your symphony.

Self-reflection is an echo that resounds within the chamber of significance. Regularly tune into the echoes of your own thoughts, feelings, and motivations. Giving a f*ck that matters involves an awareness of your internal echoes, ensuring they align with the values and aspirations that define your symphony.

Embrace the harmony of personal growth echoes. Every choice made in the pursuit of self-improvement adds a resonant note to your life's symphony. Giving a f*ck that matters involves a commitment to continuous growth, allowing the echoes of learning and development to enhance the overall harmony of your existence.

Discern between solo and ensemble echoes in the symphony of life. Some f*cks are solitary notes, influencing your personal journey. Others are ensemble notes, contributing to the collective resonance of shared experiences. Understand the dynamics between solo and ensemble echoes, finding a balance that enriches both.

Consider the echoes of legacy within your symphony. Giving a f*ck that matters extends beyond the present, creating echoes that resonate through time. Reflect on the kind of legacy you wish to leave—the enduring echoes that continue to influence and inspire generations beyond your own.

Your echoes are seeds of inspiration planted in the minds of others. Giving a f*ck that matters involves sowing seeds that have the potential to grow into flourishing gardens of positive change.

Be mindful of the inspirational potential of your echoes, nurturing a legacy that blossoms with purpose.

Compassion creates echoes with a unique resonance. When you give a fck with genuine compassion, the echoes carry a melody of empathy and understanding. Foster compassionate resonance within the echo chamber, allowing your fcks to be a source of comfort and connection for others.

Adversity weaves its own tapestry within the echo chamber. When facing challenges, the echoes of your fcks define the narrative of resilience and determination. Giving a fck that matters involves contributing notes of strength and fortitude to the tapestry of echoes in times of adversity.

Strategically amplify positive echoes within the chamber of significance. Recognize that some notes deserve to be louder, resonating more prominently. Giving a f*ck that matters involves intentional amplification of positive echoes, ensuring that the melodies of kindness, empathy, and love ring out above the noise of negativity.

Present-moment awareness enhances the clarity of echoes. When you give a fck to the present moment, the echoes become crisp and resonant. Avoid the distortion caused by dwelling on the past or worrying about the future. Cultivate a mindful presence, allowing your fcks to create echoes that contribute to the beauty of the now.

Harmonize your echoes across the dimensions of time, space, and relationships. Giving a f*ck that matters involves creating a symphony that transcends boundaries. Let your echoes harmonize with the echoes of others, creating a collective resonance that reverberates across the interconnected fabric of existence.

Wholehearted living is the symphony's crescendo. Giving a f*ck that matters means living with your whole heart, allowing its beats to synchronize with the rhythm of your choices. The symphony of wholehearted living is a powerful anthem within the chamber of significance, a melody that resounds with authenticity, purpose, and love.

"The Echo Chamber of Significance" delves into the profound impact of our choices and actions on our life's narrative. It contrasts the negative spiral of overthinking with the empowering realm of making meaningful contributions. Let's expand on these lessons and offer an action plan to help focus on creating a life of significance:

Cultivate Authentic Resonance
- Regularly assess if your actions align with your true self. Journal about moments when you felt most authentic and seek to understand what drove those experiences.
- Before making decisions, ask yourself, "Is this in harmony with my genuine self?"

Navigate Away from Inauthentic Echoes
- Create a list of your core values. With each significant choice, refer to this list to ensure alignment.
- Learn to recognize when you're acting against your values and take steps to realign.

Amplify Positive Influence
- Visualize how your actions impact others. You may want to create a mind map showing the ripple effect of your significant choices.

- Set specific goals for how you can positively influence your environment and relationships.

Strategic Emotional Investment in Relationships
- Assess your relationships based on the emotional return they offer. Focus on nurturing the ones that are mutually beneficial and fulfilling.
- Keep track of how you distribute your emotional energy among your relationships.

Harmonious Life Soundtrack Creation
- Imagine your life as a soundtrack. What kind of music does it play? Create a playlist that represents the values and emotions you want to echo in your life.
- At the end of each day, reflect on whether your 'soundtrack' played the tunes you intended.

Filter Out White Noise
- Identify 'white noise' in your life – distractions or trivial pursuits. Commit to reducing these.
- Practice mindfulness or meditation to enhance your ability to concentrate on what truly matters.

Maintain Symphonic Integrity
- Establish regular checkpoints to assess whether your actions maintain the integrity of your 'life symphony'.
- After making decisions, analyze if they contributed harmoniously to your life's overall composition.

Conscious Orchestration of Life's Impact
- Start each day by setting intentions that align with the impact you wish to create.
- Regularly review the 'echoes' you've created and adjust your actions to ensure they contribute positively to your and others' lives.

Altruistic Echo Enhancement
- Seek and engage in altruistic activities that resonate with your values.
- Reflect on how these activities make you feel and the impact they have on others.

Embrace Present-Moment Awareness
- Engage in daily mindfulness exercises to enhance your present-moment awareness.
- Write about your experiences of being fully present and the clarity of echoes it creates.

Select the strategies that truly speak to your heart and align with your personal journey. By embracing these strategies, you will be actively participating in the "Echo Chamber of Significance," towards a life resonating with purpose, authenticity, and meaningful impact. Each action and choice becomes a note in your symphony, contributing to a legacy of significance and positive influence.

The Echo Chamber of Significance is the opposite of the Inner Critic's Echo Chamber from Hell. The key distinction lies in transforming potentially negative overthinking into positive, constructive reflection. If you ever find yourself in the Inner Critic's Echo Chamber from Hell emphasize positive, purposeful contemplation rather than detrimental overthinking. Here are some strategies to do this:

Constructive Reflection vs. Negative Overthinking
- Instead of ruminating over problems, use journaling to reflect constructively on challenges and brainstorm solutions.
- When you catch yourself overthinking negatively, consciously shift your focus to what you can learn and how you can grow from the situation.

Convert Challenges into Opportunities for Growth
- Identify current challenges and map out ways they can lead to personal growth or positive outcomes.
- Regularly practice identifying the hidden opportunities in difficult situations.

Proactive Decision-Making
- Create a decision-making framework based on your core values to guide you in making choices that contribute positively to your life.
- Set clear action steps for decisions to prevent prolonged overthinking.

Foster Positive Relationship Dynamics
- Shift from critiquing relationships to exploring how they can be improved and nurtured.
- Practice balancing giving and receiving emotional energy in relationships to create mutually supportive dynamics.

Create a Life Soundtrack of Positive Echoes
- Create a daily practice of noting things you are grateful for, adding these positive notes to your life's soundtrack.
- Regularly acknowledge and celebrate small achievements to reinforce positive echoes.

Mindful Engagement with Challenges
- Incorporate mindfulness practices when addressing challenges to ensure a balanced and thoughtful approach.
- Schedule times for constructive critique, limiting the scope and duration to prevent negative spiraling.

Align Actions with Personal Integrity
- Regularly review your actions to ensure they align with your personal integrity and values.

- Develop affirmations that reinforce your commitment to living with integrity.

Intentional Impact and Influence
- Visualize the positive impact of your actions on yourself and others to reinforce the purpose behind your choices.
- Reflect on the influence you have in various spheres of your life and how you can use it positively.

Cultivate Altruism through Positive Actions:
- Plan and execute regular acts of kindness, big or small, to cultivate a habit of altruism.
- Reflect on how your contributions to your community create positive ripples.

Embrace the Present with Optimism:
- Engage in activities that encourage a positive and optimistic view of the present.
- End each day by noting optimistic thoughts or experiences to cultivate a positive outlook.

Choose strategies that resonate with you. By adopting these strategies, you transform potential negative overthinking into positive, constructive contemplation. This approach not only contrasts with but also counters the destructive patterns of the Inner Critic's Echo Chamber from Hell, paving the way for a life filled with growth, positivity, and meaningful impact.

Beyond Superficial Echoes

Step beyond the shallows into the depths of the echo chamber. Giving a f*ck that matters involves a commitment to explore the profound, to dive into the richness of experience, and to create echoes that resonate with depth and authenticity.

Superficial echoes are often mistaken for meaningful resonance. Society may applaud the loud splashes on the surface, but giving a f*ck that matters means recognizing the illusion. It's about acknowledging that the quiet, profound echoes beneath the surface carry more weight and significance.

Cultivate inner resonance that transcends superficiality. Giving a f*ck that matters is an inward journey, an exploration of your own depths. Let the echoes you create emerge from the wellspring of authenticity within, forming ripples that touch the essence of your existence.

Transform your echoes into impactful waves. Superficial echoes dissipate quickly, like ripples in a pond. Giving a f*ck that matters involves converting these ripples into waves—waves of influence, kindness, and purpose that extend far beyond the immediate moment.

Superficial echoes often align with societal trends, but giving a f*ck that matters requires sounding the depths of personal values. Your values are the echoes that resonate with the core of who you are. Make choices that amplify these resonances, creating a symphony of authenticity.

The noise of superficiality can be deafening. Giving a f*ck that matters involves intentional drowning out of this noise. Choose depth over distraction, substance over spectacle. Let the echoes of your life be a resounding declaration of purpose and meaning.

Embark on a journey of self-discovery within the echo chamber. Superficial echoes often drown out the whispers of your true self. Giving a f*ck that matters means paying attention to these whispers, allowing the echoes of self-discovery to shape the narrative of your existence.

Superficiality lacks authenticity, but giving a f*ck that matters is your sonic signature of authenticity. Let your echoes be the true representation of your values, passions, and beliefs. In a world that values the fake, authenticity becomes a revolutionary act.

Superficiality thrives on simplicity, but giving a f*ck that matters embraces the complexity of echoes. Life is not a one-note melody; it's a symphony of diverse echoes. Embrace the intricacies, contradictions, and nuances within your own echoes, creating a composition that reflects the richness of human experience.

Relationships built on superficial echoes lack depth. Giving a fck that matters transforms connections into profound relationships. Engage in conversations that echo with vulnerability, empathy, and understanding. Let your relationships be a testament to the depth of your fcks.

Superficiality is ephemeral, here today and gone tomorrow. Giving a f*ck that matters transcends the transient. Seek echoes that resonate with enduring values, leaving a lasting impact that outshines the fleeting trends of the superficial echo chamber.

In a world fixated on appearances, giving a f*ck that matters shifts the focus to substance. Substance is the core resonance that withstands the test of time. Let your echoes carry the weight of substance, forging a path that goes beyond the surface-level echoes of the superficial.

Superficial echoes often blend into the sea of facades. Giving a f*ck that matters is the beacon of authenticity in this vast expanse. Rise above the superficiality, let your echoes be a lighthouse that guides others toward the authenticity within themselves.

Superficiality lacks the depth of empathy and compassion. Giving a f*ck that matters involves infusing your echoes with these profound qualities. Let your empathy be an echo that resonates with the struggles and joys of others, creating a compassionate symphony.

Trends are fleeting echoes in the chamber of superficiality. Giving a f*ck that matters transcends trends, creating timeless echoes that endure. Let your choices reflect values that stand the test of time, becoming echoes that continue to inspire and resonate across generations.

Superficiality can be confining, like shackles that limit your potential. Giving a f*ck that matters is a declaration of freedom. Break free from the superficial shackles, allowing your echoes to reverberate with the liberated spirit of authenticity.

Superficial pursuits rarely lead to inner fulfillment. Giving a f*ck that matters redirects your echoes toward the sources of genuine satisfaction. Let your choices resonate with the echoes of inner fulfillment, creating a symphony that is deeply satisfying to your soul.

Superficial pursuits lack the depth found in the pursuit of passion. Giving a f*ck that matters means directing your echoes toward your true passions. Let your pursuits be guided by the profound resonance of what truly ignites your spirit.

Superficiality stunts personal growth, but giving a f*ck that matters elevates personal growth echoes. Embrace the transformative power of growth, allowing your echoes to reflect the continuous evolution of your authentic self.

Superficial echoes often remain confined within the echo chamber. Giving a f*ck that matters transcends these boundaries. Let your echoes reverberate beyond the chamber, reaching corners of the world where authenticity and depth are welcomed and celebrated.

Going beyond superficial echoes, challenges us to transcend superficiality, urging us to create meaningful and authentic resonances in life. Let's expand on these ideas with exercises to help cultivate depth and authenticity.

Cultivate Depth Over Superficiality
- Keep a daily diary where you reflect on moments you chose depth over superficiality. Record how these choices impact your emotions and thoughts.
- Regularly analyze your actions and decisions to distinguish whether they are driven by depth or superficiality.

Authentic Resonance Amplification
- Periodically audit your behaviors and choices. Ask yourself, "Are these reflective of my true self?"
- Practice meditation focusing on your core values and authentic self, visualizing how these can be amplified in your daily life.

Transform Echoes into Impactful Waves
- Create a plan for actions or projects that have a lasting, positive impact on your community or environment.
- Visualize the ripple effect of your actions, understanding how even small actions can create significant waves.

Navigate Societal Trends with Personal Values
- When faced with societal trends, reflect on how they align with your personal values. Choose actions that resonate more with your values than with passing trends.
- Critically analyze current trends and their impact on your life choices. Decide consciously which trends to engage with and which to avoid.

Build Depth in Relationships
- Challenge yourself to have deeper, more meaningful conversations with friends, family, or colleagues.
- Assess your relationships based on the depth and authenticity they offer. Focus on nurturing those that are mutually enriching.

Transcend Transient Superficiality
- Set and focus on long-term goals that transcend transient trends and superficial achievements.
- Regularly consider the legacy you wish to leave behind. Let this guide your choices and actions.

Embrace Complexity and Contradictions
- Engage in activities or discussions that challenge your thinking and embrace complexity.
- Journal about contradictions you observe in life and how they add richness and depth to your understanding.

Cultivate Empathy and Compassion
- Engage in exercises like active listening or perspective-taking to enhance your empathy.
- Incorporate daily practices of compassion, both towards yourself and others.

Pursue Passion and Personal Growth
- Dedicate time to projects or activities that align with your passions.
- Track and celebrate your personal growth milestones, focusing on how they contribute to your deeper self-understanding.

Break Free from Confinement of Superficiality
- Visualize and manifest scenarios where you break free from superficial constraints.

- Celebrate moments when you live authentically, regardless of societal expectations.

Choose strategies that resonate with you. By integrating these strategies, you'll be better equipped to move beyond superficial echoes, fostering a life rich in depth, authenticity, and meaningful resonance. This approach not only enhances personal fulfillment but also contributes positively to the world around you.

The Sculpture of Priorities

The sculpture of priorities is an intentional act of carving, not a passive chiseling away. Giving a f*ck that matters involves deliberate choices, where each chip of the chisel shapes the contours of a life aligned with purpose.

Consider your priorities the clay of life, waiting to be molded. Giving a f*ck that matters is an artistic endeavor where you, as the sculptor, shape this clay into a masterpiece that reflects your values, passions, and aspirations.

Just as a sculptor chips away at excess stone, giving a f*ck that matters requires chiseling away the unnecessary. Identify what doesn't contribute to the essence of your life sculpture and carve it out with precision.

Your priorities are the embodiment of your core values. Giving a f*ck that matters means prioritizing in alignment with these values. Let your life sculpture be a testament to the unwavering commitment to what truly matters to you.

Reflection is the sculptor's mirror. Giving a f*ck that matters involves regular reflection, examining the contours of your life sculpture. Use the reflection to adjust, refine, and ensure that every carve aligns with your evolving vision.

A sculptor leaves space intentionally, allowing the masterpiece to breathe. Giving a f*ck that matters means creating space for meaningful priorities. Avoid cluttering your life sculpture with the insignificant; instead, let each priority occupy a space that resonates with purpose.

Selective carving is an art. Giving a f*ck that matters requires precision in choosing where to carve deeply and where to let the surface remain untouched. Be intentional in your choices, knowing that each carve contributes to the final form.

Time is the sculptor's most valuable tool. Giving a f*ck that matters involves carving out ample time for your passions. Let the priorities aligned with your passions be the prominent features of your life sculpture, shaping its overall form.

A skilled sculptor balances dimensions, ensuring harmony in the final piece. Giving a f*ck that matters requires balancing various aspects of life. Harmonize work, relationships, personal growth, and leisure to create a life sculpture with depth and balance.

Relationships are the pillars of the life sculpture. Giving a f*ck that matters involves prioritizing relationships as foundational pillars. Carve out space for meaningful connections, recognizing their role in supporting the structure of your life masterpiece.

Just as a sculptor says no to unnecessary additions, giving a f*ck that matters requires mastering the art of saying no. Learn to decline what doesn't contribute to the essence of your priorities, ensuring that each yes resonates with significance.

A sculptor's decisions are precise and intentional. Giving a f*ck that matters involves adopting a similar precision in decision-making. Assess each decision's impact on your life sculpture, ensuring it aligns with your overarching vision.

A sculpture withstands the elements of nature. Giving a f*ck that matters means preparing your life sculpture for the challenges ahead. Carve resilience into its structure, ensuring that it stands strong against the winds of adversity.

The sculptor begins with an abstract vision, gradually bringing it into concrete form. Giving a f*ck that matters involves transitioning your abstract aspirations into tangible priorities. Carve out the steps needed to manifest your dreams into reality.

Intricacies distinguish a masterpiece from a mere creation. Giving a f*ck that matters requires attention to detail. Carve out the intricacies that add depth and richness to your priorities, making your life sculpture a work of art that captivates.

A sculptor adapts as the sculpture takes form. Giving a f*ck that matters involves evolving with your life sculpture. Embrace change, be flexible in your priorities, and allow the masterpiece to transform over time.

Boundaries define contours in a sculpture. Giving a f*ck that matters means setting clear boundaries. Carve out spaces that protect your priorities, preventing external influences from distorting the form of your life sculpture.

A sculptor revels in the unfinished, seeing potential in the incomplete. Giving a f*ck that matters involves embracing the ongoing process. Carve out time for growth, revel in the journey, and recognize that the beauty lies in the continuous carving.

A sculptor signs their work with authenticity. Giving a f*ck that matters means leaving the signature of authenticity on your life sculpture. Let each carve reflect the real you, creating a masterpiece that resonates with genuine purpose.

A sculptor displays their masterpiece proudly for the world to see. Giving a f*ck that matters involves showcasing your life sculpture with pride. Let the world witness the intentional priorities that shape your existence, a living masterpiece in progress.

"The Sculpture of Priorities" guides you in crafting a life that resonates with your deepest values and aspirations. By viewing life as a sculpture in progress, you can shape a reality that is both meaningful and fulfilling. You can:

- Recognize that shaping your life is an active process. It involves deliberately carving out non-essentials and accentuating what truly matters to manifest a life aligned with your purpose.
- Embrace the art of focusing your efforts. Prioritize carving deeply where it counts and maintaining the surface in other areas. This selective focus ensures that your energy is spent on what genuinely adds value to your life.
- Let your core values be the base of your life's sculpture. Every choice to chip away or build up should align with these values,

ensuring your sculpture is a true representation of what you stand for.
- Regularly step back to view your life's sculpture. Use reflection as a tool to assess and adjust your priorities, ensuring they are in sync with your evolving goals and aspirations.
- Understand and appreciate that your life's sculpture is a work in progress. Embrace the ongoing process of carving and shaping, finding beauty in the journey of continuous improvement and growth.
- Strive for a balanced sculpture that harmoniously integrates various life aspects like work, relationships, personal growth, and leisure. This balance contributes to a well-rounded and fulfilling life.
- Recognize the importance of relationships in your life sculpture. Carve out time and space for these connections, understanding their foundational role in supporting and enriching your life.
- Develop the skill of tactfully saying no to additions that don't enhance your life's sculpture. This skill is crucial in maintaining the integrity and focus of your priorities.
- Incorporate resilience into your sculpture to withstand life's adversities. Carve out strategies and strengths that enable you to face challenges confidently.
- Transition your abstract aspirations into concrete forms. Break down your dreams and goals into actionable steps, carving out these aspirations into your life's sculpture.
- Pay attention to the fine details in your life. The small touches and intricate carvings add depth and richness, making your life sculpture captivating and unique.
- Be open to evolving your sculpture as life unfolds. Adaptability ensures that your priorities and actions remain relevant and impactful, even as circumstances change.

The Canvas of Time

The canvas of time is ever-present, stretching before you with each passing moment. Giving a f*ck that matters involves recognizing this canvas as the medium through which the strokes of your life are painted.

Every moment is a vivid stroke of color on the canvas of time. Giving a f*ck that matters means infusing each stroke with presence. Be fully immersed in the act of living, allowing your existence to paint a vibrant and memorable masterpiece.

Time offers a limited palette of moments, each precious and irreplaceable. Giving a f*ck that matters involves understanding the scarcity of this palette. Choose your fcks wisely, ensuring that each one contributes to the richness of your life's composition.

The canvas of time allows you to craft a timeless composition. Giving a f*ck that matters means being intentional in your strokes, creating a composition that transcends the fleeting nature of individual moments and leaves a lasting impact.

Just as an artist adds depth to a painting, giving a f*ck that matters involves adding depth to the narrative of your life. Each fck contributes to the layers of meaning, creating a textured and nuanced masterpiece.

The canvas of time is a reminder of impermanence. Giving a f*ck that matters involves embracing this impermanence with grace. Recognize that each stroke is a fleeting expression, urging you to savor the beauty of the present.

Time is a precious resource, a finite quantity that cannot be replenished. Giving a f*ck that matters means treating time with the reverence it deserves. Invest your moments in pursuits that align with your values and aspirations.

In the art of giving a f*ck, avoid wasteful splatters on the canvas of time. Mindless distractions and trivial concerns can be like errant drops of paint—splattering without purpose. Direct your fcks with intention, ensuring they contribute to the overall composition.

The hues you choose define the mood of your life's painting. Giving a f*ck that matters involves selecting the right hues—

priorities that resonate with your true self. Let the colors reflect the authenticity of your values and passions.

Each fck is a note in the symphony of your life. Giving a fck that matters means composing a beautiful and harmonious symphony. Consider the composition of your priorities as the arrangement of these notes, creating a melody that resonates with purpose.

Balancing the elements on the canvas is an art. Giving a f*ck that matters involves maintaining equilibrium. Distribute your fcks across various aspects of life, ensuring that no section of the canvas is overwhelmed or neglected.

A masterpiece resonates through time. Giving a f*ck that matters involves ensuring that your priorities have timeless resonance. Choose pursuits and concerns that are not bound by the constraints of the present but contribute enduring value to your life's narrative.

Every fck is a brushstroke on the canvas of time. Giving a fck that matters requires mindfulness in each stroke. Be deliberate in your choices, making sure that each brushstroke contributes to the overall beauty of your life's artwork.

Too many brushstrokes can lead to overwhelm. Giving a f*ck that matters involves guarding against excessive clutter. Choose your priorities thoughtfully, allowing each one to shine individually while contributing to the cohesive whole.

Life is a play of contrasts. Giving a f*ck that matters involves embracing the contrast of moments—the light and the dark, the highs and the lows. Let each stroke on the canvas contribute to the rich tapestry of your life's experiences.

Some strokes intentionally fade into the background. Giving a f*ck that matters involves recognizing the transient nature of certain concerns. Allow some priorities to gently fade away, making space for new and more relevant strokes on the canvas.

Layers add depth to a painting. Giving a f*ck that matters involves understanding the depth that layers bring to your life. Each fck represents a layer, contributing to the complexity and richness of your existence.

Blank spaces on the canvas are opportunities for new meaning. Giving a f*ck that matters means actively filling these blank spaces with pursuits that hold significance. Let your priorities fill the canvas with purpose and fulfillment.

The canvas of time invites contemplation. Giving a f*ck that matters involves periodically stepping back to contemplate the finished piece. Reflect on the composition of your life, appreciating the beauty of the strokes and considering adjustments for an even more meaningful masterpiece.

Brushstrokes endure beyond the artist. Giving a f*ck that matters involves considering the legacy of your brushstrokes on the canvas of time. How will your priorities resonate in the lives of others? Aim to leave a legacy of inspiration and authenticity.

"The Canvas of Time" offers a contemplative approach to how we spend our time, emphasizing the importance of intentionality, presence, and the lasting impact of our choices. The lessons can be distilled into a thoughtful series of reflections and an action plan for time management:

Reflections

- **Moment as Medium** Recognize that each moment is a medium for creating your life's artwork, urging a mindful presence in every act.
- **Scarcity of Moments** Understand the finite nature of time, prompting a selective approach to how and where you invest your energy.
- **Impermanence and Grace** Embrace the impermanence of each moment, encouraging an appreciation of the present.
- **Purposeful Strokes** Approach each decision as a deliberate stroke on the canvas, creating a meaningful and cohesive life composition.
- **Depth of Narrative** Add depth to your life's narrative by infusing each action with layers of meaning and significance.
- **Reverence for Time** Treat time with the utmost respect, investing in pursuits that align with your deepest values and aspirations.
- **Intentional Hues** Choose priorities that reflect your authentic self, painting your life in hues that resonate with your true essence.
- **Symphony of Priorities** Compose your life's priorities as a harmonious symphony, balancing various aspects to create a resonant melody.
- **Mindful Brushstrokes** Be deliberate and mindful in every action, ensuring it contributes to the beauty and purpose of your life's artwork.
- **Embracing Contrast** Appreciate the contrast of experiences, understanding that both light and dark moments add richness to your life.

Action Plan for Time Management

- **Time Inventory** Conduct a regular audit of how you spend your time. Identify areas where time is not aligned with your priorities and values.

- **Priority Setting** Clearly define your top priorities. Ensure these align with your core values and the legacy you wish to leave.
- **Mindful Elimination** Actively remove or reduce activities that contribute to 'splatter'—mindless distractions or trivial concerns.
- **Daily Intention Setting** Start each day by setting intentions. Decide the 'colors' and 'strokes' you will use on that day's canvas.
- **Time Blocking** Allocate specific blocks of time to your priorities. This helps in dedicating focused attention to what truly matters.
- **Reflection and Adjustment** End each day with reflection. Assess the strokes made on your time canvas and adjust as needed for future days.
- **Embracing Blank Spaces** Recognize and embrace blank spaces as opportunities for growth, creativity, and new experiences.
- **Legacy Consideration** Regularly contemplate the enduring impact of your time choices. Ask how each action contributes to the legacy you aim to create.
- **Balanced Composition** Strive for a balanced life composition. Ensure your time is distributed across key life areas like work, relationships, personal growth, and leisure.
- **Contemplative Pauses** Incorporate moments of stillness and contemplation to appreciate your life's canvas and make conscious choices about future strokes.

By internalizing these lessons and incorporating the action plan, you can transform your approach to time, making each moment a purposeful and enriching part of your life's masterpiece.

The Symphony of Impact

The symphony of impact begins with harmony in connection. Giving a f*ck that matters involves recognizing your interconnectedness with the world. Your notes resonate with the notes of others, creating a rich tapestry of shared experiences.

In the symphony of impact, collaborative crescendos elevate the collective melody. Giving a f*ck that matters means actively participating in collaborative efforts. Join forces with others whose notes align with yours, creating moments of powerful crescendo.

While you have your individual melody, giving a f*ck that matters is about weaving it into the collective harmony. Your notes enhance the overall composition, contributing to a symphony that transcends individual stories to create a profound and shared narrative.

In the symphony of impact, each person is a unique instrument. Giving a f*ck that matters involves respecting the diversity of instruments around you. Embrace the different sounds, recognizing that the richness of the symphony lies in the variety of its components.

Giving a f*ck that matters is like conducting change within the symphony. Lead by example, inspiring others to contribute meaningful notes to the collective composition. A small change in one instrument can create ripples that transform the entire symphony.

The symphony of impact is not just heard; it's felt. Giving a f*ck that matters adds emotional resonance to the symphony. Your heartfelt notes create a depth of feeling that lingers in the hearts of those who experience the impact.

In the symphony of life, adversity is inevitable. Giving a f*ck that matters involves guiding others through the challenging movements. Your supportive notes can be a guiding melody, helping others navigate the complexities of their own compositions.

Compassion is an echo that reverberates through the symphony of impact. Giving a f*ck that matters means infusing your notes with compassion. Let your actions and choices create echoes of understanding and empathy, fostering a more compassionate world.

Empowerment is a powerful crescendo in the symphony of impact. Giving a f*ck that matters involves empowering others to play their notes with confidence. Your encouragement can contribute to the uplifting crescendos that define positive change.

Synchronicity is the magic that binds the symphony together. Giving a f*ck that matters involves recognizing the synchronicity in action. Your notes align with the notes of others, creating moments of profound connection and shared purpose.

The symphony of impact weaves narratives of transformation. Giving a f*ck that matters means actively participating in these narratives. Be a force for positive change, contributing notes that inspire growth, resilience, and the evolution of collective stories.

Inclusivity is a crescendo that embraces all voices in the symphony. Giving a f*ck that matters involves fostering inclusive crescendos. Ensure that every instrument, regardless of its uniqueness, has a chance to contribute to the overall melody.

Resilience is a refrain that echoes through the symphony of impact. Giving a f*ck that matters means infusing your notes with resilience. During challenging movements, let your resilient notes inspire others to persevere and find strength in adversity.

In the symphony, even silence holds transformative power. Giving a f*ck that matters involves recognizing when to let moments of silence speak volumes. Your intentional pauses can create space for reflection, growth, and the anticipation of the next powerful movement.

Empathy is the cadence that guides the symphony through moments of emotional depth. Giving a f*ck that matters means allowing your empathetic notes to influence the cadence of the collective composition. Your understanding notes can create a harmonious flow of emotions.

Social responsibility is a note that resonates loudly in the symphony of impact. Giving a f*ck that matters involves acknowledging your role in the social orchestra. Contribute notes of responsibility, advocating for justice, equality, and the well-being of the collective.

Gratitude is a recurring refrain in the symphony of impact. Giving a f*ck that matters involves expressing gratitude for the notes contributed by others. Let your appreciative notes create a harmonious atmosphere of acknowledgment and mutual respect.

The symphony of impact finds its beauty in balancing individuality and unity. Giving a f*ck that matters involves understanding this delicate balance. Contribute your unique notes while harmonizing with the greater melody of collective aspirations and shared humanity.

Diversity is celebrated in the symphony of impact. Giving a f*ck that matters involves celebrating the diversity of sound. Appreciate the different tones, rhythms, and melodies contributed by individuals, recognizing that true harmony embraces the richness of variety.

Impact echoes through generations like a timeless melody. Giving a f*ck that matters involves considering the lasting resonance of your notes. How will your contributions reverberate through the symphony of existence, influencing the narratives of future generations?

"The Symphony of Impact" revolves around the profound interconnectedness of our actions and their collective impact on the world. Let's reflect on the central themes and their implications:

- Acknowledge your deep connection with others and the world. Each action resonates, contributing to a shared experience tapestry.
- Engage in collaborative endeavors. Synergize with others whose goals and values align with yours to amplify the collective impact.
- Integrate your unique contributions into the larger tapestry, enhancing the collective narrative with your individuality.
- Embrace and respect the diverse voices and perspectives around you. The symphony's richness lies in this diversity, creating a more inclusive and comprehensive impact.
- Act as a conductor of change, inspiring and influencing others through your actions and setting an example of positive transformation.
- Infuse your actions with emotion and empathy, creating a deeper, more meaningful impact that resonates on a personal level.
- Use your influence to guide and support others through challenges, offering a beacon of hope and direction.
- Ensure your actions are empathetic and compassionate, creating an environment of understanding and care.
- Elevate those around you, encouraging them to express their unique voices confidently.
- Recognize and embrace the moments of synchronicity, where your actions align perfectly with others, creating a powerful united force.

- Be an active participant in stories of change and growth, contributing to the evolution of collective experiences.
- Strive for inclusivity, ensuring all voices are heard and valued in the collective narrative.
- Incorporate resilience into your actions, helping to fortify the collective spirit, especially in times of hardship.
- Understand the impact of intentional pauses, which can offer moments for reflection and growth.

Reflective considerations:

- **Assess Your Impact** Regularly reflect on how your actions influence the larger community. Are they adding harmony or discord?
- **Community Engagement** Actively seek collaborative projects that align with your values. Look for ways to join or initiate community efforts.
- **Diversity Appreciation** Regularly engage with diverse groups or individuals. Learn from their perspectives and experiences to enrich your understanding.
- **Empathy Practice** Incorporate daily exercises to enhance empathy, like active listening or volunteering in community services.
- **Resilience Building** Develop personal resilience through mindfulness practices or learning from challenging experiences.
- **Gratitude Expression** Make it a habit to express gratitude for the contributions of others in your life, acknowledging their part in your symphony.

"The Symphony of Impact" encourages a life lived in concert with others, where each individual's contribution enriches the collective experience, creating a harmonious and impactful existence.

The Legacy of F*ck-Giving

The legacy of f*ck-giving is akin to a symphony, a composition of impactful notes that resonate through time. Instead of leaving behind a cacophony of insignificant concerns, it's about crafting a symphony that lingers in the hearts and minds of those who inherit the melody.

In the legacy of f*ck-giving, each note is purposeful. Consider your fcks as intentional notes that contribute to the greater composition. What purpose do your notes serve in the grand symphony of existence? Let them echo with significance.

The legacy of f*ck-giving is a harmonic connection between generations. Your notes blend with those of your predecessors, creating a seamless transition of purpose and values. Ensure that your fcks contribute to a melody that harmonizes across time.

Values are the resonating core of the legacy. Giving a fck that matters means aligning your notes with your core values. Let your legacy be a reflection of the values that guided your decisions, actions, and the impact you had on the world.

A timeless melody is the essence of the legacy of f*ck-giving. Craft notes that transcend the temporal boundaries, resonating with relevance across different eras. Your fcks, when given with foresight, can contribute to a melody that withstands the test of time.

The legacy of f*ck-giving extends its influence across the narratives of individuals and societies. What stories will your fcks tell? Consider the impact your notes will have on shaping the narratives of those who come after you.

Legacy is a teacher, and f*ck-giving is the curriculum. Teach through example, showcasing the importance of giving a fck that matters. Your legacy becomes an educational symphony, inspiring others to approach life with purpose and authenticity.

In the legacy of f*ck-giving, echoes are impactful. Consider how your notes will reverberate through the lives of others. Will they create echoes of empowerment, resilience, and positive change? Ensure that your fcks leave behind meaningful and resonant echoes.

Legacy is a contribution to the collective wisdom of humanity. Give fcks that contribute to this wisdom, adding insightful notes to the evolving symphony of human understanding. Your contributions become part of a greater intellectual and emotional harmony.

Empowerment is a key theme in the legacy of f*ck-giving. Give notes of empowerment that resonate with future generations. Inspire individuals to embrace their own fck-giving journey, contributing to a legacy that uplifts and empowers.

F*ck-giving shapes cultural narratives. Consider how your notes contribute to the sculpting of these narratives. Will your legacy be one that challenges societal norms, fostering positive change? Use your fcks to sculpt a cultural narrative that aligns with your values.

Individual stories become a part of a larger narrative in the legacy of f*ck-giving. Your notes transcend the limitations of individual stories, merging with the stories of others to create a narrative of shared purpose and impact.

Legacy inspires creative expressions. Your fcks become a source of inspiration for artistic, literary, and philosophical creations. Consider how your notes can spark creative expressions that contribute to the beauty and depth of human culture.

Compassion is a theme that runs through the legacy of f*ck-giving. Cultivate compassionate echoes through your notes. Ensure that your legacy is one of understanding, empathy, and a genuine concern for the well-being of others.

The legacy of f*ck-giving plants seeds of positive change. Each note carries the potential to germinate into positive actions and transformations. Be mindful of the seeds you plant through your fcks, envisioning the positive changes they might yield.

The legacy of f*ck-giving weaves interconnected melodies. Consider how your notes harmonize with the notes of others. Embrace the interconnectedness of your legacy, recognizing that the symphony is enriched when diverse melodies converge.

Integrity is the musical score in the legacy of f*ck-giving. Your notes must align with the score of integrity to create a harmonious and impactful legacy. Be consistent in giving fcks that uphold your principles and values.

The legacy of f*ck-giving fosters a culture of giving. Encourage others to give meaningful fcks, creating a cultural environment where authenticity, purpose, and impactful actions are valued. Your legacy becomes a catalyst for positive cultural shifts.

Authenticity leaves footprints in the legacy of f*ck-giving. Ensure that your notes are authentic expressions of your beliefs and values. Let your legacy be marked by the genuine and unapologetic footprints of an authentic life.

The legacy of fck-giving transforms into an echo chamber of inspiration. Consider how your notes will inspire those who listen to the symphony of your legacy. Let the echoes be uplifting, motivating others to embark on their own journeys of purposeful fck-giving.

The ultimate goal of the legacy of f*ck-giving is to leave the world in better harmony than you found it. Give notes that contribute to the betterment of society, ensuring that your legacy is a positive force in the ongoing symphony of existence.

"The Legacy of F*ck-Giving" delves into the concept of creating a lasting and meaningful impact through intentional actions and values. This underscores the importance of shaping a legacy that resonates with authenticity, purpose, and empathy. Here's a synthesis of the key lessons and reflections:

- **Intentionality in Actions**   Treat every action as a purposeful note contributing to the grand symphony of your legacy. Reflect on the purpose and impact of your daily choices.
- **Harmony Across Generations**   Strive to create a seamless harmony that connects your legacy with past and future generations, emphasizing continuity and shared values.
- **Values as Resonating Core**   Align your actions with core values, ensuring your legacy accurately reflects your deepest beliefs and principles.
- **Timeless Impact**   Aim to craft actions that have enduring relevance, transcending temporal boundaries and remaining significant through different eras.
- **Narrative Influence**   Be mindful of how your actions shape narratives, both personal and societal, contributing to a legacy that fosters positive change.
- **Legacy as Education**   Use your legacy to educate and inspire others, showcasing the importance of purposeful living and authentic values.
- **Echoes of Empowerment**   Ensure your actions create echoes that empower and uplift, encouraging others to embark on meaningful journeys.
- **Contribution to Collective Wisdom**   Add insightful and thoughtful notes to humanity's collective wisdom, enriching the intellectual and emotional landscape.
- **Cultural Narrative Sculpting**   Use your influence to shape cultural narratives positively, challenging norms and fostering progressive change.
- **Inspiration for Creativity**   Let your actions inspire creative expressions in others, adding to the beauty and depth of human culture.

- **Seeds of Positive Change**   Be conscious of the seeds your actions plant, envisioning the growth of positive transformations they might initiate.
- **Interconnected Melodies**   Embrace the interconnectedness of your actions with others, creating a richer, more diverse symphony.
- **Upholding Integrity**   Maintain a consistent alignment with integrity, ensuring your legacy resonates with honesty and principled actions.
- **Fostering a Culture of Giving**   Encourage a cultural shift towards authenticity, purpose, and impactful actions, making your legacy a catalyst for positive change.

Reflective considerations:

- Regularly contemplate the legacy you're creating. Ask how each of your actions contributes to the symphony you wish to leave behind.
- Continuously align your actions with your core values. Conduct periodic self-assessments to ensure consistency.
- Actively seek ways to connect your actions with those of past and future generations, fostering a sense of continuity.
- Infuse empathy and compassion into your daily interactions. Reflect on how your actions affect others and strive to leave a positive impact.
- Engage in activities that positively shape cultural narratives, whether through community involvement, advocacy, or artistic expression.
- Share your journey and lessons learned with others, inspiring them to create their meaningful legacies.

"The Legacy of F*ck-Giving" encourages viewing your actions as part of a larger narrative, emphasizing the importance of leaving behind a legacy that is impactful, value-driven, and inspires future generations.

The Art of Saying No

Mastering the art of saying no is a powerful tool for setting boundaries. It's a declaration that your time, energy, and emotional resources are valuable and must be reserved for endeavors that truly matter. Saying no is a boundary that protects the sacred space of your fcks.

Your fcks are precious resources. Saying no is a strategic move to preserve these vital resources for endeavors that align with your values and contribute to your overarching goals. It's about recognizing the finite nature of your fcks and investing them wisely.

Saying no is an assertion of personal agency. It's a statement that you have the power to choose where your fcks go. By mastering this art, you empower yourself to be intentional about the causes, relationships, and activities that receive the gift of your attention and concern.

The art of saying no is synonymous with prioritizing purposeful fcks. It involves discernment in choosing causes and commitments that resonate with your values and aspirations. Every no becomes a conscious decision to channel your fcks where they matter most.

Saying yes to everything dilutes the potency of your fcks. It's akin to watering down a concentrated solution. Mastering the art of saying no is a defense against fck dilution. It ensures that your fcks remain potent, impactful, and concentrated on endeavors that truly matter.

Saying no is a cornerstone of intentional living. It's a deliberate choice to live in alignment with your values and purpose. Every no becomes a brushstroke in the canvas of intentional living, contributing to the creation of a life that is meaningful and authentic.

The art of saying no is integral to fostering authentic relationships. It involves being honest and transparent about your limitations and priorities. Saying no when necessary cultivates relationships based on authenticity, where both parties respect each other's boundaries and values.

Social pressures often push individuals to say yes to things that don't align with their values. Mastering the art of saying no is an act of resistance against these pressures. It's a refusal to conform to expectations that conflict with your purpose and authenticity.

Saying no is a key component of effective decision-making. It requires clarity about your values and goals, enabling you to make decisions that align with your overarching vision. The art of saying no enhances the quality of your decision-making process.

Your energy is a finite resource. Saying no is an acknowledgment of this fact, a recognition that you must allocate your energy to pursuits that truly matter. It's a commitment to honor and protect your personal energy for endeavors that align with your purpose.

Mastering the art of saying no is an act of self-respect. It involves valuing your time, needs, and aspirations enough to decline commitments that don't contribute to your growth and well-being. Saying no becomes a powerful affirmation of self-worth.

Saying yes to everything can lead to burnout. The art of saying no is a preventive measure against burnout, ensuring that your fcks are distributed in a way that maintains a healthy balance between your responsibilities and personal well-being.

Every yes requires a portion of your focus. Saying no is a strategic move to strengthen your focus on what truly matters. It's about directing your attention toward endeavors that align with your purpose, reducing distractions and unnecessary commitments.

Your values are the compass that guides your fck-giving. Saying no is a commitment to uphold these values. It ensures that your fcks are directed toward causes and actions that resonate with the principles you hold dear.

By mastering the art of saying no, you become a model for others. Your ability to set boundaries and make intentional choices empowers those around you to do the same. It creates a culture of respect for individual priorities and a shared understanding of the importance of saying no when necessary.

Saying no is not just about refusal; it's about creating space for meaningful yeses. Each no is a deliberate choice to free up time and energy for endeavors that truly align with your purpose and bring fulfillment. It's a positive act of curating your commitments.

As you navigate personal growth and inevitable changes, saying no becomes a skill that helps you stay aligned with your evolving values and aspirations. It's an adaptive tool for managing your fck-giving journey amidst the dynamic nature of life.

Self-care is an essential aspect of well-being. The art of saying no is a form of self-care, ensuring that you don't overextend yourself and deplete your reserves. It's a proactive step to safeguard your mental, emotional, and physical health.

Saying no authentically is an art in communication. It involves expressing your boundaries and limitations with honesty and respect. The art of saying no fosters authenticity in your interactions, setting the tone for transparent and genuine communication.

Saying no liberates you from the shackles of obligation. It's an act of liberation that frees you to give fcks with authenticity and purpose. Embracing the power of no allows you to navigate your fck-giving journey with a sense of autonomy and choice.

"The Art of Saying No" delves into mastering the skill of setting boundaries through selective refusal, emphasizing its crucial role in maintaining personal integrity and aligning actions with core values. Let's delve deeper and reflect on these ideas:

- **Strategic Preservation of Resources**   Recognize the finite nature of your emotional and mental resources. Saying no is essential for conserving these for matters that truly align with your values and goals.
- **Assertion of Personal Agency**   Understand that saying no is a powerful expression of your autonomy. It reflects your ability to make choices that serve your best interests and remain true to yourself.
- **Prioritizing Purposeful Commitments**   Develop discernment in your commitments. Prioritize engagements that resonate deeply with your values, allowing you to invest your energies meaningfully.
- **Preventing Fck Dilution**   Avoid dissipating your focus and energy on trivial or misaligned endeavors. Concentrate your efforts on what truly matters, enhancing the impact and significance of your actions.
- **Intentional Living**   Use saying no as a tool to sculpt a life that is more intentional and aligned with your purpose, ensuring each action contributes meaningfully to your overall life narrative.
- **Cultivating Authentic Relationships**   Foster relationships based on honesty and mutual respect by being clear about your boundaries. Authentic relationships thrive when both parties acknowledge and respect each other's limits.
- **Resistance Against Social Pressures**   Stand against societal expectations that don't align with your personal values. Saying no can be an act of rebellion against conformity, affirming your individuality and authenticity.
- **Enhancing Decision-Making Quality**   Refine your decision-making skills by saying no to options that don't align with your long-term vision, thereby improving the overall quality of your decisions.

- **Recognizing Energy as Finite** Acknowledge your energy limitations and use no as a tool to manage and distribute your energy effectively, focusing on activities and relationships that genuinely matter.
- **Act of Self-Respect** View saying no as an affirmation of your worth and priorities. Recognize it as an essential expression of valuing your time, energy, and aspirations. It's not merely a refusal but a powerful affirmation of your self-worth and a critical aspect of self-care.
- **Burnout Prevention** Recognize the role of saying no in balancing life's demands. Utilize saying no as a strategy to avoid overcommitment and the subsequent risk of burnout. It's crucial for maintaining balance and ensuring sustained productivity and well-being, crucial for maintaining your mental, emotional, and physical health.
- **Strengthening Focus** Channel your attention towards priorities that resonate with your purpose. Saying no to distractions enables a stronger focus on what is truly important.
- **Upholding Personal Values** Align your actions with your core values. Saying no to things that conflict with these values maintains your integrity and authenticity.
- **Creating Space for Meaningful Yeses** Understand that every no frees up space for a yes that is more aligned with your passions and goals. Saying no isn't just a refusal; it's an opportunity to embrace what truly matters, to carve out space for personal growth, rest, and activities that rejuvenate and fulfill you.
- **Adaptive Tool in Personal Growth** As your values and goals evolve, adapt your ability to say no accordingly. It's a dynamic skill that supports your growth and changing aspirations.

Reflective considerations:

- **Boundary Setting Exercise:** Identify areas in your life where you need to set stronger boundaries. Practice saying no in low-stakes situations to build confidence.

- **Values Alignment Check**   Regularly assess whether your commitments align with your core values. If they don't, consider if saying no is the appropriate response.
- **Energy Audit**   Reflect on your energy levels at the end of each day. Identify activities or commitments that drain you unnecessarily and strategize ways to say no to them in the future.
- **Assertiveness Training**   Engage in activities or workshops that enhance assertiveness. Learning to communicate your needs and boundaries assertively is key to mastering the art of saying no.
- **Mindfulness in Decision Making**   Before agreeing to a new commitment, pause and practice mindfulness. Reflect on whether this aligns with your goals and values.

The Sculptor's Chisel

Imagine your life as an uncarved block of marble, and your fcks as the sculptor's tools. Giving a f*ck that matters involves defining the sculpture—carving out the shape and form of a life that resonates with your values and purpose.

The sculptor's chisel is a tool for removing distractions. Giving a monumental f*ck means chiseling away the superfluous elements that clutter your life. It's a deliberate act of decluttering, leaving space for what truly matters.

With every strike of the chisel, you create space for significance. Giving a f*ck that matters involves making intentional choices about where to direct your energy. The sculptor's chisel clears away the unnecessary to reveal the masterpiece within.

Life is your masterpiece, and the sculptor's chisel is your tool for crafting it. Giving a f*ck that matters is an artistry—a conscious act of shaping and refining the contours of your existence. Each strike of the chisel contributes to the creation of a life well-lived.

The sculptor's chisel unveils authenticity. As you give fcks that matter, you carve away the layers of conformity and societal expectations. The authentic self emerges, revealed in the unique and intentional choices you make with each stroke of the chisel.

The sculptor's chisel shapes your values and priorities. Giving a f*ck that matters is not a haphazard process; it's a sculpting of the principles that guide your life. With precision, you chisel away the non-essential, leaving behind a foundation built on what truly matters.

In the realm of relationships, the sculptor's chisel plays a crucial role. Giving a f*ck that matters involves refining the connections that truly align with your values. The chisel may be used to sculpt away toxic influences, leaving room for healthy, meaningful relationships to flourish.

Your life's purpose is like a path waiting to be carved. The sculptor's chisel is the instrument for carving that path. Giving a f*ck that matters involves intentional strikes of the chisel, shaping a purposeful journey that aligns with your aspirations.

The sculptor's chisel is a tool for striking balance. In the intricate dance of life, balance is essential. Giving a f*ck that matters requires careful consideration and a skillful hand, ensuring that your life's sculpture is harmonious and well-proportioned.

External pressures can add unwanted details to your life's sculpture. The sculptor's chisel becomes a weapon of resistance against these pressures. It allows you to resist the imposition of societal norms and expectations, crafting a sculpture that is true to your vision.

Every detail matters in the sculpture of life. The sculptor's chisel details with purpose, ensuring that each facet of your existence contributes to the overall beauty of the masterpiece. Giving a f*ck that matters involves conscious detailing, leaving no stroke of the chisel without intention.

A master sculptor understands the beauty of imperfections. Giving a f*ck that matters is an acknowledgment that your life's sculpture may have imperfections, and that's perfectly okay. The sculptor's chisel embraces these imperfections, recognizing them as part of the unique artwork.

The sculptor's chisel has a singular focus on the essential. Giving a f*ck that matters involves a similar focus. It's about concentrating your energy on the core aspects of your life, ensuring that every strike of the chisel contributes to the revelation of the essential.

Depth and meaning are sculpted into the contours of your life with the chisel. Giving a f*ck that matters involves creating depth beyond surface-level pursuits. The sculptor's chisel delves into the layers, revealing the profound meanings that give richness to your existence.

Mediocrity is the enemy of the sculptor's chisel. Giving a f*ck that matters is a rebellion against mediocrity. With each strike, the chisel defies the ordinary, leaving behind a sculpture that stands as a testament to the extraordinary.

Your identity is the sculpture taking form. The sculptor's chisel plays a role in shaping this identity. Giving a f*ck that matters involves a conscious sculpting of the self, chiseling away influences that don't align with your true identity.

The sculptor's chisel is adaptable to change. Giving a f*ck that matters requires a similar adaptability. Life's circumstances may demand adjustments, and the chisel becomes a tool for gracefully adapting the sculpture to the evolving narrative.

Transitions in life are like chapters in a sculpture's story. The sculptor's chisel honors these transitions. Giving a f*ck that matters involves recognizing the shifts and using the chisel to ensure that each transition adds to the coherence and beauty of the overall sculpture.

The sculptor's chisel empowers self-expression. Giving a f*ck that matters is an act of self-expression. With every strike, the chisel enables you to express your values, beliefs, and individuality, creating a sculpture that reflects your unique essence.

Achievements are the milestones in the sculpture's creation. The sculptor's chisel is the tool for celebrating these achievements. Giving a f*ck that matters involves acknowledging and savoring the successes, each one a testament to the intentional strikes of the chisel.

"The Sculptor's Chisel" encapsulates the transformative journey of carving out a life that resonates deeply with one's personal values and aspirations. Let's reflect on the most pivotal lessons:

- **Intentional Carving for Authenticity** Each decision is a deliberate act of carving, revealing and refining your true self from life's raw marble. It's about removing layers of societal expectations and revealing your authentic form.
- **Strategic Decluttering** The chisel represents your ability to strategically remove distractions and non-essentials. It's about discerning what truly adds value to your life and deliberately chiseling away the rest.
- **Crafting Purposeful Relationships** Your relationships are key facets of your life's sculpture. Use the chisel to shape healthy, meaningful connections, and carve away toxic influences to let beneficial relationships flourish.
- **Balancing Life's Sculpture** The art of chiseling is also about maintaining a harmonious balance between different aspects of life. Each strike aims to create a well-rounded existence, ensuring no area is neglected or overwhelmed.
- **Resisting External Pressures** Your chisel is a tool of resistance against societal norms and pressures. It allows you to maintain the integrity of your personal vision, crafting a life that stays true to your unique path.
- **Detailing with Purpose** Paying attention to the details of your life's sculpture is crucial. Each facet, carved with intention, contributes to the overall beauty and depth of your existence.
- **Embracing Imperfections** Master sculptors know the beauty in imperfections. Accepting and embracing life's flaws as part of your unique sculpture is vital in your journey.
- **Singular Focus on Essentials** Like a sculptor focused on revealing the statue within the marble, concentrate on the essential elements of your life. Ensure every decision reveals more of what is truly important.
- **Crafting Depth and Meaning** The chisel is your tool for delving into deeper layers of existence, moving beyond superficialities to uncover the rich, meaningful textures of life.
- **Sculpting Identity and Self-expression** Your identity emerges through the act of sculpting. Every chisel strike is an

expression of your values, beliefs, and individuality, shaping a distinct personal narrative.

- **Adapting to Life's Changes**   Adaptability is key in sculpting. Life's changes are like evolving chapters in your story, and your ability to adaptively chisel ensures your sculpture remains coherent and beautiful.
- **Celebrating Milestones**   Recognize and cherish achievements in your life's sculpture. Each success, shaped by intentional decisions, stands as a testament to your purposeful journey.

"The Sculptor's Chisel" invites you to reflect deeply on the active role you play in shaping your life. It's a call to wield your chisel with purpose, awareness, and a keen eye for what matters most, crafting a legacy that is not only personal and authentic but also resonates with impact and significance.

4-Week Action Plan to Chisel Your Path, Embrace Chaos, & Find Purpose

Congratulations on completing "Chisel Your Path," the first part of "Embrace Chaos, Find Purpose." You've embarked on a journey of self-discovery, authenticity, and purposeful living. The chapters you've traversed offer insights into reshaping your perspective on life, prioritizing what truly matters, and crafting a life of significance. Now, the moment has arrived to convert these insights into tangible actions.

We recommend revisiting the chapters of the book for renewed inspiration and deeper insights. Each reading can uncover new layers of understanding and empowerment, guiding you further along your journey. To help you transition from reflection to action, here's your first action plan, designed to guide you.

Week 1 Action Plan: Unmasking and Embracing Your Authentic Self

Day 1: Reflection on Authenticity
- **Activity:** Journal about what authenticity means to you. Reflect on moments you felt most authentic and why.
- **Action:** Identify one aspect of your life where you've been less authentic due to societal expectations. Commit to one change this week to align more closely with your true self.

Day 2: The Myth of Giving a F*ck – Prioritization
- **Activity:** List down all the things you currently give a f*ck about. Categorize them into "essential" and "non-essential."
- **Action:** Choose one "non-essential" item to stop giving a f*ck about. Notice the mental and emotional space it frees up.

Day 3: Breaking the Status Quo
- **Activity:** Identify one area of your life where you're following the status quo unthinkingly.
- **Action:** Challenge the status quo by taking a small action that aligns with your true desires or beliefs.

Day 4: The Realities of F*ck-Giving
- **Activity:** Reflect on the energy and time you spend on things that don't bring you joy or value.

- **Action:** Implement a "f*ck budget" – allocate your time and energy like you would with money, only spending it on things that truly matter.

Day 5: Dancing to Your Own Rhythm
- **Activity:** Create a playlist that resonates with your personal journey and aspirations.
- **Action:** Have a solo dance party. Let loose and embody the freedom of dancing to your own rhythm, literally and metaphorically.

Day 6: Purpose Over Positivity
- **Activity:** Write down your definition of purpose. How does it differ from chasing positivity?
- **Action:** Identify one purpose-driven activity you can do today. It doesn't have to be big, just meaningful to you.

Day 7: Weekly Reflection and Planning
- **Activity:** Review your journal and activities from the week. Reflect on any shifts in your feelings or outlook.
- **Action:** Plan one bold action for next week that aligns with your core values and contributes to your symphony of impact.

Moving Forward

As you progress through these activities, remember that the journey to authenticity and purposeful living is ongoing. Each step you take is a chisel strike in sculpting the masterpiece that is your life. Embrace the process, the missteps, and the triumphs alike. Next week, we'll delve into translating your core values into actionable goals, triaging life's challenges with wisdom, and sculpting your priorities to carve out more space for what truly enriches your life. Stay committed, stay rebellious, and above all, stay true to the extraordinary path you're chiseling for yourself.

Week 2 Action Plan: Sculpting Your Path with Core Values and Boundaries

As you move into the second week of implementing the insights from "Chisel Your Path," focus on deepening your understanding of your core values, mastering the art of discernment, and learning to navigate life's challenges with resilience and purpose. Here's your guide to turning these concepts into actionable steps.

Day 8: The Lighthouse of Core Values

- **Activity:** Draft a list of your top five core values. If you're unsure, think about moments you felt proud or fulfilled—what values were you honoring?
- **Action:** Choose one core value and plan a specific way to live it out today. For example, if one of your core values is compassion, perform an act of kindness.

Day 9: Mastering the F*cking Compass

- **Activity:** Reflect on recent decisions you've made. Did they align with your core values? Write about the alignment or misalignment you discover.
- **Action:** For any decision you face today, big or small, use your core values as your compass. Make your choice based on which option best aligns with these values.

Day 10: The Currency of Feels - Emotional Investment

- **Activity:** Identify where your emotions have been most invested recently. Are these investments paying off in joy and fulfillment?
- **Action:** Redirect emotional investment from a less fulfilling area to something that aligns with your core values. Notice any shifts in your energy or mood.

Day 11: Triaging Life's Challenges with Wisdom

- **Activity:** List down three challenges you're currently facing. Use the triage method to prioritize them based on urgency and alignment with your core values.
- **Action:** Tackle the most pressing challenge first with a strategy rooted in your core values. Break down your approach into actionable steps.

Day 12: Beyond Superficial Echoes - Authentic Connections

- **Activity:** Evaluate your social interactions over the past week. Which ones felt authentic and enriching? Which felt obligatory or superficial?
- **Action:** Initiate a meaningful conversation or activity with someone who makes you feel seen and heard. Focus on depth, not breadth, in your connections.

Day 13: The Sculpture of Priorities - Carving Out What Matters

- **Activity:** Review your "f*ck budget" from the first week. Based on what you've learned, make any necessary adjustments to better reflect your core values.
- **Action:** Say no to one request or obligation that doesn't align with your priorities. Notice the feelings that come up and journal about the experience.

Day 14: Weekly Reflection and Resilience Building

- **Activity:** Reflect on the challenges you faced this week and how you applied your core values to navigate them. What worked? What didn't?
- **Action:** Based on this week's experiences, set a resilience-building goal for the coming week. This could be anything from setting firmer boundaries to dedicating more time to self-care practices that reinforce your core values.

Consolidating Your Journey

This week's activities are designed to reinforce the importance of living in alignment with your core values and practicing discernment in how you allocate your emotional and mental resources. As you continue to sculpt your path, remember that every decision, every boundary, and every step taken in authenticity strengthens the foundation of the life you're building.

Next week, we'll explore strategies for amplifying your impact, leaving a legacy of authentic f*ck-giving, and mastering the art of saying no to create space for yeses that truly matter. Keep chiseling away, one deliberate step at a time, and watch as your path becomes clearer and more purposeful with each action you take.

Week 3 Action Plan: Amplifying Impact and Legacy

Entering the third week with "Chisel Your Path" as your guide, it's time to focus on amplifying your impact and understanding the legacy you wish to create through authentic actions and meaningful contributions. This week, you'll explore the power of saying no to prioritize what genuinely matters, crafting a legacy of significance, and ensuring your actions resonate deeply with your core values.

Day 15: The Symphony of Impact
- **Activity:** Reflect on the areas of your life where you feel most compelled to make an impact. Write them down and explore why they resonate with you.
- **Action:** Choose one area to focus on today. Do one small thing that contributes to a greater good or supports a cause important to you.

Day 16: The Legacy of F*ck-Giving
- **Activity:** Imagine looking back on your life. What do you want to be remembered for? List qualities or achievements that align with your core values.
- **Action:** Implement one action that aligns with the legacy you wish to leave. This could be mentoring someone, volunteering, or starting a project that benefits others.

Day 17: The Art of Saying No
- **Activity:** Identify situations or requests you've recently agreed to that don't align with your priorities. Recognize the impact this has on your energy and time.
- **Action:** Practice saying no today. It could be to a minor request that doesn't serve you or something larger that detracts from your core focus. Notice how it feels to prioritize your needs and projects.

Day 18: The Sculptor's Chisel - Refining Your Focus
- **Activity:** Evaluate your current projects and commitments. Which ones truly align with your values and the impact you want to have?
- **Action:** Choose one project or commitment that is not serving your larger goals and take steps to conclude or exit it, freeing up space for more aligned endeavors.

Day 19: Navigating the Cosmic Garage Sale
- **Activity:** Think about the beliefs, habits, or items you've collected over the years that no longer serve you. List them out.
- **Action:** Let go of one item, belief, or habit today. This symbolic action reinforces your commitment to authenticity and purpose.

Day 20: Giving a F*ck That Matters
- **Activity:** Reflect on what giving a f*ck that matters means to you. How does it look in your daily life, in the small actions and decisions you make?
- **Action:** Act on something that deeply matters to you today, whether it's reaching out to a friend in need, advocating for a cause, or dedicating time to a passion project.

Day 21: Weekly Reflection - Carving Your Legacy

- **Activity:** Reflect on your actions this week. How did they contribute to the legacy you wish to leave? How have your definitions of impact and success shifted?
- **Action:** Write a letter to your future self, detailing the legacy you aim to create and the steps you're committed to taking to achieve it. Seal it, date it for a year from now, and set a reminder to open it.

Looking Forward

This week's journey is about recognizing and embracing the power you have to shape the world around you through authentic action and intentional living. As you progress, remember that every no is a yes to something more aligned with your core values and the legacy you wish to build.

As we move into the final week, we'll focus on integrating these lessons into a sustainable practice of authentic living and resilience. Your path is uniquely yours, and each step taken is a testament to your commitment to living with purpose and impact. Keep chiseling away, embracing the journey of authenticity and resilience.

Week 4 Action Plan: Living Authentically Every Day

Given our journey through "Chisel Your Path," the fourth week is about solidifying your newfound understanding and practices into a sustainable model of living authentically and resiliently. This week's focus is on integration and reflection, ensuring that the lessons learned become a part of your everyday life, influencing your decisions, interactions, and sense of self.

Day 22: Mastering the F*cking Compass
- **Activity:** Review your core values and assess how well your recent decisions align with them. Adjust your compass if necessary.
- **Action:** Make a decision today based solely on your core values, regardless of external pressures or opinions.

Day 23: The Currency of Feels
- **Activity:** Reflect on your emotional investments over the past few weeks. Which emotions have been most prevalent? Are they aligned with where you want to focus your energy?
- **Action:** Commit to a day of emotional mindfulness, acknowledging and directing your feelings towards constructive and fulfilling actions.

Day 24: Triaging Life's Challenges
- **Activity:** Identify a current challenge in your life. Use the triage method to determine its urgency and significance.
- **Action:** Create a plan to address this challenge, keeping in mind your lessons on resilience, authenticity, and focusing on what truly matters.

Day 25: The Echo Chamber of Significance
- **Activity:** Reflect on the voices and opinions you've allowed to influence you. How many of these truly matter to your path and growth?
- **Action:** Choose to seek out and listen to a new perspective today, one that challenges you but also aligns with your journey toward authenticity.

Day 26: Beyond Superficial Echoes
- **Activity:** Identify an area of your life where you've only engaged on a superficial level. Consider how a deeper engagement could enrich your experience.
- **Action:** Dive deeper into this area today, whether it's starting a meaningful conversation, beginning a project, or committing to learning something new.

Day 27: The Sculpture of Priorities
- **Activity:** Re-evaluate your current priorities based on the insights gained from this month's journey. Are they reflective of your true self and aspirations?
- **Action:** Adjust one area of your life to better align with your refined priorities, setting a tangible goal that reflects this alignment.

Day 28: Final Reflection - Integrating the Lessons
- **Activity:** Reflect on the past four weeks. How have you grown? What lessons have become part of your everyday life? How has your understanding of authenticity and resilience deepened?

- **Action:** Write down three commitments to yourself based on these reflections. These commitments should be actions or practices you intend to continue beyond this program to maintain your path of authentic living and resilience.

Continuing the Journey

As you conclude this structured four-week journey, remember that the path to authenticity and resilience is ongoing. The lessons learned are not just for a month but for a lifetime of exploration, growth, and fulfillment. Your action plans, reflections, and commitments are tools that you can revisit and adapt as you continue to evolve.

Keep chiseling away at the path that is uniquely yours, armed with the knowledge that every step taken is one towards living more authentically, resiliently, and with purpose. Let the symphony of your life play loudly, proudly, and most importantly, authentically.

Embrace chaos, find purpose, and remember: the journey itself is the destination. Keep moving forward with audacity and heart.

Book 2, Harmony in the Chaos: Cultivating Depth, Balance, and Resonance in Life's Symphony

Though the chapters are crafted for brisk perusal, curb your enthusiasm from consuming the book in one go or hastily within a week. Dedicate an entire day to each chapter, diving deeply into the concepts and reflections it offers. Engage intimately with the material, truly familiarize yourself with its essence, and nurture the seeds of dissent to sprout and thrive within. This journey transcends mere reading—it's a call to waltz with your inner maverick, a methodical blueprint for unleashing the grandeur of your inherent capabilities.

The Garden of Priorities

Imagine your life as a lush garden, and your priorities as the vibrant flowers within. Giving a f*ck that matters is about tending to this garden with care, cultivating an environment where your most significant priorities can flourish.

The seeds you plant in the garden of priorities determine what blooms. Giving a f*ck that matters involves choosing these seeds intentionally, aligning them with your core values and long-term aspirations. The garden becomes a reflection of the seeds you sow.

In any garden, weeds can threaten the growth of precious flowers. Giving a f*ck that matters requires diligent weeding—removing distractions and unnecessary commitments that could overshadow the priorities you've planted. It's a constant effort to keep the garden clear and focused.

Emotional energy is the water that nurtures the garden. Giving a f*ck that matters involves using this emotional water wisely. Some flowers need more care, and understanding where to direct your emotional energy ensures that the priorities receiving this nourishment are the ones that truly matter.

Pruning is an essential practice in gardening. Giving a f*ck that matters involves pruning—trimming away the excess, letting go of aspects that no longer contribute to the growth of your priorities. Pruning allows the garden to flourish with renewed vitality.

Seasons change, and so does the garden. Giving a f*ck that matters involves understanding these seasonal shifts in your life. Certain priorities may take precedence during specific seasons, and being attuned to these changes allows you to adapt your care accordingly.

A vibrant garden is one of diversity. Giving a f*ck that matters celebrates the diversity of your priorities, recognizing that each one adds a unique hue to the overall beauty of your life. It's about appreciating the different flowers that bloom in the garden.

Just as plants need the right balance of sunlight and shade, priorities need a balanced approach. Giving a f*ck that matters involves ensuring that your priorities receive the right amount of attention. It's about maintaining a delicate balance to foster healthy growth.

Values act as the fertilizer that enriches the soil of your priorities. Giving a f*ck that matters involves aligning your priorities with your core values. This fertilization ensures that your garden thrives in soil that is nutrient-rich and conducive to growth.

Pests can threaten a garden's health. Giving a f*ck that matters requires being vigilant against the pests of negativity, doubt, and external pressures. It's about guarding your priorities from influences that could undermine their growth.

The garden of priorities is your sanctuary. Giving a f*ck that matters involves creating a space where your most cherished priorities feel protected and valued. It's about fostering an environment that allows these priorities to bloom into their fullest potential.

In due time, the garden yields its harvest. Giving a f*ck that matters involves patiently tending to your priorities, knowing that the rewards will come. It's about enjoying the fruits of your intentional care and nurturing.

Not all flowers in the garden grow at the same rate. Giving a f*ck that matters involves understanding the different growth rates of your priorities. Some may require more time, while others blossom quickly. It's about acknowledging and respecting these individual paces.

Within the garden, pathways guide your journey. Giving a f*ck that matters involves creating intentional pathways among your priorities. These pathways help you navigate the garden with purpose, ensuring that each step aligns with your values and aspirations.

Time and attention are the irrigation systems for your garden. Giving a f*ck that matters involves irrigating your priorities with these precious resources. It's about dedicating time and focused attention to the aspects of your life that hold the utmost significance.

Passion acts as the bees that pollinate your priorities. Giving a f*ck that matters involves inviting the bees of passion to your garden. It's about infusing your priorities with enthusiasm and dedication, ensuring that they thrive and cross-pollinate with the energy of passion.

The garden of priorities needs boundaries to protect its integrity. Giving a f*ck that matters involves establishing clear boundaries—knowing when to say no, setting limits, and guarding against encroachments that could compromise the health of your priorities.

As the garden blooms, change is inevitable. Giving a f*ck that matters involves embracing this change with open arms. It's about recognizing that priorities may evolve, and adapting to these changes allows for continued growth and vibrancy in the garden.

The fulfillment of priorities carries a sweet fragrance. Giving a f*ck that matters involves savoring this fragrance—the joy and satisfaction that come from seeing your priorities bloom into realities. It's about relishing the moments of fulfillment within your garden.

The garden is a reflection of your care. Giving a f*ck that matters involves decorating this space with intentional reflections of your values and priorities. It's about ensuring that every corner of the garden mirrors the authenticity and significance you bring to your life.

Seeds are the promise of future growth. Giving a f*ck that matters involves preserving these seeds for the future. It's about acknowledging that the intentional care you provide today lays the foundation for the continued flourishing of your priorities in the seasons to come.

"The Garden of Priorities" provides a framework for cultivating a life where your most significant priorities can flourish. By approaching life as a garden to be tended, you can nurture a vibrant and fulfilling existence that reflects your deepest values and aspirations that includes:

- **Intentional Planting of Priorities** Recognize that the priorities in your life are like seeds in a garden. Choose these seeds thoughtfully, ensuring they align with your core values and long-term aspirations. The choices you make now will determine the future blooms of your life's garden.
- **Diligent Weeding to Prevent Overcrowding** Regularly identify and remove distractions and unnecessary commitments (weeds) that can overshadow or choke your important priorities (flowers). This continuous effort is crucial to maintain focus and clarity in your life.
- **Nurturing with Emotional Energy** Understand that emotional energy acts like water for your garden. Wisely direct this energy to nourish the priorities that are most significant, ensuring they receive the care and attention needed to thrive.
- **Pruning for Growth and Vitality** Engage in the practice of pruning – trimming away aspects and commitments that no

longer serve your growth. This not only helps in refining your focus but also allows for new opportunities and priorities to flourish.

- **Adapting to Life's Seasons**   Be attuned to the changing seasons of your life and understand that certain priorities may ebb and flow in importance. Adapt your care and attention to these shifts to ensure a continually thriving garden.
- **Celebrating Diversity in Priorities**   Appreciate the diversity in your priorities, understanding that each one contributes uniquely to the overall beauty and balance of your life. This diversity reflects the multifaceted nature of your existence.
- **Balancing Sunlight and Shade**   Strike a delicate balance in attending to your priorities. Just like plants need both sunlight and shade, your priorities require a balanced approach to ensure healthy and sustainable growth.
- **Enriching with Values as Fertilizer**   Infuse your priorities with your core values, enriching the soil of your garden. This alignment ensures that your priorities are deeply rooted and have the strength to flourish.
- **Guarding Against Pests of Negativity**   Stay vigilant against negative influences and doubts that can harm the health of your priorities. Protect your garden by reinforcing positive mindsets and surrounding yourself with supportive relationships.
- **Creating a Sanctuary of Priorities**   Transform your garden of priorities into a sanctuary where your most cherished aspirations and goals can safely and confidently grow. This space should feel protective, nurturing, and aligned with your true self.
- **Patiently Awaiting the Harvest**   Cultivate patience, understanding that the fruition of your priorities often takes time. Tend to your garden with care and consistency, and in time, you will enjoy the rewards of your dedicated efforts.
- **Respecting Individual Growth Rates**   Acknowledge that different priorities grow at their own pace. Some may quickly

bloom, while others take longer to mature. Respect and accommodate these individual growth timelines in your nurturing approach.

The Tapestry of Relationships

Much like a tapestry, relationships are woven with threads. Giving a f*ck that matters involves choosing quality threads—meaningful connections that add depth and richness to the tapestry of your life.

The art of threading relationships is a delicate dance of tension and harmony. Giving a f*ck that matters requires balancing these elements, knowing when to embrace the tension for growth and when to weave threads of harmony for stability.

Shared values are the intricate patterns that emerge in the tapestry of relationships. Giving a f*ck that matters involves embroidering these shared values into the fabric of your connections, creating a tapestry that reflects the authenticity and alignment of your shared principles.

Every tapestry encounters rips and tears. Giving a f*ck that matters means approaching these challenges with open communication, using the needle of understanding and empathy to mend the threads of connection.

Trust forms the foundation of any robust tapestry. Giving a f*ck that matters involves layering trust as the base, allowing the threads of relationships to intertwine securely, creating a tapestry that withstands the tests of time.

Relationships are a collaborative weaving process. Giving a f*ck that matters involves embarking on this weaving journey together, recognizing that each person contributes unique threads, colors, and textures to the intricate tapestry you create collectively.

Respect is the pattern that runs through every thread. Giving a f*ck that matters involves crafting patterns of respect, ensuring that each interaction, disagreement, or agreement contributes to a tapestry where mutual regard is evident.

The commitment to relationships is built thread by thread. Giving a f*ck that matters involves a meticulous commitment to each thread—acknowledging that the strength of the tapestry lies in the integrity of every connection.

Empathy adds vibrant colors to the tapestry of relationships. Giving a f*ck that matters involves coloring each thread with empathy, understanding the perspectives and emotions of those woven into the intricate design of your life.

Knots and tangles are inevitable in any tapestry. Giving a f*ck that matters requires the patience to untangle these knots, approaching challenges with a calm and composed demeanor to preserve the beauty of the woven connections.

Life's seasons influence the tapestry of relationships. Giving a f*ck that matters involves stitching through these seasons together—celebrating joys, weathering storms, and adapting to the changing hues of the woven fabric.

Weaving relationships involves setting boundaries with respect. Giving a f*ck that matters means recognizing the importance of personal space, consent, and autonomy in the weaving process.

Shared memories are the embellishments that make the tapestry memorable. Giving a f*ck that matters involves consciously creating and cherishing these shared moments, weaving them into the fabric of your relationships.

Every person brings their individuality to the tapestry. Giving a f*ck that matters involves navigating these threads of individuality with acceptance and appreciation, recognizing that diversity enhances the richness of the woven connections.

The texture of presence is felt in every thread. Giving a f*ck that matters involves reveling in the richness of being present in your relationships, actively participating in the weaving process rather than being a passive observer.

Tension in relationships can be adjusted for growth. Giving a f*ck that matters involves a mindful adjustment of this tension, recognizing that a certain level is necessary for stretching and strengthening the threads of connection.

Vulnerability is the raw material of authentic connection. Giving a f*ck that matters involves spinning threads of vulnerability, allowing for openness and honesty in the weaving process.

When threads fray, forgiveness is the needle that repairs. Giving a f*ck that matters involves the ability to forgive, understanding that mistakes and imperfections are part of the weaving journey.

Shared dreams are the grand designs within the tapestry. Giving a f*ck that matters involves weaving threads of shared aspirations and dreams, ensuring that the tapestry reflects the collective vision of a connected and meaningful life.

Not every part of the tapestry is finished. Giving a f*ck that matters involves appreciating the beauty in the unfinished sections, understanding that the weaving process is ongoing, and each moment contributes to the evolving masterpiece of your relationships.

The Catalyst for Change

Passion kindles the furnace of purpose within. Giving a f*ck that matters involves igniting this furnace, recognizing that the flames of passion are essential for forging a purposeful and meaningful life.

Engagement fueled by passion transforms mundane actions into extraordinary experiences. Giving a f*ck that matters is embracing the alchemy of passionate engagement, infusing enthusiasm and dedication into every endeavor.

Passion is the catalyst for change. Giving a f*ck that matters involves catalyzing positive change through the fervor of your convictions, allowing your passionate energy to fuel movements and initiatives that align with your values.

Passion distills the essence of authenticity. Giving a f*ck that matters means tapping into this distilled essence, allowing your genuine and unbridled passions to shine through, creating an authentic and unapologetic existence.

Enthusiasm is the forge where connections are forged. Giving a f*ck that matters involves forging meaningful connections with enthusiasm, recognizing that passion has the power to create bonds that withstand the tests of time.

Passion transmutes challenges into opportunities for growth. Giving a f*ck that matters means embracing challenges with passion, understanding that the alchemy of overcoming difficulties leads to personal and collective evolution.

Zeal is a potent tool for empowerment. Giving a f*ck that matters involves empowering others through the contagious energy of your passion, inspiring them to pursue their own dreams and causes with fervor.

Passion contributes to emotional resilience. Giving a f*ck that matters is understanding the alchemy of emotional resilience, where the passionate pursuit of your goals provides a shield against the adversities of life.

Creativity and innovation emerge from the alchemy of passion. Giving a f*ck that matters involves tapping into this wellspring of creativity, allowing passion to be the muse that inspires innovative solutions and groundbreaking ideas.

Motivation is a flame ignited by passion. Giving a f*ck that matters means fanning these flames, ensuring that the fire of motivation continues to burn brightly, propelling you forward in the pursuit of your aspirations.

Passion is the sculptor of purpose. Giving a f*ck that matters involves allowing your passions to sculpt a purposeful existence, chiseling away the superfluous to reveal the masterpiece of a life aligned with what truly matters.

Time spent in passionate pursuits is time well-spent. Giving a f*ck that matters involves understanding the alchemy of time, recognizing that dedicating your time to what you're genuinely passionate about enriches the fabric of your life.

Passion has the power to elevate the mundane to the extraordinary. Giving a f*ck that matters involves infusing passion into everyday activities, transforming routine tasks into opportunities for joy, creativity, and fulfillment.

Passion fuels intentional action. Giving a f*ck that matters means embracing the alchemy of intentional action, where every step is guided by the passionate intention to contribute positively to your own life and the lives of others.

Passion is a compass that guides self-discovery. Giving a f*ck that matters involves navigating the alchemy of self-discovery through passionate pursuits, allowing your interests and curiosities to lead you toward a deeper understanding of yourself.

Alchemy of Impactful Contribution:

- Passion magnifies the impact of your contribution. Giving a f*ck that matters involves understanding the alchemy of impactful contribution, recognizing that your passionate efforts can create ripples of positive change far beyond your immediate sphere.

- Passion is the seed that grows into fulfillment. Giving a f*ck that matters involves cultivating a garden of fulfillment, planting the seeds of passion and nurturing them into a vibrant landscape of purpose and satisfaction.

- Passion fuels fearless pursuit. Giving a f*ck that matters means embracing the alchemy of fearless pursuit, allowing your passion to be the driving force that propels you beyond fear and limitations toward the fulfillment of your dreams.

Endurance becomes joyful through the alchemy of passion. Giving a f*ck that matters involves infusing passion into your endurance, transforming challenges and obstacles into opportunities for growth and joyful perseverance.

Beyond the Shallows

Beyond the shallows lies the abyss, an expanse waiting to be explored. Giving a f*ck that matters requires the courage to dive into the abyss, where the waters are deep and the mysteries profound.

In the depths, you discover hidden realms of yourself. Giving a f*ck that matters involves plumbing the depths of your soul, uncovering facets of your being that may have remained obscured in the shallows.

Shallow relationships lack the depth that gives them meaning. Giving a f*ck that matters means nurturing the depth of connection, forging bonds that go beyond surface-level interactions to create relationships rich with understanding and empathy.

The shallows are littered with trivial pursuits. Giving a f*ck that matters involves submerging these superficial endeavors, redirecting your energy toward pursuits that carry weight and significance.

Values are the bedrock of the ocean of significance. Giving a f*ck that matters requires fathoming the sea of values, understanding the principles that guide your decisions and actions as you navigate the depths.

Shallows conceal your true passions. Giving a f*ck that matters involves unveiling these hidden passions, acknowledging the pursuits that resonate with the deepest parts of your being and infusing them with purpose.

Purpose resides in the abyss of significance. Giving a f*ck that matters is about navigating this abyss, discovering the currents that lead you toward a purposeful existence and steering clear of the aimless drift in the shallows.

In the shallows, growth is stunted. Giving a f*ck that matters means immersing yourself in transformative growth, allowing the currents of experience and learning to shape you into a more evolved and resilient individual.

Authenticity resonates in the depths. Giving a f*ck that matters involves resonating with authenticity, allowing your true self to surface in the profound waters where societal masks and pretenses dissolve.

Empathy is a rare treasure in the shallows. Giving a f*ck that matters means plumbing the depths of empathy, understanding the experiences of others in a profound way that transcends surface-level sympathy.

The shallows seek superficial validation. Giving a f*ck that matters involves casting aside this shallow pursuit of external approval, finding validation in the depth of your convictions and the authenticity of your actions.

Meaning resides in the abyss of life. Giving a f*ck that matters involves exploring this abyss, seeking profound meaning in your relationships, endeavors, and contributions to the world.

In the depths, there's a dance between darkness and light. Giving a f*ck that matters means embracing both aspects, understanding that life's complexities are more nuanced in the profound ocean of existence.

Shallows are noisy, but depths are silent. Giving a f*ck that matters involves reveling in the silence of depth, finding solace and introspection in the profound quietude that accompanies meaningful pursuits.

Shallow connections lack authenticity. Giving a f*ck that matters involves forging a sea of authentic relationships, where the tides of genuine understanding and mutual respect ebb and flow.

Shallows limit self-discovery. Giving a f*ck that matters involves descending into the abyss of self-discovery, where you confront the shadows and unveil the true dimensions of your identity.

In the shallows, storms are fleeting. Giving a f*ck that matters means navigating the enduring storms of significance, weathering challenges with resilience and embracing the transformative power of adversity.

Purpose often languishes in the shallows. Giving a f*ck that matters involves rescuing purpose from these shallow waters, bringing it into the depths where it can thrive and guide your journey.

Shallow experiences yield few pearls of wisdom. Giving a f*ck that matters means treasuring these pearls, the insights and lessons gained from the profound depths of life's experiences.

Intentions are purified in the depths. Giving a f*ck that matters involves bathing your intentions in these waters, ensuring that your actions are guided by a deep and unwavering commitment to what truly matters.

The Map of Purpose

The map of purpose is your guide through the vast landscapes of life. Giving a f*ck that matters involves charting your course intentionally, aligning your actions and decisions with the coordinates of your deepest purpose.

On this map, there are waypoints of significance. Giving a f*ck that matters means recognizing and cherishing these waypoints, moments and experiences that align with your purpose and contribute to the meaningful narrative of your life.

Authenticity is the landmark that guides your way. Giving a f*ck that matters involves navigating towards the landmarks of authenticity, staying true to yourself in a world that often tempts conformity.

Your convictions serve as the compass on this journey. Giving a f*ck that matters requires following the compass of your convictions, ensuring that your moral needle points unwaveringly towards the true north of your principles.

In this map, there are swamps of distraction. Giving a f*ck that matters involves skillfully avoiding these swamps, the places and pursuits that divert you from the purposeful path and swallow your energy without yielding meaning.

Peaks of fulfillment rise on this terrain. Giving a f*ck that matters means climbing these peaks, reaching the summits of experiences and accomplishments that resonate with the echoes of your purpose.

Valleys of challenge may shadow your route. Giving a f*ck that matters involves traversing these valleys, facing challenges with resilience and viewing them not as obstacles but as opportunities for growth on the path of purpose.

On this journey, you'll encounter purposeful companions. Giving a f*ck that matters involves forging alliances with those who share your map, building relationships that support and enhance the collective pursuit of purpose.

The map of purpose has unexplored territories. Giving a f*ck that matters is about pioneering into these uncharted realms, embracing the unknown with a spirit of curiosity and a commitment to discover new dimensions of significance.

Life's map isn't static. Giving a f*ck that matters involves updating your coordinates as you evolve, recognizing that your purpose may shift and unfold, and adjusting your course accordingly.

At crossroads, decisions shape your journey. Giving a f*ck that matters requires standing at these crossroads with intention, choosing paths that resonate with the symphony of your purpose rather than succumbing to the allure of the easier route.

Values are the North Star on your map. Giving a f*ck that matters involves navigating by this star, ensuring that your choices align with the unwavering brightness of your core values.

Forests of temptation may entice you off course. Giving a f*ck that matters involves skillfully navigating these forests, resisting the allure of short-term gratifications that might veer you away from the purposeful path.

Rivers of passion run through this landscape. Giving a f*ck that matters means sailing these rivers, allowing the currents of passion to carry you toward purposeful pursuits and infusing every endeavor with the vitality of genuine enthusiasm.

Bridges of connection span the gaps. Giving a f*ck that matters involves building and crossing these bridges, connecting with others who share your purpose, creating networks of mutual support, and fostering collaborations that amplify the impact of collective purpose.

In your toolkit are navigational tools of self-reflection. Giving a f*ck that matters requires using these tools regularly, taking moments to recalibrate, reassess, and ensure that your journey aligns with the evolving contours of your purpose.

The winds of intention fill your sails. Giving a f*ck that matters involves harnessing these winds, steering your ship with clear intention, and letting the breezes of purpose propel you forward.

The landscape bears the etchings of legacies. Giving a f*ck that matters involves considering the impact you leave on this map, ensuring that the trails you blaze contribute to a landscape that is enriched with purpose and significance.

Footsteps echo on this journey. Giving a f*ck that matters involves walking with purpose, leaving behind footsteps that resonate with the echoes of your convictions, creating a path that others may choose to follow in the pursuit of their own meaningful maps.

Monuments rise on the map of purpose. Giving a f*ck that matters involves contributing to the construction of these monuments, markers of impact and positive change that endure as testaments to a life lived with purpose and intention.

Calibrating Your Moral Compass

Living authentically in a world teeming with chaos requires a finely tuned moral compass. In this carnival of chaos, the lighthouse of truth stands tall. Calibrating your moral compass is like adjusting that lighthouse, ensuring its light cuts through the fog of societal expectations, revealing the shores of authenticity.

Picture this: life as a wild symphony, each note played by your choices, actions, and, most importantly, your integrity. Calibrating your moral compass is the conductor's wand, guiding the orchestra of your existence through the chaos.

In a celestial dance, integrity is your North Star. Calibrating it ensures you're not led astray by the fleeting comets of compromise. Integrity doesn't waver; it's a cosmic constant in the ever-shifting cosmos of life.

Beware the sirens of compromise, those seductive melodies that beckon in the dark waters of expediency. Calibrating your moral compass is your earplugs against these tempting tunes, keeping you true to your course.

Life's terrain is rugged, a chaotic mosaic of choices. Calibrating your moral compass is like having a trusty map, guiding you through the treacherous landscapes, ensuring you don't lose your way.

Now, let's talk about the art of selective fckery. Calibrating your moral compass is not about caring about everything. It's about choosing your battles wisely, giving a fck where it truly matters.

In the stormy seas of chaos, authenticity is your ship, and integrity, the rudder. Calibrating ensures that your vessel doesn't succumb to the tumult but glides through, cutting through the waves with the precision of truth.

Consistency is the echo of integrity. Calibrating your moral compass ensures that this echo reverberates through your actions, creating a harmonious melody in the grand cosmic orchestra.

Easy routes often wind through murky waters. Calibrating your moral compass is your guide, preventing you from being enticed by the shortcuts that lead to the chaotic quagmires of compromised values.

In the spotlight of authenticity, integrity takes center stage. Calibrating it is like fine-tuning the spotlight, ensuring it shines bright on your genuine self, banishing the shadows of pretense.

Life loves throwing dilemmas, those challenging dance partners in the chaotic ballroom. Calibrating your moral compass is mastering the dance, navigating the intricacies without stepping on the toes of your values.

Your moral compass is the prism through which your values refract into actions. Calibrating it ensures that the spectrum of your integrity paints a vivid picture, unfazed by the storm clouds of external pressures.

In the grand tapestry of existence, integrity is the cosmic glue. Calibrating your moral compass ensures that this glue holds your unique threads together, creating a masterpiece that withstands the chaotic winds of change.

Authenticity, our battle cry, echoes through the corridors of integrity. Calibrating your moral compass is like ensuring this battle cry resounds through your choices, actions, and the very essence of your being.

Ethical quagmires are the muddy pitfalls of life. Calibrating your moral compass is the compass that steers you clear, ensuring you don't get stuck in the chaotic mire of compromised values.

Trust, a precious currency in the chaotic marketplace of relationships. Calibrating your moral compass is minting this currency, ensuring that your integrity bank remains rich, immune to the inflation of deceit.

In the tempest of temptations, where desires clash with values, calibrating your moral compass is your anchor. It keeps you grounded, preventing you from being swept away by the chaotic currents.

Criticism, a storm that often tests the strength of your integrity ship. Calibrating your moral compass is reinforcing the hull, ensuring that your vessel not only weathers the storm but sails proudly in the aftermath.

Accountability is a dance, and integrity, your partner. Calibrating your moral compass is synchronizing your steps, ensuring that your dance through life is not a chaotic stumble but a graceful waltz of responsibility.

Calibrating your moral compass is the standing ovation, the applause for a life well-lived, authentically danced, and unapologetically given. So, fellow cosmic voyagers, calibrate away and navigate the chaos with the unwavering light of your moral compass. The seas may be wild, but with integrity as your guiding star, you're destined for a f*ckwell-lived existence!

Avoiding the Temptation of Drift

Set sail through the cosmic waves, and explore the art of avoiding the temptation of drift. Life is a vast sea, and without purpose, we risk being adrift in the chaos. So, let's unfurl the sails and embark on a journey to discover the compass that steers us through the tumultuous waters of purposeful living.

Picture this: purpose as your North Star in the cosmic sky. Avoiding the temptation of drift means fixing your gaze on this guiding light, ensuring your journey through the chaotic galaxy of life is intentional and meaningful.

Beware the seductive sirens of mediocrity, their songs luring you toward the treacherous rocks of a purposeless existence. Avoiding the temptation of drift is your earplugs against these tunes, keeping you on course toward a life of significance.

In the grand tapestry of existence, purpose is the cosmic current that propels you forward. Avoiding the temptation of drift means diving into this current, letting it carry you with intentionality through the chaotic currents of daily life.

Driftwood is what remains when the waves of conformity carry away your purpose. Avoiding the temptation of drift means resisting the current of societal norms, refusing to be whittled down into a purposeless piece of societal flotsam.

Life's terrain is vast and often uncharted. Avoiding the temptation of drift is akin to having a celestial map, guiding you through the unexplored territories and helping you navigate the chaotic landscapes toward the shores of meaning.

Life, when lived purposefully, is a symphony. Avoiding the temptation of drift is ensuring that each note played by your actions resonates with the intentional melody of purpose, creating a harmony in the chaotic orchestra of existence.

In the heartbeat of the cosmos, purpose is the rhythmic pulse that echoes through your being. Avoiding the temptation of drift means aligning your heartbeat with this cosmic pulse, infusing every moment with the intentionality of purpose.

Shallow waters may be tempting, offering the illusion of safety. Avoiding the temptation of drift is the courage to sail into the deeper, chaotic seas of purpose, where the waters may be turbulent but the journey is profoundly meaningful.

Aimlessness is the quicksand that can swallow the unwary traveler. Avoiding the temptation of drift means equipping yourself with the purposeful boots that help you traverse the chaotic landscapes without sinking into the quagmire of aimlessness.

In the stormy seas of chaos, purpose is your guiding beacon. Avoiding the temptation of drift is ensuring that this beacon shines bright, cutting through the fog of confusion and illuminating the path toward a life well-lived.

Life's dance floor is crowded with distractions. Avoiding the temptation of drift means mastering the dance, stepping away from the chaotic rhythms of meaningless diversions and swaying to the purposeful beat of your own intentions.

Aimless wanderings are a mirage, promising fulfillment but leading to desolation. Avoiding the temptation of drift means recognizing these mirages for what they are, steering your ship away from the chaotic illusions of purposelessness.

In the celestial voyage of life, purpose is your rudder. Avoiding the temptation of drift is the art of steering with conviction, ensuring that your ship sails through the chaotic currents with a sense of direction.

Intrinsic motivation is the map that leads to purposeful treasures. Avoiding the temptation of drift means rejecting the chaotic allure of external rewards, navigating instead by the inner compass that points toward meaningful goals.

Impact, when purposeful, echoes through time. Avoiding the temptation of drift is ensuring that your actions leave a lasting imprint on the cosmic canvas, creating ripples that resonate through the chaotic currents of history.

In the vastness of time, purpose is your cosmic clock. Avoiding the temptation of drift means recognizing the precious ticking moments, using them wisely in the midst of life's chaotic chronology.

A purposeless existence is a cosmic quandary. Avoiding the temptation of drift means confronting this existential question, choosing instead to sail through the chaotic unknowns with the compass of purpose as your trusted guide.

In the cosmic darkness, purpose is your flickering flame. Avoiding the temptation of drift is shielding this flame from the chaotic winds that seek to extinguish it, allowing it to shine brightly through the tumultuous journey.

A purposeless void is a chaotic abyss. Avoiding the temptation of drift means steering clear of this abyss, filling the cosmic space with the meaningful constellations of your purposeful pursuits.

The North Wind in your cosmic sails is purpose. Avoiding the temptation of drift means hoisting these purposeful sails, allowing the celestial breeze to carry you through the chaotic tides toward the shores of a life lived with profound meaning.

Resist the allure of aimless drift, and set forth with purpose as our guiding star through the cosmic chaos. May your journey be intentional, your sails filled with purposeful winds, and your course charted through the tumultuous seas toward a life well-lived.

Storms of Distractions

Storms, not of the meteorological kind, but storms of distractions, can whip through the intricacies of our lives. Adaptability is our compass, and we're about to learn how to navigate the tempests in the cosmic symphony of existence.

Picture distractions as tempestuous weather systems in the cosmic symphony. Adaptability is your anchor, your compass, and your skillful dance partner as you navigate through the unpredictable and sometimes turbulent currents of life's storms.

Beware the illusion of calm seas. Distractions can lurk beneath the surface, waiting to surge forth unexpectedly. Adaptability is your ship, designed not just for serene waters but also for the tumultuous seas where distractions roam freely.

Life's distractions perform a cosmic ballet, demanding your attention with pirouettes of urgency. Adaptability is your choreography, helping you pirouette with grace, choose your own dance, and stay centered amid the celestial performance.

In the vast digital seas, distractions are the seductive sirens calling your name. Adaptability is your digital lifeboat, helping you navigate these perilous waters without succumbing to the hypnotic calls that lead you astray.

Distractions can become a whirlwind, sweeping you into the vortex of overwhelm. Adaptability is your sturdy tornado shelter, providing refuge in the storm and guiding you through the chaos with resilience.

Picture adaptability as your cosmic umbrella, shielding you from the distractions that rain down like drops of cosmic chaos. With this adaptable shield, you can weather the storm and emerge unscathed on the other side.

Life's distractions often crescendo like chaotic symphony movements. Adaptability is your conductor's wand, allowing you to direct the tempo, choose your own rhythm, and conduct the symphony of your life with purpose.

Distractions may appear as fleeting shooting stars, captivating your attention with their transient brilliance. Adaptability is your telescope, helping you focus on the constellations of your goals while letting shooting stars pass without derailing your cosmic journey.

In the toolbox of cosmic survival, adaptability is your multifunctional tool. It's the Swiss Army knife that equips you to dismantle distractions, cut through the noise, and build a path through the cosmic chaos.

Distractions can be like nebulous clouds, obscuring your vision of the cosmic path ahead. Adaptability is your celestial wind, blowing away these clouds and revealing the clear skies of focus and purpose.

Life's dance floor is crowded with distractions, each vying for your attention. Adaptability is your dance partner, helping you move gracefully through the cosmic waltz without stepping on the toes of your priorities.

Distractions exert a gravitational pull on your attention, threatening to pull you into their orbits. Adaptability is your cosmic rocket thruster, allowing you to escape these gravitational pulls and stay in control of your trajectory.

Imagine adaptability as your cosmic GPS, recalculating routes when distractions throw you off course. With this adaptable navigation system, you can course-correct and stay on the path toward your cosmic destination.

Life's maze is filled with distractions, each path leading to a different cosmic destination. Adaptability is your cosmic map, guiding you through the maze and helping you choose the routes aligned with your purpose.

Distractions often create cosmic noise, drowning out the melodies of focus and clarity. Adaptability is your noise-canceling headphone, allowing you to tune in to the cosmic frequencies that matter and drown out the distractions.

In the stormy seas of distractions, priorities are your guiding lighthouse. Adaptability is your sturdy ship, helping you navigate toward the beacon of priorities and avoid the rocky shores of aimless distraction.

Distractions can be like dazzling cosmic fireworks, captivating your gaze with momentary brilliance. Adaptability is your telescope, helping you appreciate the cosmic display without losing sight of the long-term cosmic journey.

Life's tightrope is strung between distractions on either side. Adaptability is your cosmic tightrope walker, maintaining balance, focus, and grace as you traverse the precarious path through the cosmic circus.

Life's distractions aim to splatter paint across the canvas of cosmic focus. Adaptability is your artistic brush, allowing you to create intentional strokes, blend distractions into the background, and craft a masterpiece of undistracted purpose.

In the cosmic chaos, every flap of adaptability's wings creates ripples—a cosmic butterfly effect. Navigating storms of distractions with adaptability doesn't just impact your present; it creates a ripple effect that shapes the vast cosmos of your future.

Rogue Waves

Resilience is the secret sauce that transforms us into surfers of rogue waves, not victims drowning in adversity. Life's adversities are unpredictable and capable of tossing us into the stormy seas. Resilience is not just a life jacket; it's your surfboard, empowering you to ride the waves of adversity with skill and style.

Imagine life as a vast ocean, its waves unpredictable and at times, surprisingly ferocious. Resilience is your trusty surfboard, designed not just for the calm waters but for mastering the art of riding the rogue waves life throws your way.

In the realm of resilience, adopting a wave rider's mindset is key. Instead of resisting the incoming waves of adversity, resilient individuals learn to embrace them, seeing each challenge as an opportunity to showcase their surfing skills.

Riding rogue waves demands balance. Resilience acts as your stabilizing force, helping you find equilibrium on the surfboard of life, preventing you from toppling over when adversity hits.

Adversity has a seductive lure, tempting you to believe that it can overpower you. Resilience is your defiant response, turning that temptation into an invitation to showcase your prowess in the face of life's challenges.

Resilience is not just about surviving the rogue waves; it's about carving your own path through them. Picture resilience as your wave-carving skill, allowing you to navigate adversity with finesse and deliberate movement.

When you ride the rogue waves with resilience, the impact goes beyond personal triumph. Resilient ripples radiate outward, affecting not just your journey but influencing the wider ocean of collective human experience.

A surfer's tenacity is not about avoiding rogue waves but about eagerly seeking them. Resilience gives you that tenacity, the courage to seek challenges, knowing that every wave conquered is a victory in the making.

Within the heart of adversity lie hidden opportunities. Resilience is your lens, helping you see beyond the turbulence, recognizing the chances for growth, learning, and a triumphant ride amidst the chaos.

In the face of adversity, resilience is your rebellion. It's the bold statement that says, "I won't merely survive; I'll conquer and thrive." It transforms every challenge into a canvas for the rebellious strokes of your surfboard.

Resilience turns you into a wave dancer, someone who doesn't just weather the storm but dances through it. Picture yourself as the resilient dancer on the surfboard, mastering the art of movement amid life's tempest.

Like a skilled artisan shaping raw material, adversity sculpts character. Resilience is your sculptor's chisel, allowing you to actively participate in shaping your character through the trials and tribulations you encounter.

To ride rogue waves, patience is your virtue. Resilience fosters this patience, teaching you to wait for the opportune moment, to time your moves with precision, and to trust that every wave will eventually lose its ferocity.

Life's adversities compose a symphony of unpredictable notes. Resilience is your conductor's baton, allowing you to lead this symphony, turning chaos into a harmonious melody that narrates your story of strength.

In the tumult of adversity, resilient individuals develop sea legs. These metaphorical legs provide stability, allowing you to stand tall on the surfboard, unshaken by the stormy waves that threaten to knock others off balance.

Each wave conquered, each adversity faced, marks a chapter in the resilient surfer's evolution. Resilience isn't just about survival; it's a commitment to evolving, growing, and becoming a masterful surfer on the unpredictable seas of life.

Adversity's symphony can be temperamental, throwing unexpected crescendos your way. Resilience is your instrument, giving you the ability to adapt to the changing rhythms of life.

Imagine not only riding the surface waves but also diving deep into the ocean's mysteries. Resilience equips you with the scuba gear necessary for deep-sea exploration, enabling you to uncover hidden strengths and treasures buried beneath the surface of your consciousness. This exploration emphasizes the depth of resilience, revealing insights and wisdom that surface-level challenges cannot provide.

Life's storms are not merely obstacles but navigational aids. They point you towards your inner compass, guiding you through the darkest nights and fiercest winds. Resilience becomes your compass needle, steadfastly pointing toward your true north—your most authentic self and deepest values.

Beyond riding and dancing on the waves, resilience teaches you the art of wave sculpting. You learn to shape the very adversities that confront you, molding them into experiences that refine and define you. With resilience as an art form, each stroke of hardship sculpts a masterpiece of personal growth and transformation.

Just as the ocean is part of a larger ecosystem, your personal resilience is interconnected with the resilience of those around you. You are both influenced by and a contributor to this resilience eco-system. By sharing your stories of overcoming rogue waves, you offer hope and inspiration to others, fostering a collective resilience that uplifts and sustains your community.

Resilience invites you to gaze beyond the immediate tumult, towards the horizon of possibilities. It encourages you to dream of shores yet unseen, to envision a future shaped by your deepest aspirations. This forward-looking perspective transforms resilience from a reactive stance to a proactive journey towards realizing your full potential.

Action Plan for Time Management in the Face of Adversity

- **Prioritize Your Waves**   Just as not all waves are worth riding, not all tasks and challenges deserve your immediate attention. Prioritize based on what aligns with your values and goals.
- **Time Blocking for Surfing Sessions**   Allocate specific blocks of time to tackle challenges head-on, just as a surfer dedicates time to practice. This focused approach ensures that you're fully present for each task, turning challenges into opportunities for mastery.
- **Rest Between Sets**   In surfing, waiting for the next set of waves is as crucial as riding them. Similarly, incorporate intentional breaks between challenging tasks to recharge and reflect. This rest is vital for sustaining your resilience over the long haul.
- **Surfing in Sprints**   Approach large adversities in sprints, breaking them down into manageable sections. Tackle each part with full intensity, followed by a period of rest, mirroring the rhythm of intense surfing sessions followed by moments of calm.
- **Reflective Journaling**   After each "surfing session" or challenging period, engage in reflective journaling. This practice helps consolidate the lessons learned, deepening your understanding of resilience and preparing you for future waves.

By embracing resilience as both our surfboard and sculptor's chisel, we learn to navigate and shape the rogue waves of life with grace, courage, and purpose. This journey of resilience is not just about enduring the storm but about becoming the storm, transforming every challenge into a testament of our unyielding spirit and boundless capacity for growth.

Beyond the Known

Venture into the uncharted territories of the mind, the unexplored landscapes where conventional wisdom fears to tread. This isn't a leisurely stroll; it's a wild expedition into the realms of possibility, where open-mindedness is not just a virtue but a rebellious art form.

Imagine your mind as the untamed frontier, and open-mindedness as the compass guiding you into the unexplored. It's not about sticking to well-trodden paths; it's about blazing trails into the wilderness of ideas, where the air crackles with the excitement of the unknown.

Open-mindedness is the rebel's map, crumpled and torn from countless adventures, marking the spots where curiosity clashed with convention. We're not navigating with a pristine, folded map; we're waving the tattered banner of open-minded rebellion, declaring that the unexplored is our playground.

Life's a curiosity expedition, and open-mindedness is the machete that hacks through the thick undergrowth of assumptions. We're not here to tiptoe around the edges; we're wielding the machete with a rebellious gleam, carving paths into the jungle of preconceived notions.

Open-mindedness is the taboo trek, where you venture into the forbidden territories of thought, questioning the sacred cows that graze in the fields of tradition. We're not tip-toeing around taboos; we're kicking down the fences, inviting ourselves to the feast of forbidden fruits.

Imagine open-mindedness as the rebel's telescope, aimed at the cosmos of ideas, revealing galaxies of possibilities beyond the limited scope of narrow minds. We're not squinting through a conventional spyglass; we're peering through the rebel's telescope, exploring the vastness of uncharted intellectual space.

Open-mindedness is the iconoclast's toolkit, equipped with sledgehammers to shatter the statues of dogma. We're not delicately chiseling away at the edges; we're swinging the iconoclast's sledgehammer, turning the rigid monuments of closed-mindedness into rubble.

Life's a maverick's odyssey, and open-mindedness is the ship that sails into uncharted waters. We're not hugging the familiar shores;

we're casting off, letting the winds of curiosity fill our rebellious sails as we journey into the unexplored seas of thought.

Open-mindedness is the trailblazer's toolbox, stocked with compasses that point in every direction. We're not following a single, well-worn trail; we're using the trailblazer's compasses to forge new paths, leaving a labyrinth of possibilities for those who dare to follow.

Open-mindedness is the rebel's almanac, filled with uncharted constellations and celestial events that defy the predictions of closed-minded astronomers. We're not consulting the conventional stargazers; we're flipping through the rebel's almanac, discovering our own cosmic truths in the unexplored skies of possibility.

Imagine open-mindedness as the explorer's code, a rebellious set of guidelines that defy the restrictions of conventional cartography. We're not bound by the lines on the map; we're following the explorer's code, venturing into the unexplored with the audacity to redraw the boundaries.

Open-mindedness is the mapmaker's anarchy, a celebration of chaos that defies the neat lines of established maps. We're not here to color within the lines; we're wielding the brush of mapmaker's anarchy, splattering vibrant hues across the canvas of unexplored territories.

Life's a pioneer's playlist, and open-mindedness is the eclectic mix of tunes that defy the monotony of mainstream thinking. We're not sticking to a single genre; we're curating the pioneer's playlist, letting the rebel beats guide us through the uncharted rhythms of unconventional ideas.

Imagine open-mindedness as the rebel's symposium, a gathering where minds collide, ideas combust, and the unexplored is the stage for intellectual fireworks. We're not sitting in a polite debate; we're part of the unexplored symposium, where the sparks of open-minded rebellion ignite the fireworks of unconventional wisdom.

Open-mindedness is the heretic's journal, a chronicle of thoughts that challenge the orthodoxies of the status quo. We're not writing in the margins of conventional textbooks; we're filling the heretic's journal with rebellious scribbles, daring to question, explore, and redefine the boundaries of knowledge.

Imagine open-mindedness as the anarchist's library, shelves stacked with books that have been banned, burned, or overlooked. We're not reading the bestsellers; we're diving into the anarchist's library, exploring the unexplored volumes that challenge, provoke, and expand the limits of our understanding.

Open-mindedness is the radical's observatory, equipped with telescopes that peer into the far reaches of unconventional wisdom. We're not gazing through the conventional lenses; we're stationed at the radical's observatory, scanning the unexplored skies for the celestial wonders that elude the narrow-minded gaze.

Life's a maverick's carnival, and open-mindedness is the carousel that spins with unexplored possibilities. We're not riding the conventional Ferris wheel; we're twirling on the maverick's carousel, embracing the dizzying thrill of the unexplored as it whirls us into realms of unconventional thinking.

Open-mindedness is the rebel's echo chamber, where dissenting voices resonate, ideas clash, and the unexplored is the fertile ground for intellectual anarchy. We're not nodding in polite agreement; we're part of the rebel's echo chamber, where the cacophony of diverse thoughts creates a symphony of uncharted brilliance.

Imagine open-mindedness as the nomad's atlas, a map that unfolds into uncharted territories with every turn of the page. We're not tracing the familiar contours; we're unfurling the nomad's atlas, venturing into the unexplored landscapes where curiosity is the compass and rebellion is the north star.

Open-mindedness is the anthem of the uncharted, a rebellious melody that defies the monotony of the known. We're not humming the tunes of convention; we're singing the uncharted anthem, letting our voices join the chorus of open-minded rebels who celebrate the wild, untamed territories of the mind.

As you navigate the uncharted landscapes of ideas, let open-mindedness be your compass, curiosity your machete, and rebellion your guiding star. The journey into the unexplored is not for the faint of heart, but for those who dare, the rewards are boundless.

The Art of Reflection

The untamed territory of self-reflection awaits. We're embarking on a journey through the hall of mirrors, where truths and revelations await those bold enough to face their own reflections. This isn't a leisurely stroll; it's a reckoning, an irreverent rendezvous with the most complex, fascinating subject in the universe — you.

In a world that often encourages distraction, we're not here to look away. This is the reflective rebellion, a revolution against the noise, a call to confront the unvarnished reality of who we are.

Picture a grand hall, lined with mirrors reflecting every facet of your existence. We're not here to admire a carefully curated image; we're entering the hall of mirrors to witness the raw, unfiltered truth, even when it's uncomfortable.

Superficiality whispers the illusion of perfection, encouraging us to present flawless reflections. But we're shattering that illusion; we're exploring the beauty in imperfection, the cracks in the mirror that make us unique.

In a world where filters reign supreme, we're not airbrushing our reflections. We're embracing the unfiltered truth — the laugh lines, scars, and imperfections that tell the story of a life fully lived.

Reflection isn't about echoing societal expectations; it's about amplifying the echoes of authenticity. Each reflection is a rebellion, a declaration that we won't conform to a distorted image crafted by external forces.

Picture a dance with shadows as we navigate the intricacies of self-reflection. We're not avoiding the shadows; we're waltzing with them, understanding that even the darkest corners contribute to the masterpiece of our being.

Self-reflection is a book with unwritten chapters, waiting for the ink of our experiences. We're not afraid to turn the pages, even when the narrative takes unexpected twists. Each chapter adds depth to the evolving story of self.

In a world drowning in pretense, self-reflection is the truth serum we willingly ingest. We're not diluting the potion; we're embracing the bitter truths that lead to genuine self-awareness.

Imagine a garden where self-discovery blooms. We're not avoiding the weeds; we're tending to the garden with ruthless honesty, knowing that growth requires both nurturing and pruning.

Self-reflection paints a canvas of emotions — vibrant and tumultuous. We're not sticking to pastels; we're using the bold strokes of anger, joy, sorrow, and love to create a masterpiece that reflects the kaleidoscope of our inner world.

In a society addicted to external validation, self-reflection is the mirror of introspection. We're not seeking approval in external gazes; we're gazing deeply into the mirror, finding validation within ourselves.

Reflect on the echoes of choices reverberating through the corridors of time. We're not prisoners of our past decisions; we're architects of our future, learning from reflections that guide us toward wiser choices.

Imagine a symphony where self-reflection conducts the orchestra. We're not afraid of dissonance; we're composing a melody that encompasses the highs and lows, creating a harmonious composition of self.

Self-reflection is the unveiling of masks, exposing the raw, unadulterated self. We're not masquerading as someone we're not; we're embracing authenticity, confident in the beauty of our unmasked, genuine identity.

In the vast ocean of self, reflection is the diving expedition to unexplored depths. We're not skimming the surface; we're plumbing the profound, mysterious waters where our truest selves reside.

Picture standing on the mirror's edge, teetering between comfort and discomfort. We're not avoiding the precipice; we're boldly stepping to the edge, knowing that growth occurs in the realm of discomfort.

Self-reflection is a dialogue, a conversation with the most significant person in our lives — ourselves. We're not dodging the tough questions; we're engaging in a candid conversation that leads to profound self-discovery.

In the loom of self-reflection, lessons are woven into the tapestry of our existence. We're not dismissing the threads of discomfort; we're recognizing that each thread contributes to the rich, intricate pattern of personal growth.

Join the introspective revolution, where self-reflection is a radical act of self-love. We're not conforming to societal scripts; we're rewriting our narratives with the ink of authenticity and the audacity to embrace our true selves.

The art of reflection is an expedition into the soul's wilderness, a deep dive into the waters of introspection where the pearls of wisdom are hidden. This journey isn't for the faint of heart; it requires courage to face the raw truths that lie within, to confront the shadows and the light that shape our inner landscape. But fear not, for this voyage promises the treasure of self-understanding, a prize beyond measure.

- **The Mirror of Authenticity**   Cast aside the veils of pretense and peer into the mirror with honesty. It's time to engage with the person staring back at you, not with judgment, but with curiosity and compassion. This mirror reflects not just your face but the essence of your being.

- **Dialogue with the Self**   Reflection is a dialogue, a sacred conversation with oneself. It's about asking the hard questions and being open to the answers, however unsettling they may be. This dialogue is the key to unlocking the chambers of self-awareness and understanding.
- **Embracing the Shadows**   In the art of reflection, every shadow, every dark corner of the psyche, is an opportunity for enlightenment. These shadows are not our enemies but guides leading us to the light of deeper understanding and acceptance.
- **The Symphony of the Soul**   Just as a symphony is composed of contrasting notes and harmonies, so too is our inner world. Reflection allows us to conduct this symphony, to bring harmony to the dissonance, and to appreciate the music of our soul.
- **The Landscape of Emotions**   Our emotions are the colors with which we paint our inner landscape. Through reflection, we learn to use these colors wisely, blending joy with sorrow, anger with love, to create a masterpiece that is uniquely ours.
- **The Garden of Growth**   Self-reflection is the gardener's tool, used to prune the weeds of negativity and to nurture the blossoms of positive traits. In this garden, every thought, every feeling, is a seed that, with care, can grow into something beautiful.
- **The Path of Purpose**   Reflection illuminates the path of purpose, guiding us through the maze of life's choices. It helps us to discern which paths are worth pursuing, which are dead ends, and which lead to the fulfillment of our deepest aspirations.
- **The Forge of Resilience**   In the fire of reflection, resilience is forged. By facing our fears, our failures, and our flaws, we emerge stronger, more adaptable, and ready to face life's challenges with grace and determination.
- **The Tapestry of Connection**   Reflection reveals the threads of connection that weave us into the fabric of the universe. It

shows us that we are not isolated beings but part of a greater whole, interconnected with all of existence.
- **The Horizon of Possibility** Reflection opens our eyes to the horizon of possibility. It shows us that, no matter our past, the future is a canvas awaiting our brush, ready to be painted with the vibrant hues of our hopes, dreams, and untapped potential.

Remember that the mirror holds no judgments. It reflects, without bias, the canvas of your being. So, gaze unflinchingly, dear rebel, and let the mirror of truth be your guide in the eternal quest for self-discovery. By embracing the art of reflection, we embark on a lifelong journey of self-discovery and growth. This journey enriches not just our own lives but also the lives of those around us, as we become more authentic, compassionate, and purposeful beings. Let the hall of mirrors be your classroom, and let the lessons learned illuminate the path to your truest self.

Tools of Wisdom

Ahead is the treasure trove of insights, where we're not just handing out maps but forging a pirate's toolkit for navigating the uncharted waters of abundance. Grab your compass and a shovel; we're about to dig into the gold mines of wisdom in a way that's as irreverent as it is impactful.

In a world obsessed with scarcity, let's embrace the pirate's paradox. We're not searching for treasure with clenched fists; we're open-handed, recognizing that the more we share, the more we receive in the grand dance of abundance.

Navigate the seas of life with the wisdom compass. We're not charting a fixed course; we're adapting to the ever-changing tides, understanding that flexibility is the North Star of an abundant mindset.

Picture gratitude as the shovel that unearths treasures. We're not digging for discontent; we're excavating the gems hidden beneath the surface of our experiences, even in the seemingly mundane.

See the world through the spyglass of perspective. We're not fixated on a narrow view; we're widening our scope, recognizing that abundance isn't just about material wealth but the kaleidoscope of experiences.

Peer into the future with the telescope of vision. We're not predicting lottery numbers; we're envisioning a future abundant in purpose, passion, and meaningful connections, shaping our destinies with intention.

Craft your map with the ink of intentions. We're not leaving our destinies to chance; we're steering our ships toward intentional destinations, understanding that clarity breeds abundance.

Raise the sails of adaptability. We're not sailing rigidly against the winds of change; we're harnessing the breeze, adapting our course to ride the waves of uncertainty towards the shores of abundance.

Drop the anchor of mindfulness in the present moment. We're not casting anchor in stagnant waters; we're savoring the richness of now, understanding that abundance flourishes in the soil of present awareness.

Unlock the treasure chest of self-compassion. We're not hoarding self-criticisms; we're embracing our imperfections, recognizing that the greatest treasures lie in the depths of self-love.

Navigate self-doubt with the sextant of self-belief. We're not sailing uncharted seas with trepidation; we're trusting in our abilities, knowing that self-belief is the magnetic force that attracts abundance.

Steer through storms with the rudder of resilience. We're not avoiding tempests; we're navigating them with strength, understanding that adversity is but a temporary fog in the sea of abundance.

Sail with a crew of connections. We're not lone pirates in this adventure; we're fostering relationships, knowing that abundance is multiplied when shared with those who matter.

Illuminate the way with the lighthouse of generosity. We're not hoarding our light; we're casting it wide, understanding that the more we give, the brighter our own path becomes in the realm of abundance.

Walk the plank of risk-taking. We're not clinging to the safety of the ship; we're daring to step into the unknown, knowing that true abundance lies on the other side of calculated risks.

Consult the jester's map of playfulness. We're not navigating with stoic seriousness; we're injecting joy into the journey, understanding that a playful heart is a magnet for the abundance that springs from pure, unbridled delight.

Ignite the flames of reinvention with the phoenix feather. We're not chained to old identities; we're embracing the transformative power of change, rising from the ashes of stagnation into the boundless skies of abundance.

Sip from the alchemist's elixir of learning. We're not gulping down stagnation; we're savoring the brew of knowledge, understanding that the more we learn, the richer our understanding of the world, and the greater our capacity for abundance.

Consult the almanac of reflection. We're not sailing without navigation; we're periodically charting our course, recognizing that reflection is the compass that keeps us on track in the vast ocean of abundance.

Wade into the waters of possibility, where mythical creatures abound. We're not dismissing the fantastical; we're inviting the extraordinary into our lives, understanding that in the realm of abundance, possibilities are as boundless as the ocean.

Remember, sometimes, the telescope isn't just pointed at the stars; it's turned inward. Peer into the vastness of your own potential, embrace the audacious spirit of a pirate, and set sail into the abundant unknown with the winds of wisdom filling your sails.

Where Mavericks Reign

Forget the superficial pursuit of positivity; we're here to chase purpose like a bandit chasing the sunrise. Get ready for a purposeful escapade that'll leave you breathless, exhilarated, and hungry for the uncharted territories of a life well-lived.

In a world obsessed with the fleeting high of positivity, the purposeful rebel stands tall. We're not here to chase rainbows; we're here to embark on a purposeful rebellion against the mundane. Buckle up, purpose pursuers, for this is no ordinary journey—it's a wild, purpose-fueled escapade.

Positivity is a mirage, shimmering on the horizon, promising an oasis in the desert of life. But purpose, purpose is the cool, refreshing spring hidden deep within. Don't be fooled by the illusion of constant sunshine; purpose thrives in the storms, in the dance of light and shadow.

Become the bandit of purpose, robbing life of its mundane treasures and leaving behind a trail of meaningful exploits. Positivity may be a fleeting smile, but purpose is the daring heist that echoes through the ages. Embrace the bandit's spirit, and let purpose be your stolen bounty.

Positivity is a short-lived vacation; purpose is the never-ending odyssey. Choose the epic journey over the temporary getaway. Sail through purposeful seas, explore uncharted purposeful lands, and let your life be a tale of heroic purpose rather than a brief stint of positive vibes.

In the grand peaks of life, be a purposeful mountaineer, scaling the heights of meaning rather than chasing the shallow summits of fleeting joy. Positivity may be the oxygen of the moment, but purpose is the sturdy rope that anchors you to the majestic cliffs of significance.

Positivity is a solo melody; purpose is the symphony that echoes through the chambers of your soul. Choose to compose a purpose-infused symphony, where every note resonates with meaning, every crescendo celebrates your journey, and every pause carries the weight of purposeful reflection.

Turn the base metal of life into the gold of purpose. Positivity may be a temporary sparkle, but purpose is the alchemical transformation that turns every experience, every challenge, into a precious nugget of wisdom. Be the purposeful alchemist, transmuting the ordinary into the extraordinary.

Positivity is a well-trodden path; purpose is the trail waiting to be blazed. Step off the beaten track, purposeful trailblazer, and venture into the wilderness of your dreams. Leave behind the breadcrumbs of your purposeful journey for others to follow.

Life's coals may burn with both positivity and negativity, but it's purpose that turns you into the firewalker, dancing through the flames unscathed. Positivity is a gentle breeze; purpose is the unyielding fire that tempers your soul and forges your character.

Positivity is conformity, purpose is rebellion. Embrace the spirit of the purposeful maverick, challenging the norms, questioning the status quo, and riding the winds of purposeful change. Life's too short for the shackles of positivity; be the maverick who dares to live with purpose.

Positivity whispers, but purpose roars. Start a revolution, purposeful warriors, overthrowing the tyranny of superficial smiles and chasing the thunderous applause of a life lived with intent. Positivity may be a gentle breeze, but purpose is the hurricane that reshapes landscapes.

Tend to the garden of your life with purposeful care. Positivity may be the sunshine, but purpose is the nurturing rain that allows your dreams to bloom. Be the purposeful gardener, cultivating a vibrant and diverse ecosystem of experiences that thrive with meaning.

In the vast desert of existence, be a purposeful nomad, wandering with intent and seeking the oasis of significance. Positivity may be a temporary mirage, but purpose is the life-giving spring that quenches your thirst for a life well-lived.

Rise from the ashes of mere positivity like a purposeful phoenix. Positivity may be the fleeting flames, but purpose is the eternal essence that transcends every setback. Be the purposeful phoenix, soaring above the trivial fires of momentary joy.

Positivity may paint a pretty picture, but purpose is the brush that creates a masterpiece. Become the purposeful legacy-builder, crafting a narrative that transcends the canvas of time. Your purpose is not a passing stroke; it's the enduring masterpiece etched into the tapestry of eternity.

Dare to be a purposeful daredevil, leaping off the cliffs of routine into the exhilarating abyss of meaningful living. Positivity may be a safety net, but purpose is the wings that allow you to soar. Take the plunge, purposeful daredevil, and let the winds of intent carry you to new heights.

In the vast cosmos of possibilities, be the purposeful voyager charting your course through the galaxies of significance. Positivity may be a fleeting comet, but purpose is the celestial body that guides your journey. Navigate with purpose, purposeful voyager, and let the constellations of intent light your way.

Life is an uncharted territory waiting to be explored with purposeful enthusiasm. Positivity may be the compass, but purpose is the map that guides your expedition. Embrace the unknown, purposeful explorer, and let the thrill of discovery be your constant companion.

Live by the code of the purposeful maverick. Reject the superficial allure of constant positivity; instead, embrace the raw, untamed power of purpose. Let your purpose be your North Star, guiding you through the stormy seas and leading you to the shores of a purposeful existence.

Don't chase the fleeting specter of positivity; chase the enduring force of purpose. Positivity may be the short-lived applause, but purpose is the standing ovation of a life well-lived. May your journey be purposeful, your endeavors meaningful, and your spirit forever ignited by the relentless pursuit of living with intent.

Weathering Emotional Storms

Embark on a turbulent voyage into the heart of emotional storms. In the tempest of feelings, you are not a mere passenger; you are the captain of your emotional vessel, navigating the wild seas with the finesse of a seasoned sailor and the audacity of a storm-chaser.

Picture your emotions as a tempest, a swirling maelstrom within. It's not about calming the storm but learning to dance in the rain. Emotional regulation isn't about muting the thunder; it's about conducting a symphony with every lightning strike.

Emotions are the barometer of your internal weather. When the storm clouds gather, it's not about denial; it's about acknowledging the weather report. Emotional regulation starts with understanding the forecast, recognizing the winds of joy, sorrow, anger, and everything in between.

In the alchemist's cauldron of emotional regulation, transform the base metal of negative emotions into the gold of self-awareness. Stir the cauldron with the ladle of introspection, letting the brew of emotional alchemy simmer to perfection.

A weathered mariner doesn't fear the storm; they respect it. In the realm of emotions, wisdom lies in acknowledging the turbulence without being consumed by it. Navigate with the prowess of a seasoned mariner, steering through emotional waves with resilience.

Emotions are not discordant notes but a symphony, each playing its part in the grand composition of your soul. Emotional regulation is the conductor's wand, guiding the symphony to a harmonious crescendo. Embrace the highs and lows, let them compose the melody of your existence.

Become the emotional surfer riding the waves of your feelings with grace. It's not about avoiding the waves but skillfully riding them. Emotional regulation isn't about a calm sea but mastering the art of surfing through the emotional tempests with finesse.

In the heart of emotional storms, listen to the whispers of thunder. The thunder whisperer doesn't silence the storms; they interpret the messages within. Emotional regulation is about deciphering the thunderous emotions, finding the gems of insight within the cacophony.

When the emotional rain pours, don't hide; dance. The rain dance of release is the essence of emotional regulation. Let the emotions flow like raindrops, cleansing the landscape of your soul. In the dance, discover the freedom of expression.

Your emotions are the garden of your being. Emotional regulation isn't about eradicating the weeds but tending to the garden with care. Nurture the blossoms of joy, acknowledge the thorns of sorrow, and let the emotional gardener within flourish.

Create a map of your emotional terrain. The emotional cartographer doesn't fear uncharted territories; they explore them. Emotional regulation is about knowing the lay of the land, navigating through valleys of despair and scaling peaks of ecstasy.

A storm rider doesn't seek shelter; they ride through the tempest. Emotional regulation is the skill of the storm rider, embracing adversity with resilience. Let the winds of challenge be the wings that carry you higher.

Train like an emotional athlete, building endurance for the marathons of feelings. Emotional regulation isn't a sprint; it's a marathon. Strengthen your emotional muscles through mindfulness, meditation, and the relentless pursuit of self-awareness.

Forage through the emotional wilderness, seeking the wisdom hidden in its depths. Emotional regulation is the art of the forager, discovering the nourishment of self-awareness amid the emotional flora. Every emotion is a fruit to be savored.

In the forge of emotional regulation, become the blacksmith shaping the raw ore of feelings into resilient armor. Temper the emotions with the fires of self-awareness, crafting a shield that protects without imprisoning.

Balancing emotions is a tightrope walk in the circus of the soul. The tightrope walker of emotional regulation doesn't fear the heights; they dance with the uncertainty. Each step is deliberate, an intricate ballet of equilibrium.

Your emotions are the compass in the vast sea of existence. Emotional regulation is about steering your ship with intention, using the emotional compass to navigate the tumultuous waters. Let purpose be the northern star guiding your emotional voyage.

Weave a tapestry of emotions, each thread contributing to the vibrant mosaic of your life. Emotional regulation is the art of the emotional weaver, creating a masterpiece that reflects the diversity of your emotional palette.

Take the daredevil's leap into the abyss of your emotions. Emotional regulation isn't about tiptoeing around the edge; it's about the exhilarating freefall into the unknown. Embrace the uncertainty, for within it lies the thrill of authenticity.

Design the blueprint of your emotional architecture. Emotional regulation isn't about constructing walls; it's about creating open spaces for emotional expression. Let the emotions flow freely, shaping the contours of your authentic self.

In the crucible of emotional storms, be the phoenix rising from the ashes of intensity. Emotional regulation is the alchemy of transformation, turning emotional turbulence into the fuel for rebirth. Let every emotional storm be the catalyst for your majestic rise. Success means you've not only weathered the storms but also learned to dance in the rain.

Enriching Reflections

- **Emotional Weather Journal**   Keep a daily journal of your emotional weather, noting the changing patterns, storms, and calms. This practice enhances your emotional literacy, helping you to recognize and name your feelings, understand their origins, and appreciate their impact on your life.
- **Emotional Alchemy Workshop**   Engage in activities that transform negative emotions into creative expression. Whether through art, writing, music, or movement, explore ways to channel your emotional energy into projects that reflect and transcend your inner experiences.
- **Garden of the Psyche Meditation**   Practice regular mindfulness meditation, visualizing your emotions as plants in a garden. Contemplate their colors, textures, and what they need to grow. This meditation encourages a nurturing attitude toward all your feelings, recognizing their value in your emotional ecosystem.
- **Compass Calibration Exercise**   Periodically assess the alignment of your emotional compass. Reflect on recent decisions and experiences to determine whether they're leading you closer to or further from your core values and life goals. Adjust your course accordingly.
- **Emotional Architecture Blueprint**   Create a visual blueprint of your emotional resilience structure. Identify the materials (strengths, coping strategies, support systems) you'll use to build it and the rooms (aspects of your life) it will contain. This exercise helps visualize and plan for a resilient emotional life.

Embrace your emotions as allies in your journey toward authenticity, resilience, and unbridled joy. Fear, joy, sorrow, love, and all other emotions are not merely reactions; they are essential ingredients for sculpting a life that is richer and more nuanced.

Your Inner Scholar

Your brain is not a dusty old library; it's a rebellious maverick's den, hungry for fresh ideas and daring discoveries. Continuous learning transforms your mental space into a dynamic repository of insights, with every neuron firing like a spark in the night.

In the guerrilla warfare of wisdom, continuous learning arms you to the teeth. Knowledge isn't a burden but a weapon of mass enlightenment. Become the guerrilla scholar, launching an insurgency against ignorance with each page turned and every idea embraced.

Continuous learning is not a slow waltz; it's a rock and roll concert of revelations. Let the music of newfound knowledge reverberate through your soul. Dance in the mosh pit of ideas, where epiphanies crowd-surf and inspiration is the headlining act.

Craftsmanship isn't reserved for physical artifacts; it extends to the artistry of awareness. Continuous learning turns you into the artisan of your own enlightenment, sculpting self-awareness with the chisel of new perspectives and the brushstrokes of diverse knowledge.

Step into the time-traveling machine of continuous learning. History, science, philosophy—pick your era and let the journey commence. Every book is a portal, every podcast a time machine. Explore the epochs, converse with the great minds, and return to the present a seasoned time-traveling scholar.

Continuous learning is not a bland, predictable meal; it's a brainiac's buffet of eclectic flavors. From the spicy tang of astrophysics to the sweet richness of literature, indulge your intellectual palate. Be a glutton for knowledge, savoring the diverse delicacies that the banquet of learning has to offer.

Beware the rebel reader, for continuous learning is an act of subversion. Revolt against intellectual conformity, challenge the status quo of your own beliefs, and incite a riot of ideas. In the library of rebellion, every book is a manifesto, and every page turned is an act of defiance.

Continuous learning is a serendipity safari, where each expedition into the unknown unveils unexpected treasures. Let curiosity be your guide through the dense jungles of information. The most enchanting discoveries often lie off the beaten path.

In the shadows of ignorance, be the wisdom ninja. Continuous learning is not about flaunting your knowledge but wielding it with stealth. Move through life's challenges like a shadow, using your acquired wisdom to navigate the intricate dance of existence.

Continuous learning is your personal Wonderland, where the White Rabbit of curiosity leads you down rabbit holes of infinite possibilities. Embrace the "whys" that echo through your mind, for in each question lies the key to unlocking new dimensions of understanding.

Your brain is not a silent library but a symphony of synapses, playing the melody of perpetual curiosity. Continuous learning orchestrates this symphony, ensuring that every neuron contributes to the harmonious crescendo of intellectual expansion.

Join the maverick's rebellion against mental stagnation. Continuous learning is the battle cry of those who refuse to be imprisoned by the status quo. Break free from the chains of intellectual complacency, and let the rebel within rise.

Continuous learning is not a rigid march; it's a daring acrobatic performance. The agile mind flips, twists, and somersaults through the dynamic landscape of ideas. Be the mental acrobat, embracing change with the grace of a trapeze artist.

Become a pirate on the seas of knowledge, plundering the vast treasures that continuous learning unveils. Each book, podcast, or lecture is a chest of intellectual gold waiting to be explored. Arm yourself with a compass of curiosity, and let the adventure begin.

Continuous learning is not a solitary pursuit; it's a grand soiree where sages from different epochs converge. Attend the intellectual ball, waltzing with Aristotle, debating with Socrates, and sharing a laugh with Mark Twain. Every book is an invitation to the sage's soiree.

In the quantum realm of continuous learning, understanding leaps from one level to another. The more you explore, the more you realize the vastness of the undiscovered. Take the quantum leap, transcending your previous intellectual boundaries with every stride.

Continuous learning transforms you into a cosmic connoisseur, sipping from the chalice of universal knowledge. Drink from the cup of astronomy, philosophy, and quantum physics. Let the intoxication of understanding propel you into the cosmic realms of enlightenment.

In the carnival of continuous learning, become the jester who mocks ignorance with a jest. Laughter is the elixir that makes learning delightful. Don the cap and bells of the intellectual jester, turning every revelation into a whimsical jest.

Take the oath of the continuous learning maverick. Promise to question, to seek, to explore the uncharted territories of your mind. Let the maverick's oath echo through your every endeavor, turning each day into an epic adventure of intellectual exploration.

Embrace Your Inner Rebel

Embark on a wild journey into the heart of rebellion. This ain't your grandma's Sunday sermon; it's a raucous celebration of embracing your inner rebel. So, fasten your seatbelts—or don't, because rebels don't always play by the rules—and let's dive into the chaos.

Waking up your inner rebel is like setting off fireworks in a library—it's loud, unexpected, and bound to ruffle some feathers. So, consider this your wake-up call, the rebel bugle playing a symphony of defiance in the face of the mundane.

To embrace your inner rebel, you must master the art of rule-breaking. Forget the guidebook; toss it out the window like yesterday's newspaper. Rebels write their own rules, and the ink is made of audacity, spontaneity, and a healthy dose of "F*ck it, I'm doing it my way."

Uniforms are for soldiers of conformity. Rebels? We wear flair, individuality, and a dash of eccentricity. So, ditch the cookie-cutter attire and let your wardrobe be a canvas for your rebel spirit. Sequins on a Tuesday? Why the hell not?

Your rebellion is your canvas, and self-expression is your brush. Splash the colors of your personality across the vast canvas of existence. Whether it's through art, words, or interpretative dance, let your rebellion be a masterpiece of self-expression.

Every rebel needs a battle cry, a rallying call that echoes through the corridors of the status quo. It doesn't have to be a literal scream; it can be the refusal to accept the ordinary, a whispered declaration that says, "I am here to disrupt the mundane."

Politeness is for tea parties and Victorian novels. Rebel with impolite audacity. Challenge the norms, flip the bird at conformity, and let your rebellion be the belch after a satisfying feast of nonconformity.

Embracing your inner rebel isn't just about chaos for chaos' sake. Rebel with purpose. Let your actions speak a language of intention, a rebellion that aims to dismantle outdated structures and build bridges to uncharted territories.

Every rebel needs a soundtrack. Craft your rebel playlist with the anthems of defiance, the ballads of nonconformity, and the symphonies of rebellion. Whether it's punk, jazz, or yodeling, let your playlist be the heartbeat of your rebellion.

Approval is the currency of the conformist. Rebels? We forge our own chains. Break free from the suffocating embrace of approval-seeking. The only validation you need is the fierce drumbeat of your rebel heart.

Rebels don't emerge unscathed; we wear our battle scars with pride. Each scar tells a story of a skirmish with the status quo, a rebellion waged and won. So, let your battle scars be the badges of honor on your rebel uniform.

In the rebel's toolbox, creativity is the hammer, and courage is the wrench. Together, they dismantle the rusty structures of conformity and build the bridges to innovation. So, wield your tools with audacity, and let the world witness the construction of your rebellion.

Labels are for jars, not for rebels. Don't let society slap a convenient sticker on your forehead. Rebel against the limiting labels that threaten to box you in. You are not a product on a shelf; you're a dynamic, ever-evolving force of nature.

The rebel's code is written in the ink of integrity, not popularity. It's about staying true to your convictions even when the world raises an eyebrow. Popularity is fleeting; the rebel's legacy is eternal.

Ordinary is the enemy of the rebel. Outlaw the ordinary; let your rebellion be the outlaw riding into the sunset of nonconformity. Reject the mundane, embrace the extraordinary, and let your life be a wild, unpredictable adventure.

Silence is the ally of the status quo. Break the sound barrier with the roar of your rebellion. Speak up when others hush, challenge when others nod in agreement, and let your words echo in the caverns of conformity.

Fear is the shadow that looms over the status quo. The rebel doesn't cower; we rebel against fear itself. Turn your fears into fuel for your rebellion, and watch as the shadows dissipate in the blaze of your audacity.

Apologies are for mistakes, not for being a rebel. Write your manifesto with the bold strokes of "No Apologies." Apologize for the accidental spilled coffee, but never for the intentional splash of your rebellion.

The rebel's battle plan is written in the ink of adaptability. The status quo is a shifting landscape, and rebels dance through its ever-changing terrain. Be adaptable, and let your rebellion be a fluid, ever-evolving masterpiece.

The fringe is where the rebel thrives. Embrace the fringes of society, the edges of conventions, and let your rebellion be a dance on the periphery. The center is for the faint-hearted; the fringe is where the maverick finds home.

Your rebellion is not a whisper; it's a thunderclap reverberating through the corridors of time. Leave a legacy of unapologetic impact. Let your rebellion be the earthquake that reshapes the landscapes of conformity.

The rebel's journey is not a sprint; it's a marathon of audacity, and the finish line is wherever the hell you want it to be. Embrace your inner rebel, let the wild winds of nonconformity tousle your hair, and ride the waves of rebellion with unbridled enthusiasm. The world awaits your unique brand of chaos.

Liberate Your Choices

Welcome to the rebellion against the tyrant 'Should.' Buckle up because we're about to journey into the realm of 'Could,' where the landscapes are painted with the hues of limitless possibilities. Grab your compass, toss away the rulebook, and let's explore the uncharted territories of choice.

'Should' is the autocrat ruling over the kingdom of conformity. It dictates, demands, and enforces a rigid code of supposed obligations. Well, guess what? It's time to mount the rebellion, tear down the banners of 'Should,' and reclaim the sovereignty of 'Could.'

Picture 'Could' as the rebel's battle cry echoing through the valleys of decision-making. It's the audacious declaration that choices are not shackled by obligation but freed by the wings of possibility. So, let your battle cry be a resounding 'Could.'

Choosing 'Could' is not a mere rebellion; it's a liberation. It's breaking free from the chains of societal expectations and dancing in the open field of uncharted choices. 'Could' is the key that unlocks the doors to a world where your decisions are guided by desire, not duty.

In the rebel's lexicon, 'Should' is a dirty word, whispered by the conformists and embraced by the cautious. It's time to wash your mouth free of its residue, cleanse your vocabulary, and replace it with the resounding chorus of 'Could.'

Revolutionaries don't march to the beat of 'Should'; they waltz to the melody of 'Could.' It's time to join the 'Could' revolution, where choices are not obligations but invitations to adventure, where the road less traveled becomes the highway of possibilities.

Imagine a world where every time someone mentions 'Should,' you reply with a rebellious "F*ck 'Should,' Hail 'Could'!" It's a mantra, a declaration of independence from the oppressive regime of expectations. Let your battle cry be heard, and let 'Could' be your guiding star.

Sure, 'Should' feels safe, like a well-paved road. But what about the fear of 'Could'? What if you make the wrong choice? Well, fear not, fellow rebel, because 'Could' is not about right or wrong; it's about the exhilarating journey of exploration.

'Should' is a fixed point, a dot on the map of expectations. 'Could' is a constellation, a vast expanse of sparkling opportunities.

Navigate by the stars of 'Could,' and let the map of your life be an ever-evolving masterpiece.

Think of your life as a canvas, waiting for the strokes of your choices. 'Should' is a monochrome palette, but 'Could'—oh, 'Could' is a riot of colors, waiting to splash across the canvas of your existence. Dip your brush in the hues of 'Could' and paint boldly.

'Should' is a creator of expectations, a relentless taskmaster. 'Could' is a spark of curiosity, an invitation to peek behind the curtains of possibility. Choose curiosity over expectation, and let your choices be guided by the thrill of 'Could.'

Picture 'Could' as your passport to the grand adventure of life. Stamp it liberally with experiences, encounters, and the unexplored. With 'Could' as your guide, every decision becomes a visa to a new destination on the map of your journey.

'Should' is a monotonous hum, a drone in the background. 'Could' is a symphony, a harmonious blend of notes that crescendo with every courageous choice. Let your life be a masterpiece, composed in the grand symphony of 'Could.'

Blueprints are for buildings, not for lives. Tear up the blueprint of 'Should' and navigate by the constellation of 'Could.' Your life is not a construction project; it's a cosmic voyage, and 'Could' is your celestial navigation.

'Should' is a jigsaw puzzle, demanding every piece to fit in its predetermined place. 'Could' is a mosaic, each piece unique, contributing to the vibrant tapestry of your story. Embrace the messiness of 'Could' and let your life be a living artwork.

'Should' is the lead in the alchemist's workshop—heavy, unyielding. 'Could' is the philosopher's stone, turning the mundane into the extraordinary. Embrace the alchemy of 'Could,' and witness the transformation of your choices into golden moments.

'Should' is a straightjacket, confining you to the narrow corridors of expectation. 'Could' is a pair of wings, allowing you to soar into the limitless sky of possibility. Choose wings over straightjackets, and let your spirit take flight.

'Should' is a cage, enclosing you in the bars of societal norms. 'Could' is the call of the wild, inviting you to venture beyond the fenced boundaries. Answer the call, break free from the cage, and let your wild heart roam.

'Should' is a monologue, a dictation from the authoritarian voice within. 'Could' is a dialogue, a conversation with your deepest desires and wildest dreams. Engage in the dialogue of 'Could' and let your choices be a collaborative masterpiece.

'Should' is a cul-de-sac, a dead-end street with limited possibilities. 'Could' is an infinite highway, stretching into the horizon of limitless choices. Step onto the highway of 'Could' and let the journey unfold endlessly.

Inscribe your manifesto in the bold strokes of 'Could.' Let it be a proclamation of your allegiance to possibility, a declaration of independence from the chains of 'Should.' The Art of 'Could' is not a doctrine; it's a living, breathing manifesto of your liberated choices.

Guided by the audacity of 'Could,' paint the canvas of your life with the vibrant strokes of limitless possibilities. Run with the wind of 'Could' at your back; revel in the freedom of choosing your own adventure. The world awaits the masterpiece that only you can create.

The Dance of Integrity

Imagine the dance of integrity as a symphony, where each step is a note in harmony with your core values. Giving a f*ck that matters involves ensuring that every move in this dance resonates with the melody of your integrity.

Authenticity is the rhythm that guides your dance. Giving a f*ck that matters means moving to this rhythm, embracing your true self and expressing it boldly in every sway and turn.

Your integrity creates a choreography of purpose. Giving a f*ck that matters involves crafting this choreography deliberately, ensuring that your actions align with the purposeful narrative you wish to unfold.

Values are the dance floor on which this integrity dance takes place. Giving a f*ck that matters involves guarding this dance floor, ensuring that it remains untainted by compromises and aligned with the principles that define your existence.

Consider the dance as a reflection in a mirror. Giving a f*ck that matters involves gazing at this reflection, ensuring that the image staring back at you is one of authenticity, purpose, and integrity.

Temptations may try to pull you offbeat in this dance. Giving a f*ck that matters involves skillfully navigating these temptations, resisting the allure of shortcuts that compromise the integrity of your dance.

Life is a waltz of choices. Giving a f*ck that matters involves choosing each step wisely, understanding that every move in this dance has the potential to create a beautiful or discordant melody.

Convictions add syncopation to the dance. Giving a f*ck that matters involves embracing this syncopation, allowing your convictions to introduce unexpected rhythms and patterns into the dance of integrity.

Balance is the foxtrot in this dance. Giving a f*ck that matters involves maintaining equilibrium, ensuring that your commitment to your values doesn't lead to rigidity but allows for fluidity and adaptability.

Authenticity expresses itself in turns. Giving a f*ck that matters involves allowing authenticity to guide your turns, ensuring that your dance is not rehearsed but a spontaneous expression of your true self.

Adversity may attempt to disrupt the dance. Giving a f*ck that matters involves twirling resiliently in the face of challenges, using each obstacle as an opportunity to showcase the strength and integrity of your dance.

Accountability is the quickstep in this dance. Giving a f*ck that matters involves taking swift and purposeful steps to be accountable for your actions, acknowledging missteps, and adjusting the dance accordingly.

Transitions between steps require elegance. Giving a f*ck that matters involves transitioning between different aspects of your life with grace, ensuring that the integrity of your dance remains unwavering through every shift.

Courage leads the tango in this dance. Giving a f*ck that matters involves dancing with courage, confronting challenges with a bold and intentional stride, and never letting fear dictate the pace of your steps.

Adaptability is the cha-cha-cha in this dance. Giving a f*ck that matters involves cha-cha-chaing through the twists and turns of life, adjusting your steps without compromising the integrity of your dance.

Imagine each ethical choice as a balletic movement. Giving a f*ck that matters involves performing this ballet with precision, ensuring that each choice is in harmony with the ethical composition of your values.

Passion is the whirling dervish in this dance. Giving a f*ck that matters involves allowing passion to fuel your dance, infusing each movement with the vibrant energy that comes from aligning with what truly matters to you.

Purpose infuses joy into the salsa. Giving a f*ck that matters involves dancing the salsa with joyful purpose, celebrating every step on the path of significance and acknowledging the fulfillment that comes from living with integrity.

This dance is an unscripted waltz of freedom. Giving a f*ck that matters involves reveling in this freedom, recognizing that the dance of integrity allows you to move in ways that are uniquely your own, unrestricted by external expectations.

Against inauthenticity, perform the Haka. Giving a f*ck that matters involves expressing the Haka, a defiant and powerful dance against anything that threatens to compromise the authenticity and integrity of your purposeful existence.

Consider this dance as a legacy. Giving a f*ck that matters involves ensuring that the dance you perform leaves behind a legacy of integrity, inspiring others to dance their own dances with authenticity and purpose.

The F*ck Jar

Get ready for a crash course in emotional accounting that will redefine the way you invest your emotional capital. Enter the revolutionary concept—the Fck Jar. Picture it as your emotional piggy bank, but instead of coins, it stores your most valuable currency: fcks.

Imagine your emotions as a bustling marketplace. The Fck Jar is your personal economic system, where each fck is a unit of currency. Welcome to the f*ck economy, where emotional investments yield dividends of joy or despair.

The F*ck Jar demands savvy budgeting skills. Like a financial planner for your feelings, it encourages you to allocate your emotional funds strategically. No more reckless spending on unworthy emotional impulse buys.

Some fcks are premium, like the champagne of emotions. The Fck Jar introduces you to the concept of premium f*cks—those rare, exquisite emotions that deserve a reserved spot in your jar. Don't waste them on emotional fast food; savor them for the emotional Michelin-star experiences.

Beware of fck inflation. The Fck Jar warns against the devaluation of your emotional currency. When you throw fcks around carelessly, their value diminishes. Keep your fcks rare and precious to maintain their purchasing power.

Emotions have trends, akin to the stock market. The F*ck Jar encourages you to be a wise emotional investor, recognizing when to buy, sell, or hold. Don't get caught in the emotional equivalent of a market crash.

Diversify your emotional portfolio. The Fck Jar suggests spreading your emotional investments across various fcks, minimizing the risk of an emotional recession. A diversified portfolio ensures resilience in the face of life's inevitable downturns.

Ever heard of compound fcking interest? The Fck Jar knows the secret sauce to emotional wealth is letting your f*cks accumulate and compound over time. Each mindful investment paves the way for a richer emotional future.

Life occasionally presents liquidation events—moments demanding a withdrawal of your emotional assets. The F*ck Jar is your guide, helping you navigate these events without going bankrupt emotionally. Choose your liquidations wisely; some are worth the investment.

In times of emotional crisis, you might be tempted to seek fck bailouts. The Fck Jar cautions against relying on external sources for emotional rescue. Instead, cultivate a robust emotional reserve to weather the storms independently.

Wise investments yield dividends. The Fck Jar promises emotional dividends for judicious fck allocation. Experience the joy of returns on your emotional investments, reinforcing the wisdom of your emotional portfolio.

Emotional impulse buys are the equivalent of emotional fast food—satisfying in the moment but detrimental to your emotional health. The F*ck Jar teaches you to resist the allure of instant emotional gratification and opt for the nutritious emotional choices.

No crystal ball can predict emotional markets, but the Fck Jar encourages you to make informed forecasts. Anticipate your emotional needs and allocate your fcks accordingly. Strategic emotional planning is the key to a thriving F*ck Jar.

Beware of emotional fraud. The F*ck Jar equips you with fraud detection tools to identify counterfeit emotions that may infiltrate your jar. Authenticity is the currency that holds value in the emotional market.

Emotional bankruptcy is a real threat. The F*ck Jar urges you to be vigilant about your emotional expenditures. When you're on the verge of an emotional deficit, it's time for a strategic emotional bailout, not a reckless bankruptcy.

Hedge your emotional bets. The F*ck Jar advises against putting all your emotional eggs in one basket. Hedge against emotional downturns by diversifying your emotional investments and embracing the volatility of the emotional market.

Venture into the realm of emotional futures trading. The F*ck Jar challenges you to forecast your emotional needs and invest in the emotional assets that will appreciate over time. Strategic emotional futures trading ensures a bountiful emotional harvest.

Maintain a meticulous Fck Ledger. The Fck Jar encourages you to track your emotional transactions. Reflect on your emotional investments, learn from the emotional losses, and celebrate the emotional gains.

Like any robust economic system, the F*ck Jar comes with emotional taxation. Some emotional investments require emotional taxes in the form of vulnerability and self-reflection. Embrace the emotional taxation; it's the price of admission to a fulfilling emotional economy.

Engage in emotional philanthropy. The F*ck Jar invites you to share your emotional wealth with others. Acts of emotional kindness and generosity contribute to the collective emotional prosperity, fostering a more emotionally abundant world.

Consider your Fck Legacy. The Fck Jar prompts you to reflect on the emotional inheritance you're leaving behind. Will your F*ck Legacy be one of mindful investments, wise emotional choices, and a wealth of shared emotional experiences?

Remember, emotional wealth isn't about the quantity of fcks but the quality of emotional investments. Audit your F*ck Jar wisely, and may your emotional capital lead you to a life rich in authentic, meaningful experiences.

Your Most Potent Sorcery

Welcome to the realm of alchemy, where the mundane transforms into the extraordinary, and the ordinary into the exceptional. Here, we embark on a journey to unlock the secrets of The Alchemy of Passion, a journey that involves not just setting goals but infusing them with the fervor and fire of your deepest passions.

Imagine your passion as a cauldron bubbling with untamed enthusiasm. Now, toss in your goals—those raw, unshaped ambitions waiting to be forged. The alchemical reaction begins, and the spark of passion ignites the transformative process.

In the alchemy of passion, clarity is the philosopher's stone. You can't transmute the ordinary into the extraordinary without a clear vision. Take the formless lead of vague aspirations and refine it into the gold of well-defined goals that resonate with your soul.

Passion is the elixir that fuels your motivation. It's the potion you sip when the journey gets tough, and the road ahead seems treacherous. Let your passion be the North Star, guiding you through the darkest nights of self-doubt and uncertainty.

Goal setting in the alchemy of passion is an art of distillation. Like a master distiller crafting the finest whiskey, distill your ambitions to their purest essence. Remove the impurities, the unnecessary, and what remains is the concentrated elixir of your true desires.

In the alchemy lab, we use WISE goals as our alchemical equations. Well-Defined, Inspiring, Sustainable, and Empowering —these elements create the perfect formula for transformation. Your goals aren't just wishes; they're alchemical reactions waiting to happen.

> **Author's Note**   We delve into the intricacies of WISE goals in our publications, "Emotional Resilience Now: A Resilience Action Plan for Leaders" and "Hands-On Leadership Resilience: Practical Techniques for Self-Assessment, Meditation, and Goal Attainment." Leadership transcends the conventional boundaries of managing teams; it embodies a comprehensive approach to living. Through these texts, we illuminate the essence of leadership as an integrated lifestyle, emphasizing self-awareness, strategic planning, and the cultivation of resilience. Our exploration into WISE goals isn't just about achieving objectives; it's about nurturing a mindset that embraces adaptability, mindfulness, and purpose-driven action, positioning leadership as a transformative journey rather than a mere role.

Fear is the lead that weighs down our ambitions. In the alchemy of passion, you wield the philosopher's stone to transmute fear into courage. Fear becomes the raw material for growth, the catalyst for transformative change.

Alchemy is an experimental science. Likewise, the journey of passion-fueled goal setting involves a laboratory of trial and error. Mix your aspirations, observe the reactions, and refine your approach. Failure is not an obstacle; it's a necessary step in the alchemical process.

Resilience is the crucible where your goals are tested and forged. Like molten metal, your ambitions face the fire of challenges. The alchemy of passion teaches you to withstand the heat, emerging stronger and more resilient on the other side.

In the alchemy of passion, focus is your most potent sorcery. Channel your energy into the crucible of your goals, eliminating distractions and side quests. The more focused the energy, the more potent the alchemical reaction.

Visualization is the mystic art in the alchemy of passion. Envision your goals not as distant dreams but as tangible, achievable realities. Paint vivid mental pictures, infusing them with the colors of your passion. The mind is the canvas; let it be a masterpiece.

The dance of adaptability is a core principle in the alchemy of passion. Goals, like elements, can change states. Be fluid, adjust to the evolving landscape, and understand that the unexpected is not a detour but an integral part of the alchemical journey.

Achievement is the goldsmith's workshop in the alchemy of passion. As you forge your goals in the crucible, the goldsmith meticulously shapes the raw material into the intricate design of success. Every achievement is a crafted masterpiece.

Time is the alchemist's hourglass, a constant reminder that every moment is a precious ingredient. In the alchemy of passion, time management isn't just a practical skill; it's the art of optimizing the alchemical process, ensuring that every grain of sand contributes to your transformative goals.

Dreams are the philharmonic symphony in the alchemy of passion. Each goal you set is a note in the grand composition of your life. Let your dreams create a symphony that resonates with the universe, a melody so powerful that it propels you toward your desired destination.

True alchemy goes beyond personal gain; it involves the transformative power of giving back. As you pursue your passions, consider how your goals can contribute to the greater good. The alchemy of passion extends its magic when shared with others.

Reflection is the casting of mystic runes in the alchemy of passion. Regularly assess your journey, read the signs, and decipher the messages. Reflection is not about dwelling on mistakes but about learning from the alchemical experiments that shape your path.

Celebrate every milestone as you would a potion brewed to perfection. In the alchemy of passion, acknowledgment is the potion that amplifies your motivation. Each step toward your goals is a sip of success; savor the taste, and let it fuel your journey.

In the alchemy of passion, reinvention is the phoenix rising from the ashes. Goals achieved are not endpoints but catalysts for new beginnings. Embrace the cycles of growth and renewal, understanding that every end is a prelude to a fresh alchemical experiment.

Look to the stars in the alchemy of passion. Your goals are not confined to earthly limitations. Aim for the cosmos, dream big, and let your passion be the rocket fuel propelling you toward the galaxies of your wildest aspirations.

Step back and witness the unveiling of your masterpiece—the confluence of passion and goal setting. This isn't just the achievement of objectives; it's the alchemical transformation of your existence. May your goals be the gold that enriches your journey, and may the alchemy of passion be your perpetual guide.

Journey into the heart of where passion meets purpose, and transform the raw materials of your aspirations into the gold of realized dreams. This is a spellbook for the courageous, ready to harness their deepest desires and channel them into the creation of a life that echoes with the vibrancy of true fulfillment.

1. **The Cauldron of Clarity** Begin with absolute clarity. Like the alchemist seeking the philosopher's stone, your journey requires a clear vision. Distill your desires to their purest form, ensuring that your goals are not just reflections of fleeting wishes but beacons guiding you towards your authentic self.

2. **The Elixir of Motivation** Let passion be the elixir that sustains you. When the path becomes difficult, and shadows lengthen, sip from this potion to renew your spirit. Passion is not just fuel; it's the very essence of your journey, imbuing your actions with meaning and your goals with the possibility of achievement.

3. **WISE Goals as Alchemical Equations**   Employ WISE (Well-Defined, Inspiring, Sustainable, Empowering) goals as your formula for transformation. This framework is your spell for turning leaden aspirations into golden outcomes, ensuring that each goal is a step towards the extraordinary.

4. **The Philosopher's Stone of Courage**   Use courage to transmute fear. In the alchemical process of pursuing your passions, fear often emerges as the base metal. With courage, however, you possess the philosopher's stone capable of turning this fear into the gold of opportunity and growth.

5. **The Laboratory of Life**   Embrace life as your alchemical laboratory. Experimentation is the essence of discovery. Mix, try, fail, and refine. Each attempt, each failure, is a precious ingredient in the potion of success, leading you closer to the masterpiece you seek to create.

6. **The Crucible of Resilience**   Let resilience be your crucible, within which the true strength of your goals is tested and forged. Face the flames of adversity with the knowledge that what emerges will be stronger, more beautiful, and infinitely more precious.

7. **The Sorcery of Focus**   Harness the sorcery of focus, directing your energies with laser precision. In the realm of goal achievement, distraction is the enemy. Focus your powers on what truly matters, allowing your passions to guide you through the fog of the inconsequential.

8. **The Mystic Art of Visualization**   Visualization is your mystic art, the practice of seeing the unseen, of bringing the future into the present through the power of your mind's eye. Visualize not just the goals but the steps, the challenges, and the triumphs. Let this vision be the map that guides you through the uncharted territories of your ambitions.

9. **The Dance of Adaptability** Master the dance of adaptability. Goals, like the alchemist's elements, can change states. Fluidity is not a sign of weakness but of wisdom, allowing you to navigate the ever-changing landscape of life with agility and grace.

10. **The Goldsmith's Workshop of Achievement** View each goal as a piece in the goldsmith's workshop. Here, raw ambitions are carefully shaped, refined, and polished until they shine with the luster of achievement. This meticulous process turns goals from mere intentions into tangible successes.

11. **The Alchemist's Hourglass** Time is your alchemist's hourglass, reminding you that each moment is a finite resource to be utilized with intention. Manage this resource wisely, allocating your moments to pursuits that will shape the masterpiece of your life.

12. **The Symphony of Dreams** Let your goals compose the symphony of your life, a harmony of dreams that sings with purpose and passion. Each goal, each achievement, is a note in this melody, contributing to the opus that is your legacy.

Embrace this journey not as a mere pursuit of goals but as an alchemical transformation. Let the passion that fuels your desires be the fire that transmutes your dreams into reality, crafting from the ordinary an existence that resonates with the extraordinary. In this sorcery, find not just the achievement of goals but the unveiling of your true masterpiece: a life lived with purpose, passion, and profound fulfillment.

The Comfort Zone

Tear down the walls of familiarity, embrace the chaos of growth, and declare that the most profound transformations occur in the crucible of discomfort. The Comfort Zone is that deceptive snuggle, a warm, fuzzy prison that convinces you that safety is better than adventure. F*ck that. True liberation lies beyond the confines of the familiar.

The safety net below the Comfort Zone is an illusion, a flimsy parachute that prevents the exhilarating free fall into the unknown. F*ck the false security; growth demands a daring dive into uncertainty.

Comfort is the silent assassin of dreams, lurking in the shadows of routine. F*ck the seductive whispers of familiarity; let discomfort be your ally in the pursuit of extraordinary dreams.

The predictable routine of the Comfort Zone is a graveyard of innovation. F*ck the monotony; let the unpredictable rhythm of growth be the soundtrack to your rebellion against stagnation.

Comfort steals potential, handcuffing it to the radiator of the familiar. F*ck the thief; unlock your potential by stepping into the uncharted territories where discomfort is the key.

The illusion of contentment within the Comfort Zone is a mirage that evaporates upon closer inspection. F*ck the counterfeit joy; discover the authentic bliss that comes with confronting challenges head-on.

The Comfort Zone is a magnet for mediocrity, pulling dreams down to its level. F*ck the magnetic force; let the gravitational pull of ambition rocket you toward the cosmos of extraordinary achievement.

The fear of discomfort is a paper tiger, roaring louder than its bite. F*ck the false alarms; walk through the discomfort like a warrior stepping over fallen foes.

Comfort is a chalice filled with the poison of complacency. F*ck the toxic sips; let the elixir of discomfort be the tonic that invigorates your spirit.

The Comfort Zone breeds an echo chamber of sameness, where every voice echoes the status quo. F*ck the dull hum; let the cacophony of diverse challenges be the symphony of your personal revolution.

Comfort sings a lullaby of stagnation, a hypnotic melody that numbs the senses. F*ck the lullaby; let the dissonance of growth be the wake-up call to a vibrant reality.

The chains of routine within the Comfort Zone are subtle, but their weight is immense. F*ck the shackles; dance in the wild turbulence of change where freedom is your partner.

Comfort is a false haven, a mirage that evaporates when life's storms hit. F*ck the illusion; build your fortress in the storm, where resilience is the cornerstone.

The Bubble Wrap Mentality within the Comfort Zone shields you from bruises but leaves you untested and fragile. F*ck the bubble wrap; let the scars of growth be the tattoos of your resilience.

The Comfort Zone is a false summit, convincing you that you've reached the peak when the real summit is obscured by clouds. F*ck the illusion; climb higher, where the air is thin, and the view is breathtaking.

The Couch Potato Comfort within the Comfort Zone is the graveyard of ambition. F*ck the inertia; rise and sprint toward the horizon where challenges await with open arms.

Comfort tricks you into believing you're in control, a puppet master of a predictable puppet show. F*ck the strings; embrace the spontaneity of chaos where true control lies in your adaptability.

The fear of failure, incubated in the Comfort Zone, is a phantom menace. F*ck the apparition; let failure be your battle scars, proving that you fought in the arena of growth.

Comfort seduces with sameness, an intoxicating perfume that masks the scent of potential. F*ck the allure; walk into the unfamiliar where the fragrance of growth is both thrilling and intoxicating.

The inertia of comfort is a heavyweight champion, difficult to defeat but not impossible. F*ck the inertia; be the revolutionary heavyweight, throwing punches of change until the bell of transformation rings loud.

Let this be your battle cry, a manifesto against the marshmallow embrace of the Comfort Zone. F*ck the familiar; embrace the chaos, for within it lies the sculptor's chisel carving the masterpiece of your becoming.

The Canvas Isn't Infinite

Sharpen your mental chisels. We're about to sculpt the masterpiece of your existence by diving headfirst into the chaotic art of time management—a sculpting session where you decide what deserves a place in the marble of your day and what's better left as abstract space. So, grab your chisel, don your creative cap, and let's carve out a life worth living.

Imagine your day as a blank canvas, and time as the paint waiting to be splattered across it. Your life is the art you create. But here's the kicker: the canvas isn't infinite. You've got a finite space to work with, so make each brushstroke count.

Multitasking is the magician's sleight of hand in the world of productivity—it looks impressive, but it's all smoke and mirrors. Let's debunk the myth; multitasking is a time-thief, robbing moments of focus and leaving you with a haphazard jumble of unfinished tasks.

Ah, the to-do list—a mythical creature that promises order but often leads to chaos. Don't let your list mutate into a monster. Instead, wield your time chisel and sculpt a realistic plan. Prioritize, break it down, and conquer one task at a time.

Procrastination is the fire-breathing dragon lurking in the caves of productivity. But fear not, intrepid time sculptors! Equip yourself with the sword of discipline and face the dragon head-on. Slay the procrastination beast, and watch your time kingdom flourish.

Enter the Zen garden of time blocking, where each pebble represents a task. Arrange your stones strategically, creating a harmonious balance between work, leisure, and the occasional cat video. It's a meticulous process, but the result is a tranquil landscape of productivity.

Life without routines is like a clock without gears—chaotic and ultimately useless. Craft your daily gears with intention, creating a well-oiled machine that propels you toward your goals. Routine isn't the enemy; it's the silent ally that keeps your time sculpture in motion.

Imagine time as a buffet, with each minute a delectable dish waiting to be savored. But, alas, you have a finite plate. Be selective at the time buffet; pile on what truly matters, and leave the tasteless tidbits of triviality behind.

Deadlines are the metronome of productivity, setting the rhythm for your creative orchestra. Embrace the symphony of deadlines; let the ticking clock be the driving force behind your magnum opus. Procrastination, meet your match.

Enter the matrix, not the sci-fi one, but the Eisenhower Matrix. It's your time management dojo. Slice through the tasks with the precision of a ninja. Urgent and important? Do it now. Not urgent but important? Schedule it. Urgent but not important? Delegate. Neither urgent nor important? Hit the delete button.

If you could time travel, would you go back to correct your mistakes or forward to glimpse the future? Time travel is a fantasy, but effective time management lets you dictate the narrative of your story. Learn from the past, plan for the future, and make the present a damn good chapter.

In the frenetic dance of seconds and minutes, sometimes all it takes is a mindful minute to reset. Pause, breathe, recalibrate. It's the mental floss your brain craves, clearing out the clutter and making room for focused productivity.

Time vampires are real, and they're not as glamorous as the ones in fiction. Identify the culprits—endless social media scrolls, mindless meetings, or the abyss of internet rabbit holes. Stake your time vampire heart and reclaim those stolen hours.

Rest is not the enemy of productivity; it's the Renaissance period of your day. A well-rested mind wields the chisel more effectively. Sculpting your time doesn't mean relentless toil; it means honoring the ebb and flow, knowing when to carve and when to step back.

Priorities are the quantum physics of time management—ever-changing, elusive, and sometimes confusing. But fear not, fellow quantum sculptors! Identify your priorities, take the quantum leap, and watch your daily reality shift in alignment with your goals.

"No" is a complete sentence, a punctuation mark in the paragraphs of time. Master the art of saying no to the time-thieves disguised as obligations. Guard your schedule like a fierce dragon guards its treasure.

Small wins are the butterflies that create the whirlwind of productivity. Celebrate these delicate creatures, for they have the power to set in motion a chain reaction of positive momentum. Your time sculpture thrives on the flutter of small victories.

Your calendar is not a confounding puzzle; it's a map to undiscovered territories. Navigate the calendar conundrum with purpose. Schedule your priorities, pencil in moments of joy, and leave room for the unexpected adventures that make life a thrilling expedition.

A time machine may be sci-fi, but a reflective moment is a powerful tool. Carve out time for introspection, review your time-sculpting endeavors, and adjust the chisel for future creations. The past is your quarry, the present your chisel, and the future your masterpiece.

No, we're not advocating forgery, but the art of time forgery involves bending the rules. Sometimes, breaking free from the rigid structure of time management can unleash bursts of creativity. Forge your path, break a few rules, and see where the winding road takes you.

Your time management skills aren't just for the present; they're the legacy sculpture you leave behind. Carve your time with intention, let the chisel of priorities shape your days, and watch as your life becomes a timeless masterpiece, admired by those who follow in your footsteps.

Let the echoes of efficient chiseling, intentional carving, and the occasional rebellious stroke linger in the air. Carry the masterpiece of your time sculpture with pride, for it's a testament to your ability to craft a life that reflects your priorities. Onward, skilled sculptors of time to the action plan for mastering time management where you select strategies that genuinely resonate with you and your unique path in life.

Action Plan and Activities for Mastering Time Management

- **Daily Canvas Evaluation** Each morning, visualize your day as a blank canvas. Decide on three main "brushstrokes" (tasks) that will most significantly contribute to your masterpiece (goals). Sketch these out in your planner or a dedicated app.
- **Multitasking Myth-Busting Challenge** For one week, consciously avoid multitasking. Tackle tasks sequentially, noting any differences in productivity and the quality of work.
- **Taming the To-Do List Beast** Transform your to-do list into a prioritized action plan. Divide tasks into "Must Do," "Should Do," and "Could Do" categories. Focus on completing the "Must Do" tasks first to prevent your list from becoming overwhelming.
- **Time Blocking Garden** Schedule your week using the time blocking method. Assign specific tasks to dedicated blocks of time, including blocks for breaks and leisure. This helps create a balanced "garden" of productivity and relaxation.
- **Routine Reinforcement** Establish a morning routine that kickstarts your day on a positive note. Include elements such as

meditation, exercise, or reading. Note how this impacts your mood and productivity throughout the day.
- **Buffet-Style Time Management Reflection** At the end of each day, reflect on how you "filled your plate" with activities. Were you selective, or did you overindulge in time-wasting activities? Plan adjustments for the next day.
- **Deadline Symphony** For each project or task with a deadline, create a mini-symphony. Break down the project into movements (phases) and set mini-deadlines for each. This helps maintain a rhythmic progression toward your final goal.
- **Urgent-Important Matrix Dojo** Apply the Urgent-Important Matrix to your tasks weekly by drawing lines that divide a piece of paper into quadrants. Label Quadrant 1: Urgent and Important (Do First), Quadrant 2: Important but not Urgent (Schedule), Quadrant 3: Urgent but Not Important (Delegate) and Quadrant 4: Not Urgent and Not Important (Eliminate). Sort tasks into the matrix's quadrants and tackle them according to their categorization. Reflect on how this clarifies your priorities and enhances decision-making.
- **Mindful Minute Resets** Incorporate regular "mindful minutes" into your day. Use these moments to breathe deeply, center yourself, and realign with your goals. Observe how this practice affects your focus and stress levels.
- **Identify and Banish Time Vampires** Keep a log of activities for a week. Identify "time vampires" that drain productivity. Develop strategies to minimize or eliminate these from your schedule.
- **Rest Renaissance** Schedule regular rest periods and activities that rejuvenate you. Acknowledge these as crucial for sustaining long-term productivity.
- **Quantum Leap Prioritization** Periodically reassess your priorities. Visualize them as elements in a quantum field, flexible and adaptable. Adjust your focus and actions to align with any shifts in priorities.

- **The Art of Saying "No"**   Practice saying no to new commitments that don't align with your priorities. Reflect on the empowerment this brings and its impact on your time management.
- **Celebration of Small Wins**   At the end of each day, jot down small victories. Acknowledge how these contribute to your larger goals and enhance your motivation.
- **Calendar Cartography**   Treat your calendar as a map of your personal journey. Ensure it reflects a balance of tasks, personal time, and unplanned adventures.
- **Reflective Time Sculpting:** Dedicate time each week to reflect on your time management practices. Adjust your strategies and techniques based on insights gained from these reflections.
- **Rule Breaking**   Once a month, deliberately break away from your structured time management plan. Engage in spontaneous or creative activities, noting the impact on your creativity and overall well-being.
- **Legacy Time Management Reflection**   Consider how the way you manage your time contributes to the legacy you're building. Align your time management practices with the legacy you wish to leave behind.

The Procrastination Dragon

Welcome, brave souls, to the battlefield where many a warrior has faced their most formidable foe: the Procrastination Dragon. This beast isn't just a thief of time; it's a master of deception, luring you into the illusion that tomorrow holds endless possibilities for productivity. But fear not, for today, we arm you with a powerful weapon: The Triple Sprint Method. This isn't just a strategy; it's your battle plan for reclaiming your kingdom of productivity from the clutches of procrastination.

Before we dive headlong into the fray against the procrastination dragon, let's take a moment to understand this beast that lurks in the shadows of our ambitions. This isn't just about tactics and strategies; it's about peering into the heart of the dragon, understanding its origins, and facing it with the wisdom of a sage and the courage of a warrior. So, buckle up, for we're about to embark on a journey into the psyche of procrastination.

Procrastination isn't born out of laziness; it's the offspring of fear. Fear of failure, fear of success, and the overwhelming dread of the unknown. Every time you delay, you feed this dragon a morsel of your potential, letting it grow stronger on your doubts.

The procrastination dragon makes its lair in the comforting shadows of your comfort zone. It whispers sweet nothings of "later" and "someday," lulling you into a false sense of security where nothing changes, and therefore, nothing risks failure. It thrives on the illusion of perfection, convincing you that if you can't do it perfectly, then why do it at all? But here's the truth: perfection is the dragon's lie, a mirage that keeps you parched in the desert of inaction.

Procrastination tricks you into believing that time is both infinite and immediate. It seduces you with the promise of an endless tomorrow while stealthily stealing today. It's a paradox that binds you in chains of "later" while the sands of "now" slip through your fingers.

The dragon feasts on your feelings of overwhelm. When tasks mount like an insurmountable peak, procrastination whispers, "Why start at all?" But remember, even the tallest mountains are climbed one step at a time.

In its cunning, the dragon employs sirens that sing the sweet song of distractions. Social media scrolls, aimless web surfing, and binge-watching become the lullabies that soothe you into stasis, away from the shores of productivity.

Procrastination armors itself in excuses, a shield forged from "not enough time," "not the right moment," and "I'm not ready." This armor is formidable but not invincible. Your weapon against it? Action, no matter how small.

The dragon forces you to gaze into the mirror of self-doubt, where every reflection questions your capability, worth, and the validity of your dreams. Break this mirror; your reflection is distorted by the dragon's breath. This beast is a master of deception, tricking your brain with the quick fixes of dopamine hits from easy tasks or pleasures, leaving the meaningful quests—the ones that require effort and yield long-term fulfillment—by the wayside.

Procrastination establishes a ritual of avoidance, a ceremonial dance that distances you from your goals. Recognize this ritual for what it is—a delay tactic—and choose to disrupt the pattern with intentional action.

Busywork is the dragon's shield, a barrage of inconsequential tasks that protect it from the strikes of meaningful action. It's a shield that sparkles with the illusion of productivity but guards the entrance to the cave of stagnation.

"Tomorrow," whispers the dragon, a seductive promise that tomorrow holds more promise, more motivation, more courage. Yet, tomorrow becomes today, and the cycle repeats, a Groundhog Day of unfulfilled potential.

The dragon lures you onto the easy path, where effort is minimal, and rewards are fleeting. It's a path that circles the mountain of your ambitions but never ascends. The climb may be hard, but the view from the summit is worth it.

Within the dragon's lair lies a maze of rationalization, where every turn justifies delay and every dead end feels like a reasoned choice. Navigating this maze requires the compass of honesty and the map of your values.

The most tragic treasure hoarded by the procrastination dragon is the legacy of the unlived life—dreams unchased, goals unreached, and potentials unfulfilled. It's a treasure that, once taken, can never be reclaimed.

The rebellion against procrastination starts with the power of now. It's a rebellion that doesn't require weapons or armor, just the sheer force of will to say, "Not later, not tomorrow, but now." Now is the time to act, to live, to create.

Ultimately, facing procrastination is a dance with the dragon—a dance where you lead. It's a dance of courage, of stepping into the arena despite the fear, and of moving to the rhythm of your purpose and passion. This battle isn't just about time management; it's about soul management. It's about conquering the fears, doubts, and illusions that feed the dragon and reclaiming the kingdom of your potential. The time to act is now. The place to start is here. The person to do it is you. Let's dance, for today, we arm you with a powerful weapon: The Triple Sprint Method. This isn't just a strategy; it's your battle plan for reclaiming your kingdom of productivity from the clutches of procrastination.

1. **Identifying the Beast.** Your first step in this epic quest is to identify the task you've been avoiding—the dragon lurking in the shadows of your to-do list. It's that one task

that seems so daunting, you'd rather face an actual dragon than tackle it. But here's the twist: break down this monstrous task into smaller, more manageable dragons. These mini-beasts won't seem nearly as intimidating.

2. **The Art of the Triple Sprint.** Armed with your segmented task, initiate the Triple Sprint. Set a timer for 20 minutes, and dive into battle against the first segment of your task. During this sprint, all distractions must be banished to the realm of "Not Now." Your focus is your sword, cutting through excuses and delays.

3. **The Sacred Pause.** After your first 20-minute sprint, the bell tolls for a sacred pause. This isn't a retreat; it's a strategic regrouping. Take deep breaths, stretch your limbs, and refresh your surroundings. This brief respite is the magical elixir that rejuvenates your spirit for the next charge.

4. **Charging Forward.** Reset your timer and plunge back into the fray, attacking the next segment of your task or continuing your assault on the first if the beast is stubborn. With each 20-minute cycle, you're not just working; you're weaving a spell of productivity, turning daunting tasks into achievable victories.

5. **The Reward of Rest.** After three cycles of relentless pursuit (totaling 60 minutes of focused effort), grant yourself the boon of a 15-minute break. This is your time to wander the castle grounds, feast, or simply bask in the glory of your efforts. This is essential to replenish your energy for the battles ahead.

6. **The Cycle of Momentum.** Continue the rhythm of 20-minute focused work intervals followed by 15-minute rejuvenating breaks, diligently progressing through the steps of your task until its completion. Each cycle is a balanced blend of concentrated effort and meaningful relaxation, designed to optimize both productivity and well-being.

7. **Reflection in Victory.** With each task conquered, take a moment to stand atop the mountain of your achievement and reflect. How did the Triple Sprint Method serve you in battle? Were the dragons of distraction kept at bay? Did the rhythm of focus and rest invigorate your spirit?

8. **Adjusting Your Armor.** No warrior remains clad in the same armor for all battles. Reflect on the pacing of your sprints, the effectiveness of your breaks, and the overall strategy. Adjust your approach as needed, for the Procrastination Dragon is cunning and ever-changing in its tactics.

Let the Triple Sprint become your rhythm in the dance of productivity. With each task approached in this manner, you're not just doing work; you're performing a ritual that celebrates focus, discipline, and well-being. The journey doesn't end with one task. The Procrastination Dragon has many heads, and your quest is ongoing. But fear not, for you now possess a powerful strategy that transforms overwhelming battles into series of victorious sprints. In the end, what you're fighting for is time—precious, irreplaceable time. The Triple Sprint Method doesn't just help you win battles; it helps you reclaim your time, allowing you to spend it on the pursuits that truly matter in the grand saga of your life.

Purpose is not a Unicorn

Purpose is not a unicorn; it's not some elusive creature that frolics in the meadows of self-help books. No, purpose is the quest for meaning, the relentless pursuit of a life that resonates with the very core of your being. It's time to give a f*ck about what truly matters to you.

Let's clear the air; purpose isn't a buzzword you sprinkle on your Instagram bio. It's not about appearing profound to your virtual audience. Purpose is the backbone of your existence, the spine that keeps you standing tall when the winds of life blow hard. It's about giving a f*ck when it's easier not to.

In the realm of purposeful living, your pursuits should be fckworthy. Don't waste your emotional currency on endeavors that leave you empty. Choose the battles that ignite a fire within you, the causes that make your heart beat a little faster. That's the essence of giving a fck that matters.

Imagine purpose as your North Star, not a distant, unattainable light but a guiding force that helps you navigate the vast expanse of your existence. When you're lost in the fog of uncertainty, purpose shines brightly, reminding you of your unique journey.

Purposeful living is a symphony of passion, not a monotone humdrum of existence. Give a f*ck about the notes that compose your melody. Whether it's art, science, community service, or making the world's best pancake, let your passion play the lead.

You've got a limited budget of fcks, so allocate them wisely. Purposeful living is about directing your fcks toward the areas that align with your values. It's not about frivolous spending but about investing your emotional currency in the ventures that yield meaningful returns.

Purpose isn't a static concept; it's a verb, an action. Live your purpose every damn day. Let it be the force that propels you out of bed in the morning and the reason you smile before drifting off to sleep. Give a f*ck about the active pursuit of your purpose.

As you navigate the twists and turns of life, let your purpose evolve. It's not a rigid script but a dynamic narrative that unfolds with each chapter. Give a f*ck about adapting your purpose to the changing landscapes of your growth and experiences.

In a world that often values conformity, purposeful living is an act of rebellion. Rebel against the notion that your purpose should fit neatly into predefined boxes. Give a f*ck about carving your unique path, even if it means trampling on the well-manicured lawns of societal expectations.

Sometimes, purposeful living involves a purposeful disconnect. Give a f*ck about recognizing when certain paths no longer align with your true north. It's okay to sever ties with endeavors that no longer contribute to the symphony of your purposeful existence.

Your purpose isn't just a personal affair; it's a call to make a purposeful impact. Give a f*ck about how your existence ripples through the lives of others. It's the acknowledgment that your purpose, when lived authentically, becomes a beacon inspiring those around you.

Picture your purpose as a stone tossed into the pond of humanity, creating ripples that extend far beyond your immediate surroundings. Give a f*ck about the ripple effect, understanding that your purpose has the power to influence, inspire, and create meaningful change.

In purposeful living, alignment is the name of the game. Give a f*ck about aligning your actions, choices, and relationships with your purpose. It's the fine-tuning of your existence to resonate with the symphony you're composing.

Challenges are not adversaries sent to derail you but companions on the journey of purposeful living. Give a f*ck about embracing challenges as opportunities for growth. They're the resistance that strengthens the muscle of your purpose.

Craft a rebellion playlist for your purposeful journey. Let it be the soundtrack of your fck-giving escapades. Whether it's the anthem of resilience, the ballad of perseverance, or the punk rock of defying the odds, give a fck about curating a playlist that fuels your purposeful rebellion.

Your purpose isn't a solitary affair; it thrives in the soil of purposeful relationships. Give a f*ck about cultivating connections with those who align with your purpose, individuals who contribute verses to the symphony of your existence.

Set aside moments for purposeful reflection. Give a f*ck about reviewing your journey, celebrating the victories, and learning from the detours. It's in the reflective pauses that you recalibrate your purpose, ensuring it continues to be a driving force in your life.

Your purpose isn't confined to the duration of your existence; it extends into the legacy you leave behind. Give a f*ck about the imprint you're crafting on the pages of history. What narrative are you inscribing into the collective memory of humanity?

Gratitude is the silent partner of purposeful living. Give a f*ck about expressing gratitude for the opportunities, challenges, and relationships that shape your purpose. It's in acknowledging the richness of your journey that you deepen your connection to your purpose.

Remember, the tapestry of your existence is ever-unfolding. Give a fck about the masterpiece you're creating. It's a canvas painted with the strokes of passion, resilience, and purpose—a testament to a life lived authentically and unapologetically.

March Headlong into the Chaos

Strap on your metaphorical armor, grab the shield of adaptability, and march headlong into the chaos of existence. Life throws challenges like confetti at a parade, and it's time to learn the ancient art of triage — separating the paper cuts from the broken bones with finesse, and maybe a touch of irreverence.

Life is a grand theater of chaos, and you're the lead actor dodging metaphorical tomatoes and occasional curveballs. Adaptability is your backstage pass, allowing you to navigate the unexpected plot twists without losing your cool.

Think of life as a relentless emergency room, and you're the overworked doctor. Adaptability isn't just a skill; it's your trusty scalpel for expertly triaging the stream of challenges that rush through the ER doors. Some issues demand immediate attention, while others can wait in the queue.

Life serves up a buffet of challenges: a plate of relationship woes, a side of career conundrums, and the dessert of existential dilemmas. Adaptability is the culinary skill that lets you savor each challenge, knowing when to nibble and when to devour.

Every adaptable warrior needs a Triage Toolkit. It includes humor as a painkiller, resilience as a bandage, and a healthy dose of perspective as the ultimate cure-all. This toolkit isn't sold in stores; you assemble it through trial, error, and a pinch of audacity.

Ever had a day ruined by a broken shoelace? It's the perfect example of life's micro-challenges that, when mishandled, can spiral into major mood disasters. Adaptability is the art of whipping out the spare lace and carrying on with a swagger despite the absurdity.

Life throws a barrage of flaming chainsaws at your priorities. Adaptability is the circus act that lets you juggle with finesse, deciding which priorities are rubber balls (bouncing back) and which are delicate crystal (requiring utmost attention).

Picture a Zen master facing a typhoon with tranquility. That's the essence of the adaptability Zen. It's not about controlling the storm; it's about surfing its wild waves, occasionally doing a flip for style points.

Life's grand circus is led by the ringmaster, Uncertainty. Adaptability is your VIP ticket, letting you enjoy the acrobatics of the unknown without breaking into a cold sweat. After all, who wants to be caught without a safety net?

Balance is the tightrope walker of life. Adaptability whispers, "Spread your arms wide, embrace the wobble, and revel in the thrill of defying gravity." It's not about avoiding the tightrope; it's about dancing along its precarious length.

Think of adaptability as a dance — a wild, unchoreographed dance where you twirl with unpredictability and two-step with change. It's not about knowing every step but feeling the rhythm and adjusting your moves accordingly.

Chameleons change colors to adapt, and so should you. Life isn't black and white; it's a kaleidoscope of hues. Adaptability is your color palette, allowing you to blend into different environments while staying true to your vibrant core.

Life is Shakespearean in its comedy of errors. Adaptability is your script doctor, turning misadventures into plot twists, and tragicomedies into tales of resilience. It's not about avoiding errors but turning them into standing ovation-worthy performances.

Life is an improv show, and adaptability is your ability to roll with the punches and seamlessly weave unexpected plotlines. It's the audacity to say "yes, and" when faced with life's spontaneous prompts.

Change is the only constant, like an uninvited guest crashing on your couch. Adaptability is your survivalist's guide, teaching you to offer change a cup of tea, find common ground, and maybe even become friends.

In a world that craves order, adaptability is your silent rebellion. It's the audacious act of thriving in chaos, refusing to conform to the script, and writing your own narrative with a defiant grin.

Life's challenges are peaks on an unpredictable mountain range. Adaptability is your climbing gear, enabling you to scale the summits with grit and a fearless spirit. It's not about conquering the mountain but embracing the climb.

Adaptability involves the delicate art of surrender, not to defeat, but to the wisdom that some battles aren't worth fighting. It's the discernment to know when to stand your ground and when to let the river of life chart its course.

Life's challenges can be torrential downpours or gentle rains. Adaptability is your umbrella, letting you dance in the storm or stroll leisurely, depending on the intensity of the shower. It's about choosing your pace amidst life's weather patterns.

In the grand tapestry of life, adaptability is the vibrant thread that weaves through challenges, creating a mosaic of resilience and growth. It's the intricate pattern that transforms adversity into a masterpiece.

Let the anthem of the adaptable echo in your spirit. It's a melody of audacity, a rhythm of resilience, and a chorus of embracing life's beautiful chaos. Raise your shield of adaptability high, fearless reader, for the battlefield awaits, and you are the triumphant warrior of the ever-adapting tale of existence.

The Busyness Epidemic

Embrace the rhythm of your own journey. Tear down the walls of the busyness epidemic, and reveal the raw reality beneath the façade of perpetual motion. It's time to liberate ourselves from the chains of constant activity and redefine what it truly means to live.

Busyness has become a deity we unwittingly worship. F*ck the deity; unmask it. Living in a constant state of frenzy doesn't make you a high priest of productivity; it makes you a slave to chaos.

Wearing busyness as a badge of honor? F*ck the badge; rip it off. Exhaustion isn't a status symbol; it's a cry for respite. True rebels revel in balance, not in the burnt-out embers of relentless activity.

Competing in the Busyness Olympics leads to nowhere. F*ck the competition; opt out. Your value isn't measured by the number of tasks you juggle but by the authenticity you infuse into each moment.

Feeling guilty about downtime? F*ck the guilt; shed it. Downtime isn't laziness; it's the necessary pause between life's verses, the silent beats that compose the symphony of your existence.

A calendar bursting at the seams? F*ck the overbooking; edit it boldly. A rebel's calendar is a canvas, not a checklist. Paint your days with purpose, leaving ample white space for spontaneity.

Saying yes to everything is a fool's errand. F*ck the reluctance; master the art of saying no. Your time is a finite resource; spend it on pursuits that align with your rebel heart.

Frenzy leads to fatigue. F*ck the fatigue; embrace stillness. In the quiet moments, you'll discover reservoirs of strength, and it's from these reservoirs that rebels draw their power.

Urgency is often an illusion. F*ck the illusion; see through it. Rebels discern between what's truly urgent and what's fabricated urgency designed to hijack their attention.

Multitasking is a mirage, promising productivity but delivering chaos. F*ck the mirage; shatter it. Focus on one thing at a time, for true rebels master the art of undivided attention.

FOMO isn't just about social events; it's also about fearing missed productivity. F*ck the fear; embrace missing out. Sometimes, the most productive thing is to miss out on busyness and delve into meaningful idleness.

Burnout is the breakdown of rebels. F*ck the breakdown; prevent it. Pace yourself in the marathon of life; rebels know that the race isn't won by sprinting but by enduring.

More isn't always better. F*ck the quantity; choose quality. Rebels understand that a handful of meaningful experiences outweigh a multitude of superficial engagements.

Digital chaos ensnares. F*ck the overload; disconnect. Rebels recognize the value of unplugging, reconnecting with the analog world, and savoring the simplicity of a tech-free moment.

Busyness blinds us to the richness of life. F*ck the blindfold; remove it. Rebels open their eyes to the beauty in the ordinary, finding fulfillment in the spaces between the hectic intervals.

In the rush, pleasure often dissipates. F*ck the haste; savor slowness. Rebels take pleasure in the unhurried moments, allowing life's flavors to linger on the palate of experience.

Hyper-productivity is a myth. F*ck the myth; demolish it. Rebels understand that true productivity lies in the alignment of actions with purpose, not in the quantity of tasks.

Reflection is a rebel's sanctuary. F*ck the neglect; cultivate the ritual. Regular pauses for introspection allow rebels to navigate life's labyrinth with intention and grace.

Legacy isn't forged in busyness but in presence. F*ck the notion; build the legacy. Rebels know that their impact on the world is most profound when they're fully present in each moment.

Rest is an act of rebellion. F*ck the sleep deprivation; sleep like a rebel. In the embrace of rest, rebels rejuvenate, and in their rejuvenation, they find the strength to defy the gravitational pull of the busyness epidemic.

The busyness epidemic has entrenched itself in the very fabric of modern existence, heralding a false dawn of productivity that often leads to burnout rather than genuine achievement. In this relentless pursuit of doing more, we've unwittingly surrendered the reins of our lives to a ceaseless cycle of tasks, meetings, and notifications, each clamoring for our dwindling attention. This epidemic, however, is not an invincible foe; it's a construct of our collective making, and just as we have built it, so too can we dismantle it. The journey towards reclaiming our time and essence begins with a conscious decision to prioritize depth over breadth, meaning over mere activity.

1. **Prioritize Depth Over Breadth** Embrace the art of doing less but better. This means making the tough choices about what truly deserves your time and energy. It's about digging deeper into fewer pursuits that resonate with your core values rather than skimming the surface of many.
2. **Cultivate Mindfulness and Presence** In a world that glorifies busyness, the act of being fully present becomes a radical form of resistance. Mindfulness practices not only counteract the scatterbrain syndrome induced by chronic busyness but also enhance our capacity to engage deeply with the task or moment at hand.

3. **Establish Boundaries** The busyness epidemic thrives in the absence of clear boundaries. By setting firm limits on work hours, technology use, and even the types of engagements we commit to, we can create a sanctuary for focus, creativity, and rest.
4. **Embrace the Art of Slow Living** Slow living is not about doing everything at a snail's pace; it's about doing things at the right pace. This means allowing ourselves the time to immerse fully in activities, to savor experiences, and to perform tasks with care and attention.
5. **Redefine Productivity** Productivity should not be measured by the quantity of tasks completed but by the significance of our contributions. This shift in perspective encourages us to focus on impact rather than activity, on creating lasting value rather than ticking off to-do lists.

Action Plan for Tackling the Busyness Epidemic:

- **Daily Mindfulness Practice** Dedicate at least 10 minutes each day to mindfulness or meditation to cultivate presence.
- **Weekly Priority Review** At the start of each week, identify your top three priorities that align with your values and goals. Focus your energy on these areas.
- **Technology Time-Outs:** Implement regular technology breaks throughout your day. Consider "tech-free" evenings or weekends to disconnect and recharge.
- **Slow Living Rituals** Incorporate rituals into your routine that encourage slow living—this could be a leisurely walk, cooking a meal from scratch, or practicing a craft.
- **Reflection and Journaling** End your day with a reflection session. Use journaling to contemplate the day's activities, what you learned, and how you felt. This practice fosters mindfulness and helps you stay aligned with your core values.

By adopting these strategies and embracing the principles laid out, you can begin to carve out a life marked not by busyness but by meaningful engagement and purposeful living. Challenge the prevailing winds of the busyness epidemic and chart a course towards a more intentional, fulfilled existence.

In the rebellion against busyness, you'll discover the profound art of living authentically, unburdened by the chains of perpetual motion. The rebel's path is one of intentional action, not mindless reaction. It's time to reclaim your time, your sanity, and your essence. Turn the page; the rebellion begins now.

The Theatre of Judgement

In the theater of judgment, the critics in your life have secured the best seats in the house. As we raise the curtain on this cosmic performance, remember, this isn't a tragedy; it's a dark comedy. So, grab your popcorn, and let's explore the grand spectacle of judgment.

The critics sit in the front row, armed with opinions sharper than daggers. They're ready to dissect your every move, like theater aficionados analyzing a Shakespearean play. But remember, their reviews don't define your script.

In the theater of judgment, master the dramatic pause. Let the critics hang on the edge of their seats, waiting for your next scene, while you revel in the power of keeping them in suspense.

Your authenticity takes center stage. In a world craving originality, don't let judgment censor your true character. Let your authenticity be the standing ovation your critics never saw coming.

Critics love a good monologue. They'll dissect your choices, narrate your flaws, and deliver a soliloquy about what you should have done. Let their monologue play out, and then steal the scene with your unwavering self-belief.

In the theater of judgment, choose bold performances over stage fright. Don't let the fear of critique keep you backstage. Strut onto the stage of life with the confidence of a seasoned actor.

Critics thrive on the illusion of perfection. Rebel against their expectations. Embrace your imperfections; they are the brushstrokes that paint the masterpiece of your uniqueness.

Tear up the script that seeks approval. The theater of judgment is no place for conformity. Let your performance be an unrehearsed rebellion, breaking free from the chains of societal expectations.

The whispers of the stagehands are the rumors critics thrive on. Ignore the gossip. Let them speculate while you steal the show with your enigmatic performance, leaving them to unravel the mystery.

When the critics unleash their harshest reviews, let resilience be your standing ovation. Your ability to weather the storm is the epic finale, leaving the critics in awe of your unwavering spirit.

Life's script is full of unexpected plot twists. In the theater of judgment, embrace improv. When the plot takes an unexpected turn, let your spontaneous brilliance shine, leaving the critics bewildered.

Cheers and jeers echo in the theater of judgment. Let neither inflate your ego nor shatter your confidence. Walk the middle path, where your self-worth isn't determined by the applause or the criticism.

Backstage is where revelations unfold. In the quiet moments away from the spotlight, reflect on your performance, adjust your costume, and emerge stronger for the next act.

Behind the critic's mask is often insecurity. They project their fears onto your stage. Don't let their masks fool you. Beneath the veneer of judgment lies a vulnerability they'd rather keep hidden.

Critics have biases; it's part of the theater's charm. Rebel against their biases. Let your performance challenge their preconceptions, forcing them to confront the limitations of their own narratives.

Encores are earned, not given. In the theater of judgment, let your exit be a masterpiece. Leave them yearning for more, with the echoes of your applause lingering in their minds.

Craft the dramaturgy of self-love. In a world where judgment seeks a spotlight, make self-love the leading character. Let it overshadow the critics, leaving them in the wings of irrelevance.

Critics love to compare, creating a labyrinth of expectations. Rebel against comparisons. Your journey is unique; let the spotlight be on your narrative, not the shadows of others.

The stage manager commands the chaos backstage. Be your own stage manager. Take charge of your narrative, cue the moments that matter, and let the theater of judgment bow to your directorial prowess.

In the final act, seek catharsis. Let the theater of judgment be a cathartic release, where you shed the weight of external opinions and emerge, reborn, as the architect of your destiny.

The curtains close on the theater of judgment; the critics fade into the background. What remains is your performance—a bold, unapologetic masterpiece that transcends the fleeting opinions of the audience. So, dear protagonist of the theater of judgment, take a bow. Your performance is a revelation—a testament to the art of giving a f*ck where it truly matters, and to the unwavering strength found in the spotlight of your authenticity. The theater may be judgmental, but you, my friend, are a virtuoso.

The Photoshop Rebellion

Grab your sledgehammers, because we're about to shatter the facades of superficiality. This isn't a beauty pageant; it's a rebellion against the shallows, a call to arms for authenticity in a world drowning in the glossy veneer of the superficial.

Picture the world as a grand masquerade ball, where everyone wears masks of perfection. Superficiality is the charade, the illusion that these masks define us. But we're not here to waltz behind the facade's charade; we're here to tear those masks off and dance to the rhythm of authenticity.

Superficiality is the Photoshop rebellion, where imperfections are airbrushed away, leaving behind a sanitized version of reality. But life isn't a filtered photo; it's a messy, beautiful collage of experiences. We're not here to smooth out the rough edges; we're here to embrace the authenticity that arises from life's unfiltered chaos.

Imagine a world where everyone is a mannequin, striking poses dictated by societal norms. Superficiality is the mannequin's protest, the rigid adherence to postures that lack depth. We're not here to be lifeless replicas; we're here to break free from the mannequin's pose and dance to our authentic rhythm.

Superficiality is the illusionist's deception, where smoke and mirrors create a false sense of reality. But we're not sitting in the audience, applauding the illusion; we're stepping onto the stage to reveal the raw, unfiltered truth. Authenticity is our spotlight, exposing the genuine magic of imperfection.

In a world obsessed with the beauty myth, superficiality dictates standards that are as elusive as a mirage. We're not chasing after the unattainable; we're flipping the script, rewriting the beauty narrative with authenticity as our guiding principle. Because real beauty lies in the quirks, scars, and idiosyncrasies that make us unique.

Superficiality is the high-definition rebellion, where the quest for clarity blurs the line between reality and fantasy. We're not turning up the resolution on life; we're embracing the beautiful blur, where authenticity thrives in the fuzzy, unscripted moments that define our existence.

In the realm of social media, superficiality is the mirage that distorts reality into carefully curated feeds. But we're not here to curate a fictional story; we're here to disrupt the narrative, sharing the messy, unfiltered chapters that showcase the authenticity of our lives.

Superficiality is the plastic fantastic fallacy, the notion that a surgically altered appearance equates to happiness. We're not going under the knife of conformity; we're celebrating the beauty of authenticity, where genuine smiles, laughter lines, and scars tell stories that no cosmetic procedure can replicate.

Picture a world enamored with the glossy pages of Vanity Fair, where superficiality reigns supreme. We're not posing for the cover shoot; we're staging a revolt against the superficial narrative, embracing the gritty, unfiltered stories that deserve the spotlight.

Superficiality is the emoji rebellion, reducing complex emotions to cartoonish symbols. But we're not communicating in hieroglyphics; we're using the rich language of authenticity, expressing the depth and nuance of our feelings without the need for superficial shortcuts.

Imagine life as a perpetual runway, where everyone struts in conformity to superficial trends. Superficiality is the fashion police dictating the rules. We're not here to conform; we're walking our own runway of authenticity, wearing the garments of genuine self-expression, regardless of societal fashion norms.

Superficiality is the masquerade of filters, where reality is obscured behind a digitally altered veil. But we're not hiding behind layers of illusion; we're peeling back the filters to reveal the authenticity beneath—the unfiltered, unapologetic version of ourselves.

In a world burdened by unrealistic standards, superficiality dictates a measure of worth that's as substantial as a soap bubble. We're not inflating ourselves to fit these ephemeral standards; we're shedding the weight of superficial expectations, embracing the authenticity that comes from accepting ourselves as we are.

Superficiality is the obsession with magazine covers, where airbrushed perfection becomes the benchmark. We're not striving for cover model status; we're tearing down the glossy pages and replacing them with a rebellion of authenticity, where real stories and unfiltered faces take center stage.

In a world where superficiality writes the glossy pages of self-doubt, we're not reading that narrative. We're penning our own story, embracing authenticity as the protagonist. Because real self-worth isn't found in conformity; it's discovered in the courage to be authentically, unapologetically ourselves.

Superficiality is the runway where flaws are airbrushed away, creating a sterile beauty devoid of character. We're not walking the runway of flawlessness; we're celebrating the flawsome—the beauty that arises from embracing our imperfections, quirks, and idiosyncrasies.

In a world saturated with superficial selfies, we're not capturing moments that conform to societal expectations. We're clicking the selfie of authenticity, capturing the unfiltered, unposed versions of ourselves, each photo telling a story that goes beyond the surface.

Superficiality is the masquerade ball where masks hide authentic expressions. We're not here to wear masks; we're engaging in the art of unmasking, allowing our true selves to step into the spotlight. Because authenticity is the real masterpiece, and we're the artists who paint with the colors of vulnerability.

Picture a world trapped in the superficial echo chamber, where the same glossy narratives reverberate endlessly. We're not amplifying those echoes; we're disrupting the superficial symphony, introducing new, authentic notes that create a melody of diversity, depth, and genuine human experience.

We raise our banner against superficiality; we let the rebellion's battle cry echo: "Authenticity, not perfection! Real, not retouched! Flawsome, not flawless!" It's time to break free from the shackles of superficiality, forging a path where authenticity reigns supreme. In the rebellion against the superficial, we emerge as the champions of realness, celebrating the beauty that arises from the unfiltered, unapologetic truth of our existence.

The Validation Revelation

F*ck the permission slips, the rebellion against self-limitations begins. Buckle up; this is not a gentle stroll through the park of self-approval—it's a roaring rollercoaster breaking through the barriers of your own limitations and an invitation to the wildest carnival where you grant yourself the ultimate permission to be unapologetically you.

The permission slips we seek are often disguised as external validation. But let's unravel this illusion—it's time to become the arbiter of your worth, tearing up the notion that someone else's stamp of approval determines your value. We conjure up imaginary gatekeepers who hold the keys to our desires. Spoiler alert: those gatekeepers don't exist. It's time to be your own gatekeeper, unlocking the doors to your dreams without waiting for permission from the nonexistent authorities.

Seeking permission is a comfortable trap, a cozy blanket of safety that cocoons you from the risks of the unknown. But life is not lived in the safety net of permissions; it's a high-wire act without a safety harness. It's time to step onto the wire and dance without seeking approval.

Permission slips are the invisible handcuffs of conformity. They bind you to the mundane, forcing you into the neatly drawn lines of societal expectations. It's time to break free, snapping those cuffs and painting outside the lines of your unique canvas.

Creativity thrives in the wilderness of unrestricted thought. Tear up the permission slips that confine your imagination. Be the renegade artist of your life, creating masterpieces that defy the norms without waiting for a nod from the critics.

Paradoxically, seeking permission becomes a limitation. It's like trying to fly with clipped wings. So, let's rip up the imaginary flight restriction notices, spread your wings, and soar to heights unknown. Granting yourself permission is an act of self-love. It's a declaration that your desires, dreams, and quirks are not only valid but deserving of pursuit. Give yourself the love you've been seeking from external sources by handing out permission slips like confetti.

Waiting for the perfect moment is a mirage. The right time is a fiction we use to delay our dreams. Tear up the permission slip that says you must wait for the stars to align. Create your own cosmic spectacle.

Fear of rejection often lurks behind the quest for permission. But here's a revelation: rejection is a phantom, a ghost without substance. Tear up the permission slip that binds you to the fear of this spectral illusion. In a world that thrives on conformity, granting yourself permission is a revolutionary act. It's a declaration that you refuse to be a cog in the machine, opting instead to be the mad scientist creating your own unconventional experiments.

Permission-less living is liberation in its purest form. It's a dance in the rain without checking the weather forecast. It's the exhilarating freedom of being unapologetically yourself. Tear up the permission slips and join the rebellion.

The irony is that permission, while seemingly empowering, is a double-edged sword. It's time to wield that sword, cutting through the illusions and restrictions that it imposes. Be the warrior who battles for the right to live authentically.

The permission slip paradox is that the more you seek external validation, the less you grant it to yourself. Break free from this paradox by tearing up the slips and giving yourself the green light, not just at intersections but at every twist and turn of your journey.

The facade of permission is fragile, built on the shaky grounds of societal norms. It's time to be the wrecking ball that brings down this facade, revealing the raw, unfiltered authenticity beneath.

Expectations come with permission slips—permission to conform, to meet predetermined standards. Tear them up. Your life is not a standardized test. It's a choose-your-own-adventure novel with endless plot twists.

Life is an ongoing reinvention, not a static sculpture. Grant yourself permission to evolve, transform, and embrace the ever-changing masterpiece that is you. Tear up the permission slip that says you must remain stagnant. Unbeknownst to many, permission can be a silent saboteur, whispering doubts and planting seeds of hesitation. It's time to expose this saboteur, tear up its scripts, and pen your own narrative.

Waiting for permission is like holding a blank check to happiness hostage. It's time to cash in on joy by tearing up the notion that someone else must endorse your happiness. Be your own happiness advocate. Life is a perpetual work in progress, an unfinished masterpiece. Grant yourself permission to be incomplete, imperfect, and beautifully unresolved. Tear up the perfectionist permission slips, allowing the messy authenticity of your existence to shine.

The rebellion against self-limitations starts with a torn permission slip. Embrace the chaos, uncertainty, and the raw beauty of a life unscripted. Be the author, the director, and the lead actor of your narrative. Toss away the permission slips, for your existence needs no validation. So, in the grand carnival of life, let your banner proudly declare, "F*ck the Permission Slips!" The show is yours; go steal the spotlight.

The Eternal Now

In the rebellion against the ticking hands of the clock, the concept of time transforms from a relentless taskmaster into a playful companion in the eternal dance of now. Thus, we embark on a journey to dismantle the chains of deadlines and liberate the spirit from the oppression of schedules.

F*ck the illusion that time is a linear progression. The eternal now is the only reality, where past and future converge into this exquisite moment. Embrace it like a lover you thought you'd lost. Clocks are tyrants that dictate our routines, reducing life to a series of obligations. F*ck the clock; reclaim your sovereignty over time. Life isn't a scheduled sentence; it's an unscripted masterpiece.

Imagine the eternal now as a blank canvas, inviting you to paint your experiences without the constraints of past regrets or future anxieties. F*ck the clock's insistence on predefined strokes; let spontaneity be your brush. The "not enough time" myth is a sneaky saboteur, convincing us that we're perpetually racing against an invisible adversary. F*ck that. In the eternal now, time expands to accommodate the richness of experience.

Picture a wonderland where clocks are obsolete relics, and every moment is an eternity. F*ck the pressure to fit your joy into designated slots; let the wonderland of now be your boundless playground. The eternal now is the rebel's sanctuary, a place where deadlines and expectations dissolve. F*ck the demands of yesterday and tomorrow; bask in the present rebellion against the tyranny of time.

Rushing through life is a disservice to the soul. F*ck the pressure to hurry; savor the pace of the eternal now. Each moment is a delicacy; let it linger on your palate. Creativity flourishes in the fertile ground of the eternal now. F*ck the notion that inspiration can be scheduled; let the spontaneous bursts of now be the seeds of your most profound creations.

Passion defies the tick-tock of clocks. F*ck the idea that your zeal should be confined to predefined hours; let passion be your guiding compass in the boundless terrain of the eternal now. The fear of running out of time is a shadow that eclipses the brilliance of the now. F*ck that fear. In the eternal now, time is an infinite resource, and every heartbeat is a treasure trove.

Relationships blossom in the playground of the eternal now. F*ck the scheduled togetherness; let connections unfold organically, like the petals of a flower responding to the sun. Freedom isn't found in the regimented beat of the clock; it resides in the eternal now. F*ck the illusion that time binds you; spread your wings in the limitless sky of this moment.

Calendars wield a dictatorship over our plans and dreams. F*ck the pressure to conform to the calendar's expectations; let your journey unfold naturally, guided by the rhythm of the eternal now. The eternal now is the fountain of youth, where age is just a number, and enthusiasm knows no bounds. F*ck the countdown to aging; let the now rejuvenate your spirit endlessly.

The "too late" syndrome is a myth concocted by the clock-worshippers. F*ck the notion that opportunities have an expiration date; the eternal now is the perpetual opening for new beginnings. Mindfulness paints its masterpiece on the canvas of the eternal now. F*ck the distractions that pull you away; immerse yourself in the brushstrokes of this present masterpiece.

Fantasies of time travel distract us from the beauty of now. F*ck the desire to escape to a different era; the eternal now is the most captivating destination, where past, present, and future coalesce. Picture the clock as a comedic prop in the grand theater of life. F*ck the seriousness of its ticking; let it be the amusing sidekick in your personal comedy.

Growth thrives in the gymnasium of the eternal now. F*ck the rush to achieve milestones; every now is a weight to lift, a challenge to overcome, and a victory to savor. F*ck the obsession with a future that's yet to unfold. Embrace the now as the destination and the journey—a timeless adventure where the clock's hands are powerless against the infinite canvas of your existence. The rebellion against time is your eternal anthem; sing it loud.

Embracing the eternal now is akin to stepping into a river where time flows, not linearly, but in a mesmerizing dance around you. Here, in the heart of the present, we uncover the profound truth that life's essence is not measured by the ticking of a clock but by the depth of the moments we inhabit fully. This realization is not just a philosophical musing; it's a call to action, a directive to immerse ourselves completely in the fabric of now.

- **The Illusion of Time** Recognize that the conventional perception of time as a linear progression from past to future is a mental construct. Instead, see time as a series of present moments, each fully capable of holding the vastness of life's experiences.
- **Mindful Presence** Cultivate a practice of mindfulness, where each task, conversation, and thought is approached with full attention. By being fully present, you transform mundane activities into profound experiences, enriching your life with depth and meaning.
- **Joy in Spontaneity** Break free from the rigidity of schedules and embrace spontaneity. Let the joy of unplanned moments guide your day. It's in these spaces of freedom that creativity and happiness often flourish, revealing the beauty of living unbounded by the clock.
- **Savoring Moments** Slow down and savor each experience, whether it's a simple meal, a walk in the park, or a conversation with a loved one. By fully engaging with the present, you deepen your connection to life, finding richness in simplicity.
- **Letting Go of Fear** Release the fear of not having enough time. In the eternal now, every moment is an opportunity, a space for action, reflection, and growth. Understand that time is not running out; it's unfolding in an endless series of nows.

- **Nurturing Relationships**   Invest in relationships with the understanding that the most precious gift you can offer is your presence. Quality time spent in the company of loved ones is infinitely more valuable than any measure of time spent distracted or disengaged.
- **Freedom from Calendars**   Challenge the tyranny of calendars and to-do lists by prioritizing activities that bring you joy and fulfillment. While planning is necessary, ensure it serves your wellbeing, not the other way around.
- **Embracing Agelessness**   View life through the lens of the eternal now, where age is irrelevant to your capacity for wonder, learning, and joy. Let your spirit be guided by curiosity and resilience, defying the societal constraints on age and time.
- **Seizing Opportunities**   Understand that it's never too late to pursue dreams, change paths, or start anew. The eternal now is a field ripe with potential, where every moment is a fresh start, a new opportunity to craft the life you desire.
- **Living Mindfully**   Make each decision, each action, and each thought a testament to your commitment to the now. This doesn't mean forsaking the future but recognizing that the foundation for tomorrow is laid in the mindfulness of today.

Action Plan and Activities

- **Daily Mindfulness Meditation**   Dedicate time each morning or evening to meditate, focusing solely on your breath and the sensations of the present moment. This practice grounds you in the now, enhancing your awareness throughout the day.
- **Gratitude Journaling**   At the end of each day, write down three things you were grateful for. This encourages a focus on the positive moments of the day, anchoring you in the present.
- **The "One Task" Experiment**   For one week, commit to doing one task at a time, giving it your full attention. Notice the difference in the quality of your work and your mental state.
- **Technology Sabbatical**   Allocate one day a week as a technology-free day, or set specific hours each day without

digital devices. Observe how this affects your engagement with the present moment.
- **Nature Walks** Regularly spend time in nature, observing the details of the environment around you. Use all your senses to fully experience the moment, fostering a deep connection with the now.

In the eternal now, every breath, every heartbeat, is a symphony of existence played in real-time. The art of living becomes a masterful dance where we are fully awake, alive, and attuned to the richness of each moment. Let us embrace this rebellion against the tyranny of time, discovering in the process that the true essence of life is not in how many moments we capture but in how deeply we are captivated by each moment.

4-Week Action Plan for Harmony in the Chaos: Cultivating Depth, Balance, and Resonance in Life's Symphony

Congratulations on completing "Harmony in the Chaos," the second part of "Embrace Chaos, Find Purpose." This journey has taken you through the complexities and nuances of balancing the multifaceted aspects of your life while cultivating depth and resonance within your personal and professional spheres. You've explored how to weave the intricate tapestry of relationships, navigate the ever-changing landscape of life's challenges, and march confidently into the chaos with purpose and integrity.

As you move forward, remember that each chapter you've encountered serves as a guidepost, offering strategies, reflections, and insights to help you achieve a more harmonious existence. The path to balance and depth is ongoing, a dynamic dance that evolves with every step you take. To ensure these insights become integrated parts of your journey, we invite you to revisit the chapters for further exploration and to deepen your engagement with the concepts presented.

To bridge the gap between understanding and application, we've crafted a four-week action plan. This plan is your roadmap to applying the lessons learned, designed to foster growth, encourage self-reflection, and empower you to create a life that resonates with your deepest values and aspirations. It's your guide to transforming the chaos into a symphony of purposeful action.

Week 1 Action Plan: Laying Foundations for Harmony

As you embark on the journey to cultivate depth, balance, and resonance in your life's symphony, the first week is about setting the stage for transformative growth. Let's dive into actionable steps and reflections drawn from the initial chapters of "Book 2, Harmony in the Chaos."

Day 1: The Garden of Priorities
- **Activity:** Create your Garden of Priorities. List your current top five priorities on paper, then assess if they genuinely reflect your values and the life you wish to lead.
- **Reflection:** Consider the soil of your garden—is it nourishing your priorities, or is it time to re-till and plant anew?

Day 2: The Tapestry of Relationships
- **Activity:** Identify the key threads in your Tapestry of Relationships. Reach out to at least one person who strengthens your tapestry with joy, support, or wisdom.
- **Reflection:** Reflect on the diversity of threads in your tapestry—are there colors missing, or threads that no longer serve you?

Day 3: The Catalyst for Change
- **Activity:** Embrace one small change today that can act as a catalyst for larger transformation. This could be a new habit,

breaking an old pattern, or making a decision you've been postponing.
- **Reflection:** How did initiating this change make you feel? Empowered, anxious, excited?

Day 4: Beyond the Shallows
- **Activity:** Dedicate at least 30 minutes to an activity that deepens your understanding or skills in a particular area of interest. This could be reading, a creative endeavor, or learning a new skill.
- **Reflection:** Explore how diving deeper into this area can add richness and depth to your life's symphony.

Day 5: The Map of Purpose
- **Activity:** Draft a basic map of your life's current path. Include your passions, dreams, and goals. Highlight areas where you feel off-course.
- **Reflection:** Contemplate the roads taken and not taken. How does this map guide you towards your true purpose?

Day 6: Calibrating Your Moral Compass
- **Activity:** Reflect on a recent decision. Was it aligned with your moral compass? Write down thoughts or feelings that influenced your decision-making process.
- **Reflection:** Consider the alignment of your moral compass. Does it need recalibration to better reflect your authentic self?

Day 7: Avoiding the Temptation of Drift
- **Activity:** Identify areas of your life where you're merely drifting. Set one actionable goal to regain direction and momentum.
- **Reflection:** Reflect on the forces that cause you to drift. How can you better anchor yourself in purposeful action?

Week 1 Closing Reflection:

At the end of this week, take a moment to reflect on the foundational work you've begun. Harmony in life's chaos doesn't arrive overnight, but each step you've taken this week is a note in the right direction. How do you feel about the path unfolding before you? What insights have emerged from this week's activities and reflections?

Remember, the journey to harmony is uniquely yours. Embrace the chaos, dance with complexity, and cultivate a life symphony that resonates with depth, balance, and authenticity. Continue to build on these foundations as you progress through the next weeks of transformative action.

Week 2 Action Plan: Deepening Connections and Embracing Change

As we move into the second week of "Harmony in the Chaos," our focus shifts towards deepening our connections and embracing the inevitable changes life presents. This week's activities and reflections are designed to strengthen your tapestry of relationships and navigate through life's transformations with grace.

Day 8: Storms of Distractions

- **Activity:** Identify your main sources of distraction and commit to a two-hour block where you consciously avoid them. Use this time to engage in a focused activity that contributes to your goals.
- **Reflection:** How did the absence of these distractions affect your focus and productivity? What did you learn about your distraction triggers?

Day 9: Rogue Waves

- **Activity:** Reflect on a recent "rogue wave" event in your life—an unexpected challenge that caught you off guard. Write down how you responded and what you might do differently next time.

- **Reflection:** How can preparing for life's rogue waves make you more resilient and adaptable?

Day 10: Beyond the Known
- **Activity:** Step out of your comfort zone today. Try something new that challenges you, whether it's a new skill, a conversation with a stranger, or a different route to work.
- **Reflection:** Explore the feelings and outcomes from stepping beyond the known. Did this experience reveal anything new about yourself?

Day 11: The Art of Reflection
- **Activity:** Dedicate 30 minutes to silent reflection. Contemplate where you are in life, where you want to go, and what might be holding you back.
- **Reflection:** What insights emerged from this quiet reflection? How can these insights guide your steps moving forward?

Day 12: Tools of Wisdom
- **Activity:** Seek out a new tool of wisdom—a book, podcast, or seminar that aligns with your goals for growth and learning. Spend at least an hour engaging with this new resource.
- **Reflection:** What wisdom did you uncover, and how can it be applied to your journey towards harmony and balance?

Day 13: Where Mavericks Reign
- **Activity:** Embrace your inner maverick. Do one thing today that breaks from convention but feels authentic to you.
- **Reflection:** How did it feel to act on your maverick instincts? What does this tell you about the balance between conformity and authenticity in your life?

Day 14: Weathering Emotional Storms
- **Activity:** Think of an emotional storm you're currently navigating. Write down strategies you're using or could use to weather it with resilience.
- **Reflection:** Reflect on the strength and wisdom gained from weathering past emotional storms. How do these experiences fortify you for current and future challenges?

Week 2 Closing Reflection:

Reflect on the progress you've made in deepening your connections and embracing change. This week was about pushing boundaries, seeking wisdom, and learning to navigate through life's unpredictable waves with a maverick spirit. Consider how these experiences are weaving new patterns into your tapestry of relationships and shaping your journey through the chaos.

What lessons stood out most vividly? How have these activities and reflections helped you move closer to achieving harmony in the chaos? Carry these insights forward as you continue to cultivate depth, balance, and resonance in your life's symphony.

Week 3 Action Plan: Embracing Integrity and Liberating Choices

In the third week of "Harmony in the Chaos," we'll focus on embracing our inner integrity and liberating our choices. This journey involves recognizing our core values, challenging our comfort zones, and embracing your inner rebel. Here's your guide to unlocking the next level of depth, balance, and resonance in your life's symphony.

Day 15: Your Inner Scholar
- **Activity:** Dedicate an hour to learning something new that aligns with your interests or goals. This could be through a book, online course, or documentary.
- **Reflection:** How does continuous learning enrich your life and support your journey toward authenticity and resilience?

Day 16: Embrace Your Inner Rebel
- **Activity:** Identify one societal expectation that doesn't align with your true self. Today, consciously choose to rebel against this norm in a small, personal way.
- **Reflection:** Reflect on the liberation that comes from not conforming. How can embracing your inner rebel lead to a more authentic life?

Day 17: Liberate Your Choices

- **Activity:** Think of a decision you've been postponing because you're worried about others' opinions. Make that choice today, based solely on what's best for you.
- **Reflection:** How does it feel to make decisions based on your own needs and desires rather than external expectations?

Day 18: The Dance of Integrity

- **Activity:** Write down three core values that are most important to you. For each, list a way you can more fully integrate these values into your daily life.
- **Reflection:** How does living in alignment with your core values impact your sense of self and your interactions with others?

Day 19: The F*ck Jar

- **Activity:** Create a physical or digital "F*ck Jar." Whenever you find yourself stressing over something insignificant, write it down and "put" it in the jar as a way to let it go.
- **Reflection:** At the end of the day, review the contents of your F*ck Jar. How many of your worries were truly worth the energy you gave them?

Day 20: Your Most Potent Sorcery

- **Activity:** Identify a talent or skill that you often take for granted. Find a way to share or celebrate this "sorcery" with others today.
- **Reflection:** How does acknowledging and sharing your unique talents contribute to your sense of authenticity and purpose?

Day 21: The Comfort Zone

- **Activity:** Step outside your comfort zone in a significant way. This could be initiating a difficult conversation, trying a new activity, or exploring a place you've never been.

- **Reflection:** What did you learn about yourself by stepping outside your comfort zone? How can pushing these boundaries fuel your growth?

Week 3 Closing Reflection:

This week was about tapping into our inner scholar, embracing the rebel within, and making choices that reflect our true selves. Each day's activity and reflection were steps toward a more integrated, authentic existence, challenging us to live in alignment with our deepest values and to explore the edges of our comfort zones.

Reflect on the shifts in your perspective and behavior over the past week. How have these actions and reflections helped you to see yourself and your place in the world differently? What insights will you carry forward as you continue to cultivate a harmonious symphony of depth, balance, and resonance in your life?

Embrace these lessons as you prepare for the final week of our journey through "Harmony in the Chaos," where we'll confront procrastination, address the busyness epidemic, and explore the eternal now.

Week 4 Action Plan: Conquering Procrastination and Embracing the Moment

In our final week of "Harmony in the Chaos," we delve into the art of conquering procrastination, challenging the busyness epidemic, and embracing the eternal now. This phase is dedicated to actionable strategies that encourage us to live more fully in each moment, prioritize what truly matters, and cultivate a life of purpose and depth.

Day 22: The Procrastination Dragon
- **Activity:** Identify one task you've been procrastinating on. Break it down into smaller, manageable steps. Tackle the first step today using the Triple Sprint Method (20-minute sprints, followed by a 15-minute rejuvenating break).
- **Reflection:** Reflect on the barriers that have been holding you back from completing this task. How does addressing procrastination directly change your approach to challenges?

Day 23: Purpose is not a Unicorn
- **Activity:** Spend time today defining or refining your purpose. Write a mission statement for your life that includes your passions, values, and the impact you wish to have.

- **Reflection:** How does having a clear sense of purpose guide your decisions and actions? In what ways does it serve as a compass during times of uncertainty?

Day 24: March Headlong into the Chaos
- **Activity:** Choose an area of your life currently in chaos. Instead of avoiding it, confront it head-on with a plan to bring order or understanding to the situation.
- **Reflection:** How does facing chaos directly, rather than avoiding it, provide you with a sense of empowerment and resilience?

Day 25: The Busyness Epidemic
- **Activity:** Conduct a time audit of your day to identify periods spent on unproductive busyness. Choose one activity to eliminate or reduce, reallocating that time to something more meaningful.
- **Reflection:** How does reducing busyness affect your stress levels and overall satisfaction? What benefits do you notice from reallocating time to activities that align with your purpose?

Day 26: The Theatre of Judgement
- **Activity:** Reflect on a recent situation where you felt judged by others. Write a letter to yourself from the perspective of a compassionate observer, offering support and understanding.
- **Reflection:** How does changing your perspective on judgment help you to cultivate a stronger sense of self-compassion and resilience?

Day 27: The Photoshop Rebellion
- **Activity:** Identify an aspect of your life or self-image you've been "photoshopping" for the sake of others. Commit to one action that celebrates this aspect authentically, without alteration or apology.

- **Reflection:** What does rebelling against the pressure to present a "photoshopped" version of yourself reveal about your values and the importance of authenticity?

Day 28: The Eternal Now
- **Activity:** Practice mindfulness or meditation for 15 minutes, focusing solely on the present moment. Alternatively, engage in an activity that fully absorbs your attention, bringing you into the "now."
- **Reflection:** How does embracing the eternal now impact your ability to appreciate life's moments? What shifts do you notice in your stress levels, attention, and overall wellbeing?

Week 4 Closing Reflection:

This week was a journey through confronting procrastination, challenging societal pressures, and embracing the beauty of each moment. As you reflect on the past seven days, consider the shifts in your perception and actions. How have these exercises helped you to engage more deeply with your life, prioritize effectively, and live in alignment with your authentic self?

Reflect on the entire four-week journey through "Harmony in the Chaos." What lessons have resonated most deeply with you? How will you integrate these insights into your daily life to continue cultivating depth, balance, and resonance?

As we close this chapter, remember that the quest for harmony in life's chaos is ongoing. Each day presents new opportunities to weave the threads of your existence into a tapestry of meaning and beauty. Carry forward the lessons learned, the practices adopted, and the insights gained, and let them guide you in orchestrating a life of purpose, balance, and profound impact.

Book 3, Orchestrating Impact: Conducting Life's Symphony with Purpose and Resilience

6-Week Action Plan for Orchestrating Impact: Conducting Life's Symphony with Purpose and Resilience

Congratulations on reaching the crescendo of "Orchestrating Impact," the concluding volume of "Embrace Chaos, Find Purpose." This journey is an exploration into how you can lead with purpose, build resilience against life's adversities, and create a lasting impact in your world. The chapters serve as individual notes in the grand symphony of your life, teaching you to embrace leadership, impact, resilience, and the relentless pursuit of purpose.

As you stand on the threshold of this journey's end, it's time to translate the symphony of insights into a concerto of action. Each chapter is crafted for quick engagement, but hold back from consuming the entire book in one session or even within a brief week. Dedicate a whole day to delve into each chapter, deeply connecting with the insights and reflections it provides. Embrace the content thoroughly, become intimately familiar with its messages, and let the seeds of transformation take root and grow within you. This journey is more than just reading; it's an invitation to sync with your inner rebel, offering a detailed path to unleash the full orchestra of your capabilities, especially as you navigate life's balancing act.

Revisiting the chapters will allow you to deepen your connection with each theme, uncovering new nuances and empowering you to fine-tune your approach to life's complex score. To bridge the gap between reflection and action, we've interwoven a six-week action plan throughout the text. This integrated approach, distinct from the standalone action plans in the earlier books, is designed to facilitate a smoother assimilation of strategies, practices, and insights, ensuring the harmony of your actions aligns with the melody of your aspirations. Consider this plan as your conductor's baton, guiding you towards a life marked by meaningful impact and resonant fulfillment.

The Symphony Within

It's time to dive into the soul-stirring symphony that is your inner strength. In a world drowning in cacophony, this is your chance to conduct a masterpiece. So, grab your baton, throw on your metaphorical cape, and let's explore the symphony within, where we say, "F*ck the Noise" and discover the powerful chords of your own inner strength.

Life, my friends, often feels like an overbearing orchestra of external expectations, each instrument playing a relentless tune of societal norms, family pressures, and the relentless hum of comparison. It's time to plug your ears to that noise and tune in to the symphony within.

Picture the symphony within as an overture of self-discovery. It's not about conforming to the external tunes but about embracing the unique notes that make up your inner melody. Each instrument represents a facet of your identity waiting to be explored.

As you navigate the symphony of life, let the crescendo be one of unapologetic authenticity. Don't hold back; let your unique composition reverberate through the halls of existence. This is your symphony, and it's time to play it loud.

In the midst of life's chaotic orchestra, find the timpani of courageous choices. It's not about following the crowd; it's about beating your own drum. Each courageous choice is a resounding thump that echoes through the corridors of your journey.

Envision the strings section as the embodiment of your resilience. Life may pluck at them with challenges and setbacks, but they reverberate with strength. It's not about avoiding the discord; it's about turning it into a melody that speaks of your ability to endure.

The brass section symbolizes bold self-assertion. Let the trumpets declare your presence, and the trombones amplify your convictions. It's time to drown out the noise of doubt with the bold declaration of who you are and what you stand for.

Life, much like a symphony, requires flexibility. The woodwinds represent your ability to bend without breaking, to adapt without losing your essence. It's not about rigidity; it's about the graceful dance of flexibility in the face of life's unpredictable melodies.

The percussion section embodies tenacity. Imagine the relentless beat of the drums and the steady pulse of determination. Life's challenges are the rhythm, and your tenacity is the driving force that keeps the symphony within marching forward.

As the symphony unfolds, let the choir be one of self-compassion. It's not about harsh self-criticism but about harmonizing with your imperfections. Each note of self-compassion adds depth to the symphony, creating a melody that acknowledges both strengths and vulnerabilities.

In the quiet moments between movements, indulge in the solo of introspection. The symphony within is ever-evolving, and introspection is your chance to fine-tune the melody. It's about understanding the nuances of your own composition.

The symphony within is a complex arrangement, and acceptance is the harmony that ties it all together. Embrace the different sections—the high notes of joy, the low tones of sorrow—and let them coalesce into a harmonious whole that reflects the beauty of being human.

Within the symphony, discover the rhythm of emotional intelligence. It's about recognizing the various emotional instruments playing in your inner orchestra and conducting them with finesse. Emotional intelligence is the art of orchestrating your feelings, ensuring they contribute to the overall melody.

As the composer of your symphony, consider the importance of boundaries. They are the sheet music that guides the orchestra. Establishing clear boundaries ensures that your symphony remains true to your vision, preventing discordant notes from disrupting the flow.

Life often throws unexpected melodies your way. Embrace the jazz improv of spontaneity. It's not about sticking rigidly to the musical score but about finding joy in spontaneous riffs and harmonizing with the unexpected twists and turns.

Hold the conductor's baton of personal power. It's not about controlling every note; it's about directing the symphony within with intention. Your personal power is the force that guides each movement, ensuring a harmonious balance between control and spontaneity.

Consider the piano sonata as a celebration of individuality. Each key represents a unique aspect of yourself. Play the piano of your individuality with passion and confidence, creating a sonata that resonates with authenticity.

In the intermezzo of your symphony, take a moment for reflection. Life moves swiftly, and reflection is the pause button that allows you to appreciate the beauty of your journey. It's not about rushing through movements but about savoring the music of your existence.

The symphony within extends beyond your individual composition; it's also about the symphony of connection with others. The harmonies created through shared experiences, mutual respect, and understanding amplify the beauty of your personal symphony.

As the final notes approach, embrace the cadence of lifelong learning. The symphony within is a dynamic composition that evolves with each new lesson. Lifelong learning ensures that your symphony remains vibrant, continuously enriched by the wisdom gained through experience.

The symphony within is an ongoing encore. It doesn't have a final curtain call because your journey is a continuous melody. Play on, conduct with passion, and let the symphony within be a testament to the extraordinary composition that is your life and in this grand orchestra that is life, where each day plays out in a cacophony of sounds, tasks, and interactions, remember that the moments of silence—those fleeting interludes of stillness and reflection—are the unsung heroes. They are not merely gaps in our melody; they are the spaces that allow the music of our existence to resonate, to echo, and ultimately, to be truly heard and felt.

Silence is the breath between phrases in a song. Just as a singer takes a breath to sustain the next note, moments of silence give us the breathing space necessary to continue our journey. They are the inhales and exhales of our existence, reminding us that to keep playing our melody, we must pause, breathe, and then proceed.

Silence is the blank canvas of our minds, a space devoid of immediate distraction, where the possibilities of what could be are painted in strokes of thought and contemplation. In stillness, we find the freedom to dream, to envision lives that stretch beyond the boundaries of our current reality.

In the quiet, we face the most honest mirror—one that reflects not just our faces but our souls. This mirror does not flinch or turn away; it invites us to look deeper, to see ourselves in our purest form. Here, in the silence, we confront our fears, embrace our joys, and come to understand the depths of our own being.

Silence is the fertile soil in which the seeds of personal growth are planted. It is in the quiet moments that we digest the lessons of our experiences, allowing them to take root and flourish within us. Growth often happens not in the noise of action but in the quiet of reflection.

Just as a bell's ring is most profound in a silent room, the truth of our being resonates most deeply in moments of stillness. Silence amplifies the inner voice that guides us, the intuitive whisper that often gets drowned out in the day's hustle. Listening to this resonance, we find guidance, wisdom, and the authentic path forward.

In a world incessantly connected, silence is the act of disconnection that brings us back to harmony with ourselves. It's in these quiet moments that we disconnect from the external to reconnect with the internal, finding harmony within the dissonance of daily life.

Silence is our sanctuary, a refuge from the storms of life. In this sanctuary, peace is not just the absence of noise but the presence of a profound serenity that calms the turbulent seas of our minds. Here, we are sheltered, healed, and renewed.

Against the backdrop of silence, our life's music plays with greater clarity. The notes of our desires, dreams, and destiny stand out starkly, allowing us to discern the melody of our true path. Silence grants us the clarity to see which notes are ours to play and which are noise to be ignored.

Silence invites us into a dance of intimacy with the self, a slow, introspective waltz that reveals the layers of who we are. It is in this dance that we become intimately acquainted with our strengths, our vulnerabilities, and the infinite facets of our identity.

In the profound depths of silence, we touch the echo of infinity, a sense of connection to something greater than ourselves. This echo whispers of the timeless, the eternal, and our place within the vast tapestry of existence.

To come full circle, silence is the deliberate pause in our life's symphony, a momentary cessation that makes the return to music all the more sweet. It reminds us that the beauty of the symphony lies not just in the notes played but in the spaces between them, where the potential for new music lies in wait.

Embrace these moments of silence, for they are the sacred pauses in the composition of our lives. Let them be the spaces where you rest, reflect, and ready yourself for the next note. In the embrace of stillness, discover the music of your existence—a melody unique to you, waiting to be played in the symphony of the eternal now.

The Circus Tent

Life, at times, feels like a smoke and mirrors show where everyone's tossing around fcks like confetti. But let's dim the spotlight, sweep away the glitter, and expose the illusion that giving a fck about everything is the secret to a fulfilled existence.

Authenticity isn't a rare gem hidden in a mythical cave. It's the alchemy that transforms the base metal of societal conformity into the gold of genuine expression. Giving a f*ck about authenticity means abandoning the costume of societal roles and parading around in the nakedness of your true self.

The illusion whispers that there's a universal checklist of things we must give a f*ck about—careers, relationships, the neighbor's judgment, and the brand of coffee we sip. Authenticity scoffs at this checklist, urging us to create our own, filled with the things that genuinely resonate with our souls.

Picture a budget, not for money, but for fcks. Authenticity introduces the fck budgeting system—a mindful allocation of your emotional currency. It's not about bankrupting yourself by overspending on trivialities; it's about investing where it truly matters.

Society loves to play puppeteer, dangling societal expectations as strings, dictating when and where we should give our f*cks. Authenticity hands us a pair of scissors and invites us to cut the strings, to dance to the rhythm of our own emotions rather than society's manipulative tune.

To be authentic is to be a rebel. It's a revolution against the cookie-cutter molds society attempts to press us into. Authenticity doesn't politely ask for permission; it crashes through the door, leaving societal norms trembling in its wake.

Not all fcks are created equal, contrary to the myth perpetuated by societal norms. Authenticity encourages us to be discerning in our fck-giving, to reserve the VIP section for the matters that genuinely resonate and consign the rest to the nosebleed seats.

The circus tent of social approval is a chaotic spectacle where the audience cheers for conformity. Authenticity is the tightrope walker who dares to balance on the thin line between societal applause and individual truth, ignoring the roars of the crowd.

Much like in The Wizard of Oz, the wizard behind the f*cking curtain isn't a mythical force but a mere mortal playing tricks. Authenticity pulls back the curtain, revealing the vulnerability behind the illusions of societal expectations.

Picture authenticity as the court jester, giggling in the face of societal seriousness. It laughs at the absurdity of conforming to norms that stifle our genuine expressions, urging us to join the mirthful rebellion against the seriousness of societal expectations.

Navigating life without an atlas is like sailing uncharted waters. Authenticity provides the compass and map—an atlas that guides us through the landscapes of self-discovery, encouraging us to explore the uncharted territories of our true selves.

Authenticity is an unmasking ritual, a shedding of the layers society heaps upon us. Picture it as a masquerade ball where everyone wears societal masks. Authenticity is the bold soul who tears off the mask, inviting others to unmask their true selves.

The myth of giving a f*ck implies a quest for perfection—a pursuit as elusive as catching moonbeams in a net. Authenticity discards the illusion of perfection, embracing the beauty in imperfection, the charm in flaws, and the richness in the raw and unpolished.

Life has a soundtrack, and authenticity curates a rebellion playlist. It's a mixtape of courage, vulnerability, and unapologetic self-expression. Picture it blaring through the speakers of societal norms, drowning out the monotonous hum of conformity.

Authenticity is an art gallery displaying the masterpieces of genuine expression. It's a space where individuality is celebrated, where the canvases bear the brushstrokes of uniqueness. Picture walking through this gallery, each painting telling a story of authenticity and self-discovery.

In the arid desert of societal expectations, authenticity is the fountain—gushing forth the refreshing waters of genuine expression. It invites us to drink deeply from its waters, quenching the thirst that conformity could never satisfy.

Society's approval is the mythical unicorn, forever elusive and vanishing just when we think we've caught it. Authenticity invites us to stop chasing unicorns, to recognize that the only approval that matters is our own. Picture a world where the mythical unicorn becomes irrelevant in the face of self-acceptance.

Staring into the authenticity mirror is like gazing into the reflection of your true self. It doesn't Photoshop away flaws or airbrush imperfections. Instead, it celebrates the authenticity of every line, every wrinkle, and every scar.

Imagine a bonfire fueled by societal expectations, where the flames dance in celebration of authenticity. It's a cleansing fire, burning away the illusions and leaving behind the raw, untamed essence of our true selves.

Take a solemn pledge. A pledge to step out of the circus tent, to dance to your own rhythm, and to give your f*cks only to the matters that genuinely resonate with the beating of your heart. Let authenticity be your guiding light, illuminating the path to a life that's true, unfiltered, and uniquely yours.

The Messy Threads That Weave Our Lives

Ah, relationships—the intricate, messy threads that weave the tapestry of our lives. In life's loom, we're about to create a masterpiece with the threads of connection, laughter, and the occasional tear. So grab your metaphorical needle, and let's stitch together the vibrant Tapestry of Relationships.

Relationships are the yarn of life, and we're all just amateur weavers trying not to tangle ourselves in knots. Each thread represents a connection, a shared moment, a laugh, or even an awkward silence. The Tapestry of Relationships is the quilt that warms us on the cold nights of existence.

Friendship is the cha-cha of the weaving dance. It's the two-step of shared secrets and inside jokes. As you twirl through life, let the dance floor of camaraderie be your sanctuary. Don't worry about stepping on toes; real friends forgive bad dance moves.

Acquaintances are the patches in the tapestry—some small, some large, and occasionally a bit frayed around the edges. Cherish the diversity of patches, for even the tiniest square might hold the key to unexpected joy or a serendipitous adventure.

Trust is the silk thread that binds the Tapestry of Relationships. It's delicate yet resilient, easily damaged but also repairable. The loom of trust requires careful weaving; one loose thread, and the entire tapestry might unravel. Handle it with care.

Shared moments are the stitches that hold the tapestry together. Whether it's a belly laugh over a terrible joke or a tear shed in solidarity, these stitches form the patterns of the relationships. Don't be afraid to experiment with bold stitches; they often create the most beautiful designs.

Balancing acts are essential in the weaving process. You're juggling threads of work, family, friends, and personal time. It's like trying to juggle flaming torches while riding a unicycle—chaotic but oddly satisfying when you find your rhythm.

Boundaries are the tug-of-war ropes in the Tapestry of Relationships. Sometimes you need to pull back, establish a line, and protect your territory. Other times, loosen your grip and let others in. Finding the right tension is an ongoing art, a dance of give and take.

Family is the intricate embroidery in the tapestry—a bit more elaborate, a touch more complicated. These threads run deep, connecting generations and weaving stories that become the family folklore. Embrace the quirks; they add character to the design.

Laughter is the symphony playing in the background. It's the cheerful soundtrack of the tapestry. Whether it's the melodic laughter of friends, the hearty guffaws of family, or the contagious chuckles of colleagues, let the symphony play on.

Solitude is a patch in the tapestry that often goes unnoticed. Like negative space in art, it defines and enhances the beauty of the whole. Don't fear the empty spaces; they provide room for individual growth and self-discovery.

Conflicts are the dramatic plot twists in the Tapestry of Relationships. They add tension, test the strength of the threads, and sometimes lead to unexpected resolutions. Don't shy away from the drama; embrace it as a catalyst for growth and understanding.

Support is the warmth that radiates from the tapestry. Be the cozy blanket for others, and allow them to wrap you up in return. A network of support is like a patchwork quilt; each square contributes to the overall comfort and resilience.

Tangles are inevitable in the weaving process. Relationships, like threads, can get twisted and knotted. The untangling ritual requires patience, communication, and sometimes a good sense of humor. Remember, a well-untangled thread can be woven into the most beautiful patterns.

Conversation is the jazz improvisation in the tapestry. It's spontaneous, unpredictable, and occasionally a bit chaotic. Let the notes of dialogue flow freely, and don't be afraid to explore new rhythms and harmonies.

Shared stories are the hidden treasures woven into the fabric. They are the anecdotes, the legends, and the whispered tales passed down through the generations. Each story adds richness and depth to the Tapestry of Relationships.

Listening is the fine art of weaving. Pay attention to the subtle nuances of the threads; sometimes the most delicate whispers carry the most profound meanings. The loom of relationships is enhanced when every thread feels seen and heard.

In the modern era, social media is the mosaic section of the tapestry. It's a collection of digital threads, connecting us across vast distances. Use it wisely, as too much digital noise can distract from the tangible warmth of face-to-face connections.

Shared goals are the quilt squares that align the threads of relationships. When individuals collaborate toward a common purpose, a beautiful design emerges. Identify the shared goals in your tapestry, and stitch them together with purpose.

Change is the dyeing process that alters the hues of the tapestry. Embrace the vibrant colors of growth, even when change feels like a bold splash of unexpected dye. The evolving shades add depth and vibrancy to the overall design.

As you continue weaving, step back and admire the masterpiece that is the Tapestry of Relationships. It's a living, breathing work of art, ever-changing and infinitely fascinating. Cherish each thread, for they contribute to the richness of your life's woven narrative.

And there you have it—a glimpse into the intricate artistry of relationships, where every thread, every knot, and every patch contributes to the ever-evolving Tapestry of Relationships. May your loom be forever vibrant, and your connections ever resilient. Keep weaving, my friend.

The Echo Chamber

The echo chamber is the sanctuary of comfort, a padded cell where your beliefs bounce back, never challenged. But comfort is a lullaby that sings the melody of stagnation. It's time to wake up and disrupt the soothing rhythm.

Validation within the echo chamber is a mirage, an illusion of progress. It's time to recognize that real growth requires the sharp edges of discomfort, not the padded cushions of constant agreement.

In the echo chamber, every note sounds familiar, creating a repetitive symphony that lulls you into complacency. It's time to break free from the loop and compose a new, dynamic score that challenges and inspires.

The ego loves the echo chamber; it's a playground where it's always the star. But beware, for the ego's stage is not the arena of authentic evolution. It's time to dim the spotlight on the ego and embrace the vulnerability of growth.

In the echo chamber, you're the one-man show, the writer, director, and protagonist. But a great story involves collaboration and diverse perspectives. It's time to invite new characters onto the stage of your narrative.

Too much comfort is like drowning in still waters. It's time to make waves, to disrupt the serene surface and swim in the unpredictable currents of challenge and diversity.

Validation and growth are often mistaken for allies, but they can be adversaries. It's time to decide whether you seek the echo of agreement or the roar of personal evolution.

The echo chamber thrives on a feedback loop of validation. It's time to break the loop, disrupt the pattern, and invite dissonance as the precursor to a more harmonious understanding.

Stagnation lurks in the corners of the echo chamber, patiently waiting for its next victim. It's time to escape the trap, to venture into the unknown, even if it means stumbling in the darkness of uncertainty.

The echo chamber is seductive, a siren's call to the comfort of the familiar. But growth lies in the uncharted territories beyond the known. It's time to resist the allure and embark on an expedition of self-discovery.

In the echo chamber, validation becomes a crutch, supporting your beliefs but weakening your legs. It's time to toss away the crutch and stand tall on the sturdy foundation of self-awareness.

Disagreement is the specter haunting the echo chamber. It's time to confront the fear of dissent, for within the clash of ideas, true growth emerges.

Echoes are feeble whispers bouncing off walls; thunderclaps, on the other hand, resonate with power. It's time to trade the echoes of self-validation for the thunderous applause of genuine achievement.

The echo chamber is a bubble, an illusion of safety. But bubbles burst, and it's time to let the shards of illusion pave the way for the solid ground of authenticity.

Growth is a symphony, not a monotonous drone. It's time to introduce contrasts and crescendos into your life's music, moving beyond the echo chamber's repetitive melody.

Discomfort is the catalyst for growth, the fertilizer that nourishes the seeds of progress. It's time to embrace the awkwardness, the unease, and let them fuel the blossoming of your potential.

Agreement in the echo chamber is a myth; it's a deceptive illusion of unity. It's time to acknowledge that real unity emerges from the cacophony of diverse voices.

Authenticity resides in the wild terrains beyond the echo chamber, where validation is not a prerequisite. It's time to prioritize the authenticity of your journey over the applause of the echo.

Disagreement is not a shackle but a key to liberation. It's time to unlock the door, step into the unknown, and relish the freedom that comes with embracing diverse perspectives.

Mark your departure from the echo chamber. The horizon beyond is uncharted, unknown, and brimming with the potential for genuine growth. It's time to break the sound barrier of self-validation and venture into the symphony of a life well-lived. The echoes are fading; the crescendo of authenticity awaits.

Not Your Grandma's Etiquette Class

Embark on a wild journey into the rebellious realm of "no." This ain't your grandma's etiquette class; it's a crash course in the art of saying no with the finesse of a ninja and the audacity of a rockstar.

Welcome to the No Manifesto, where we flip the script on the relentless yes culture. Saying no isn't a rejection; it's a declaration of self-worth. Get ready to sculpt your boundaries with the precision of a chainsaw-wielding artist.

In a world intoxicated with yeses, the power of a single no is a force to be reckoned with. It's not about being a negative Nancy; it's about reclaiming your sanity, your time, and your autonomy. Embrace the potency of a well-timed, unapologetic no.

Saying no is your conductor's baton in the symphony of prioritization. Picture your life as a grand orchestra; each no directs the musicians to focus on the essential notes. The art of saying no orchestrates a masterpiece of intentional living.

Let your no be a rebel yell of self-preservation. When you say no, you're not just declining a request; you're defending the fortress of your well-being. It's a battle cry that echoes through the corridors of your boundaries.

Saying no is a dance, and it's time to master the no-guilt two-step. Kick guilt to the curb; it has no place in the rhythm of your boundaries. Every refusal is a step towards the dance floor of unapologetic self-care.

Assertiveness is your artistic palette in the canvas of saying no. Splash bold strokes of "no" onto the canvas of life. Don't water it down with maybes or apologies. Own your assertiveness like a rebellious artist embracing the vivid hues of self-expression.

Like a Zen master in the dojo of life, embrace the art of selective no's. Not every request deserves a no, but the ones encroaching on your boundaries? They're in for a Zen slap of rejection. Choose your battles, and let your no's be swift and purposeful.

Equipped with the boundary sculptor's toolkit, you're armed to chisel your boundaries with finesse. The toolkit includes the chisel of assertiveness, the brush of clarity, and the hammer of conviction. Carve your boundaries into a masterpiece that reflects your unyielding self-respect.

Mastering the language of no is akin to learning a rebellious dialect. It's not about being rude; it's about being unapologetically honest. Develop your no vocabulary, peppered with phrases like "I can't commit to that" and "It's not feasible for me right now."

Saying no in relationships is an art form that requires a delicate touch. Communicate your boundaries with the finesse of a love poet. Let your no be a love note that says, "I cherish our connection, but I also honor my autonomy."

Inject a bit of comedy into your no repertoire. Humor disarms tension and adds a touch of irreverence to the art of refusal. Picture your no as a stand-up routine; make 'em laugh while you stand your ground.

Saying no is your guerrilla warfare strategy in the battlefield of time management. Each refusal is a strategic move, a guerrilla fighter defending the precious territory of your schedule. Wage war on time-wasting obligations with the weapon of no.

No isn't a shackle; it's a key to liberation. Liberating yourself from the burden of overcommitment, from the chains of people-pleasing. Picture your no as the key that unlocks the door to your sovereign kingdom of boundaries.

Understand the ripple effect of the art of saying no. Your refusal isn't just a solitary act; it sends ripples through the pond of your life. It empowers others to set their boundaries, creating a collective symphony of self-respect.

Consider the art of saying no a marathon, not a sprint. Pace yourself, build endurance in your boundary muscles. Like a marathon runner, you'll find strength in consistency and resilience in every refusal.

Craft your no-regret anthem as you navigate the labyrinth of boundaries. When you say no, let it be a resounding anthem that echoes in the chambers of your choices. No regrets, only the sweet melody of self-honoring decisions.

Add a staccato rhythm to your no symphony. Short, sharp no's punctuate your boundaries with clarity. Like a percussionist in a rebellious orchestra, let your staccato of no cut through the noise of unreasonable demands.

Discover the hidden yes within the no. Saying no isn't about closing doors; it's about opening the right ones. Your refusal paves the way for a yes to your priorities, your well-being, and your authenticity.

Think of your no as a shield of self-care. When you say no, you're not rejecting; you're safeguarding your energy, your peace, and your mental well-being. Let your no be the impenetrable armor of self-preservation.

The art of saying no is ever-evolving. It's not a static masterpiece but a dynamic creation that adapts to the shifting landscapes of your life. Embrace the ever-changing canvas of boundaries and let your no's be strokes in the ongoing painting of your unapologetic existence.

The Cookie-Cutter Catastrophe

In the rebellious sanctuary we tear apart the ill-fitting garment of the "One Size Fits All" mentality. Life isn't a clearance sale, and you're certainly not a generic, mass-produced item. It's time to embrace your eccentricities, relish in your quirks, and declare war on the suffocating idea that there's a universal mold into which we all must cram ourselves.

The "One Size Fits All" mentality is the cookie-cutter catastrophe of individuality. It suggests that we should all think, feel, and live in identical ways, as if humanity were a factory assembly line pumping out identical widgets. Spoiler alert: we're not widgets, and life isn't a conveyor belt.

Life is a bespoke suit, crafted for your unique dimensions. F*ck the notion that you should squeeze into someone else's ill-fitting attire. It's time to tailor your existence to the contours of your own soul, not the mannequin in the store window.

Averageness is the enemy of exceptional. The "One Size Fits All" mentality revels in mediocrity, celebrating the middle ground while suffocating the outliers. Let's embrace the absurdity that is each of us—gloriously exceptional, magnificently peculiar.

Happiness isn't stamped from a universal mold. F*ck the idea that there's a one-size happiness that fits all. What brings joy to one might be the bane of another's existence. Your happiness is a bespoke creation, stitched together with the threads of your unique passions and desires.

Life isn't a scripted play where we all recite the same lines. It's an improv performance, and you're the star of your own show. F*ck adhering to the pre-written narratives; grab the pen, and script your tale in a way that resonates with your truth.

The rebellion begins with individuality. Break free from the chains of conformity, for they bind the spirit. Each of us is a glorious misfit in the grand mosaic of existence, and the world deserves to witness the kaleidoscope of your uniqueness.

"One Size Fits All" is the straitjacket of societal expectations. It dictates how you should behave, what success should look like, and when you should hit life's milestones. F*ck that noise. Life's timeline is subjective; walk to the beat of your own drum.

Your rebellion uniform isn't mass-produced; it's a bespoke ensemble that encapsulates your essence. F*ck the idea that there's a standardized rebel look. Whether your rebellion is clad in leather, sequins, or flannel—it's uniquely yours.

Eccentricity is the spice of life. F*ck blending into the monotonous background. Celebrate the quirks, oddities, and idiosyncrasies that make you gloriously weird. Let the world marvel at the kaleidoscope of your eccentric existence.

Wisdom doesn't come in a one-size box. The "One Size Fits All" mentality assumes that universal maxims fit every circumstance. It's time to embrace the wisdom that's tailor-made for your unique journey—a wisdom that bends, adapts, and molds itself to your distinct narrative.

Life is beautifully chaotic, a symphony of unpredictability. F*ck the sanitized predictability of the "One Size Fits All" mindset. Embrace the glorious chaos that is uniquely yours, and revel in the spontaneity of a life less scripted.

Labels are the uniform badges of the "One Size Fits All" army. Peel them off; you're not a product on a shelf. Refuse to be confined by the limitations of labels. Your identity is a nuanced masterpiece, painted with the hues of your experiences and convictions.

Your beliefs are not off-the-rack; they're bespoke creations that align with the contours of your conscience. F*ck the notion that you should subscribe to a pre-packaged set of beliefs. Choose the ones that resonate with your soul, even if they clash with the norm.

Life is your canvas, and the "One Size Fits All" mentality hands you a paint-by-numbers kit. F*ck that. Splash bold strokes of your passions, dreams, and eccentricities. Create a masterpiece that defies the boundaries of conformity.

Conformity is the conveyor belt of a mundane existence. F*ck riding that conveyor belt. Step off, dance to your rhythm, and relish in the freedom to move in directions that defy the monotonous straight line.

Unapologetic uniqueness is an art form. F*ck apologies for being who you are. Embrace your quirks, flaunt your eccentricities, and revel in the masterpiece of your unapologetic existence.

The "One Size Fits All" mentality thrives on the comparison trap. F*ck comparing your journey to others. Your path is a bespoke trail, winding through landscapes unique to your experiences. Walk it with pride and purpose.

Relationships aren't cut from the same cloth. F*ck expecting uniformity in connections. Your relationships are a patchwork quilt, each square representing a unique bond, woven together by shared moments, not societal expectations.

Emotions aren't monochrome; they're a vibrant spectrum. F*ck restraining your emotional palette. Let the full range of your emotions paint the canvas of your experiences. Life is richer in color, not in grayscale.

Your rebellion deserves an anthem—a cacophony of diverse voices, not a monotonous hum. F*ck the standardized tunes; let your anthem be the rebellious melody that celebrates the harmonious chaos of individuality.

As you embark on this rebellious journey against the "One Size Fits All" mentality, revel in the exquisite tailoring of your existence. Life wasn't meant to be uniform; it's a kaleidoscope of individual narratives. So, f*ck conformity, embrace your eccentricity, and let the world witness the glorious spectacle of your uniquely tailored rebellion.

Week 1 Action Plan: Diving Deep into Your Symphony

This leg of your journey has been about recognizing your inner strength, leading with resilience, and making a meaningful impact. It's time to reflect, act, and amplify the impact you wish to create in the world and within yourself.

Day 1: Reflection on "The Symphony Within"
- **Activity:** Spend 20 minutes in solitude reflecting on your inner strengths and weaknesses. Write down what makes your personal symphony unique. Identify which parts of your life you're leading with purpose and where you might be merely following the crowd.
- **Reflection:** How does your inner symphony guide your daily actions?

Day 2: "The Circus Tent" Exploration
- **Activity:** Visualize your life as a circus. Identify the acts (areas of your life) that are thrilling and those that feel like they're underperforming. Sketch or write down ideas on how to bring more balance and excitement to your personal circus.

- **Reflection:** Which act of your life's circus are you most proud of, and why?

Day 3: Weaving "The Messy Threads That Weave Our Lives"
- **Activity:** List the top 5 relationships in your life. Next to each, note how these relationships contribute to your tapestry and one action you can take to strengthen each thread.
- **Reflection:** How do these relationships influence your resilience and impact?

Day 4: Entering "The Echo Chamber"
- **Activity:** Identify a recent decision influenced by external expectations rather than your own desires. Reevaluate this decision from your authentic perspective and consider any adjustments you'd like to make.
- **Reflection:** How often do you find yourself influenced by the echo chamber, and what can you do to resist its pull?

Day 5: "Not Your Grandma's Etiquette Class" - Defining Your Values
- **Activity:** Create a personal code of values that you want to live by. Consider what is non-negotiable for you and what guides your decisions.
- **Reflection:** How do these values align with the impact you wish to create?

Day 6: "The Cookie-Cutter Catastrophe" - Embracing Individuality
- **Activity:** Reflect on areas of your life where you feel you're conforming to societal norms at the expense of your individuality. Plan one action you can take to break free from one of these "cookie-cutter" molds.
- **Reflection:** How does conforming or not conforming affect your mental and emotional energy?

Day 7: Weekly Synthesis
- **Activity:** Review your reflections and activities from the week. Combine them into a personal manifesto for leading a life of purpose and resilience. Share this manifesto with someone you trust, or keep it as a personal reminder.
- **Reflection:** Reflect on how this week's activities have shifted your perspective on making an impact and leading with purpose.

This week is just the beginning. Each day has been designed to spark thought, inspire action, and lead you closer to orchestrating your life's symphony with intent and impact. Stay tuned for Week 2, where we'll explore further chapters and deepen our journey into purposeful resilience.

The Art of Creative Chaos

In a world where reactive problem-solving has become the norm, where we're conditioned to play defense against life's curveballs, it's time for a revolution. A revolution that says, "F*ck reactive solutions," and champions the cause of proactive, creative chaos. This isn't about putting out fires; it's about lighting your own flames of innovation and dancing in the glow.

Reactive problem-solving is the equivalent of playing life on a loop, responding to the same old challenges with the same old solutions. It's a merry-go-round of monotony, and frankly, it's boring as hell. You're not here to be a passive player in your own life, reacting to what's thrown at you. No, you're here to be the master of ceremonies, the creator of your destiny, and the architect of your own chaos.

The problem with reactive problem-solving is that it keeps you tethered to the past, always one step behind, always playing catch-up. It's a hamster wheel of frustration, where every solution seems like a temporary fix, a Band-Aid on a wound that needs stitches. It's time to break the cycle, to step off the wheel, and to take control.

Think of proactive problem-solving as your rebellion against the status quo. It's an act of defiance against the predictable patterns of thinking that have held you captive. It's your declaration of independence from the old ways of doing things, a manifesto for the creatively chaotic and the audaciously adventurous.

Proactive problem-solving is about anticipation, about envisioning the future and shaping it to your will. It's about being one step ahead, not just of the problems themselves, but of your own potential solutions. It's about seeing the maze from above, not just navigating it on the ground.

The key to proactive problem-solving lies in embracing the art of creative chaos. It's about recognizing that the best solutions often come from the most unexpected places, from the wild edges of your imagination where logic meets lunacy. It's about mixing the ingredients of innovation, audacity, and a healthy dose of irreverence to cook up solutions that are as delicious as they are daring.

Creative chaos is the playground of the proactive problem-solver. It's where you allow your mind to wander, to explore the realms of the ridiculous, the realms where flying pigs are not just possible but practical. It's about breaking the rules, about questioning the unquestionable, and about daring to dream the impossible.

In this journey, you'll learn to wield the tools of the trade: curiosity, courage, and a relentless desire for something better. You'll learn to see problems not as obstacles but as opportunities, not as dead-ends but as detours on the road to innovation. You'll discover that the most powerful weapon in your arsenal is your ability to think differently, to approach problems from angles that others haven't even considered. You'll learn that creativity isn't just about art; it's about solving problems in ways that leave people awestruck.

As we dive into the chaos of life, let's bid farewell to reactive problem-solving and welcome the era of proactive innovation. Let's celebrate the messy, the unpredictable, and the utterly brilliant solutions that await us. This is your invitation to join the revolution, to become a maestro of creative chaos, and to orchestrate a life that's as unique as it is impactful.

Imagine life as a chaotic circus, complete with fire-breathing dilemmas and acrobatic disasters. Proactive problem-solving isn't about being the ringmaster; it's about turning chaos into your personal sideshow. Grab your popcorn, because we're about to tame the unruly beasts of life's big top.

Proactive problem-solving begins with a maverick mindset, a rebel yell against the mundane. It's not about tiptoeing around problems; it's about waltzing with them in a tango of audacity. Strap on your problem-solving boots, for we're about to kick down the doors of convention.

Think of proactive problem-solving as the art of creative chaos. It's not about tidy solutions neatly arranged on a shelf; it's about diving headfirst into the messy, paint-splattered canvas of uncertainty. Picasso had his blue period; welcome to your chaotic masterpiece.

Life's problems are a jigsaw puzzle, and you're the irreverent jester putting the pieces together with a mischievous grin. Proactive problem-solving isn't about fitting into a pre-made picture; it's about creating your own whimsical collage. Let the jesting begin!

Consider problems as the dissonant notes in the symphony of life. Proactive problem-solving is your conductor's baton, orchestrating solutions that harmonize with the chaos. Get ready to compose your magnum opus amid the cacophony.

Proactive problem-solving tosses aside the rulebook and writes its own rebel's manual. It's not about coloring inside the lines; it's about turning the lines into doodles of brilliance. Break the rules, for only then can you discover new pathways through the labyrinth.

Daredevils face dilemmas head-on, turning fear into fuel for audacious feats. Proactive problem-solving is your daredevil's dilemma, transforming the adrenaline of challenges into the propulsion for extraordinary solutions. Embrace the thrill; the daring part is the best ride.

Sherlock Holmes didn't solve mysteries by following a linear path; he thrived in the unexpected twists. Proactive problem-solving is your Holmesian surprise, unraveling conundrums with sharp wit and a touch of irreverence. Get ready to put on your metaphorical deerstalker.

In the toolbox of a proactive problem-solver, you won't find just hammers and nails. Expect a dash of glitter, duct tape, and maybe a rubber chicken. It's not about conventional tools; it's about wielding the unexpected with flair. Let's craft solutions that sparkle in the face of adversity.

When life sets your plans ablaze, proactive problem-solving invites you to rise from the ashes like a phoenix. It's not about preventing fires; it's about learning the flamenco amidst the flames. Burn, rise, dance—repeat.

Picture problems as the audience, eagerly watching your magic show. Proactive problem-solving is the misdirection that leaves them awestruck. It's not about pulling rabbits out of hats; it's about making problems disappear in a puff of audacious innovation.

Proactive problem-solving is the juggling act of a comedic genius, tossing challenges in the air with a wink and a laugh. It's not about avoiding drops; it's about turning drops into unexpected punchlines. Ready to join the circus?

Quantum physics meets problem-solving in a dance of unpredictability. Proactive problem-solving is your quantum quotient, where uncertainty becomes the canvas for groundbreaking solutions. Get ready to defy the gravity of conventional thinking.

Life hands you a mixtape of problems; proactive problem-solving is your eclectic playlist. It's not about playing the hits; it's about introducing your own rhythm into the chaos. Dance to the beats of unconventional solutions.

Proactive problem-solving embraces the Zen of Zest, turning challenges into the spice of life. It's not about bland solutions; it's about adding a dash of irreverent flavor to transform the ordinary into the extraordinary. Get ready to savor the unexpected.

Aviators navigate the skies, rising above storms. Proactive problem-solving is your ascent through turbulent challenges, not avoiding the clouds but learning to dance among them. Buckle up; we're taking flight into the realm of audacious solutions.

Alchemy transforms base metals into gold; proactive problem-solving turns adversity into the elixir of resilience. It's not about avoiding challenges; it's about transmuting them into the building blocks of your audacious journey. Get ready to sip from the alchemist's cup.

Life's trails are filled with nuts and berries; proactive problem-solving is your trail mix, blending the unexpected for a nourishing journey. It's not about a paved road; it's about forging your own trail, munching on the challenges as you go.

Proactive problem-solving crafts a vision board of solutions, not limited to the images you've seen before. It's about pasting dreams and aspirations in the mosaic of challenges. Ready to visualize the unexpected?

Inventors thrive on spontaneity; proactive problem-solving is your improv session, turning unexpected hiccups into comedic brilliance. It's not about a scripted play; it's about embracing the unexpected lines. Welcome to the theater of audacious solutions. Armed with irreverent ingenuity, audacious wisdom, and a touch of madness, you're now ready to face life's chaotic circus with a smirk and a swagger. So, step into the ring; the show awaits your grand entrance.

The Jungle of Human Connection

Ever felt like you're drowning in the social media sea, where likes and emojis are the shallow waves that barely brush the surface? It's time to unplug the life jacket and dive into the deep waters of real connections, where vulnerability, laughter, and shared experiences create the currents.

Small talk is the fast food of human interaction—quick, convenient, but ultimately unsatisfying. Let's toss the superficial salad aside and indulge in the hearty feast of unfiltered conversations. It's time to share stories, spill truths, and savor the rich flavors of genuine connection.

Picture vulnerability as the superhero cape you never knew you needed. In the realm of connections, being vulnerable is not a weakness; it's the courageous act of unveiling your true self. So, let that vulnerability cape flutter in the wind as you soar into the uncharted skies of genuine relationships.

Friendships are not a spectator sport; they're a Ferris wheel ride with twists, turns, and the occasional upside-down loop. Embrace the unpredictability, cherish the laughter, and hold on tight when life takes you for a spin. After all, the best views come after a few thrilling revolutions.

Ever tried to fit square pegs into round holes? Relationships aren't a geometry puzzle; they're a celebration of differences. Embrace the quirks, the idiosyncrasies, and the beautifully mismatched shapes that make each person a unique piece in the puzzle of connection.

Life is an adventure, and shared experiences are the stories told around the campfire of connection. So, gather 'round, fellow wanderers, and let's swap tales of triumphs, failures, and the bizarre plot twists that make our journeys worth recounting.

Relationships are not solo performances; they're a dance of give and take, a choreography where both partners twirl in harmony. Step into the dance floor of reciprocity, where the tango of understanding, the waltz of support, and the jitterbug of shared responsibilities create a masterpiece.

Ever had a conversation that felt like navigating through a dense fog with a broken compass? Genuine connections require an upgraded GPS of authentic interest. Let curiosity be your guiding star, leading you through the labyrinth of interests, passions, and stories that make each person a unique destination.

Empathy is not a serene lake; it's a rollercoaster that plunges into the depths of another's emotions. Buckle up for the ride, feel the exhilaration of shared joys, and brace yourself for the loop-de-loops of sorrows. In the rollercoaster of empathy, every twist strengthens the bonds of connection.

Friendship is not a pre-packaged mix; it's a recipe crafted with care, laughter, and a pinch of shared secrets. So, grab your metaphorical apron, sprinkle in trust, add generous scoops of inside jokes, and bake the friendship cake that makes every moment sweeter.

Love is not a solo instrument; it's a symphony where every note contributes to the grand composition. In the orchestra of relationships, let the melody of unconditional love rise above, creating a harmonious ensemble that resonates with warmth, acceptance, and genuine connection.

Trust is not a fragile glass sculpture; it's a lighthouse guiding ships through the stormy seas of uncertainties. Build your lighthouse on the rock of reliability, let its beam pierce through the darkness, and navigate the vast ocean of connections with the assurance that you're anchored in trust.

Navigating relationships is not a blindfolded game of pinning the tail on the donkey. It's a journey with a well-drawn map of boundaries, where each person's comfort zone is respected. So, unfold the map, chart the territories of consent, and traverse the landscape of connection with respect.

Connections are not potted plants; they're a garden where mutual growth is the constant blooming. Cultivate the soil of encouragement, water the plants of shared aspirations, and watch the garden of connections flourish into a vibrant landscape of support and understanding.

Relationships are not jigsaw puzzles with predetermined pieces; they're a puzzle of compatibility where the pieces shape themselves through shared experiences. Let the puzzle unfold naturally, celebrating the unique fit that develops with time, understanding, and the occasional trial-and-error.

Laughter is not a solitary echo; it's a chorus that reverberates through the aquarium of connection. Dive into the deep waters of shared humor, explore the coral reefs of inside jokes, and witness the vibrant fish of genuine laughter swimming through the transparent walls of camaraderie.

Support is not a one-sided banner; it's a tapestry woven with threads of encouragement, understanding, and shared burdens. Each thread contributes to the strength of the tapestry, creating a resilient fabric that shields against the storms and celebrates the sunny days of connection.

Communication is not a broken telescope with a blurry lens; it's a finely tuned instrument that brings distant galaxies of thoughts closer. Polish the lens of active listening, adjust the focus of articulation, and peer through the telescope of communication to explore the vast cosmos of shared understanding.

Dreams are not solitary campfires; they're a bonfire where each spark contributes to the blaze of shared aspirations. Gather around the bonfire of connection, toss in the logs of encouragement, and let the flames illuminate the shared path towards the constellation of collective dreams.

Life is a grand symphony of comings and goings, where every farewell is the prelude to a new hello. Embrace the ebb and flow of connections, cherish the melodies created with each interaction, and let the symphony play on, an ever-evolving masterpiece of human relationships.

The Unhealthy Connections

Buckle up; we're about to sever the ties that bind and set your spirit free. Life's emotions often cling like Velcro, sticking to you long after their welcome. F*ck being a human bulletin board; unstick, unleash, and unwind. Free yourself from the weight of unnecessary emotional baggage.

Welcome to the revolution, where the chains of unhealthy connections are about to be shattered. We're not just talking about cutting ties; we're talking about transforming the very fabric of our emotional existence. Say goodbye to being a magnet for emotional clutter. It's time to declutter, detoxify, and declare your emotional independence.

Life's grand puppet show has you tangled in strings of expectations, obligations, and misplaced loyalty. F*ck being a marionette; you're not a puppet. It's time to grab the scissors of audacity and cut those strings. Own your narrative, and let others know you're scripting your own epic.

That emotional albatross hanging around your neck? It's not a badge of honor; it's a millstone dragging you to the depths. F*ck dragging it around. Let's untie that knot, set the albatross free, and watch as your soul takes flight. The skies of emotional freedom await, vast and unexplored.

Attachments are like quicksand; the more you struggle, the deeper you sink. But who says you need to fight? F*ck fighting; dance atop the quicksand. Transform struggle into a ballet of liberation, twirling on the surface with the grace of someone who knows their worth.

Guilt, that relentless blacksmith, keeps hammering chains around you, each link forged from remorse. Enough. It's time to cool the forge and break those chains. F*ck forging more links; break the existing ones. Learn from guilt, but don't let it define you. Your journey is one of growth, not imprisonment. Allow guilt to be a teacher, not a jailer, as you navigate the path.

Emotional vampires lurk, cloaked in charm while draining your vitality. F*ck being a blood bank; drive the stakes. Guard your emotional life force and let the vampires starve. It's not your job to be their sustenance. Boundaries are your armor. Illuminate your boundaries with the daylight of assertiveness, and watch these vampires dissolve into the shadows.

Expectations can be a trap, ensnaring you in a web of disappointment. F*ck the trap. Light the torch of self-determination, burn down the traps, and walk away. Embrace the beauty of the unpredictable, the unexpected twists of your story.

Attachments offer a thrill like a bungee jump without the freefall, but it's the cut of the cord that brings true exhilaration. F*ck the entanglements; cut the cord. Experience the free fall of letting go, and find in that space the wings of independence. Soar on the updrafts of self-discovery, higher and freer than ever before.

Leeches latch onto your emotions, draining the lifeblood of joy. F*ck being a host; extract and heal. Allow the wounds to mend, cultivating a reservoir of emotional vitality, a testament to your resilience.

Drama, that treacherous lighthouse, beckons with the promise of excitement, but delivers only stormy seas. F*ck shipwrecks; change your course. Navigate by the stars of peace and contentment, and find safe harbor in the tranquil waters of emotional stability.

Envy, that intricate web-spinner, often whispers tales of inadequacy as we gaze upon the success of others. But here's the secret: You're the spider, not the fly. F*ck the whispers. Spin a new web, one of inspiration and individual achievement not measured against others but by the milestones of your personal journey. Applaud the triumphs of your peers, but craft a unique masterpiece from the threads of your aspirations.

Resentment is a bonfire fueled by grievances. F*ck stoking the flames; let it burn out. Allow the ashes to fertilize the soil of forgiveness and new beginnings. Watch as new life springs forth, lush and thriving.

An emotional house of cards is fragile, susceptible to collapse. F*ck tip toeing around. Don't brace that house of cards; knock it down. Build anew with the bricks of resilience and wisdom, structures that withstand the gales of life's challenges.

Validation, that elusive jailer, holds you captive in a cell of external approval. F*ck being an inmate in a self-imposed prison. It's time for a jailbreak; pick the lock. Liberate yourself from the need for external approval. Find validation within, and step into the sunlight of self-reliance.

Life's a constant tug-of-war of emotions that exhaust without purpose. F*ck the rope; drop it. Step out of the battlefield. Conflict is a choice, not a necessity. Refuse to engage in unnecessary emotional skirmishes.

A backpack of grudges weighs you down, a collection of resentment stones gathered from the road of life. F*ck the weight; unload and walk light. Continue your journey unburdened, collecting instead memories of joy, lessons learned, and the beauty of forgiveness.

Comparison lays a snare that entices you towards the edge of self-doubt. F*ck the descent; barricade that door. Plant your feet firmly on the solid ground of self-appreciation, rejecting the lure into the chasm of not-enoughness. Stand tall, recognizing your value and journey are incomparable, and let the trapdoor of comparison remain forever closed behind you.

Emotional tornadoes can whirl chaos through your life, threatening to upend your world. F*ck the havoc; seek the calm. Find the eye of the storm, the place of calm within. Here, in the center of turbulence, find your balance, your clarity, and your strength.

Regret is a rollercoaster of missed chances and what-ifs. F*ck the loops; get off and walk the path of redemption. Learn from the twists, turns, and take control of the ride.

Consider this the funeral for unhealthy attachments. Bury them, grieve their passing, and move on. Life's too short for graves of emotional baggage. The eulogy for the attachments that once bound you, and the anthem for your emancipation, begins. F*ck the unhealthy attachments; your spirit is now unshackled, soaring freely into the vast expanse of emotional liberation.

The collapse of this house of cards, while seemingly a catastrophe, is an essential step towards genuine emotional strength. It's in the ruins of our most fragile selves that we discover the materials needed for reconstruction. The fall is not a failure but a liberation, clearing the ground for something more substantial to take its place.

Sweeping away the remnants of this collapse means letting go of the illusions that once defined us. It involves a conscious decision to move beyond the ephemeral and seek out the enduring. This act of clearing is both literal and metaphorical, requiring us to examine what beliefs, relationships, and values we've allowed to dictate our emotional stability.

In place of the fallen cards, we lay bricks—solid, enduring, and reliable. These bricks are made from our experiences, our learned resilience, and the wisdom garnered from each challenge faced. Unlike the cards, these bricks are not easily swayed by the opinions of others or the changing winds of fortune. They are the embodiment of our growth, each one a testament to a lesson learned or a trial overcome.

With these bricks, we begin to construct our emotional fortress. This fortress does not isolate us from the world but instead provides a sanctuary of strength from which we can engage with life more fully. Its walls are built with self-esteem, its foundation laid on self-awareness, and its battlements fortified by a deep-seated belief in our own worth.

The design of this fortress is unique to each individual, reflecting personal values, goals, and the essence of who we are. Some might construct towering spires of ambition, while others build expansive courtyards of openness and vulnerability. The architecture of our emotional fortress is a reflection of our deepest self, designed not for show but for genuine living.

Within the fortress, we create rooms for reflection, halls of celebration, and gardens of tranquility. These spaces are carved out for the various aspects of our emotional lives, each designed to nurture and sustain us. They remind us that strength does not come from avoidance but from the ability to face life with courage and grace.

The emotional fortress is not impervious to the gales of life's challenges, but it is infinitely more resilient than the house of cards. When storms approach, as they inevitably will, this fortress stands firm, its foundations deep, and its walls sturdy. We may feel the wind and rain, but we remain unbroken, sheltered within the strength of our own construction.

Building this fortress is not a one-time endeavor but a lifelong project. With each new experience, we add another brick, expand a room, or fortify a wall. It is a testament to our ongoing growth, a structure that evolves as we do, ever becoming stronger, wiser, and more resilient.

While built for strength, our emotional fortress is not a place of solitude. The gates are open to those who respect its boundaries and cherish its creator. Within its walls, we forge connections that are deep and meaningful, relationships built on mutual respect, understanding, and genuine affection.

Ultimately, the emotional fortress we build is the greatest symbol of our inner strength. It stands as a monument to our journey from fragility to resilience, from chaos to clarity. It is here, within these walls, that we find our true selves, unshaken by the world outside, and fully prepared to engage with life from a place of strength, wisdom, and peace.

The Emotional Stock Exchange

In the emotional stock exchange, your feelings are the currency, and you're the trader. Explore the intricate world of emotional regulation, the Wall Street of your inner landscape. Invest wisely, hedge against emotional crashes, and become the Warren Buffett of your own emotional energy.

Picture your emotions as stocks, each with its own market value. Emotional regulation is your personal Wall Street, where you decide which stocks to buy, sell, or hold. It's a tumultuous market, but with the right strategies, you can navigate the highs and lows like a seasoned trader.

Within your emotional stock exchange, you play the roles of both the emotional broker and the market analyst. You analyze market trends in your feelings, deciding when to invest heavily in joy, diversify into calmness, or short-sell the anxiety stock. It's a delicate balance, and emotional regulation is the key to keeping your portfolio in the green.

Emotions, like stocks, have their bulls and bears. The bull market of happiness and the bear market of sorrow ebb and flow. Emotional regulation isn't about eradicating the bears but about managing them wisely, understanding that both are essential players in the emotional stock exchange.

Ever had an emotional margin call? It's that moment when your emotional debts exceed your emotional assets, and you're at risk of an emotional crash. Emotional regulation involves making strategic investments to avoid these margin calls, ensuring your emotional portfolio remains robust.

Some days, you're a day trader in the stock market of emotions. Emotional regulation means recognizing that not every feeling requires a long-term investment. Some are fleeting, and attempting to hold onto them indefinitely is like trying to day trade in a volatile market—risky and often counterproductive.

Beware of emotional insider trading—those moments when you let external influences dictate your emotional investments. Emotional regulation requires an internal compass, guarding against the whims of societal trends, ensuring your emotional trades align with your authentic values.

Just as a savvy investor diversifies their financial portfolio, emotional regulation involves diversifying your emotional assets.

Don't put all your emotional eggs in one basket. Spread your investments across joy, resilience, love, and yes, a few carefully chosen risks.

Think of emotional regulation as long-term financial planning for your inner self. What emotional goals do you have for the future? Where do you want to be emotionally in five, ten, or twenty years? Strategic emotional regulation involves aligning your daily trades with these long-term objectives.

Emotional regulation encounters its own interest rates—the rates at which you invest emotional energy in various aspects of your life. Some emotions may have high interest rates, demanding significant attention and care. Others may have lower rates, allowing you to allocate emotional resources more freely.

Imagine an Emotional Dow Jones, an index that reflects the overall health of your emotional portfolio. Emotional regulation ensures that, despite the inevitable market fluctuations, your Emotional Dow Jones remains resilient, weathering the storms and bouncing back with a bullish spirit.

Ever find yourself emotionally bankrupt in the wrong currency? Emotional regulation involves navigating the currency exchange of feelings, ensuring that your emotional investments are aligned with your authentic self rather than being swayed by external pressures.

Create emotional hedge funds to protect your emotional investments. Emotional regulation is about anticipating potential emotional downturns and having strategies in place to mitigate risks. These hedge funds act as a safety net, preventing emotional crashes and fostering overall emotional stability.

Introduce Emotional IPOs (Initial Public Offerings) when you're ready to share new emotional aspects of yourself with the world. Emotional regulation allows you to carefully select which emotions to take public, ensuring that your emotional stock doesn't experience a sudden crash on the emotional market.

Your Emotional 401(k) is your long-term emotional investment plan. Emotional regulation involves contributing regularly to this plan, making conscious decisions that align with your emotional retirement goals. It's the recognition that emotional wealth isn't built overnight but through consistent, intentional investments.

Develop emotional trading strategies that suit your unique risk tolerance and preferences. Emotional regulation isn't a one-size-fits-all endeavor. Experiment with different strategies—value investing in gratitude, momentum trading in joy, or contrarian investing in self-compassion.

Even the most skilled emotional traders may face bankruptcy at times. Emotional regulation is about acknowledging these moments, allowing yourself to recover, and learning from the experience. It's a dynamic process that embraces the highs and lows of emotional capitalism.

Enjoy the emotional dividends of your wise investments. Emotional regulation leads to a portfolio that pays dividends in the form of well-being, resilience, and a profound sense of self-awareness. It's the enduring reward for consistently making shrewd emotional choices.

Conduct ongoing emotional market research. Emotional regulation requires staying informed about your internal market conditions. Regularly assess the performance of your emotional stocks, adjust your strategies, and remain vigilant for emerging emotional trends.

Celebrate the emotional bull markets—the periods of heightened positivity and flourishing emotions. Emotional regulation involves savoring these moments, allowing them to bolster your emotional wealth and provide a buffer against the inevitable emotional downturns.

As we conclude our exploration of the emotional stock exchange, consider the legacy of your emotional investments. Emotional regulation isn't just a present-day endeavor; it's a gift to your future self. With strategic investments and conscious trading, you're creating a lasting legacy of emotional well-being and resilience. May your emotional stock continue to rise, and may your inner trader navigate the twists and turns of the emotional market with wisdom and audacity.

Forging Your Own Path

Society hands us a worn-out script, a dog-eared manual of how to seamlessly blend into the mundane background of the status quo. It's the same script passed down through generations, and it's about time we tossed it into the bonfire of rebellion. Welcome to the unruly pages of "F*ck the Status Quo," where we'll strip naked, dive into the deep end of nonconformity, and emerge baptized in the refreshing waters of unapologetic authenticity.

The status quo is a symphony of sameness, a predictable melody that echoes through the corridors of tradition. It's the comfort zone where everyone is handed the same sheet music, and deviations are met with disapproving glances. But here's the truth: the most extraordinary compositions are born when the notes dance to the rhythm of rebellion.

Picture a carnival where conformity is the headlining act, and we're all reluctantly wearing matching clown costumes. It's a masquerade where individuality is sacrificed on the altar of societal expectations. "Fit in or be cast out" echoes through the carnival speakers, but we've got our own playlist, and it's time to crank up the volume.

Deep within every soul, there's a rebel waiting to break free. It's the part of us that craves authenticity, that hungers for the unconventional, and that refuses to be molded into society's predetermined mold. Let's dig deep into our rebel roots and unearth the seeds of nonconformity.

There's an undeniable allure to rebellion, a magnetic force that draws us away from the monotonous humdrum of the status quo. It's the siren song of individuality, tempting us to sail our ships into uncharted waters where the seas are rough, but the treasures are worth the risk.

From the moment we take our first steps, invisible puppet strings attach themselves to our limbs. These strings, woven from societal expectations, guide our movements and dictate our choices. It's time to grab a pair of scissors, cut those strings, and pirouette into the spotlight of our true selves.

Equipped with a rebellion toolbox, we'll dismantle the expectations, one screw at a time. It's filled with wrenches of authenticity, hammers of self-expression, and screwdrivers of unapologetic individuality. Let's tinker with the machinery of conformity until it grinds to a rebellious halt.

Liberation awaits on the other side of unconformity. It's a vast landscape where the air is thick with the scent of freedom and the ground is fertile for the seeds of authenticity. Liberation through unconformity is a journey of self-discovery, an expedition into the unexplored territories of our true selves.

The playbook society hands us is dog-eared and outdated, a relic of a bygone era. It's time to shred that playbook, tear it to pieces, and use its remnants to fuel the flames of rebellion. In the absence of a script, we become the playwrights of our own narratives.

In the rebellion against the status quo, chaos becomes our trusted companion. It's an unpredictable dance where missteps are celebrated, and wrong turns lead to unexpected discoveries. Embracing the unpredictable chaos is like salsa dancing through a hurricane—wild, exhilarating, and utterly freeing.

Defying normalcy is an art form—a brushstroke of defiance on the canvas of the mundane. It's about turning ordinary into extraordinary, mundane into extraordinary, and normal into a rebellious masterpiece. Let's dip our brushes in the paint of nonconformity and create our own vivid strokes.

Every rebel needs a rebellion wardrobe, a collection of attire that screams individuality. Say farewell to the uniformity of the status quo and embrace a wardrobe filled with eclectic pieces that tell the story of your rebellion. It's time to strut down the runway of life, draped in the fabrics of nonconformity.

On the frontline of rebellion, fearlessness is our armor. It's a shield that deflects the arrows of judgment and ridicule, allowing us to march forward with heads held high. The fearless frontline is where the battle against the status quo unfolds, and victory belongs to those unafraid to stand out.

The status quo clings to an unwritten rulebook—a set of guidelines etched into the collective consciousness. In our rebellion, we'll write our own rulebook, a manifesto of authenticity, creativity, and the audacity to be different. Let's toss the status quo's rulebook into the fire and watch the flames of our rebellion roar.

Eccentricity is the rebel's anthem, a melody that resonates with the unconventional. It's the heartbeat of nonconformity, the rhythm that propels us forward in our journey against the status quo. Let's compose an ode to eccentricity, celebrating the beautifully bizarre and the wonderfully weird.

In the rebellion against the status quo, we're not just breaking chains; we're breaking norms. It's a symphony of shattered expectations, a cacophony of societal restrictions crumbling to the ground. Breaking chains, breaking norms—this is the rhythm of our liberation.

Authenticity paints our rebellion with bold brushstrokes, each stroke a declaration of selfhood. It's time to dip our brushes into the vibrant hues of our true selves and unleash the artistry of authenticity. The canvas of rebellion awaits, and every stroke adds to the masterpiece.

In the rebellion against the status quo, we usher in a renaissance—a rebirth of individuality, creativity, and unbridled freedom. It's a cultural shift where the mundane is replaced by the extraordinary, and the echoes of rebellion reverberate through the corridors of societal norms.

As rebels, we form an unseen alliance—a coalition of nonconformists united by the desire to shatter the chains of the status quo. Together, we amplify our voices, creating a chorus of rebellion that echoes across the landscapes of conventionality. The unseen rebel alliance is a force to be reckoned with.

In the wake of our rebellion, echoes linger—whispers of nonconformity that inspire others to embark on their own journeys against the status quo. These echoes are the legacy of our rebellion, a testament to the indelible mark we leave on the canvas of societal expectations.

As we gaze toward the uncharted horizon of nonconformity, a sense of exhilaration courses through our veins. It's a frontier waiting to be explored, an expansive territory where the compass of rebellion points us toward new possibilities. The uncharted horizon beckons, and with every step, we redefine the boundaries of what's possible. This is the essence of "F*ck the Status Quo"—a relentless exploration of the uncharted, a rebellion against the ordinary, and a celebration of the extraordinary.

The Drumbeat You Can't Ignore

Unfurl your banner, don your armor of self-expression, and charge into the battlefield of life. This act is not for the faint-hearted; it's a battle cry, a rallying call to embrace your truest self, adorned with the badge of courage. So, tighten your bootstraps and prepare to raise your f*cking banner high.

Before we charge into the battlefield, let's establish the preamble: personal truth. Your banner is not a flag of conformity; it's a symbol of personal truth. It's time to cut through the noise and declare, "This is who I am, unapologetically."

Imagine your banner as a tapestry woven with threads of individuality. Each thread represents a unique trait, a quirky passion, a scar earned through life's battles. This tapestry is not about perfection; it's about the rich, messy beauty of being authentically you.

As you raise your banner, listen to the drumbeat of authenticity. It echoes the rhythm of your genuine self, drowning out the cacophony of societal expectations. This drumbeat is the pulse of your courage, propelling you forward with every heartfelt step.

The battlefield is strewn with norms and expectations, but your battle cry against them reverberates like thunder. Let the world know that your authenticity is a force to be reckoned with. Shatter the norms and dance amidst the debris.

In the thick of battle, your banner becomes a shield of unwavering self-respect. It deflects the arrows of judgment and criticism. Courage is not about being impervious; it's about standing tall despite the wounds and scars.

Authenticity wears the armor of vulnerability. It's a paradox—exposing your true self requires courage, and yet, vulnerability is the strongest armor against the superficial arrows aimed at your authenticity. Raise your banner, vulnerable and unafraid.

Picture your banner as the gauntlet of unfiltered expression. It's time to throw down the gauntlet and declare that you won't be shackled by societal filters. Authenticity is not a whisper; it's a roar that echoes across the battlefield.

As your banner flutters in the winds of adversity, it becomes a battle-tested crest of resilience. The storms of life may sway it, but it stands firm. This resilience is the backbone of authenticity, refusing to be broken by the turbulence of external judgment.

Before entering the battlefield, don the war paint of self-love. It's not about arrogance; it's about acknowledging your worthiness. As you raise your f*cking banner, let the world see the colors of self-love streaked across your face.

In the chaos of the battlefield, your banner serves as a beacon of belonging. It attracts those who resonate with your authenticity, creating a tribe bound by the shared language of genuine self-expression. Courage is not a solitary pursuit; it's a collective battle.

At the top of your banner, fly the pennant of imperfection. Embrace the truth that authenticity is not flawless—it's beautifully imperfect. Your battle cry echoes with the acceptance of your quirks, scars, and the unpolished edges that make you uniquely human.

As you march forward, recognize that the battlefield is also the trenches of self-discovery. Each step is an exploration, revealing more layers of your authentic self. Courage is not a destination; it's the continuous journey of self-unveiling.

Your banner carries the horn of defiance, a clarion call challenging the status quo. Authenticity is an act of rebellion against the prescribed roles and masks imposed by society. Let the horn blare, announcing your refusal to conform.

Fearlessness is your battle standard, carried high on your banner. It's not the absence of fear but the audacity to confront it head-on. Courage thrives in the face of fear, and your banner is a testament to the fearless authenticity you embody.

In the heat of battle, listen for the echoes of battle cheers. Those who witness your authenticity will raise their own banners, creating a symphony of cheers that reverberates across the battlefield. Authenticity is not a solo act; it's a chorus of individual voices rising in unison.

Hold the scepter of unapologetic authority as you raise your f*cking banner. This is not about dominance over others; it's about asserting your right to be authentically, unapologetically you. The scepter signifies the sovereignty of your self-expression.

As you charge forward with your banner, infuse each step with the valiant charge of intention. Authenticity is not a passive state; it's a deliberate choice. With every stride, declare your intention to live authentically, even if it means navigating the thorns of discomfort.

Above your banner shines the guiding star of conviction. It illuminates the path of authenticity, casting light on the darkest corners of self-doubt. Authenticity requires conviction—the unwavering belief that being true to yourself is worth the battles fought.

In the aftermath of the battlefield, let your banner lead the victory march of self-approval. This is not seeking external validation; it's about approving of the authentic self you see in the mirror. The greatest victory is the one you achieve within.

As you lower your banner at the end of each day, recognize its legacy in the tapestry of humanity. Your authenticity contributes a unique thread, weaving into the larger narrative of human experience. The courage to raise your f*cking banner is not just a personal triumph; it's a gift to the collective story of authenticity.

Congratulations, fearless warrior. You've not only raised your banner but also left an indelible mark on the battlefield of authenticity. The world is richer for your courage, and your banner will forever flutter in the winds of genuine self-expression. Until the next battle, keep marching to the beat of your own drum, with your f*cking banner held high.

Week 2 Action Plan: Cultivating Connections and Creative Chaos

Welcome to Week 2 of "Orchestrating Impact: Conducting Life's Symphony with Purpose and Resilience." This week, we delve into the heart of human connections, embrace the beauty of creative chaos, and learn to navigate the complex emotional landscapes of our lives. Let's continue to build your resilience and impact with purpose.

Day 1: "The Art of Creative Chaos"
- **Activity:** Identify a current problem or project. Spend 30 minutes brainstorming creative, unconventional solutions or ideas. Embrace wild, out-of-the-box thinking without judgment.
- **Reflection:** How did embracing creative chaos shift your perspective or approach?

Day 2: "The Jungle of Human Connection"
- **Activity:** Reach out to someone with whom you want to deepen your connection. This could be through a meaningful conversation, a shared activity, or a heartfelt message.

- **Reflection:** Reflect on the nature of this connection. How does it contribute to your life's symphony?

Day 3: "The Unhealthy Connections"
- **Activity:** Reflect on your relationships and identify any that may be draining or counterproductive to your well-being. Plan a gentle but firm conversation or action to redefine or release these connections.
- **Reflection:** How does the process of addressing or releasing unhealthy connections make you feel?

Day 4: "The Emotional Stock Exchange"
- **Activity:** Track your emotional investments throughout the day. Note moments or interactions that significantly lift or lower your spirits. Evaluate if these investments align with your values and goals.
- **Reflection:** Which emotional investments are yielding positive returns, and which are costing you?

Day 5: "Forging Your Own Path"
- **Activity:** Spend time visualizing your ideal path forward in life or career. Create a vision board or write a detailed description of this path, focusing on what feels authentic and fulfilling.
- **Reflection:** In what ways does this vision challenge the status quo of your current trajectory?

Day 6: "The Drumbeat You Can't Ignore"
- **Activity:** Identify a passion or cause that resonates deeply with you but you've been neglecting. Outline the first three steps you can take to integrate this more fully into your life.
- **Reflection:** How does focusing on this passion or cause reinvigorate your sense of purpose?

Day 7: Weekly Integration
- **Activity:** Review your activities and reflections from the week. Write a letter to your future self, describing what you've learned and how you hope to apply these insights moving forward.
- **Reflection:** Reflect on the growth you've experienced this week. How has your understanding of human connections and creative chaos deepened?

This week has been a journey through the landscapes of connection and creativity, crucial components of orchestrating impact with resilience. Each step taken is a note added to your symphony, enriching its melody and harmony. Prepare for Week 3, where we will explore further dimensions of your purpose and resilience.

Where Every Voice is Heard

Life is not a monochrome canvas; it's a riot of colors, and each hue represents a unique human experience. The Rainbow Coalition of significance is not about conformity but celebrating the kaleidoscope of diversity that paints the canvas of existence.

Imagine life as a grand symphony, and every individual is a note contributing to the overture of uniqueness. Diversity is not a discordant cacophony; it's the harmonious blend of varied melodies creating a masterpiece that resonates through the ages.

The echo chamber is not a confined space; it's a boundless expanse where every voice reverberates, creating a rich tapestry of significance. Respect for diversity is the key that opens the door to this chamber, inviting in perspectives that broaden the horizons of understanding.

In the great tapestry of humanity, each thread represents a human story. Some threads are bold and vibrant, while others are subtle and intricate. Respect for diversity is the loom that weaves these threads into a tapestry that tells the tale of our shared existence.

Life is not a one-dimensional painting; it's a mosaic of perspectives, each piece contributing to the larger picture. Respect for diversity is the glue that holds this mosaic together, ensuring that every shard, no matter how different, finds its place in the intricate design.

Picture the garden of human experience, where every flower, no matter how unconventional, adds to the overall beauty. Respect for diversity is the gardener's touch, nurturing each unique bloom and allowing the fragrance of individuality to permeate the air.

In the symphony of life, contrasts create the most captivating movements. Respect for diversity is the conductor's wand, orchestrating a harmonious dance between the high notes and the low, the fast beats and the slow, to compose a melody that resonates with richness.

Cultures are not separate entities; they're ingredients in the grand recipe of human existence. Respect for diversity is the culinary skill that blends these ingredients, creating a feast of cultural fusion where every flavor is savored, and no palate is left untouched.

Life's cauldron is not about homogenizing; it's about simmering with the diverse ingredients that give it flavor. Respect for diversity is the flame beneath the pot, ensuring that each element retains its distinct taste, contributing to the delectable stew of existence.

Consider life as an ever-expanding canvas waiting to be painted by the brushes of diverse perspectives. Respect for diversity is the palette that offers an array of colors, allowing each stroke to create a masterpiece that reflects the intricate beauty of collective human artistry.

Diversity speaks a language that transcends words; it's a silent conversation where gestures, expressions, and experiences become the dialects. Respect for diversity is the translator that decodes this language, fostering understanding and building bridges where communication flows effortlessly.

Life's dance floor is vast, and every individual is invited to twirl to the rhythm of their own song. Respect for diversity is the open invitation, ensuring that no one is left sitting on the sidelines, and the dance becomes a celebration of varied styles, steps, and stories.

Picture a quilt where every patch is a unique identity, stitched together to create warmth and comfort. Respect for diversity is the needle and thread, sewing a quilt of acceptance that wraps around us all, offering solace in the embrace of collective understanding.

Belonging is not about fitting into a mold; it's about finding your place in the vast panorama of humanity. Respect for diversity is the panoramic lens that captures the breadth of this landscape, ensuring that every individual is seen, valued, and embraced.

Life is a voyage where we sail on the seas of each other's emotions. Respect for diversity is the compass that guides this voyage, steering us towards the shores of empathy where we anchor our understanding and embark on shared journeys of compassion.

In the echo chamber of significance, every voice is not just heard; it's empowered to resonate. Respect for diversity is the amplifier that ensures each voice, no matter how soft, carries weight and contributes to the powerful reverberation that defines our collective significance.

Life is a prism that refracts the light of experiences into a spectrum of colors. Respect for diversity is the prism itself, allowing the light of varied perspectives to shine through, creating a dazzling display of understanding, acceptance, and shared humanity.

At the crossroads of diversity lies intersectionality, where identities intersect and weave a complex tapestry. Respect for diversity is the cartographer's pen, mapping the intricacies of this terrain and ensuring that every intersection is acknowledged, celebrated, and navigated with care.

Imagine an open-air forum where ideas, no matter how unconventional, are welcomed, debated, and celebrated. Respect for diversity is the moderator, ensuring that this forum remains a space where every idea, opinion, and perspective contributes to the robust exchange of thoughts.

Let the anthem of unity in diversity echo in your spirit. It's a melody of acceptance, a rhythm of understanding, and a chorus of embracing the rich tapestry of human experience. Stand tall, fearless reader, in the kaleidoscope of significance, where every voice, every story, and every identity contributes to the symphony of shared humanity.

That Dissonant Note

Welcome to the tempest, the rollercoaster, the cosmic carnival of chaos we affectionately call life. Today, we're strapping on our boots, adjusting our sails, and diving headfirst into the turbulent waters of adversity. This ain't your grandma's tea party; it's a gritty, irreverent exploration of how to ride the storm with the swagger of a resilient badass.

Picture this: adversity is the thunderous overture in life's symphony. It's the part where the sky cracks open, and you're drenched in rain, yet you stand there, middle fingers to the heavens, ready for whatever chaotic melody life decides to throw your way.

Adversity, my friend, is the sh*tstorm, the unexpected downpour that leaves you drenched in challenges. But guess what? We're not here with umbrellas; we're here to dance in the rain, to revel in the absurdity of the storm, and emerge on the other side with stories that would make the gods themselves jealous.

Adversity is the uninvited guest that crashes your carefully planned party. It stumbles in, spills red wine on your white carpet of tranquility, and laughs in the face of your well-orchestrated plans. But hold up, because we're not reaching for the broom to sweep it away. No, we're offering it a seat and saying, "Pour yourself a drink, adversity, let's see what you've got."

Resilience is the rumble in the pit of your stomach when adversity throws its best punches. It's the gut-check moment, where you decide whether to cower or unleash the beast within. We're not talking about a polite tap dance; we're talking about a full-blown mosh pit of resilience, where you come out bloody, but victorious.

Adversity, my friend, is the opponent on the mat, ready to grapple. Resilience, on the other hand, is the slick jiu-jitsu master, flipping adversity on its head with grace and precision. We're not here to shy away from the fight; we're here to execute a flawless jiu-jitsu move and emerge with a triumphant grin.

Life is a novel, and adversity is the plot twist that leaves you questioning the author's sanity. But here's the kicker: we're not tossing the book aside in frustration; we're flipping the pages with anticipation, eager to see how this unexpected twist propels the narrative forward.

Resilience is the rebellion, the middle finger raised against the unjust regime of adversity. It's the refusal to be crushed, the insistence on standing tall when everything around you crumbles. This ain't a passive resistance; it's a full-blown rebellion, and you're the fearless leader.

Life's a comedy, and adversity is the punchline that catches you off guard. Resilience, however, is the stand-up comedian who turns the joke on its head, transforming tears into laughter. We're not sitting in the audience; we're stealing the mic and delivering the punchline with a comedic finesse that leaves the universe in stitches.

Adversity may be the storm, but resilience is the rock anthem that blares through the thunder. It's the guitar solo that pierces through the chaos, reminding you that, in the face of adversity, you're the headlining act. So, grab that air guitar, my friend, and let's rock through the challenges like the resilient rockstars we are.

Life throws adversity at you like a relentless boot camp, testing your mettle and pushing you to your limits. Resilience, then, is the badass drill sergeant who turns your pain into strength, your struggles into muscle. We're not here to whimper through boot camp; we're here to conquer it, emerge battle-hardened, and flex our resilience muscles.

Adversity is the adventure that takes unexpected turns, complete with plot twists and cliffhangers. Resilience, however, is the daring adventurer who navigates the treacherous terrain with a smirk, embracing the thrill of the unknown. We're not seeking the safe and predictable path; we're diving headlong into the adventure, ready for whatever the journey throws our way.

Resilience, my friend, is the battle cry that echoes through the valleys of adversity. It's the roar that shakes the foundations of despair, the call to arms that rallies your inner warriors. We're not whispering sweet lullabies to adversity; we're screaming our battle cry, declaring that we're here for the fight, and we're here to win.

Life's a symphony, and adversity is the dissonant note that threatens to derail the melody. Resilience, however, is the conductor who transforms that dissonance into a powerful crescendo. We're not covering our ears to drown out the disharmony; we're conducting the symphony, turning adversity's chaos into our masterpiece.

Adversity may be the harsh winter, but resilience is the spring that follows, ushering in the renaissance of your spirit. It's the blossoming of strength from the frozen ground of challenges. We're not shivering in the cold of adversity; we're basking in the warmth of resilience, knowing that the seasons of life may change, but our resilience remains evergreen.

Life's a rollercoaster, and adversity is the stomach-churning drop that leaves you breathless. Resilience, however, is the fearless rider who throws their hands in the air, embracing the exhilaration of the freefall. We're not gripping the safety bar with white-knuckled fear; we're throwing ourselves into the twists and turns, relishing the unpredictable ride.

Adversity leaves its scars, but resilience turns them into badges of honor. They're not wounds to be concealed; they're marks of survival, reminders that you've stared adversity in the face and emerged undefeated. We're not covering our scars with shame; we're wearing them proudly, like battle-scarred warriors with stories etched into our skin.

Life throws adversity at you like raw material, and resilience is the alchemist who turns the base metal into gold. It's the transformation of challenges into opportunities, the ability to find the hidden gems in the rubble. We're not drowning in the raw material of adversity; we're wielding the alchemist's wand, turning it into the gold of resilience.

Adversity may be the oppressive regime, but resilience is the rebellion that refuses to be oppressed. It's the uprising against the tyranny of challenges, the fight for freedom from the chains of despair. We're not cowering in the face of adversity's dictatorship; we're leading the rebellion, unfurling the banner of resilience, and marching towards victory.

Adversity is the raw canvas, and resilience is the artisan who paints a masterpiece with the vibrant hues of survival. It's the creation of beauty from the chaos, the ability to turn adversity into a work of art. We're not staring at the blank canvas with trepidation; we're picking up the brush of resilience and creating a masterpiece that tells the story of our strength.

Adversity may set the race, but resilience runs the victory lap. It's the triumphant sprint across the finish line, arms raised in celebration of the challenges conquered. We're not limping to the end with exhaustion; we're sprinting with the energy of resilience, crossing the finish line with a grin that says, "I faced adversity, and I emerged victorious."

So, fellow adventurer, embrace the storm, dance in the rain, and let resilience be your swagger in the face of adversity. Life may throw its challenges, but with resilience as your compass, you'll ride the waves, conquer the mountains, and emerge on the other side stronger, wiser, and unapologetically resilient.

Investing in Vintage Experiences

We're about to embark on a celestial decluttering journey, sorting through the cosmic junk and investing in the vintage experiences that make our souls sing. It's time to set some intergalactic boundaries and ensure that the only baggage we carry is a suitcase full of epic memories. Grab your stardust broom; we're sweeping away the unnecessary and making room for the extraordinary.

Picture the universe as your cluttered attic, filled with boxes of f*cks you never needed. It's time to toss those boxes into the black hole of irrelevance. The cosmic clutter conundrum ends here, and we're stepping into the spacious expanse of a clutter-free cosmos.

We're at the galactic garage sale, where f*cks are the items on display. Picture yourself as the savvy shopper, strolling through the aisles of cosmic junk. The goal? To declutter your emotional space and invest in experiences that outshine even the rarest celestial gems.

Celestial decluttering is an art form, my friends. It's about letting go of the emotional bric-a-brac that's been collecting cosmic dust. Imagine yourself as the curator of your own museum, carefully selecting the exhibits that deserve a place in your heart's gallery.

Envision a black hole, not as a cosmic menace, but as a magnificent vacuum cleaner sucking up the unnecessary f*cks. Watch as they spiral into oblivion, leaving behind a trail of stardust that forms a new constellation—a constellation of freedom from irrelevant worries.

Think of your past f*cks as items tossed into the intergalactic dumpster fire of irrelevance. Picture the flames dancing with the ferocity of your determination to be free from the emotional baggage. Stand back, marvel at the blaze, and feel the warmth of newfound liberation.

Have your own celestial Marie Kondo moment. Hold each f*ck in your emotional hands and ask, "Does this spark joy?" If the answer is no, toss it into the cosmic recycling bin. Streamline your emotional space until it's a minimalist masterpiece, devoid of unnecessary clutter.

Imagine creating an interstellar no-f*cks zone around your mental space. This force field repels the irrelevant, leaving only the essential. It's your cosmic fortress against emotional clutter, a sanctuary where vintage experiences can flourish without the interference of cosmic noise.

As you declutter, witness the birth of the nebula of emotional freedom. Picture it as a vibrant cloud of colors, each hue representing a f*ck you've liberated yourself from. This nebula becomes your emotional masterpiece, a breathtaking display of boundary-setting prowess.

Set astral boundary stones in the cosmic terrain of your life. Envision them as markers that delineate the territory where your f*cks are invested. Anything beyond these stones is the great unknown, an expanse free from the gravitational pull of unnecessary emotional baggage.

Once the decluttering is complete, step into the vintage experience bazaar. Picture it as a bustling marketplace where the currency is meaningful moments. Invest your emotional energy in the rare, the extraordinary, and the vintage experiences that appreciate with time.

Imagine a time-traveling carousel, each horse representing a vintage experience. As the carousel spins, the horses carry you through the corridors of cherished memories. This is the ride of a lifetime, fueled by the energy of well-invested f*cks and vintage experiences.

Consider your emotional energy as a cosmic investment portfolio. Allocate your f*cks wisely, diversify into vintage experiences, and watch your emotional wealth grow. It's the interstellar version of a financial advisor whispering, "Invest in what truly matters."

Create a celestial meditation garden within the landscape of your mind. Picture it as a serene space adorned with vintage experiences, a place where you can retreat to find solace. As you meditate, let the energy of well-spent f*cks rejuvenate your cosmic essence.

Become a pioneer in the emotional minimalism movement. Envision a world where everyone declutters their emotional spaces, investing in vintage experiences rather than drowning in unnecessary f*cks. It's a cosmic revolution, and you're leading the charge.

Host a stargazing soiree within the galaxy of your soul. Picture the stars as vintage experiences, each one with its own tale to tell. Invite fellow celestial travelers to share in the cosmic feast, and bask in the glow of well-spent emotional energy.

Imagine your empowered boundaries as a quasar—a powerful, radiant force in the cosmic landscape. As you declare your emotional sovereignty, watch the quasar pulsate with the energy of self-respect and the refusal to be bogged down by unnecessary cosmic debris.

Nurture your nebula of emotional freedom with a cosmic ritual. Picture yourself as the guardian of this celestial masterpiece, ensuring that each vintage experience is tended to with care. This ritual becomes a sacred practice of honoring the moments that truly matter.

As you navigate the cosmic garage sale, install the warp-drive of emotional resilience. Picture it as the engine propelling you through the universe of life's challenges. With vintage experiences as your fuel, you'll traverse the galaxies with a speed and grace that transcends the gravitational pull of negativity.

Consider the legacy you're leaving in the cosmic archives. Envision it as a tapestry woven with the threads of vintage experiences and well-spent f*cks. This legacy is a testament to your commitment to live authentically, unburdened by the cosmic clutter that ensnares so many.

As you sail into the cosmic sunset of liberation, feel the gentle breeze of emotional freedom. Picture the horizon painted with the hues of vintage experiences, each one contributing to the masterpiece of your life. This, my celestial comrades, is the journey of navigating the cosmic garage sale—decluttering f*cks and embracing the boundless beauty of well-chosen, vintage moments.

Life Without Rose-Tinted Glasses

The grittiest corner of self-help, where the air is thick with realism, and rose-tinted glasses are banned at the door is where we find ourselves. In a world drowning in positivity, we're here to throw you a lifeline of unfiltered reality. Buckle up for a journey through the messiness of life, where we embrace the chaos with a dose of realistic optimism.

Positivity, like glitter, seems to be sprinkled over everything these days. It's a pandemic infecting self-help aisles, promising a perpetual state of bliss. Well, we're the immune response, the rebels with antibodies against the positivity pandemic. It's time to peel off the glitter and face the messiness underneath.

Life isn't a neatly wrapped gift; it's a messy package with frayed edges and unexpected contents. Let's unveil the messy truth, strip away the shiny paper, and confront the raw and unfiltered reality lurking beneath the surface. Realistic optimism starts with acknowledging the mess.

If life were a sitcom, perpetual happiness might be plausible. But alas, it's more like a tragicomedy with plot twists that leave us questioning the screenwriters. Realistic optimism doesn't promise eternal sunshine; it hands us an umbrella and teaches us to dance in the rain of life's unpredictability.

Imagine a duel between the positivity fairy and the reality check goblin. Spoiler alert: the goblin wins every time. Realistic optimism isn't about banishing the goblin; it's about acknowledging its existence, having a cup of coffee with it, and learning to appreciate its dark humor.

Life's emotions aren't confined to a neatly organized color wheel. They're a messy palette, a Jackson Pollock painting of joy, sorrow, anger, and everything in between. Realistic optimism isn't about whitewashing the canvas; it's about embracing the vivid and chaotic strokes that make the masterpiece of our existence.

In the realm of self-help, realistic optimism often feels like the ugly duckling—an outlier among the glossy swans of unbridled positivity. Let's celebrate our ugly duckling, for it grows into a swan that can navigate the murky waters of life with resilience and authenticity.

Realistic optimism introduces us to the Zen of chaos—a philosophy that doesn't seek to eliminate chaos but teaches us to find serenity within it. Life's messiness is the chaotic symphony we learn to appreciate, not a problem to be solved. Grab your conductor's baton; we're composing a masterpiece.

Life is often described as a dumpster fire, and we're the firefighters armed with realism. Realistic optimism doesn't extinguish the flames; it teaches us to roast marshmallows in the heat, finding moments of warmth and camaraderie amid the chaos.

Imperfection is the fingerprint of authenticity. Realistic optimism is the art of finding beauty in the cracks, appreciating the flawed pottery of our lives. Let's raise a glass to the perfectly imperfect, for in our messiness, we discover the true masterpiece.

Balance, that mythical balance beam, is a challenge we're all expected to master. Realistic optimism replaces the beam with a wobbly tightrope—a thrilling, nerve-wracking journey where occasional falls are not failures but lessons in equilibrium.

Resilience isn't about bouncing back from setbacks as if they were mere speed bumps. Realistic resilience acknowledges that some potholes are deep, and the road to recovery might include detours. It's not the absence of struggle but the ability to wade through the mess with determination.

In the world of realistic optimism, we're dumpster divers, scavenging for lessons amid life's discarded challenges. Each bruise, each scrape is a treasure waiting to be unearthed. We don't fear the mess; we dive into it headfirst, equipped with curiosity and a flashlight.

Life is a jigsaw puzzle with missing pieces, and we're the realists patiently sifting through the scattered fragments. Realistic optimism is about acknowledging that some pieces may never be found, and the incomplete picture is still a masterpiece worth appreciating.

In the gym of raw reality, we're not pumping iron to achieve perfection. Realistic optimism is the personal trainer urging us to lift the weights of life's challenges, acknowledging that some days, the dumbbells feel heavier than usual. It's not about flawless fitness but enduring strength.

Life's soundtrack is a bittersweet symphony—a melody that echoes the highs and lows. Realistic optimism teaches us to savor the sweetness without denying the bitterness. It's a symphony where the minor notes are as crucial as the major ones, creating a harmonious whole.

Compassion meets realism on the canvas of life. Realistic optimism doesn't demand perfection; it extends a compassionate hand to our imperfect selves. It's a hug in the face of failure, a nod in acknowledgment of our messy endeavors.

Self-help often peddles the myth of the perfect self—a flawless, Instagram-filtered version of who we should be. Realistic optimism scrapes off the filters, revealing the unedited self, scars and all. It's not about self-improvement but self-acceptance.

Look into the unfiltered mirror of realistic optimism. Life's messiness stares back, and instead of turning away, we embrace the reflection. Realistic optimism isn't about pretending the mirror is flawless; it's about seeing the beauty in the cracks and crevices.

Realistic optimism acts as a truth serum—a potion that strips away the illusions and reveals life's messy truths. It's not a magic elixir that erases difficulties but a tonic that fortifies us to face the messiness with open eyes and resilient hearts.

As we journey through the manifesto of realistic optimism, let's swear an oath—not to avoid the messiness, not to wear rose-tinted glasses, but to confront life authentically. We pledge allegiance to the messy truth, embracing it with a realistic optimism that transforms chaos into a beautifully imperfect masterpiece.

Blind to the Gems

In the vast ocean of life, it's time to dive beyond the shallows and explore the depths of an Abundance Mindset. Forget the kiddie pool of scarcity thinking; we're about to embark on a deep-sea expedition into a world where limitations dissolve, and the currency is boundless optimism.

Picture scarcity thinking as the abyss, a place where every opportunity seems like a shipwreck waiting to happen. It's the Bermuda Triangle of the mind, where dreams vanish into thin air. But fear not; we're navigating beyond this treacherous territory.

As we set sail into the ocean of possibility, let's embrace the concept that abundance isn't just a mindset—it's a lifestyle. Abundance is the recognition that the sea of opportunities is vast and unexplored, and you're equipped with a ship that can weather any storm.

Your perception is the ship sailing these waters. Scarcity thinking is like navigating with a leaky dinghy; it'll get you somewhere, but you'll be bailing water the whole way. Abundance mindset? That's a sleek, state-of-the-art vessel cutting through waves with purpose.

Beware the pirates of limitation that lurk in scarcity waters. These thieves steal dreams, plunder potential, and leave you with the scraps of what could have been. It's time to raise the Jolly Roger of abundance and repel those who'd hijack your aspirations.

In the treasure chest of abundance, gratitude is the map leading to the riches of contentment. Scarcity thinkers are blind to the gems scattered around them; abundance thinkers recognize and appreciate the treasures, no matter how small.

Opportunities are the coral reefs of abundance, teeming with life and vibrant potential. While scarcity thinkers avoid these reefs, fearing they might get stuck, abundance thinkers dive in, knowing that every twist and turn holds a chance for growth and discovery.

Generosity echoes through the abundance mindset like sonar guiding a pod of dolphins. Scarcity thinkers hoard their provisions, fearing they'll run out. Abundance thinkers understand that the more they share, the more they receive in return.

Resilience is the rising tide that lifts the abundance ship. Scarcity thinkers are shipwrecked by setbacks; abundance thinkers ride the waves, knowing that each ebb and flow brings new opportunities to set sail again.

Creativity is the submarine exploring the depths of abundance. Scarcity thinkers fear the unknown, staying afloat in the shallows. Abundance thinkers dive deep, discovering uncharted territories and unveiling the wonders hidden beneath the surface.

Positivity is the deep-sea current propelling the abundance vessel forward. Scarcity thinkers are adrift in the stagnant waters of negativity. Abundance thinkers catch the currents, navigating challenges with a forward momentum fueled by optimism.

Fear, the leviathan of the mind, lurks in scarcity-infested waters. Abundance thinkers don't deny the existence of this sea monster; instead, they face it head-on, using its presence as a compass guiding them toward uncharted territories.

Self-belief is the bioluminescence illuminating the dark expanses of abundance. In scarcity's shadows, self-doubt reigns. Abundance thinkers, however, radiate with the inner glow of confidence, lighting their path even in the murkiest depths.

Beware the sirens of comparison singing their scarcity lullabies. Abundance thinkers plug their ears to the tune of "not enough" and chart their course based on the compass of personal fulfillment.

Purpose is the celestial navigation system guiding the ship of abundance. Scarcity thinkers drift aimlessly, at the mercy of unpredictable currents. Abundance thinkers set their course by the stars of purpose, knowing exactly where they're headed.

Mindfulness are the shoals that protect the ship of abundance from crashing into the rocks of anxiety. Scarcity thinkers navigate blindly, crashing into obstacles. Abundance thinkers, aware of every ripple, navigate the waters with mindful precision.

Affirmations echo through the abundance mindset like sonar guiding a pod of dolphins. Scarcity thinkers believe in the scarcity of positive outcomes. Abundance thinkers use affirmations to create positive echoes, attracting opportunities like a magnet.

Growth is the archipelago that dots the abundance seascape. Scarcity thinkers fear change; abundance thinkers see each challenge as a new island to explore, every experience a stepping stone toward personal evolution.

Fulfillment is the song echoing across the abundance horizon. Scarcity thinkers hear only silence. Abundance thinkers, however, let the melody of fulfillment guide them, composing a life that resonates with joy, purpose, and accomplishment.

In the northern lights of abundance, possibility dances across the sky. Scarcity thinkers see a barren night; abundance thinkers witness a celestial spectacle of potential. It's not about the scarcity of stars; it's about the abundance of constellations.

As we conclude our deep-sea exploration, the once daunting abyss of scarcity thinking transforms into the cosmos of abundance. Beyond the shallows, where scarcity anchors dreams, lies an infinite universe where optimism reigns, opportunities abound, and the abundance mindset becomes the guiding star in the navigation of life's boundless ocean.

No Rehearsed Speeches

The dance floor of authenticity awaits, where the beats are raw, the moves are genuine, and the spotlight reveals the unfiltered you. This isn't about tiptoeing around the rhythm of societal norms; it's about grooving to your unique melody and tossing conformity out the window.

Imagine this dance as the ballad of Unapologetic You. It's not about striking poses for an invisible audience; it's about throwing open the doors of your authenticity and waltzing to the tune of your true self.

The Cha-Cha of Self-Expression awaits, and the dance floor is yours. Authenticity isn't a carefully choreographed routine; it's the spontaneous sway of hips, the twirls of unfiltered thoughts, and the rhythm of courageous self-expression.

Step into the Tango with Vulnerability, where authenticity isn't a mask but a dance with exposed hearts. It's about embracing the raw beauty of imperfection and daring to lead with your truest self, flaws and all.

The Breakdance of Transparency is where authenticity spins on its head. No smoke, no mirrors—just the raw, unfiltered truth. It's about exposing the gritty details, showcasing the bruises, and letting the world see the real you.

In the Waltz of Unfiltered Thoughts, authenticity takes the lead. No scripted lines, no rehearsed speeches—just the genuine sway of your ideas pirouetting across the dance floor. It's a dance where thoughts waltz freely, unburdened by societal filters.

Let's hit the Jive of Fearless Choices. Authenticity isn't about playing it safe; it's about kicking up dust, leaping into the unknown, and making choices that resonate with the beat of your heart.

Dip into the Salsa of Genuine Emotions, where authenticity isn't a poker face but a dance of real feelings. It's about swaying to the rhythm of joy, twirling with passion, and stomping through the storms of authentic emotions.

Enter the Hip-Hop of Radical Acceptance. Authenticity doesn't judge; it embraces. It's about accepting yourself, your quirks, your scars, and letting them become part of the freestyle dance that is your life.

Swing into the Swing of Bold Declarations. Authenticity is loud, proud, and unafraid to declare its presence. It's about boldly announcing your values, standing firm in your beliefs, and orchestrating a symphony of authenticity that reverberates through the crowd.

Now, slide into the Electric Slide of Unwavering Integrity. Authenticity and integrity are dance partners. It's about maintaining consistency in your values, gliding through challenges with grace, and illuminating the dance floor with the unwavering light of your principles.

In the Foxtrot of True Connections, authenticity leads. It's about forging connections without a mask, engaging in genuine conversations, and creating a dance of meaningful relationships that stand the test of time.

Reggae to the Reggae of Soulful Purpose. Authenticity finds its groove in purpose. It's about dancing to the rhythm of a purposeful life, swaying with the melody of meaningful goals, and letting your life be a reggae anthem of authenticity.

Now, pirouette into the Ballet of Compassionate Understanding. Authenticity isn't a solo act; it's a duet with compassion. It's about understanding others, gracefully gliding through differences, and creating a ballet of harmony on the dance floor of relationships.

Line dance into the Line Dance of Boundless Creativity. Authenticity thrives in creativity. It's about expressing your unique dance moves, stepping outside the prescribed choreography, and creating a line dance of boundless possibilities.

Feel the Breakbeat of Unconventional Choices. Authenticity doesn't follow a set rhythm; it's the breakbeat that disrupts the monotony. It's about making choices that defy expectations, breaking free from conformity, and composing your own rebellious soundtrack.

In the Samba of Fearless Self-Love, authenticity takes center stage. It's about swaying to the rhythm of self-love, celebrating your uniqueness, and samba-ing through life with confidence and a heart full of self-appreciation.

Jazz it up with the Jazz of Unapologetic Boundaries. Authenticity isn't afraid to set boundaries. It's about improvising the notes of self-respect, creating a jazz of assertiveness, and ensuring that the dance floor of your life respects your rhythm.

Embark on the Charleston of Genuine Resilience. Authenticity waltzes through challenges with resilience. It's about swinging through adversity, tap-dancing through setbacks, and performing the Charleston of genuine strength.

Sway into the Rumba of Ever-Evolving Growth. Authenticity embraces growth. It's about slow-dancing with change, twirling with new experiences, and engaging in the rumba of continuous, ever-evolving self-improvement.

Conclude with the Rock 'n' Roll of Authentic Rebellion. Authenticity rebels against the status quo. It's about headbanging to your own anthem, rocking the boat of conformity, and concluding the dance of authenticity with a rebellious encore.

So, dance on, authentic soul. Let your rhythm be the guiding light, and may your dance floor be filled with the unapologetic authenticity that sets your spirit free.

Week 3 Action Plan: Deepening Authenticity and Embracing the Uncharted

Welcome to Week 3 of "Orchestrating Impact: Conducting Life's Symphony with Purpose and Resilience." This week, we focus on deepening our authenticity, embracing life's uncharted territories, and fostering resilience amidst life's unpredictability.

Day 1: "Where Every Voice is Heard"
- **Activity:** Host a small group discussion with friends or family, focusing on a topic where diverse opinions are encouraged. Practice active listening and ensure each voice is heard and valued.
- **Reflection:** How did this activity challenge or change your perspectives?

Day 2: "That Dissonant Note"
- **Activity:** Reflect on a recent experience that felt uncomfortable or challenging. Explore the lessons it offered and how it contributed to your growth.

- **Reflection:** What beauty or growth can you find in the discomfort of dissonant notes in your life?

Day 3: "Investing in Vintage Experiences"
- **Activity:** Identify one experience you've longed to invest in but have postponed or neglected—something that promises to enrich your life significantly, akin to a celestial gem. Commit to making this experience a reality, planning the first step you will take to bring this gem into your life's constellation.
- **Reflection:** Reflect on the celestial gem you've chosen to invest in. Why is this experience valuable to you, and how do you anticipate it will enrich your life?

Day 4: "Life Without Rose-Tinted Glasses"
- **Activity:** Spend the day consciously avoiding the tendency to romanticize or gloss over the more challenging aspects of your life. Face them head-on with honesty and courage.
- **Reflection:** How does embracing life's realities, without the rose-tinted glasses, alter your approach to challenges?

Day 5: "Blind to the Gems"
- **Activity:** Identify something or someone in your life you've taken for granted. Acknowledge its/his/her value and express gratitude in a meaningful way.
- **Reflection:** How does shifting your focus to the overlooked gems in your life change your feelings of gratitude and appreciation?

Day 6: "No Rehearsed Speeches"
- **Activity:** Engage in a conversation where you consciously avoid planning what to say next and be vulnerable and transparent. Allow the dialogue to flow naturally, responding authentically in the moment.

- **Reflection:** How does the absence of rehearsed speeches and daring to lead with your truest self, flaws and all affect the authenticity and depth of your conversations?

Day 7: Weekly Integration
- **Activity:** Review the week's activities and reflections. Create a piece of art (writing, painting, music) that represents your journey into deeper authenticity and embracing life's realities.
- **Reflection:** Reflect on your growth this week. How has embracing authenticity and life's uncharted territories enriched your experience?

This week's journey has been about embracing the full spectrum of life's experiences, learning to listen deeply, and celebrating the authenticity that each moment brings. As you prepare for Week 4, remember that each step taken is a step closer to conducting a life's symphony that resonates with the depth, balance, and resonance of your true self.

The Humble Reminder

We boldly declare independence from the shackles of the fear of failure. This isn't just about brushing off apprehension; it's about turning fear into fuel, failure into fertilizer for growth, and proving that the journey matters as much as the destination.

Failure is not an adversary; it's your rogue companion on the journey of life. Embrace it like the unpredictable ally it is, always teaching, always pushing you toward evolution.

F*ck the myth that failure puts you under an unforgiving spotlight. In reality, the spotlight is on those who dare greatly, even if it means stumbling in the process. Let them watch; you're too busy conquering.

Fear of failure is fearing the unknown. Yet, every adventurer knows the allure of uncharted territory. Consider failure your map to the undiscovered lands of personal triumphs.

The fear of failure often stems from a society fixated on cookie-cutter success stories. F*ck that narrative. Your story is an original masterpiece, with plot twists and setbacks that make it uniquely yours.

Failure holds up an honest mirror, reflecting where you stumbled, where you need to grow. Embrace this mirror; its clarity is the first step toward self-improvement.

Picture failure as a musical note in the symphony of resilience. It's not the end; it's a transition to the next powerful chord. Let the symphony play on; your resilience is the melody.

Fear of failure can induce stagnation, trapping you in a comfort zone that's more like a padded cell. F*ck that. Life's an adventure, not a prison sentence.

Consider failure the university where wisdom is earned. The tuition is high, but the lessons are priceless. The most enlightened souls proudly display their scars from this university.

The fear of failure makes you avoid shooting for the stars. Become the fearless stargazer who, even if they miss, lands on a moon of unexpected victories.

Fear of failure births mediocrity. Break free from the mediocre chains, aim for the extraordinary, and let failure be the stepping stone, not the stumbling block.

Failure is the fertile soil where innovation grows. Let your failures be the seeds that sprout into the innovative landscape of your life.

Fear of failure often stems from the illusion of perfection. F*ck perfection. Embrace the messy, the flawed, the beautifully imperfect reality that is uniquely yours.

Fear of failure is like hesitating on a tightrope. F*ck that. Become the fearless tightrope walker, arms wide open, ready to embrace the exhilarating dance of success and failure.

Fear of failure is a self-imposed prison. Embrace failure, and suddenly the cell door swings open, offering liberation from the confines of fear.

Fear of failure often echoes the doubts of others. F*ck that noise. Let your courage be the booming voice that silences the echoes and forges a path of audacious endeavors.

Consider failure the canvas on which your character is painted. Each stroke of failure adds depth, resilience, and a unique hue to the masterpiece that is you.

Fear of failure makes you hesitate as the architect of your dreams. F*ck hesitation. Grab the blueprints, design the grandest structures, and let failure be the scaffolding that elevates your dreams.

Failure humbly reminds you that you're human. It's not a mark of weakness; it's a testament to your willingness to strive, to dream beyond the safety of the known.

Fear of failure is essentially fear of the unknown. F*ck fearing the unknown. Embrace it. Dance with it. Let the unknown be the thrilling backdrop of your daring adventures.

Rise fearlessly from the ashes of failure, let the doubters watch in awe, and soar to heights you once thought unreachable. The fear of failure has met its match—you. The odyssey continues.

It Glitters Like the Sun

Distractions are the shiny objects that glitter in the sun, tempting you to veer off your course. They're the sirens of the modern age, singing songs of immediate gratification and pulling you into the rocky shores of procrastination. But fear not, for the adaptable sailor knows when to plug their ears and steer clear of the mesmerizing melody.

Picture this: distractions are the Bermuda Triangle of productivity. Sail too close, and your time, energy, and focus disappear without a trace. The adaptable sailor, armed with a map of priorities, knows how to navigate these perilous waters and emerge unscathed.

Distractions are cunning pirates, silently boarding your ship of productivity when you least expect it. They plunder your time and make off with the treasures of your attention. But the adaptable sailor is no stranger to a well-placed cannonball of focus, ready to fend off these marauders and protect the ship's precious cargo.

In the digital age, distractions are the digital sirens, singing songs of notifications, social media, and endless cat videos. The adaptable sailor, with a firm grip on their smartphone wheel, sails through these treacherous waters with purpose, refusing to be lured by the siren call of the virtual abyss.

Ah, multitasking, the deceptive dance of distractions. It promises efficiency but leads to a chaotic jig of half-done tasks and a shipwreck of focus. The adaptable sailor knows when to put on the brakes, opting for the deliberate waltz of single-tasking, steering clear of the frenetic distractions on the dance floor.

Distractions are the mermaids of procrastination, beckoning you to the sunlit shores of delay. The adaptable sailor, wise to the enchanting melody of procrastination, stays the course with a steadfast gaze on the horizon of deadlines and goals.

Ah, FOMO, the whispers of distractions. Fear of Missing Out tugs at your anchor, urging you to set sail for every social gathering and online trend. The adaptable sailor, with a sturdy anchor of priorities, knows when to say "no" to FOMO and "yes" to the journey they've charted for themselves.

Distractions are rogue waves, rising unexpectedly to rock your ship of concentration. The adaptable sailor, nimble on their mental feet, learns to ride these waves with grace, maintaining equilibrium and ensuring that their ship sails true.

Distractions often wear the disguise of urgency, masquerading as matters demanding immediate attention. The adaptable sailor, with a discerning eye for genuine urgency, doesn't let the illusion divert them from their true course. They navigate the waters of urgency with precision, distinguishing between the tempest and the mere ripples.

Distractions are chameleons, blending seamlessly into the background of your day. The adaptable sailor, with a keen eye for the ever-changing hues of distractions, spots these sneaky creatures and adjusts their course accordingly.

Picture focus as a symphony, each instrument playing in harmony to create a masterpiece. Distractions, then, are the off-key notes threatening to disrupt the symphony. The adaptable sailor conducts this symphony with finesse, silencing the discordant distractions to ensure a harmonious performance.

Distractions are mischievous winds, blowing you off course with their whims. The adaptable sailor, skilled in the art of trimming sails and adjusting the rigging, harnesses these winds to propel their ship forward rather than being tossed aimlessly.

In the sea of distractions, purpose is your GPS, guiding you to your destination with unwavering precision. The adaptable sailor, firmly plugged into their purpose, navigates through the cluttered waters, making intentional course corrections and avoiding the magnetic pull of distractions.

Distractions are mirage islands, promising respite but revealing themselves as illusions upon approach. The adaptable sailor, well-versed in the art of navigation, recognizes these mirages and stays focused on the true landmarks of their journey.

Distractions are the juggling balls of the overwhelmed performer, threatening to drop and scatter your focus. The adaptable sailor, a master juggler, keeps their eye on the most important balls, gracefully tossing aside the distractions that don't contribute to the grand performance of their goals.

Distractions are the quicksand of productivity, pulling you down with their subtle allure. The adaptable sailor, with a lifeline of discipline, knows how to traverse this tricky terrain, avoiding the sinking pitfalls and forging ahead with purpose.

Imagine distractions as the battlefield, and your focus as the warrior fighting for dominance. The adaptable sailor, armed with the sword of resilience, charges into the fray, cutting through the distractions that threaten to overpower their attention.

Distractions are time bandits, pilfering precious moments when you least expect it. The adaptable sailor, a vigilant guardian of time, fends off these bandits, ensuring that each moment contributes to the epic tale of their journey.

Distractions create a maze of endless options, enticing you to wander aimlessly. The adaptable sailor, equipped with a mental compass, follows their true north, slicing through the maze with purpose and direction.

Distractions are shooting stars, brief and dazzling but ultimately fleeting. The adaptable sailor, with their eyes on the constellations of long-term goals, appreciates the beauty of distractions without being blinded by their transient glow.

In the ever-shifting seas of distractions, the adaptable sailor remains the master of their ship, navigating with purpose, resilience, and a steadfast commitment to the course they've charted. Stay vigilant, fellow sailor, for in the mastery of adaptability, you find the true compass that guides you through the unpredictable tides of life.

Courageous Self-Expression

It's time to grab the sledgehammer of authenticity and smash to bits the delicate china around us. Imagine this as a rebellious act of redecorating your life—tossing out the generic IKEA furniture and replacing it with the bold, handcrafted pieces of courageous self-expression. Ready to embark on this wild journey of liberation? Let's dive in.

Society loves to play interior designer with our lives, handing us a mood board labeled "Expectations." Well, guess what? This isn't an episode of HGTV, and you don't need to follow their renovation plans. It's time to demolish the expectation trap and build a home that screams, "This is me!"

The IKEA Syndrome is a common ailment, infecting us with the belief that life comes with a one-size-fits-all manual. But who wants a life that looks like every other cookie-cutter existence on the block? F*ck that noise. It's time to assemble our lives with the unique pieces that resonate with our souls.

Imagine life as a DIY project, and you're the fearless craftsman. F*ck the prefabricated blueprints society hands you. Courageous self-expression is about sketching your own damn blueprint, complete with trapdoors, secret passages, and rooms painted in the vibrant hues of your individuality.

Life is a symphony, and societal expectations are the off-key notes threatening to ruin the melody. Courageous self-expression is the conductor's wand, orchestrating a symphony that resonates with the authentic beats of your heart. Picture it: a standing ovation for the uniqueness of your composition.

If societal expectations were a fortress, courageous self-expression is the battering ram crashing against its walls. It's the rebellion of individuality, refusing to be confined within the narrow parameters of what society deems acceptable. Tear down the walls; let the sunlight of your authenticity flood in.

Imagine a manifesto written with middle fingers held high, a declaration that societal expectations can go take a long walk off a short pier. Courageous self-expression is the ink that scrawls this manifesto, proclaiming that you're not here to meet anyone's expectations but your own.

Visualize a bonfire fueled by societal expectations. Throw in the rulebook, the "shoulds" and "musts" that society loves to prescribe. Watch the flames dance with the ferocity of your defiance. Courageous self-expression is the fuel, turning the expectation bonfire into a blaze of liberation.

Courageous self-expression is the banner of the authenticity revolution. It's about waving that banner high, leading the charge against the conformity militia. Picture a sea of people, each brandishing their unique flags of self-expression, marching to the rhythm of their own rebellious drumbeats.

In a world obsessed with paint-by-numbers, courageous self-expression follows the Picasso Principle. It's about embracing the chaos of individuality, allowing the paint to splatter where it may. Reject the paint-by-numbers life; instead, wield your paintbrush like a fearless artist creating the masterpiece of your existence.

Courageous self-expression is a guerilla warfare campaign against the regimented army of expectations. It's about guerrilla gardening your own life, planting seeds of authenticity in the barren soil of societal conformity. Watch as your garden blossoms into a riot of colors that defy the grayscale expectations.

Picture a demolition derby where societal expectations are the rusty old cars and courageous self-expression is the powerhouse on wheels. Rev up your engines and crash through the expectations, leaving behind a trail of liberated dust. Let the roar of your authenticity echo through the arena.

Courageous self-expression is the couture fashion show of your life. Strut down the runway wearing garments made of audacity, draped in the fabrics of your unique personality. F*ck the off-the-rack expectations; this is a bespoke fashion show where you're the designer, the model, and the roaring applause.

Ever feel trapped in a labyrinth of societal expectations? Courageous self-expression is the map leading to the exit. It's about carving your escape route with a machete of authenticity, hacking through the suffocating vines of "shoulds" and "supposed tos" until you're standing in the open field of your own liberation.

Courageous self-expression is the graffiti sprayed across the walls of societal norms. Grab your cans of authenticity paint and tag the cityscape of conformity. Let your rebellious graffiti be a reminder to everyone that the streets are meant to be painted in the vibrant hues of individuality.

Imagine courageous self-expression as the exorcism ritual, casting out the societal demons that possess your authenticity. It's about wielding the authenticity crucifix and banishing the expectations that haunt your every step. Picture the liberation as the demons dissipate into the ether.

Courageous self-expression is a serenade played with a sledgehammer. It's the melody that shatters the glass walls of expectations, letting the symphony of your authenticity reverberate through the shattered pieces. Grab your sledgehammer; it's time to play your courageous tune.

Picture a rebellion anthem, echoing through the streets, inspiring others to join the expectation rebellion. Courageous self-expression is the bassline that reverberates in the chests of the rebels, inviting them to dance to their own beats and sing their own anthems of defiance.

Courageous self-expression is the thunderstorm that breaks the oppressive heat of societal expectations. Picture the lightning of your authenticity illuminating the dark clouds of conformity. Let the rain wash away the societal residue, leaving behind the cleansed landscape of your liberated life.

From the ashes of societal expectations, courageous self-expression births the expectation phoenix. Watch as it rises, its wings made of the feathers of your audacity. Let it soar through the skies, leaving a trail of fiery rebellion in its wake. The phoenix is your emblem, a symbol of your resurrection from the expectations' ashes.

Courageous self-expression is the grand finale of the freedom fireworks. Picture the night sky ablaze with the colors of your individuality. Each explosion is a declaration of your independence from the dull, monotonous expectations. As the last firework fades, stand in the radiant glow of your courageous self-expression, knowing you've forged your own path, painted your own masterpiece, and danced to the rhythm of your own rebellious drum.

The Wild, Unrestrained Extravaganza of Life

On the dance floor of life, we're about to tango. This isn't your grandma's tea dance; it's a wild, unrestrained extravaganza where generosity takes the lead. So, grab your cosmic dance shoes, because we're about to groove.

Imagine life as an intergalactic dance floor, pulsating with the beats of opportunities, challenges, and unexpected twists. You're not a wallflower; you're the star of this cosmic ball. The dance floor is where the magic happens, where the art of conscious f*ck-giving transforms each step into a masterpiece.

Visualize generosity as the galactic DJ spinning tunes that resonate with the rhythm of the universe. It's not about throwing handfuls of f*cks like confetti; it's about choosing the perfect moments to sprinkle that cosmic generosity, creating a symphony of goodwill and positive vibes.

Picture the dance of conscious fck-giving as an intricate tango. It's not about stumbling through the steps; it's about the mindful, intentional exchange of energy. Each fck given is a deliberate step, a twirl that adds grace to the dance of life.

Contrary to the rigid routines of traditional dances, imagine the dance floor of life as an unchoreographed chaos of authenticity. It's about throwing away the rulebook and dancing to the beat of your own heart. Authenticity becomes your signature move, and generosity is the rhythm that guides your steps.

For too long, many of us have been cosmic wallflowers, hesitant to hit the dance floor of generosity. It's time for liberation. Shed the self-consciousness, kick off the doubts, and waltz into the center of life's dance floor with the radiant glow of generosity illuminating your every move.

Visualize the dance of conscious fck-giving as a free-form waltz, unrestricted by societal norms. This isn't about following the rigid patterns of expectation; it's about twirling through life with the freedom to give a fck where your heart truly calls for it.

Imagine selfless acts as the salsa beats reverberating through the cosmic dance floor. The sizzle of generosity spices up the routine, infusing your every move with passion and purpose. It's not about performative gestures; it's about a genuine desire to contribute to the rhythm of positivity.

Envision the dance floor illuminated by the disco ball of random acts of kindness. Each glint of light represents a small f*ck given selflessly, creating a dazzling display of compassion. It's not about choreographed sequences; it's about the spontaneous brilliance of making someone's day.

Picture bold benevolence as the breakdance moves that defy gravity on life's dance floor. It's about flipping the script, challenging the status quo, and giving a f*ck in ways that leave an indelible mark on the cosmic dance of existence.

See charitable contributions as the cha-cha-cha beats that add rhythm to your life's dance. It's not about dancing around issues; it's about confidently stepping into the arena of giving, cha-cha-cha-ing through obstacles, and leaving behind a trail of positive impact.

Imagine transformative giving as the tango that leads to profound change on life's dance floor. Each deliberate step of generosity becomes a pivot point, turning the ordinary into the extraordinary. It's the dance that doesn't just follow the rhythm; it orchestrates it.

Visualize fearless compassion as the flamenco, where each stomp on the dance floor resonates with the courage to give a f*ck even in the face of adversity. It's about dancing through challenges with the fiery passion of unwavering compassion.

See anonymous acts of kindness as the moonwalk, gliding through the dance floor without seeking recognition. It's not about spotlight moments; it's about the smooth, subtle gestures that leave a lasting imprint on the cosmic dance of human connection.

Envision helping hand grooves as the hiphop beats that sync with the pulse of generosity. It's about the rhythmic cadence of offering assistance, aligning your movements with the beats of compassion, and creating a vibe that encourages others to join the dance.

Picture benevolent boundaries as the ballet leaps that gracefully navigate the dance floor. It's not about overextending; it's about the elegance of giving a f*ck within the bounds of self-care. Each plié becomes a reminder that generosity can coexist harmoniously with personal limits.

Imagine joyful contribution as the jitterbug, infusing the dance floor with infectious energy. It's about the joy that emanates from giving a f*ck where it matters most. The jitterbug of generosity is a celebration, a dance that radiates positivity in every swing and sway.

Visualize empathy as the electrifying electric slide that sends shockwaves through the dance floor. It's about gliding into the shoes of others, feeling the rhythm of their experiences, and responding with a compassionate slide into their emotional space.

See loving gestures as the Lindy Hop, a dance of genuine affection that adds a skip to your cosmic step. It's about the joyful bounces of expressing love and care, creating a rhythm that resonates with the interconnectedness of the human experience.

Imagine well-timed fcks as the waltz, a dance of precision and purpose. It's not about the frantic pace of constant giving; it's about the deliberate, well-timed steps that align with the music of meaningful moments. The waltz of conscious fck-giving is a masterpiece of intentional generosity.

The cosmic swan song of generosity echoes through the vast expanse of existence, leaving an indelible mark on the cosmic dance floor of life. It's not just a dance; it's a legacy of meaningful fcks given, a testament to the profound impact one can have by choosing to dance with generosity in every step. Now, my fellow cosmic dancers, go out there and create your own masterpiece on life's dance floor, where the art of conscious f*ck-giving becomes a symphony of connection and compassion.

Not Your Grandma's Library

Alright, knowledge junkies and wisdom seekers, buckle up because we're about to embark on a wild ride through the landscape of continuous learning. This isn't your grandma's library visit; it's a rebellious expedition into the uncharted territories of intellectual growth.

Let's shatter the illusion right out of the gate. The myth of the know-it-all is a one-way ticket to intellectual stagnation. Think you've got it all figured out? Well, think again. The sculptor's chisel is ever-sharp, ready to carve new insights into the marble of your mind.

Consider the sculptor's chisel has many uses. It's also the ultimate tool in the pursuit of continuous learning. Its purpose? To chip away at the block of ignorance and reveal the masterpiece of a well-informed, ever-evolving individual. Embrace the chisel; let it be the soundtrack to your intellectual symphony.

Your mind is an unfinished sculpture, and the sculptor's chisel is your instrument of refinement. Don't settle for a lumpy, half-formed statue of knowledge. Let the chisel dance across the contours of your mind, shaping and reshaping until your intellectual masterpiece emerges.

In the world of continuous learning, be the humble stonecutter, not the arrogant sculptor. The chisel is your ally, not your weapon. Approach the vast quarry of knowledge with humility, ready to chisel away the excess and embrace the beauty of discovery.

Picture the continuous learner as a conductor in the symphony of curiosity. The sculptor's chisel is your baton, guiding the orchestra of your interests. Let the music of discovery play on, and conduct your intellectual pursuits with the passion of a maestro.

Your library isn't a dusty, forgotten space; it's the rebel's headquarters for continuous learning. The sculptor's chisel rests on the shelves, waiting for you to pick it up and chisel away at the layers of ignorance. Make your library the fortress of intellectual rebellion.

The sculptor's chisel encounters resistance in the form of challenges and difficulties. Embrace the resistance; it's the tension that sharpens the chisel. The path of continuous learning isn't always smooth, but the chisel becomes more effective with every obstacle it overcomes.

Continuous learning isn't just about acquiring; it's also about unlearning. The sculptor's chisel is versatile—it chips away at outdated beliefs and carves space for fresh perspectives. Unlearn the obsolete, and let the chisel sculpt a mind open to new possibilities.

Knowledge isn't a flat canvas; it's a sculpture with curves and edges. The sculptor's chisel navigates the nuanced terrain of diverse subjects, carving intricate details into your understanding. Explore the nooks and crannies of knowledge with the precision of a seasoned sculptor.

Become the artisan of adaptability with the sculptor's chisel as your tool of transformation. The world evolves, and so should your mind. Let the chisel be the catalyst for adapting to new information, molding your intellect into a dynamic and resilient masterpiece.

Continuous learners are living encyclopedias, not dusty tomes on forgotten shelves. The sculptor's chisel is the quill that updates your pages with the ink of fresh insights. Transform into a walking, talking compendium of knowledge, the embodiment of the sculptor's ongoing work.

Learning is a collage of perspectives, and the sculptor's chisel assembles the pieces. Embrace diversity in thought; let the chisel carve pathways between different viewpoints. Your mind's collage should be vibrant, a testament to the sculptor's ability to weave threads of understanding.

Every stroke of the chisel echoes through the corridors of your intellect. Make each reverberation count. With every book read, every course taken, and every conversation engaged in, let the chisel's echo resonate with the harmonious melody of intellectual growth.

Continuous learning is the Sisyphean task of pushing the boulder of ignorance up the hill. The sculptor's chisel is your secret weapon against the weight of the unknown. Keep pushing, keep chiseling; the view from the peak is worth the effort.

Like a signature on a masterpiece, the chisel leaves its mark on your evolving intellect. Cherish the marks of growth, the scars of challenges met and conquered. Let the sculptor's chisel be the artist's tool that signs your name on the ever-expanding canvas of knowledge.

Become the Atlas of learning, carrying the weight of knowledge on your shoulders. The sculptor's chisel is your map, guiding you through the vast terrain of information. Shoulders squared, chisel in hand, venture into the intellectual wilderness with the confidence of a seasoned explorer.

Even the sculptor's chisel needs rest. Continuous learning isn't a sprint; it's a marathon. Allow the chisel moments of respite, where the mind can absorb and integrate the lessons learned. A rested chisel is a sharper, more effective tool in the pursuit of wisdom.

Expertise is a mosaic crafted by the sculptor's chisel. Each shard of knowledge contributes to the masterpiece of your understanding. Don't be afraid to explore different facets; let the chisel shape you into a polymath, a mosaic of intellectual versatility.

Your mind is the sculptor's workshop, a bustling space of intellectual creation. The chisel isn't gathering dust; it's in constant motion, shaping the raw material of information into a work of art. Transform your mental workshop into a haven for the continuous pursuit of wisdom.

The legacy of a continuous learner is written in the strokes of the sculptor's chisel. What will your intellectual sculpture reveal about the journey of continuous learning? Let the legacy be one of insatiable curiosity, relentless growth, and a mind sculpted by the unwavering dedication to the art of knowledge.

And there you have it, disciples of the sculptor's chisel, the symphony of continuous learning. May your minds be ever-malleable, your chisels ever-sharp, and your intellectual sculptures an ongoing testament to the vibrant journey of the eternal learner.

The Oracle Within

Get ready to plunge into the mystical depths of intuition, the secret compass that guides us through the uncharted waters of self-awareness. Picture this as your own personal fortune telling, but with a penchant for irreverence and a splash of swashbuckling wisdom.

Intuition, my fellow seekers, is the mystic's brew, not a concoction of eye of newt and dragon scales, but a subtle elixir brewed in the cauldron of self-awareness. Drink deep, for this potion reveals the hidden currents beneath the surface of our consciousness.

Ever felt the whispering winds of intuition brushing against your soul? It's not some ethereal breeze; it's the universe sharing its secrets. Tune in, dear reader, and let the winds carry you to realms unknown, guided by the quiet nudges of your inner sage.

Think of intuition as a pirate's parley, a clandestine meeting between your conscious mind and the mysterious depths within. It's not a negotiation; it's an understanding—an unspoken pact that propels you forward on your journey with the wisdom of your inner captain.

Sailors of old had a sixth sense for imminent storms. Intuition is your seafarer's sixth sense, not predicting the weather, but navigating the storms of life. Listen keenly to its warnings, and you'll steer clear of treacherous waters.

Imagine your life as a grand symphony. Intuition is the conductor, not rigidly following the sheet music, but improvising, leading the orchestra of your experiences into harmonious melodies. Let your inner symphony play, and dance to the rhythm only you can hear.

In the vast darkness of uncertainty, intuition is the unseen lighthouse guiding ships home. It's not a fixed beacon; it's a flickering light that urges you to trust your inner navigation. Sail confidently into the unknown, for your intuition is your guiding star.

Intuition speaks in riddles, not because it enjoys playing games, but because the language of the soul is nuanced. Decipher the riddles with patience, and you'll unravel the mysteries of your own existence, charting a course through the enigmatic depths within.

Think of intuition as a dowsing rod searching for authenticity. It's not leading you to hidden springs; it's guiding you to the wellspring of your true self. Trust in its movements, for authenticity is the source of unyielding strength.

Gaze into the oracle's mirror, not to glimpse the future, but to reflect on the present. Intuition is the mirror that reveals your deepest desires and fears. Look unflinchingly, for self-awareness is the first step towards mastery.

Sometimes intuition wears the mask of an inner jester, not to trick you, but to nudge you towards joy. Embrace the playfulness, dance with the jesters of intuition, and let laughter be the wind in your sails.

Intuition echoes the wisdom of your experiences. It's not a detached oracle; it's a mirror reflecting the lessons learned from the tapestry of your past. Let those echoes guide you, for within them lies the map to self-awareness.

Gut feelings are the alchemy of intuition, not mere stomach rumblings but the transformation of subtle whispers into instinctive knowing. Digest these feelings, and you'll metabolize the elixir of profound self-awareness.

Just as sailors navigated by the stars, let intuition be your navigational stars. They're not distant suns; they're the celestial guides within, mapping the constellations of your desires and dreams. Sail confidently by their light.

Opportunities carry a distinct scent only intuition can detect. It's not a fragrance in the conventional sense, but a nuanced aroma of possibilities. Inhale deeply, follow the scent, and you'll find yourself on the shores of newfound potential.

For the rebellious souls, intuition is the compass that defies the conventional maps. It's not pointing north; it's guiding you off the beaten path. Trust the rebel within, for sometimes the detours are the most enlightening.

Creativity dances in the whispers of intuition. It's not a silent muse; it's a relentless companion inspiring your artistic endeavors. Listen intently, for within the muse's whispers lies the wellspring of boundless creativity.

In the symphony of life, intuition conducts the movements of silence. It's not a void to be feared; it's the pregnant pause before the crescendo. Embrace the silence, for within it, you'll hear the most profound truths.

Sometimes intuition leads in silent rebellion against the noise of societal expectations. It's not a protest; it's a gentle reminder to chart a course authentic to your own desires. Rebel quietly, and you'll find your true north.

Navigators had a code; intuition has its own. It's not etched in stone; it's written on the parchment of your soul. Follow its unwritten rules, and you'll discover the uncharted territories of your self-awareness.

Envision yourself as the captain of your own ship, standing tall with a salute to the guiding force within. Sail forth, intrepid captains, through the seas of self-awareness, with intuition as your eternal compass. May your journey be as vast and mysterious as the boundless ocean itself.

Week 4 Action Plan: Embracing Your Unique Journey and Mastering Balance

Welcome to the final week of "Orchestrating Impact: Conducting Life's Symphony with Purpose and Resilience." This week, we focus on celebrating your unique journey, mastering the balance in life's complexities, and solidifying the lessons learned for lasting impact.

Day 1: "The Humble Reminder"

- **Activity:** Identify a recent setback or failure you've encountered. Reflect on the journey that led there, acknowledging where you started, the progress and growth you experienced, and the lessons learned. Recognize and honor the journey, not just the endpoint.
- **Reflection:** Consider the value of this setback as a "humble reminder". Reflect on how acknowledging and learning from our failures can help maintain a grounded perspective and

foster gratitude for the journey, regardless of its ups and downs. How does embracing these humble reminders contribute to your personal growth and resilience?

Day 2: "It Glitters Like the Sun"

- **Activity:** Consciously confront your Fear Of Missing Out (FOMO) for the entire day. Whenever you feel the tug of FOMO—perhaps when seeing social media posts or hearing about events you're not attending—acknowledge it, then redirect your focus to the value of your current activities or the choice to enjoy solitude or different company.
- **Reflection:** Reflect on your experience. How did recognizing and standing up to FOMO change your perspective on your day's activities? Did this exercise reveal any deeper insights about what truly matters to you, beyond social trends or the fear of missing out? How can you apply this awareness to cultivate more meaningful, distraction-free moments in your life?

Day 3: "Courageous Self-Expression"

- **Activity:** Do something that requires you to express yourself courageously, whether it's sharing your art, speaking your truth, or standing up for your beliefs.
- **Reflection:** Reflect on the power of courageous self-expression. How does it feel to share your true self with the world?

Day 4: "The Wild, Unrestrained Extravaganza of Life"

- **Activity:** Actively seek out opportunities to perform acts of kindness, big or small, for the entire day. Whether it's complimenting a stranger, volunteering your time, or simply offering a helping hand, let generosity guide your actions.
- **Reflection:** Reflect on your day of deliberate generosity. How did engaging in selfless acts alter the rhythm of your daily routine? Did you notice a shift in your own energy or mood?

Consider how these moments of generosity resonate with your core values and enhance your life's melody. How can incorporating regular acts of kindness into your life transform the way you navigate your personal "dance floor"?

Day 5: "Not Your Grandma's Library"
- **Activity:** Explore a new book, podcast, or documentary on a topic outside your usual interests. Expand your horizons and knowledge base.
- **Reflection:** How does diversifying your sources of knowledge and inspiration influence your perspective on life?

Day 6: "The Oracle Within"
- **Activity:** Spend quiet time in reflection or meditation, seeking the guidance of your inner oracle. Bring to mind a situation or decision that's been weighing on you. Instead of analyzing it with logic alone, close your eyes, take deep breaths, and ask your inner oracle for guidance. Pay attention to the first feeling, image, or thought that arises, even if it seems unconnected. Jot it down if it helps you focus.
- **Reflection:** Reflect on the insight you received during your moment with your inner oracle. Was the guidance surprising, or did it affirm what you already felt? Consider the difference between this intuitive insight and your rational thoughts on the matter. How can integrating this intuitive wisdom enrich your decision-making process and enhance your journey forward?

Day 7: Weekly Integration and Balance Mastery
- **Activity:** Create a balance wheel for your life, dividing it into segments that represent different areas (work, relationships, personal growth, health). Assess and plan how to balance these areas moving forward.
- **Reflection:** Reflect on the journey through this book and the past four weeks. How have the insights and activities helped you master the balance in your life?

This week's journey marks the culmination of your exploration into harmony, balance, and resonance within life's symphony. As you move forward, remember the lessons learned, the growth experienced, and the resilience built. Your ability to orchestrate impact, navigate chaos, and cultivate depth in your life's symphony will continue to grow as you apply these principles daily. Carry forward the courage, wisdom, and authenticity you've nurtured, and let them guide you in conducting a life of meaningful impact and resilient harmony.

The Red Button Syndrome

You've seen that red button in cartoons, right? The one you're never supposed to touch? Fck that. Smash it. The Fck Reset Button isn't a delicate tap; it's a full-blown demolition.

Pressing the reset button is a ritual of reinvention. Rebels shed old skins, old patterns, and old expectations. It's not a timid change; it's a metamorphosis.

Imagine standing at the edge of a cliff, ready to leap into the unknown. Fck the fear; take the liberation leap. The Fck Reset Button is your parachute, not your anchor.

We accumulate identities like dusty old books on a shelf. Fck the dusty shelf; flush it out. The Fck Reset Button is a detox for the soul, a cleanse of outdated labels.

Quantum leaps aren't reserved for subatomic particles. Fck the limitations; shift your reality. The Fck Reset Button propels you into a dimension where possibilities aren't probabilities; they're certainties.

Life's a symphony, and rebels don't play by the conventional notes. Fck the sheet music; compose your subversion symphony. The Fck Reset Button is your baton, conducting a rebellion against the mundane.

Ever felt like a puppet tangled in society's strings? Fck the puppetry; cut the cords. The Fck Reset Button is your scissors, setting you free from the entanglement of societal expectations.

Tabula rasa isn't just a philosophical concept; it's your rebel manifesto. Fck the old narratives; embrace the blank slate. The Fck Reset Button is your paintbrush, and life is your canvas.

Time travelers have a dilemma—where to go next. Fck the dilemma; embrace now. The Fck Reset Button doesn't transport you to the past or future; it grounds you firmly in the present.

Resetting isn't calm; it's a storm. Fck the tranquility; embrace the chaos. The Fck Reset Button stirs the winds of change, and in the storm, rebels find clarity.

Burn those permission slips society handed you. Fck the permissions; shred them ceremoniously. The Fck Reset Button is your declaration of autonomy, a rebellion against seeking approval.

Life can feel heavy, like lead. Fck the weight; become the alchemist. The Fck Reset Button transmutes the lead of your existence into the gold of your aspirations.

Resetting is a tumble through uncertainty. Fck the fear; embrace the quantum tumble. The Fck Reset Button is your parachute, not your anchor.

Eclipses aren't just celestial events; they're symbolic. Fck the shadows; redefine them. The Fck Reset Button is your celestial body, casting a new light on the narratives you've outgrown.

Phoenixes rise from their ashes. Fck the ashes; embrace the flames. The Fck Reset Button is your ignition, and from its spark, rebels emerge anew.

Life isn't binary code. Fck the binary; break the code. The Fck Reset Button dismantles the preconceived notions, letting rebels create their own script.

Serendipity isn't a chance encounter; it's a dance. Fck the rigid steps; dance with chance. The Fck Reset Button is your partner, leading you through the unpredictable waltz of life.

In the silence, rebels find their melody. Fck the noise; listen to your inner symphony. The Fck Reset Button is your tuning fork, attuning you to the resonance of authenticity.

Gravity is for the ordinary. Fck the gravity; defy it. The Fck Reset Button is your wings, propelling you to heights where rebels soar.

Resetting shatters the echo chamber. Fck the confinement; break free. The Fck Reset Button is your sledgehammer, demolishing the walls that echo only the mundane.

Smashing the button isn't just about resetting; it's about reclaiming control, rewriting your narrative, and giving a giant middle finger to the expected. So, rebel, ready to smash that button? The journey awaits, and it begins with a resounding Fck yeah!

The Unsung Hero of Life

In the exhilarating realm of open-mindedness stands the unsung hero in the symphony of life. Buckle up, because we're diving deeper into the art of discernment. It's time to flex those mental muscles, discard the rusty old goggles of narrow-mindedness, and embrace the panoramic view of possibility.

Discernment isn't just a passive act; it's a mental gymnastics routine that flips and twirls through the landscape of ideas. Picture it as a dynamic dance between curiosity and critical thinking, a choreography that opens the doors to unexplored territories.

Consider yourself the intrepid explorer of the intellectual realm, armed not with a compass but with an open mind. The journey of discernment is an expedition through the jungles of perspectives, scaling the peaks of ideologies, and occasionally getting lost in the valleys of conflicting opinions.

Let's get one thing straight—discernment is not the twin sibling of indifference. It's not about apathy or a laissez-faire attitude toward ideas. Instead, it's a dynamic engagement with diverse thoughts, a willingness to navigate the complex landscape of perspectives.

In the world of discernment, certainty is the illusion we bid farewell. Give a nod to the uncertainty; it's the breeding ground for growth. Discernment involves acknowledging the shades of gray, embracing the ambiguity, and reveling in the questions without always demanding answers.

To master discernment, one must become an artist of unlearning. It's about peeling away the layers of preconceived notions, societal conditioning, and self-imposed limitations. Imagine yourself shedding the layers of an onion, each peel revealing a clearer, more nuanced perspective.

Consider your discernment like a wardrobe of eclectic garments. Each piece represents a different viewpoint, and you have the liberty to choose what to wear when navigating the runway of ideas. It's a sartorial celebration of intellectual diversity.

Picture discernment as a toolbox filled with an array of cognitive tools. There's the screwdriver of skepticism, the wrench of empathy, and the pliers of critical thinking. The discerning craftsman knows when to use each tool, crafting a masterpiece of understanding.

Balancing on the tightrope of discernment requires finesse. It's the delicate act of weighing ideas without toppling into the chasm of dogma. Imagine yourself as the tightrope walker, gracefully navigating between openness and critical evaluation.

In the playground of discernment, every idea is a swing, waiting for you to take it for a spin. It's about embracing the playfulness of exploration, swinging between perspectives, and occasionally doing intellectual somersaults.

At the core of discernment lies humility—the acknowledgment that your mental playground is but a small corner in the vast expanse of human thought. It's about recognizing that every swing in the playground contributes to the collective laughter of shared understanding.

Imagine hosting a dinner party for ideas. Each thought is a guest, bringing its unique flavor to the table. Discernment involves orchestrating this intellectual feast, savoring the diversity of perspectives, and occasionally spicing things up with a dash of contrarian spice.

Consider the dance floor of discernment as a pulsating club of ideas. It's where thoughts twirl, sway, and occasionally engage in a lively debate. Picture yourself as the DJ, curating the playlist of perspectives, and letting the rhythm of open-mindedness dictate the moves.

In the art of discernment, emotional intelligence is the secret sauce. It's the ability to understand not just the logic of ideas but also the emotions that underpin them. Discernment involves empathizing with the beats of emotional resonance within every thought.

Picture your mind as a yoga mat for discernment. It's about stretching your mental flexibility, assuming the poses of various viewpoints, and finding balance between strength and suppleness. In this yoga of the mind, every stretch contributes to increased intellectual resilience.

In the vast intellectual cosmos, discernment is the ability to connect the dots and form constellations of understanding. It's about recognizing patterns, understanding relationships between ideas, and occasionally discovering a new star in the galaxy of knowledge.

The discerning mind is also a mirror. It reflects not only external ideas but also engages in regular self-reflection. It's about holding the mirror to your own biases, questioning your assumptions, and occasionally wiping away the fog to see a clearer reflection.

In the jungle of ideas, discernment is your camouflage. It allows you to blend with the diverse foliage of perspectives, observe without disturbing the ecosystem, and occasionally adapt to the changing intellectual climate.

Consider discernment as your recipe book for intellectual exploration. Each idea is a culinary experiment, and you have the freedom to mix, match, and occasionally spice things up. Discernment is the chef's kiss in the symphony of diverse flavors.

It takes courage to be discerning. It's the bravery to venture into the unknown territories of thought, confront the dragons of ignorance, and occasionally challenge your own cognitive comfort zones. Discernment involves being a fearless knight in the quest for intellectual truth.

As we conclude this exploration of the art of discernment, envision your mind as an infinity mirror. Reflecting endlessly upon itself, discernment opens the door to infinite intellectual possibilities. It's an ever-expanding journey, a labyrinth of ideas where every turn reveals a new facet of understanding.

As you navigate the rich terrain of open-mindedness, remember—discernment isn't just an art; it's the compass that guides you through the labyrinth of ideas, the North Star of intellectual exploration. So, keep your minds open, your discernment sharp, and embrace the exhilarating dance of diverse thoughts. The intellectual playground awaits, and you're the discerning maestro orchestrating the symphony of ideas.

The Intent Matters

A treasure map awaits, but instead of "X marks the spot," it's "P marks your purpose." Grab your compass, dust off your explorer's hat, and let's embark on a rollicking adventure to uncover the hidden gems of a life lived with intent.

Every purposeful journey starts with a compass, an unwavering commitment to intentional living. It's not about wandering aimlessly through the forest of existence; it's about hacking through the underbrush with a machete of purpose, creating your own damn path.

Life is a series of crossroads, and purpose is your GPS. At each juncture, you're faced with choices. Purposeful living isn't about blindly following Google Maps; it's about flipping off Siri, taking the wheel, and choosing the scenic route.

As you traverse the landscapes of your purpose, your backpack is laden with values—the essentials for any intrepid explorer. These values aren't picked up at the souvenir shop of societal expectations; they're carefully chosen provisions that sustain you on your journey.

In the desert of mundane existence, purposeful living discovers an oasis of passion. It's not a mirage; it's a life source. Forget sipping droplets; dive in, splash around, and let passion quench your thirst for a life well-lived.

Hidden in the dense foliage of your journey lies the treasure chest of talents. Purposeful living is the map that leads you to unlock this chest, revealing skills and abilities you didn't know you possessed. Jack Sparrow would be jealous.

Scaling the mountains of challenges is part of the purposeful climb. It's not about avoiding the ascent; it's about relishing the difficulty, planting your flag at the summit, and yelling, "I conquered this mountain because it was there!"

Beware the quicksands of distractions that threaten to swallow your purpose whole. Purposeful living is the map that points out these treacherous territories, allowing you to sidestep the sinking traps of mindless pursuits.

In purposeful living, you'll find yourself in the river of flow. It's not about fighting the current; it's about embracing it, navigating the twists and turns with a kayak named Purpose, and enjoying the scenery along the way.

Amidst the purposeful jungle stands the Forest of Reflection, where each tree bears the marks of your personal growth. Purposeful living encourages you to sit on the mossy ground, contemplate the journey so far, and carve your initials on the bark of wisdom.

Every purposeful footstep sends ripples through the Echoes of Impact. Purposeful living isn't about tiptoeing through life; it's a dance party where you're the DJ. Throw on your favorite tunes and make the dance floor quake with the impact of your purposeful beats.

Canyons of resilience cut through the purposeful landscape. These canyons aren't obstacles; they're opportunities to build bridges. Purposeful living isn't about avoiding falls; it's about learning to fly on the wings of resilience.

As you sail the seas of purposeful living, let your values be the North Star guiding your ship. Purposeful living isn't a reckless pirate's life; it's a deliberate journey following the constellations of your deeply held principles.

In the fertile soil of purposeful living grows the Garden of Relationships. These aren't just any plants; they're the kind that bloom with mutual respect, shared goals, and the occasional dose of laughter. Purposeful living nurtures these relationships like a skilled gardener.

Perched on the cliffs of purposeful living, the Lighthouse of Legacy beams its light across the waves of time. Purposeful living isn't about leaving a mark; it's about constructing a lighthouse that continues to guide others long after you've set sail for new horizons.

The Archipelago of Curiosity is where purposeful living anchors for exploration. It's not about staying in one port; it's about sailing from island to island, driven by an insatiable curiosity that keeps the sails billowing and the compass ever spinning.

Gaze through the Telescope of Vision, and purposeful living reveals constellations not visible to the naked eye. It's not about short-sighted stargazing; it's about envisioning a future that stretches across galaxies, a future shaped by your purposeful intentions.

Gaze through the Telescope of Vision, and purposeful living reveals constellations not visible to the naked eye. It's not about short-sighted stargazing; it's about envisioning a future that stretches across galaxies, a future shaped by your purposeful intentions.

At the summit of purposeful living stands the Observatory of Introspection. Purposeful living isn't a race to the top; it's about pausing, gazing at the stars, and contemplating the vastness of your purpose.

In purposeful living, your life becomes a Symphony of Alignment. Each note played, each instrument in harmony, resonates with the melody of your purpose. It's not about solo performances; it's about the orchestration of a life in sync with your deepest intentions.

Remember this: the compass of intention, the map of purpose, leads you not to a destination but to a place called Home. Home is where your purpose resides, where the heart beats in sync with the rhythm of a life lived with intent. So, fellow explorer, set your compass, unfold your map, and venture forth into the thrilling landscapes of purposeful living. The treasure of a purposeful life awaits those brave enough to chart their course.

The Symphony of Serendipity

Imagine life as a vast, intricate web, each strand a potential pathway, each node a crossroads of choices and chances. Within this web, the Symphony of Serendipity plays its enchanting tunes, coaxing us to step into the flow of the unforeseen, to dance with the unknown. Serendipity, my friends, is not mere coincidence. It's the universe's playful whisper, a nudge towards opportunities veiled in the guise of randomness. It's the universe saying, "Trust me," with a mischievous wink, inviting you to a game where the rules are unknown but the rewards are beyond imagination.

To the untrained ear, the Symphony of Serendipity might sound like dissonant chaos. But to those who listen, truly listen, it's a masterpiece of interconnected melodies, each note a step towards discovering one's purpose, each pause a moment of introspection, and each crescendo a leap towards fulfilling one's destiny. It's the beautiful cacophony of chance that orchestrates the most unexpected yet profoundly impactful moments of our lives, where the script is unwritten, the stage is unbounded, and the actors – well, that's us – navigate the spontaneous choreography of existence.

Let's debunk a myth: Serendipity isn't passive. It doesn't mean sitting back and waiting for the stars to align. No, it demands an active listener, someone who's attuned to life's subtle cues, ready to pivot with grace and leap with courage when the moment strikes. Think of serendipity as life's improvisation. There are no rehearsals, no second takes. It's about embracing the moment, making decisions on the fly, and trusting that these choices lead you to where you need to be, even if it's miles away from where you planned to go.

The Symphony of Serendipity thrives on openness. Open your mind, open your heart, and most importantly, open your eyes to the wonder that surrounds you. The most life-altering opportunities often come disguised as mundane moments or insurmountable challenges. Remember, serendipity favors the bold. It's the brave souls who dare to dream, to step outside the comfort zone, who find themselves at the right place at the right time, not by accident, but by being open to the possibilities that lie in the unknown.

This symphony is also a solo performance. Your serendipity is yours alone, a melody unique to your life's journey. What seems like a misstep to one may be a pivotal note in another's crescendo. And yet, the Symphony of Serendipity is a shared experience. Our individual melodies intertwine, creating a complex harmony. Your chance encounter, your serendipitous moment, can set off a chain reaction, altering not just your path but the courses of those around you.

To dance to this symphony is to appreciate the beauty of fleeting moments. It's about finding joy in the journey, not just the destination. It's about celebrating the here and now, knowing that each moment is a stepping stone towards your ultimate purpose.

Navigating the Symphony of Serendipity requires a conductor's baton of mindfulness. It's about being present, attuned to the subtleties of life's rhythms, ready to adapt the tempo as the music of the universe guides you. It's also about resilience. Not every serendipitous opportunity pans out as expected. Sometimes, what appears as a fortuitous encounter can lead to a dead end. But, like any skilled musician, you must learn from the dissonance, adjust your approach, and play on.

Trust is the foundation of serendipity. Trust in the journey, trust in the chaos, and most importantly, trust in yourself. Believe that you are exactly where you need to be, doing exactly what you need to do, even if it feels like you're flying blind.

The Symphony of Serendipity is not about finding a linear path to success or happiness. It's about discovering the beauty in life's detours, the lessons in its setbacks, and the joy in its surprises.

Patience, dear reader, is a virtue in this symphony. The most magical moments often come when least expected. Like a seedling breaking through the soil, serendipity requires time to grow and bloom into something spectacular.

Courage, too, is essential. It takes guts to follow a path revealed by chance, to say yes to the unknown, and to leap into the void with nothing but faith that you'll land where you need to be.

Reflection is the quiet melody playing in the background of the Symphony of Serendipity. It's in moments of stillness that we hear the whispers of chance, guiding us towards our next adventure. As you orchestrate your life's symphony, let curiosity be your compass. It's the curious mind that discovers new paths, that sees the potential in the unexpected, and that finds the hidden threads of serendipity woven into the fabric of daily life.

Embrace the Symphony of Serendipity with a spirit of adventure. Life is not a problem to be solved but a mystery to be explored, a journey filled with hidden treasures waiting to be uncovered by those brave enough to look. And so, we circle back to the beginning, to the grand theater of life, where the Symphony of Serendipity continues to play. The music never stops; it only evolves, shifts, and transforms, guiding us through the wondrous, unpredictable, and utterly beautiful journey of existence.

Let this symphony be your guide, your inspiration, and your reminder that in the grand design of the universe, there are no accidents, only serendipitous encounters waiting to be embraced. So, take a bow, dear conductor, for the symphony is yours to command, and the music of serendipity is the soundtrack to a life lived fully, fearlessly, and with open arms.

It's Not About Likes and Emojis

Grab a compass, because we're navigating the labyrinth of relationships with the irreverence of pirates and the wisdom of philosophers. This isn't your typical lovey-dovey guide; it's a rebel's handbook to forging connections that echo through the corridors of time.

Picture this: a world where connections are measured in likes and emojis. Superficiality reigns, and genuine bonds are obscured by the social media mirage. But we're not here for virtual popularity contests; we're diving into the tangible, messy, and beautifully imperfect realm of real connections.

In a world where swipes dictate romantic possibilities, we're not dancing the Tinder tango of superficial encounters. This isn't about collecting matches like trophies; it's about forging connections that go beyond a pixelated profile, finding resonance in shared laughter, quirks, and the complexities of being human.

Superficiality is reducing emotions to emojis, but we're not expressing love with heart-eyed faces. Relationships aren't one-size-fits-all, and we're using the rich language of authentic connection—full sentences, messy emotions, and genuine expressions that emojis can never encapsulate.

Superficiality is the catfish game, where identities are masked, and connections are built on illusions. We're not donning masks to fish for shallow connections; we're unmasking the catfish, seeking genuine bonds that thrive in the vulnerability of being true to ourselves.

In a world obsessed with friend counts and follower numbers, superficiality equates connection with quantity. But we're not amassing a legion of acquaintances; we're cultivating a tight-knit crew of genuine connections—people who know the real us, flaws and all.

As we click the selfie of authenticity, it's not just about us—it's about capturing moments with those who add color to our lives. Relationships are the brushstrokes that paint the canvas of our existence, and each connection contributes to the masterpiece of shared experiences.

Superficiality is parading relationships like accessories on a runway, but we're not wearing connections as mere adornments. This isn't about showcasing a curated lineup of associations; it's about walking the runway of authenticity, where each connection is a unique, irreplaceable piece in our collection.

Superficiality seeks high-definition connections, where the quest for clarity blurs the line between real and fantasy. But we're not turning up the resolution on relationships; we're embracing the beautiful blur, where genuine connections thrive in the fuzzy, unscripted moments that define our shared stories.

In a world enamored with glossy portrayals of relationships, we're not posing for the cover shoot of superficial perfection. We're revolting against the Vanity Fair narrative, celebrating the authenticity of our connections—the messy, real, and beautifully imperfect tales that deserve to be told.

Imagine a world trapped in the echo chamber of superficial connections, where glossy narratives reverberate endlessly. We're not amplifying those echoes; we're disrupting the superficial symphony, introducing new, authentic notes that create a melody of diversity, depth, and genuine human experience.

Superficiality burdens relationships with unrealistic standards, dictating a measure of worth as substantial as a soap bubble. We're not inflating our connections to fit these ephemeral standards; we're shedding the weight of superficial expectations, embracing the authenticity that comes from accepting our connections as they are.

Superficiality is the obsession with magazine-cover relationships, where airbrushed perfection becomes the benchmark. We're not striving for cover-story connections; we're tearing down the glossy pages and replacing them with a rebellion of authenticity, where real stories and unfiltered emotions take center stage.

In a world where superficiality writes the glossy pages of relationship self-doubt, we're not reading that narrative. We're penning our own story, embracing authenticity as the protagonist. Because real connection isn't found in conformity; it's discovered in the courage to be authentically, unapologetically ourselves.

Superficiality is the runway where flaws are airbrushed away, creating a sterile beauty devoid of character. We're not walking the runway of flawlessness; we're celebrating the flawsome—the beauty that arises from embracing our imperfections, quirks, and idiosyncrasies in the dance of relationships.

Superficiality is the masquerade ball where masks hide authentic expressions. We're not here to wear masks; we're engaging in the art of unmasking, allowing our true selves to step into the spotlight. Because authenticity is the real masterpiece, and we're the artists who paint with the colors of vulnerability in the canvas of connections.

Picture a world trapped in the superficial echo chamber, where the same glossy narratives reverberate endlessly. We're not amplifying those echoes; we're disrupting the superficial symphony, introducing new, authentic notes that create a melody of diversity, depth, and genuine human experience.

Storms Don't Weaken Your Lighthouse

Life, much like the unpredictable seas, tosses us about with waves of challenges, societal currents, and occasional tsunamis of chaos. In this tempest, integrity stands tall as the lighthouse, cutting through the storm and providing a steady light to guide your way.

Imagine your core values as the vibrant light radiating from the lighthouse of integrity. These values aren't a dusty set of rules; they're the dynamic colors that pierce through the darkness, ensuring you stay true to your course, even when the seas get rough.

In the vast expanse of life's ocean, there are sirens luring you toward the treacherous rocks of compromise. Integrity acts as your earplugs, drowning out the seductive songs that might lead you astray. It's your steadfast refusal to dance with the dangerous allure of shortcuts.

Integrity isn't just a destination; it's a constant course correction. Think of it as a compass that directs you back to your true north. Regular self-reflection is the sailor's tool, ensuring that you don't drift away from the authentic path defined by your core values.

Picture the shipwrecks scattered along the coast of convenience. These are the remnants of vessels that chose an expedient route over one guided by integrity. Your lighthouse is the preventive force, warding off the allure of shortcuts that might lead to the wreckage of your principles.

Every lighthouse needs a keeper, and integrity is no different. You, dear reader, are the keeper of your integrity. Polish the lens, trim the wick, and ensure your values shine brightly through the fog of external expectations and societal pressures.

Life often shrouds us in the fog of ethical dilemmas. In these moments, your lighthouse becomes a powerful beacon, cutting through the uncertainty and helping you discern the right course. Integrity is the light that doesn't waver even when the fog thickens.

Imagine the crashing waves around the lighthouse as the cacophony of societal expectations and peer pressure. In the midst of this uproar, integrity roars silently but powerfully, a force that can't be drowned out by the noise of conformity.

Your core values aren't a monolith; they're a mosaic, each piece contributing to the vibrant picture of your integrity. It's about understanding the intricate dance between values like honesty, compassion, and resilience—arranging them in a way that creates a masterpiece of character.

Life's seas are unpredictable, and storms are inevitable. Integrity is the resilient seafarer who, despite being battered by the waves, remains steadfast in their commitment to sail authentically. It's the refusal to abandon ship when the going gets tough.

In the darkest nights, when the sky is devoid of stars, integrity becomes your guiding celestial body. It's the star you navigate by, the unwavering light that assures you that even in the pitch-black darkness, you're on the right course.

Imagine your lighthouse standing alone on a desolate shore. This solitude is the strength of your integrity—the ability to stand firm even when the coastline is barren of external validation. It's about being true to your values even when there's no audience.

Life's waters are filled with the shadows of temptation, enticing you to deviate from your course. Integrity is your guardian against these shadows, a sturdy anchor that keeps you from being swept away by the currents of compromise.

There will be moments when the flame of your lighthouse flickers—a temporary setback, a moral challenge, or a crisis of conscience. Yet, like a seasoned sailor, you tend to the flame, ensuring it burns bright once more. Integrity isn't about perfection; it's about resilience.

Consider the ship of accountability sailing toward your lighthouse. It's not a vessel of punishment but a ship that ensures you remain answerable to yourself and your values. Integrity is the harbormaster, welcoming the ship back after every journey with open arms.

The echo of your lighthouse reverberates in the waves that crash against the shore. Similarly, your integrity leaves a lasting impact on those around you. It's the subtle influence that encourages others to navigate their own seas with authenticity.

Storms don't weaken your lighthouse; they strengthen its resolve. Likewise, the challenges life throws at you aren't meant to erode your integrity but to forge it into a formidable force. Each tempest becomes a testament to your unwavering commitment.

There's a song playing in the rhythmic beam of your lighthouse—a song of consistency. Integrity isn't a sporadic melody; it's a harmonious tune that plays day in and day out. It's the rhythm of your values, the heartbeat of your authentic existence.

Imagine your lighthouse casting an anchored shadow, a legacy that extends beyond your own journey. Integrity is the legacy you leave behind—a testament to a life lived with purpose, resilience, and an unwavering commitment to the values that define you.

Week 5 Action Plan: Deepening Resonance and Strengthening Your Compass

As we step into Week 5, it's time to deepen the resonance of your life's symphony and strengthen the compass that guides you through chaos and harmony alike. This week focuses on inner wisdom, intentionality, and the power of authenticity in navigating life's unpredictable seas.

Day 1: "The Red Button Syndrome"
- **Activity:** Craft your own Fck Reset Button ritual. This could be writing down habits, thoughts, or patterns you wish to release on a piece of paper and tearing it up, symbolizing your commitment to transformation. Alternatively, create a visual representation of your reset—a button you can "press" (draw or craft one) whenever you need a symbolic restart.

- **Reflection:** Reflect on what the reset symbolizes for you. How does the act of consciously choosing to reset empower you to shed outdated aspects of yourself? Consider the potential transformations this reset can initiate. How do you feel about the changes you are inviting into your life, and what steps will you take to embody this new beginning?

Day 2: "The Unsung Hero of Life"
- **Activity:** Do something that embodies your unsung qualities, something that truly reflects the essence of who you are, without seeking recognition or validation.
- **Reflection:** How does embracing and acting on your unsung qualities affect your sense of self and fulfillment?

Day 3: "The Symphony of Serendipity"
- **Activity:** Before starting your day, get a small notebook or use a digital app dedicated to note taking. Your task is to jot down any unexpected moments, chance encounters, or seemingly random occurrences that happen throughout your day. These could range from finding a book you've long wanted at a garage sale, to a chance meeting with an old friend, or even a new opportunity that comes out of a misdialed phone number.
- **Reflection:** Reflect on how these moments made you feel, any new opportunities that arose from them, and how they might be guiding you towards paths you hadn't considered. Consider continuing your Serendipity Tracking for the next week and then deeply reflecting on the role of serendipity in your life. This deeper activity and reflection are designed to tune your senses to the Symphony of Serendipity playing around you constantly. By actively engaging with serendipity, you learn to embrace the unexpected, interpreting life's subtle cues and understanding the interconnectedness of seemingly random events. This is not just about acknowledging serendipity; it's about actively inviting it into your life, allowing it to guide you to a richer, more resonant existence.

Day 4: "The Intent Matters"
- **Activity:** Before starting your day, set a clear intention for how you want to approach the day's tasks and interactions. Revisit this intention throughout the day.
- **Reflection:** Reflect on how setting an intention influenced your day. Did it change how you approached challenges or interactions?

Day 5: "It's Not About Likes and Emojis"
- **Activity:** For one day, commit to a digital detox where you consciously avoid non-essential digital distractions. This includes social media, unnecessary internet browsing, and excessive smartphone use. Focus on real-world interactions, presence, and observe the quality of these engagements.
- **Reflection:** How does the absence of digital validation impact your mood, self-esteem, and connections with others? Did the absence of these distractions illuminate any habitual patterns or dependencies on technology? How can you integrate the insights gained from this experience to better steer through life's digital sea without losing sight of your true course?

Day 6: "Storms Don't Weaken Your Lighthouse"
- **Activity:** Write a letter to yourself about a past challenge you've overcome. Highlight the strengths you displayed and how you can apply them to current or future challenges.
- **Reflection:** In what ways are you your own lighthouse, guiding yourself through life's storms with resilience and strength? What core values make up the light of your lighthouse, and how do they guide you in difficult times? How can you maintain and strengthen your light to ensure it continues to guide you and others?

Day 7: Weekly Integration - Mastering Intentions
- **Activity:** Create a personal intention-setting ritual. Begin by writing down your core values and the intentions you wish to

manifest in your life. Place these written intentions somewhere you will see them daily. For one week, start each day by reading your intentions aloud and visualize yourself living these intentions fully.

- **Reflection:** After completing your intention-setting ritual, reflect on how aligning your daily actions with your intentions changes your perspective and actions. Consider the following questions: How does setting clear intentions influence your decisions? How do you feel when your actions are in harmony with your intentions?

This week aims to reinforce your inner strength, clarity, and resilience. By focusing on your oracle within, acknowledging your triggers, setting intentions, honoring your unsung hero, disconnecting from superficial validation, and reaffirming your resilience, you fortify your ability to navigate life's symphony with purpose and impact. Carry these lessons forward as you continue to orchestrate a life of meaningful resonance and authentic balance.

Master that Compass Already!

We're diving into the art of mastering the f*cking compass, that internal tool that guides you through the wild seas of emotions. Buckle up, because emotional resilience isn't just about weathering the storm; it's about riding the waves like a badass surfer of the soul.

Life, much like the open sea, is prone to emotional tempests. Storms of anger, tsunamis of sadness, and whirlpools of anxiety are bound to challenge your emotional vessel. Emotional resilience isn't about avoiding these storms but about navigating them with finesse.

Imagine your emotions as the vast, unpredictable sea, and your resilience as the f*cking compass. Just as a skilled sailor uses a compass to find true north, mastering emotional resilience means becoming adept at finding your emotional north amidst the chaos.

Emotional weather is as unpredictable as a cat on a pogo stick. One moment it's sunny and serene, the next it's thunderstorms and chaos. Emotional resilience is the meteorologist within you, interpreting the forecast and readying you for whatever emotional turbulence comes your way.

Surf's up, emotional warriors! Riding the waves of your feelings requires finesse, balance, and a damn good sense of humor. Emotional resilience isn't about avoiding the waves but about mastering the art of emotional surfing, gracefully riding the highs and lows.

Your internal compass needs regular calibration. Life has a way of throwing magnetic disturbances your way—a breakup, a setback, or just a really bad hair day. Emotional resilience is the ability to recalibrate your f*cking compass, ensuring it points toward your emotional true north.

Picture the rogue waves of life crashing against your emotional vessel. These can be the unforeseen challenges, the sudden setbacks, or the unexpected plot twists that catch you off guard. Emotional resilience isn't about preventing these waves but about becoming a skilled captain who steers through them.

Ever seen a stoic surfer riding a monstrous wave? Emotional resilience is about channeling your inner stoic surfer, maintaining your balance and composure even when faced with the towering emotions that threaten to engulf you. It's the art of staying on the board amidst the chaos.

Tidal waves of emotion can feel like emotional tsunamis, threatening to drown you in their intensity. Yet, emotional resilience isn't about fearing these waves but about becoming the architect of your emotional seawall, standing strong against the surges that come your way.

Emotional currents are as fluid as a lava lamp at a hippie convention. They shift, twist, and sometimes defy logic. Emotional resilience is about adapting to the fluidity of these emotional currents, understanding that, much like the sea, your emotions are in constant motion.

In the realm of emotional resilience, you are the captain of your ship. A compassionate captain doesn't berate themselves for feeling certain emotions. Instead, they acknowledge, accept, and steer through the waves with a compassionate hand on the helm, guiding themselves toward calmer waters.

Amidst the vast emotional ocean, there are hidden archipelagos of joy, islands of happiness, and atolls of laughter. Emotional resilience isn't just about navigating the storms but also about setting a course for these islands, allowing yourself to bask in the sunlight of positive emotions.

Your emotional life is a symphony—sometimes a serene sonata, sometimes a stormy symphony. Emotional resilience is about being the conductor of this symphony, orchestrating the cacophony of feelings into a harmonious melody that resonates with your internal compass.

Just as the sun sets on the horizon, emotional resilience allows you to release emotions that no longer serve you. It's the understanding that every emotional sunset paves the way for a new emotional dawn. Letting go becomes a form of emotional navigation toward a brighter tomorrow.

Life's emotional map includes uncharted territories, mysterious lands of fear, grief, and uncertainty. Emotional resilience transforms you into the intrepid explorer, bravely venturing into these uncharted emotional territories, discovering the hidden treasures of self-awareness and growth.

Alchemy isn't just about turning lead into gold; it's also about transforming emotional lead into emotional gold. Emotional resilience is the alchemical process of turning challenging emotions into opportunities for growth, wisdom, and a deeper understanding of oneself.

In the stormy seas of emotion, your internal compass acts as the f*cking lighthouse of emotional stability. It guides you back to center, helping you find your balance even when the waves threaten to knock you off course.

Imagine your emotions as the diverse crew members on your emotional vessel. Emotional resilience isn't about silencing or dismissing these crew members but about fostering a healthy relationship with each, understanding their unique roles, and ensuring they work together harmoniously.

Consider emotional resilience not just a skill but an art form. It's the masterpiece you create with every emotional ebb and flow. Much like an artist who molds clay, you mold your emotional responses, shaping them into a resilient work of art that reflects your inner strength.

In the vast sea of emotions, the siren song of self-compassion calls out to you. Emotional resilience involves heeding this song, recognizing that amidst the storms, you are deserving of kindness, understanding, and a safe harbor within yourself.

The Occasional Cosmic Curveball

Gather 'round because we're about to paint with the chaotic colors of existence. We're not just managing time; we're unleashing it on the canvas of our lives—a swirling masterpiece of deadlines, routines, and the occasional cosmic curveball. So, grab your brushes, dip them in the palette of priorities, and let's create a damn fine art piece called Your Life.

Imagine your life as a blank canvas, stretched taut across the easel of the universe. Time, your vibrant paint, waits to be slapped onto this vast, daunting surface. But hey, no pressure. It's your canvas, your brush, and your damn colors.

Contrary to what the existentialists might argue, your paint isn't infinite. You've got a finite tube of minutes, hours, and days. So, let's debunk the myth of endless paint. Each stroke counts. Wasting time is like throwing your precious hues into a black hole—avoid it.

Ever seen Picasso's art? It's a glorious mess of shapes and perspectives. Your priorities are the same—multifaceted and, at times, delightfully confusing. Don't try to be a paint-by-numbers artist. Embrace the chaos; let your priorities dance like abstract figures on the canvas.

Routine isn't the enemy; it's the reliable brush in your toolkit. Use it to create patterns, strokes of consistency that weave through the canvas. But, beware of becoming a mindless painter. Routine should be your servant, not your master.

Procrastination is the master illusionist of the art world. It promises the grand reveal, but the curtain never lifts. Beware the vanishing act of procrastination; it's a disappearing ink that erases your potential strokes. Conquer it with the wand of discipline.

Time is the Salvador Dalí of your existence—melting, warping, and occasionally playing tricks on you. But instead of being perplexed, dance with the surrealism of time. Twist it, stretch it, but make every distorted second count.

Your palette isn't limited to black and white; it's an explosion of possibilities. Don't stick to a monochrome life. Splash your canvas with the vibrant hues of experiences, challenges, and the occasional wild experiment. Monotony is the true color thief.

Deadlines are the drumbeats in the orchestra of life, keeping the rhythm and ensuring your masterpiece doesn't turn into a cacophony of procrastination. Embrace the performance art of deadlines; they're your ticket to a standing ovation.

In a world cluttered with unnecessary details, sometimes a minimalist sketch speaks volumes. Trim the excess strokes from your canvas. What remains should be intentional, impactful, and capable of conveying your message without unnecessary embellishments.

Ever seen a graffiti artist at work? Unpredictable, rebellious, and often misunderstood. Infuse your canvas with the graffiti of spontaneity. Let it be the unexpected splash that adds character to your otherwise well-planned mural.

Time blocking is the jazz improvisation of time management. Each block is a different instrument, playing in harmony to create a unique composition. Let the rhythm of time blocking guide your brush, creating a masterpiece that swings and sways.

Multitasking isn't a clean canvas; it's a messy collage of half-finished strokes. Don't fall into the trap of thinking you're creating a masterpiece by juggling too many brushes at once. Focus on one stroke at a time; it's the key to a refined masterpiece.

Distractions are the graffiti on your wall of productivity. They might seem colorful at first, but they obscure the true beauty of your canvas. Grab your paint scraper and remove the distracting tags; let your canvas breathe.

Every artist pauses to admire their work. Engage in the calligraphy of reflection. What worked? What didn't? Use the pen of self-awareness to write notes in the margins of your canvas. It's how you grow as an artist.

Life isn't a grand oil painting; it's a mosaic of small wins. Each tiny tile contributes to the overall picture. Celebrate these victories, for they are the colorful pieces that make your canvas a joyful masterpiece.

Time vampires are the sneaky street artists, splashing unwanted paint on your canvas when you're not looking. Identify these nocturnal creatures and clean up your canvas. Guard your time like a vigilant curator guards a priceless painting.

Watercolor is unpredictable, flowing where it pleases. Be the watercolor artist of your life. Adapt to unexpected splashes, and let them blend into your canvas. Rigidity is the canvas killer; flexibility is the brush that adds dynamic depth.

Life throws ink blots on your canvas; it's inevitable. Instead of seeing them as mistakes, view them as opportunities. What do they resemble? What story do they tell? The ink blot test of patience reveals the hidden narratives in your masterpiece.

Ever worn 3D glasses? Suddenly, everything leaps off the screen. Wear the 3D glasses of perspective in life. Your canvas isn't two-dimensional; it's a multidimensional experience. Embrace the depth, the layers, and the richness of your artistic journey.

Your canvas is never truly finished. It's an ever-evolving symphony of strokes, colors, and experiences. Embrace the unfinished symphony; let it be your motivation to wake up each day with the excitement of an artist facing a fresh, blank canvas.

Let the echoes of intentional strokes, rebellious splatters, and the occasional paint-spattered mishap linger in the studio of your mind. Carry the canvas of your time with flair, for it's a living, breathing testament to your ability to create a life that reflects your essence.

The Map to Liberation

Prepare to embark on a daring voyage into the uncharted waters of forgiveness, where the anchors of resentment are raised, and the sails of liberation catch the winds of redemption. This is not a mere guide; it's a treasure map leading you to the buried riches of a lighter heart and unshackled spirit.

Picture resentment as rusty anchors, dragging your ship through turbulent waters. The art of forgiveness isn't about polishing those anchors; it's about setting them free. Prepare to cast off the burdensome weight, for the seas of life await your unencumbered vessel.

Forgiveness is your map to liberation, a compass pointing you toward the open waters of serenity. It's not about forgetting the treacherous shores; it's about choosing a different course. Navigate the seas of forgiveness, and you'll find calmer, more inviting horizons.

In the pirate's code, forgiveness is the ultimate treasure. It's not a sign of weakness; it's a bold, rebellious act of choosing freedom over the shackles of resentment. Ready to wield your cutlass of forgiveness and liberate the hidden treasures within?

Carrying grudges is the burden of a buccaneer with a heart weighed down by cannonballs of anger. Forgiveness is your cannonball remover, freeing your ship from the ballast of resentment. Brace yourself for the audacious act of casting those cannonballs into the abyss.

Forgiveness is not a luxury; it's a navigational necessity. In the vast expanse of life's ocean, harboring resentment is like sailing through treacherous waters blindfolded. Unveil your eyes; forgiveness is the sextant guiding you to clearer skies.

The mariner who forgives undergoes a metamorphosis, shedding the barnacles of bitterness to emerge with a sleeker, swifter vessel. Forgiveness isn't about erasing history; it's about transforming it into a tale of resilience and growth. Ready to set sail on the seas of metamorphosis?

Compassion is the compass of the corsair who forgives, navigating the vastness of human flaws with understanding. Forgiveness isn't a pardon for the wrongs; it's a compassionate acknowledgment that even the mightiest ships encounter storms. Prepare to unfurl the sails of compassion.

In the world of forgiveness, a privateer seeks parley instead of plunder. It's not about vanquishing enemies; it's about engaging in a dialogue that transforms adversaries into allies on the unpredictable seas of life. Ready to hoist the flag of parley?

Forgiveness requires the vulnerability of a voyager exposing their underbelly to the unpredictable sea monsters of emotions. It's not about invincibility; it's about acknowledging the human vulnerability that makes the journey worthwhile. Prepare to embrace the authenticity of vulnerability.

Imagine forgiveness as a sea shanty, a melodious journey through the chapters of redemption. It's not about erasing painful verses; it's about composing a ballad that transcends the storms. Ready to sing your sea shanty of forgiveness?

To forgive is to offer clemency to the castaways of resentment stranded on the islands of past grievances. It's not about rescuing them; it's about letting them build their own rafts toward redemption. Get ready to extend the olive branch of clemency.

In the act of forgiveness, a sailor finds solace, a tranquil harbor in the tumultuous seas of emotion. It's not about erasing the storms; it's about navigating them with a heart unburdened by the weight of grudges. Prepare to dock in the safe haven of solace.

Forgiveness is the swashbuckler's surrender to the unpredictable tides of human imperfection. It's not about lowering your swords; it's about choosing battles that steer your ship toward calmer waters. Ready to surrender to the audacity of forgiveness?

The captain who forgives wields a unique compass, not pointing north but guiding toward the magnetic force of reconciliation. Forgiveness isn't a journey to forget; it's a courageous voyage to heal the wounds that mark your ship. Prepare to navigate with the captain's compass.

The true treasure hidden in the chest of forgiveness is release—the liberation from the chains that bind your spirit. It's not about searching for external riches; it's about discovering the priceless gems within. Ready to unlock the chest and revel in the treasure of release?

In forgiveness, the rogue wave is not a threat but an opportunity for reflection. It's not about avoiding the waves; it's about surfing on them with audacious grace. Get ready to ride the rogue wave of reflection toward the shores of healing.

Forgiveness is the buccaneer's blessing, a daring ritual that transforms the curse of resentment into the benediction of liberation. It's not about forgetting the battles; it's about declaring peace within. Ready to receive the buccaneer's blessing?

In forgiveness, the maritime mirror reflects not just the scars but the resilience etched on the ship's hull. It's not about hiding the battle wounds; it's about proudly displaying them as badges of audacity. Prepare to gaze into the maritime mirror of forgiveness.

Forgiveness hoists the jolly roger of redemption, not as a flag of conquest but as a symbol of audacious resilience. It's not about conquering enemies; it's about conquering the storms within. Ready to raise your jolly roger of redemption?

In the grand finale of forgiveness, avast your anchors with audacious flair. It's not about a timid release; it's about a bold declaration that your ship is unburdened and ready to sail the seas of life with audacious freedom. Avast, courageous navigator, avast!

Back to the Garden

You know it's about to get very real when you're back in the Garden of Priorities, a terrain where the flowers of balance bloom, and the weeds of unnecessary chaos are uprooted. We're not just cultivating well-being; we're growing a garden of priorities so vibrant that even Mother Nature would take notes.

Life can be an overgrown jungle, vines of responsibilities choking the sunlight of your peace. The Garden of Priorities is your machete—the tool you use to carve out paths of serenity. Hack away at the excess, and create the well-tended garden where your well-being can flourish.

In this garden, we're master gardeners, armed with the wisdom of priorities. Identify the weeds—those tasks and commitments that suffocate your joy—and ruthlessly pluck them from the soil. Leave space only for the flowers of purpose and the trees of meaningful endeavors.

Self-care is the nutrient-rich soil that nurtures the Garden of Priorities. Without it, your well-being wilts like neglected blossoms. Water your mental, emotional, and physical health, and watch the garden thrive. Remember, a garden left unattended becomes a wilderness.

Boundaries are the sunlight in this garden. They shine down, giving energy to your priorities, while preventing the invasive shade of unnecessary demands. Like a skilled horticulturist, cultivate robust boundaries so your well-being can bask in the warm rays of intentional living.

Occasionally, the Garden of Priorities needs pruning. Clip away the branches of obligations that have grown wild, stealing nutrients from your essential blooms. It's a constant process, but the well-being of your garden depends on maintaining order among the chaos.

Prioritize joy like it's the rarest orchid in the garden. These blossoms aren't just decorative; they're the essence of a well-tended life. Choose activities and pursuits that bring you joy, and watch as the entire garden lights up with the vibrant colors of fulfillment.

Relationships are the orchards in the Garden of Priorities. Nurture the bonds that bear sweet, succulent fruits. Invest time and care in those relationships, and let the well-being of shared laughter and companionship enrich the soil of your existence.

Regret and guilt are the compost bins of the garden—they break down the waste of past mistakes and transform it into fertile lessons. Don't let regret and guilt stink up your garden. Use them as the rich compost that nurtures the growth of resilience and wisdom.

The root system of the Garden of Priorities is your core values. Plant them deep, and let them anchor your decisions. When the storms of indecision rage, the strong roots of your values keep the garden from being uprooted. Tend to them regularly, and watch your well-being flourish.

Continuous learning is the greenhouse in this garden. It shelters your mind from the frost of stagnation and cultivates the seeds of curiosity. Keep the windows open, letting the breeze of new knowledge circulate. A well-fed mind is the cornerstone of holistic well-being.

In the Garden of Priorities, every mindful moment is a seed. Plant them generously, and watch a forest of peace and tranquility grow. Mindfulness is the secret fertilizer, ensuring that each moment contributes to the flourishing ecosystem of your well-being.

Gratitude is the fountain at the heart of the garden, its waters quenching the thirst of appreciation. Regularly take a sip, acknowledging the beauty of your blooms and the resilience of your garden. Gratitude keeps the well-being of your oasis in perpetual bloom.

Just like a garden needs seasons of rest, so does your well-being. Embrace the fallow periods, allowing the soil of your mind to rejuvenate. Rest isn't weakness; it's the preparation for the vibrant blooms that will burst forth in the next season of growth.

In the Garden of Priorities, flexibility is the dance of the willow tree in the wind. Be resilient, bending but not breaking in the face of life's storms. Adaptability is the key to sustaining well-being when unexpected weather threatens your carefully nurtured garden.

Stress is the labyrinth in this garden—a twisting, turning maze that threatens to obscure your path. Equip yourself with the shears of coping mechanisms, and systematically navigate the labyrinths. Remember, even the most intricate maze has an exit.

Sleep is the nightly rainfall in the Garden of Priorities. Let it drench the soil of your consciousness, replenishing the reserves of well-being. Don't compromise on this vital nutrient; allow yourself the luxury of deep, restorative sleep.

Single-tasking is the Zen meditation of the garden. Focus on one bloom at a time; give it the attention it deserves. In a world obsessed with multitasking, the art of single-tasking ensures that every petal receives your full presence.

Regularly harvest the fruits of reflection in your garden. What worked this season? What didn't? Use the bounty of insights to refine your priorities. The well-being of your garden relies on the cyclical process of planting, growing, and harvesting wisdom.

Well-being has its own melody—a song that resonates through the branches and leaves of your life. Listen to the rhythm of your heart, the harmony of your thoughts, and the melody of your actions. When you're in tune, the song of well-being echoes through the entire Garden of Priorities.

In the Garden of Priorities, the future is ever-blooming. As you tend to your well-being, envision the perpetual growth of your vibrant oasis. With each deliberate choice, each prioritized moment, you're sowing the seeds of an ever-flourishing, ever-blooming future.

There you have it, green thumbs of life—the guide to cultivating the flourishing Garden of Priorities. May your well-being blossom, and your garden be a testament to the intentional, joy-infused living that comes from tending to the seeds of priorities. Happy gardening!

Unlike Jellyfish Take Aim

We're not here to drift along like aimless jellyfish; we're here to ride the waves with intention. So, brace yourself for a journey that'll kick you in the rear and whisper sweet wisdom in your ear.

Life is an ocean, my friend, and the possibilities are vast, stretching as far as the eye can see. But here's the kicker – without purpose, you're just a lonely surfer caught in the riptide of mediocrity. Purposeful living is your surfboard, and damn, it's time to ride those purposeful waves.

Driftwood? That's for the aimless wanderers, my friend. Purposeful living is the compass in your hand, pointing you north, south, east, and west. Without it, you're just flotsam and jetsam, tossed around by the currents of other people's expectations and societal whims.

Oh, the siren song of drift, calling you to abandon ship and let the tides carry you where they may. But beware, for drift is the cousin of regret, and it loves to serenade those who chose the path of least resistance. Purposeful living? That's your earplugs, drowning out the tempting melody of a directionless existence.

Picture this: purpose is your North Star, shimmering in the vast cosmos of choices. Without it, you're lost in the wilderness, stumbling over roots and tripping on the branches of indecision. Purposeful living is your compass, your map, and your survival guide all rolled into one.

Comfortable drift, the silent assassin of dreams. It wraps its cozy arms around you, whispering sweet nothings about the safety of the familiar. But, my friend, purposeful living is the disruptor of comfortable stagnation. It's the alarm clock jolting you awake, reminding you that you've got dreams to chase.

Imagine your life as a ship, drifting aimlessly through the vastness of the sea. Now, imagine purpose as the captain at the helm, steering with determination. Without purpose, your ship is just adrift, at the mercy of unpredictable storms and capricious winds. Purposeful living is your captain, navigating you through the chaos.

Drifters collect dust, my friend. They accumulate the debris of missed opportunities and the residue of unfulfilled potential. Purposeful living? It's your duster, clearing away the cobwebs of hesitation and the grime of procrastination.

Drift is a mirage, shimmering with the illusion of ease and comfort. But once you reach out to touch it, you find emptiness. Purposeful living? It's the oasis in the desert, offering fulfillment, direction, and a damn good reason to keep marching through the sands of uncertainty.

Here's a secret: purposeful living is a rebellion. It's sticking a middle finger to the mundane and a defiant salute to the status quo. Drifters? They're the minions of conformity, marching in line. Purposeful living is your rebellion, your battle cry, and your war paint against the dull canvas of a purposeless existence.

Drifters leave no footprints, my friend. They tiptoe through life, leaving no mark on the sands of time. Purposeful living? It's your heavy boots, stomping through the wilderness of life, leaving a trail that screams, "I was here, and I mattered."

Life without purpose is like a silent movie with no music. Purposeful living? It's the blasting soundtrack of your existence, the rhythm that keeps you moving, and the melody that makes your heart skip a beat.

Drift is the seductive whirlpool that promises comfort but drags you into the abyss of regret. Purposeful living is your life jacket, your buoy, and your sturdy vessel, steering clear of the treacherous waters.

Life is a canvas, and purposeful living is your bold brushstroke, painting a masterpiece that tells a story. Drifters? They're the accidental spills, the unintended splatters that lack intention and narrative.

Drifters are unwritten novels, forever stuck in the prologue. Purposeful living? It's your epic saga, filled with plot twists, character development, and a riveting climax that keeps readers on the edge of their seats.

Life is a stormy sea, and purpose is the lighthouse guiding you through the turbulence. Drifters? They're lost sailors, tossed about by the tempest, yearning for a beacon that purposeful living provides.

Drift is a silent film, devoid of dialogue and substance. Purposeful living? It's your talkie, filled with profound conversations, impactful monologues, and the resonance of a life lived with meaning.

Imagine life as a construction site, and purposeful living is your toolbox. Drifters? They're the ones trying to build without the right tools, facing collapsed structures and unfinished projects. Purposeful living equips you with the wrenches and hammers needed to construct a life that stands tall and proud.

Drift is the whispers of regret echoing in the corridors of a purposeless mind. Purposeful living? It's the loud declarations of triumph, drowning out the regretful murmurs with the resounding cheers of a life well-lived.

Drift is discordant noise, a cacophony of missed chances and wasted time. Purposeful living? It's a symphony, each note a deliberate choice, each movement a step closer to the crescendo of a life rich with purpose.

Drifters are silent protagonists in their own story, letting life's script unfold without intervention. Purposeful living? It's your bold dialogue, your gripping monologue, and the narrative arc that keeps everyone hooked, eager to see what happens next.

And there you have it, the saga of purposeful living – a tale of deliberate choices, bold brushstrokes, and a symphony playing in the background. So, my purpose-driven companion, as you navigate the tumultuous seas of life, let your purpose be the anchor that keeps you grounded amidst the chaos. Avoid the tempting allure of drift, for you are the captain of your ship, and purposeful living is your compass in this grand adventure.

Life's Balancing Act

Ready yourself for a cosmic voyage into the mysterious realm of time management, where the seconds are the stars guiding your ship through the vast expanse of goals, priorities, and all the other celestial stuff. This ain't your average dance; it's the time tango, a symphony of chaos and order, with you as the fearless conductor.

Imagine time as the cosmic clockwork, a grand mechanism ticking away with relentless precision. But fear not, for in this celestial dance, you're not a mere spectator; you're the choreographer of your destiny, orchestrating the ballet of goals, priorities, and the whole cosmic shebang.

Goals, those elusive sirens, beckon with promises of treasure at the end of the rainbow. But beware, for not all treasures are worth the pursuit. In the time tango, discernment is your compass, guiding you to goals that harmonize with your soul's melody.

Priorities, the partners in your time tango, waltz in and out with a grace that demands attention. The art lies in mastering the priority polka, where each step is deliberate, ensuring that the dance floor of your life remains uncluttered and harmonious.

Life's a juggling act, a vivacious jive where responsibilities, passions, and the unexpected are the colorful balls in the air. The trick is not to drop the balls but to dance with them in rhythm, a jester in the court of time, entertaining chaos with grace.

As a time traveler in the time tango, dilemmas abound like portals to alternate realities. Choosing between what's urgent and what's important requires a discerning eye. The time traveler's dilemma is not about speed but about direction.

The cosmic choreography of time management is not a rigid routine but a spontaneous dance where goals and priorities pirouette across the stage of your existence. It's not about sticking to the script; it's about embracing the improvised brilliance of the moment.

Schedules are the instruments in the symphony of time, each playing a unique note. In the time tango, the symphony isn't about perfection but about creating a melody that resonates with the rhythm of your heart. Adjust the tempo, change the key, and let the symphony play on.

In the time tango, the magician's secret lies in the art of time warping. It's not about bending time to your will but about making time an ally. With a wave of your wand, transform the mundane into the magical, and let the time warp commence.

Goals are the unexplored horizons on the map of your journey. As an explorer of time, chart your course with audacious curiosity. Navigate not just towards the visible goals but also towards the hidden gems that shimmer on the edges of your perception.

Balancing goals and priorities is a tightrope walk in the circus of life. The trick is not just to stay on the tightrope but to dance on it with flair. Each step is a choice, a delicate pirouette between the gravity of obligations and the weightlessness of dreams.

A navigator in the time tango relies on a unique compass—purpose. Goals and priorities find their true north in the compass of purpose. As you navigate through the cosmic currents, let purpose be the guiding star that keeps your ship true.

Goals are the seeds, priorities are the watering cans, and time is the fertile soil. The gardener of time management doesn't just plant; they cultivate and harvest. Witness the blossoming of your efforts and savor the fruits of your well-tended temporal garden.

In the time tango, adopt the stargazer's perspective. Goals are the constellations guiding your journey, priorities are the planets aligning in your favor. Connect the dots, read the celestial signs, and navigate the vastness with the wisdom of an interstellar traveler.

Goals and priorities are the puppeteer's strings in the cosmic marionette show of life. But here, you're not a puppet; you're the puppeteer. Master the art of pulling the strings with intention, creating a dance that reflects your authenticity.

Time is the alchemist's crucible, where goals and priorities undergo transmutation. It's not about turning lead into gold but about transforming moments into memories, dreams into reality. Embrace the alchemy of time, and let each second be a drop in the elixir of your existence.

Balancing goals and priorities is an acrobatic feat, a dance on the narrow beam of existence. The acrobat doesn't fear the heights; they relish the challenge. In the time tango, become the virtuoso acrobat, executing flips of creativity and somersaults of focus.

Goals and priorities are the raw marble in the sculptor's hands. Carve with purpose, and let the sculpture of your life emerge with each intentional stroke. The sculptor doesn't rush; they savor the process, revealing the masterpiece within the uncut stone.

Listen to the whispers of time, for it holds secrets untold. The time whisperer deciphers these secrets, understanding that not every ticking second is the same. In the time tango, attune your ears to the subtle rhythms, and let time reveal its enigmatic dance.

Adopt the Magellan mindset in your time voyage. Goals are the uncharted territories, and priorities are the maps. Embrace the spirit of exploration, face the storms with resilience, and let the Magellan in you navigate the seas of time.

As a voyager in the grand time tango, pledge an oath to the cosmic clock. Let your oath be a declaration of intention, a promise to dance with purpose, and a commitment to savor every step in the intricate dance of goals, priorities, and all the other celestial stuff.

Remember, the most harmonious melodies are those that resonate deeply with the essence of who we are. The power of choice lies within your hands—or more aptly, within your heart. Not every note, technique, or method will align with the rhythm of your soul. And that's more than okay—it's expected. The beauty of this journey lies in the freedom to choose what works for you and gracefully set aside what doesn't. It's about crafting a personal symphony that reflects the depth, complexity, and uniqueness of your being.

Reflections for the Journey

Before you step out of "Orchestrating Impact: Conducting Life's Symphony with Purpose and Resilience" and into Life's Balancing Act, remember these reflections. They're the guiding lights in the concert hall of life, illuminating the path to a symphony that's uniquely yours—played with passion, conducted with purpose, and echoed with resilience.

1. **The Symphony of Now**   In the eternal dance of life, every moment pulses with music. Embrace the 'now' as your symphony plays, for it's in these fleeting beats that the essence of existence sings.
2. **Authenticity's Melody**   Let the music within you play freely, unencumbered by the world's noise. Your authenticity is your melody, a unique rhythm that defines the dance of your life.
3. **Courageous Crescendos**   Face life's challenges with the courage of a maestro facing a tumultuous orchestra. Each decision, a bold crescendo, amplifies your strength, echoing courage through the symphony of your existence.

4. **Resilience's Rhythm**   When adversity strikes, let resilience be your rhythm, keeping time in the face of discord. It's the beat that sustains you, ensuring the music never stops.

5. **The Harmony of Self-Compassion**   In the composition of life, self-compassion harmonizes the notes. It's a soothing melody that heals and nurtures, allowing you to play on with grace and strength.

6. **Flexibility's Flow**   Like a river's meander, flexibility in life's symphony ensures the music flows, uninterrupted by the rocks of rigidity. Adapt and improvise, for in flexibility, there's beauty.

7. **Tenacity's Tempo**   Let tenacity set your tempo, a steadfast beat against the storm. It's the persistent drum that resonates with determination, driving the symphony forward.

8. **Introspection's Interlude**   In the quiet spaces between life's movements, introspection offers a reflective pause. These interludes are essential, allowing you to tune into your inner symphony with clarity and purpose.

9. **Acceptance's Accord**   In life's symphony, acceptance is the chord that brings harmony. It's the understanding that all notes, whether joyful or somber, contribute to the beauty of the whole.

10. **The Conductor's Baton of Personal Power**   You wield the baton of personal power, guiding the symphony within. Direct your life's music with intention, blending the notes into a masterpiece of your making.

11. **The Sonata of Individuality:** Celebrate the sonata of your individuality, a composition that resonates with the authenticity of your being. Each key struck is a declaration of your unique presence in the world's orchestra.

12. **Lifelong Learning's Legacy**   The symphony within is enriched with each lesson learned. Lifelong learning is the

melody that evolves, a testament to your growth and the endless beauty of your internal composition.

Building the Relational Tapestry

Across these chapters, a unified theme emerges: the journey toward cultivating rich, fulfilling relationships is both intricate and essential. We're guided to weave our tapestry with intention, exploring the depths of genuine connections, and courageously unbinding ourselves from the chains of unhealthy ties. Each chapter offers unique insights and actionable steps to enrich our relational tapestry. As we draw these discussions to a close, our final reflections converge on some pivotal lessons, underscoring the journey's core insights and offering a pathway to enrich our interconnected web of life.

1. **Inventory and Reflection** Regularly assess the state of your relationships, acknowledging the beauty in each connection and identifying areas for growth or release.
2. **Cultivate Authenticity** Be genuine in your interactions, embracing vulnerability as a strength and fostering an environment where authenticity is celebrated.
3. **Practice Active Listening and Empathy** Deepen your connections through active listening and empathy, ensuring every thread in your tapestry feels seen, heard, and valued.
4. **Set and Respect Boundaries** Establish clear boundaries to protect your emotional well-being and respect those of others, fostering healthy, balanced relationships.
5. **Embrace Diversity and Change** Welcome the diverse threads that each person weaves into your life, and remain open to the growth and change that each relationship brings.

6. **Invest in Emotional Intelligence**   Enhance your relationships through emotional intelligence, understanding and managing your emotions and those of others for deeper connections.
7. **Nurture Shared Experiences**   Create and cherish shared moments and experiences, as these are the stitches that strengthen the fabric of your relationships.
8. **Let Go of What No Longer Serves You**   Courageously release connections that hinder your growth, making room for new threads that enrich your tapestry.

By integrating these lessons, we embark on a transformative journey toward a richer, more vibrant relational life. As we weave, untangle, and sometimes re-weave the threads of our connections, we create a living tapestry that reflects the depth, complexity, and beauty of human relationships.

Nurturing Your True Self

Across these chapters, a unified theme emerges: the journey to authenticity demands more than just the desire to peel away society's expectations; it requires actionable steps, reflective practices, and a steadfast commitment to nurturing our true selves. Herein lies a strategic blueprint to navigate the terrain of dispelling illusions and wholeheartedly welcoming your authentic self. This guide serves as your compass, offering direction and strategies to embark on this transformative journey, ensuring each step taken is grounded in purpose, reflection, and an enduring commitment to unveiling and celebrating the true you. As we draw these discussions to a close, our final reflections converge on some pivotal lessons, underscoring the journey's core insights and offering a pathway to enrich our interconnected web of life.

1. **Audit Your F*ck Budget**   Take inventory of where your f*cks are currently invested. List out the things, people, and pursuits you're dedicating your emotional currency to. Then, critically assess each one: Does it reflect your true values, or is it a product of societal expectation? Redirect your emotional investment towards what genuinely matters to you.

2. **Cultivate Self-Discovery**   Engage in activities that foster self-discovery. Journaling, meditation, and solo travel are potent tools for unearthing your authentic desires and aspirations. Set aside dedicated time each week to explore your inner landscape, seeking to understand the melody of your soul.

3. **Continue the Practice of Saying No**   Strengthen your ability to say no to things that don't align with your authentic self. Start small, perhaps by declining invitations or requests that don't resonate with you. Each act of saying no is a step towards reclaiming your time and energy for the things that truly matter.

4. **Embrace Vulnerability**   Authenticity and vulnerability go hand in hand. Begin sharing more of your true thoughts and feelings with others, even when it feels uncomfortable. Start with trusted friends or family, gradually expanding your circle as you become more confident in your authentic expression.

5. **Deconstruct Societal Masks**   Identify the roles and masks you wear that are more about societal approval than genuine self-expression. For each mask, ask yourself why you put it on and what fears are associated with taking it off. Begin experimenting with removing these masks in safe environments.

6. **Curate Your Influence** Assess the sources of influence in your life—social media, peer groups, family expectations. Consciously curate these influences, distancing yourself from those that reinforce the illusion and drawing closer to those that encourage authenticity.

7. **Celebrate Your Uniqueness** Identify traits, interests, and aspirations that make you unique, and find ways to celebrate and express them daily. Whether through your style, hobbies, or work, let these unique aspects shine.

8. **Reflect and Adjust** Regularly reflect on your journey towards authenticity. What felt liberating? What challenges did you encounter? Use these reflections to adjust your course, fine-tuning your approach to align more closely with your true self.

Activities for Embracing Authenticity:

- **Authenticity Journal** Keep a journal dedicated to your journey of authenticity. Use it to record insights, challenges, and victories along the way.
- **No Week Challenge** Dedicate a week to practicing saying no to things that don't align with your authentic self. Reflect on the experience.
- **Unmasking Ritual** Create a personal ritual for letting go of societal masks. This could involve a physical activity, like a symbolic burning of written fears or expectations, or a quiet meditation focused on releasing these burdens.
- **Authentic Expression Project** Start a project that allows you to express your unique self, such as writing, art, or creating a personal blog or vlog. Let this project be a testament to your individuality and a celebration of your authentic expression.

By following this roadmap and engaging with these activities, you're not just unmasking the illusion—you're stepping into a symphony of authenticity, composed by and for you. Your authentic self is the most beautiful and resonant note. Play it loud, play it proud, and let the world hear the true melody of who you are.

When you are ready for more, consider these steps for orchestrating your inner symphony:

1. **Conduct Your Day**   Start each morning by setting an intention that aligns with your inner symphony. Consider what melody you wish to play today—perhaps it's courage, resilience, or joy. Let this intention guide your actions and interactions throughout the day.
2. **Tune Out the Noise**   Dedicate a period each day to disconnect from external pressures. This could be through digital detoxes, quiet walks, or simply sitting in silence. Use this time to listen to the quieter notes of your inner melody.
3. **Self-Discovery Overture**   Journal about the different facets of your identity as if they were instruments in your symphony. What unique sound does each one contribute? How do they harmonize to create the music of 'you'?
4. **Authenticity Crescendo**   Identify moments when you feel most authentic and alive. What are you doing? Who are you with? Reflect on how you can amplify these moments in your life to let your true self play louder.
5. **Resilience Strings**   Reflect on a recent challenge and how you navigated it. Write about the 'music' you used to endure—was it a slow, steady tune or a powerful anthem? Celebrate your resilience and consider how it enriches your symphony.
6. **Bold Brass Moments**   Think of a time when you needed to stand up for yourself or make your presence known. How did you summon the courage? Create a 'bold brass' playlist that inspires you to amplify your convictions.

7. **Woodwind Flexibility** Practice flexibility by introducing small changes into your routine. Notice how adaptation feels and journal about the experience. Is it uncomfortable, liberating, or both?

8. **Percussion of Tenacity** Set a challenging goal for yourself, something that requires persistence. Break it down into actionable steps and track your progress, celebrating each 'beat' of achievement.

9. **Choir of Compassion** Perform a daily act of self-kindness. This could be forgiving a mistake, treating yourself, or simply offering words of encouragement. Note how these acts influence the harmony of your inner symphony.

10. **Solo of Introspection** Spend time in solitude reflecting on your values, dreams, and the music you want to make in the world. Consider how your actions contribute to or detract from this vision.

11. **Symphony of Connection** Reach out to someone who adds beautiful harmony to your life. Share your appreciation for their presence and explore how you can create more beautiful music together.

12. **Lifelong Learning Cadence** Commit to learning something new that resonates with your inner symphony. This could be a skill, hobby, or area of knowledge. Reflect on how this new learning enriches your music.

13. **Silence Between the Notes** Incorporate moments of silence into your daily life to appreciate the music you're creating. Use these pauses to breathe, reflect, and prepare for the next note.

14. **Reflective Encore** At the end of each week, reflect on the music you've created. What felt harmonious? What notes would you change? Use these reflections to fine-tune your symphony moving forward.

Congratulations, you've not only mastered the time tango but also conducted a symphony of purpose and audacity. May your steps be filled with purpose, your rhythms be harmonious, and your dance be an everlasting celebration of existence.

Week 6 Action Plan: Navigating Uncharted Waters

Welcome to Week 6, where we dive into the final chapters of "Harmony in the Chaos" to navigate the uncharted waters of life with agility, purpose, and balance. This week, you'll harness the full power of your internal compass, embrace life's unpredictable curveballs, and chart a course toward true liberation and balance.

Day 1: "Master that Compass Already!"
- **Activity:** Design your personal compass. On a piece of paper, draw a compass and label the four directions with your core values. Place this compass somewhere you will see it daily.
- **Reflection:** How do your core values guide your daily decisions and long-term goals?

Day 2: "The Occasional Cosmic Curveball"
- **Activity:** Reflect on a recent "curveball" life threw at you. Write about how you responded, what you learned, and how you might handle similar unexpected events in the future.

- **Reflection:** What does this curveball teach you about your resilience and adaptability?

Day 3: "The Map to Liberation"
- **Activity:** Create a "Map to Liberation" by listing resentments and grudges you are carrying. Next to each, write at least one action you can take to liberate yourself.
- **Reflection:** How does envisioning your path to liberation make you feel, and which burdensome weights you most excited to rid yourself of?

Day 4: "Back to the Garden of Priorities"
- **Activity:** Spend time in nature or a place that brings you peace. Contemplate your priorities and how they've shifted throughout this journey.
- **Reflection:** In what ways has reconnecting with your priorities in a peaceful setting provided clarity or new insights?

Day 5: "Unlike Jellyfish, Take Aim"
- **Activity:** Set a specific, measurable goal related to a personal project or aspiration. Outline the steps you need to take to achieve this goal.
- **Reflection:** How does setting a clear aim empower you to move forward with intention?

Day 6: "Life's Balancing Act"
- **Activity:** For the next week, practice a physical balance exercise (e.g., yoga, standing on one foot) as a metaphor for life's balance. While you are balancing, reflect on the areas of your life that need more balance.
- **Reflection:** What did the physical act of balancing teach you about maintaining equilibrium in your life?

Day 7: Weekly Integration - Charting Your Course

- **Activity:** Combine insights from this week into a "Life's Course Chart." This could be a visual representation, written plan, or another creative format that maps out how you'll navigate life's complexities with your newly sharpened compass.
- **Reflection:** Reflect on the journey you've undertaken during these six weeks. How have your perspectives shifted, and how do you feel equipped to handle the chaos and harmony of life?

This week's journey brings you to the helm of your life's ship, with a firm grip on your compass, eyes on the horizon, and a heart ready for whatever the seas may bring. As you continue to navigate the waters of life, remember that your compass, crafted from your deepest values and lessons learned, will always guide you back to your true north. Keep charting your course with courage, curiosity, and an unwavering commitment to your journey of growth and impact.

The Resilient Growth Self-Assessment

We're about to embark on a journey together—an unapologetic expedition into the uncharted territories of your own psyche. Buckle up for a rollercoaster ride through the rugged terrains of resilience, adaptability, and emotional fortitude. This is where we assess your prowess in weathering life's storms, dancing through the rain, and emerging stronger on the other side. Think of it as a reality check for your emotional biceps—we want to know how much heavy lifting they can do.

The Resilient Growth Self-Assessment

The Unapologetic Revolution of Self-Reflection: Unveiling Paths to Growth

In the epic saga of personal growth, the almighty tool in your rebellious arsenal is self-assessment. This unfiltered exploration invites you to dig into the trenches of your strengths, face the dragons of your weaknesses, and unearth the treasure troves of growth opportunities. But, make no mistake, this isn't a prim and proper tea party; it's a rebellious expedition into the wild terrain of your authentic self.

1. **A Riotous Inner Journey** Self-assessment is your personal rollercoaster ride. It's a no-judgment zone, and you're the sole master of your voyage. No need for

polished facades or playing to an audience. This is your wild, untamed space for brutally honest introspection.

2. **The Truth Glasses**   Slap on those truth glasses like a renegade aviator. Honesty is your co-pilot as you soar through your emotional landscape. This isn't rose-tinted glasses territory; it's the raw, unfiltered view of your reactions, coping styles, and the quirky dance of your behavioral patterns.

3. **Unveiling Rebel Fortresses**   Each honest answer is a cannon shot, tearing down the walls hiding your strengths and exposing the fortresses where growth awaits. Your self-assessment rebellion isn't just about acknowledging the good; it's about embracing the messy, uncovering the glorious imperfections.

4. **Authenticity as a Rebel Badge**   This isn't a tea cozy version of authenticity. This is the rebellion of embracing the chaos, proudly showcasing your struggles, and putting your challenges on the rebellious runway. Authenticity becomes the war paint for your personal growth battles.

5. **A Construction Site of Change**   Imagine you're not just building a house; you're erecting a fortress of personal evolution. Honest self-assessment lays the groundwork for wrecking ball-sized change. It's the rebel architect's blueprint for building something that stands the test of time.

6. **Biases, Meet Your Nemesis**   Human nature loves to sugarcoat the bitter pills. But you, rebel, you strip away the candy coating. Honesty dismantles the cognitive biases that often sugarcoat reality. It's a rebellion against self-deception, seeing yourself as you truly are.

7. **Resilience, the Rebel's Armor**   Emotional resilience isn't forged in the fires of denial. It's smelted in the furnace of self-awareness and authenticity. Honest self-assessment is

the rebel's anvil, shaping the armor that helps you weather the storms and emerge unscathed.

8. **Growth Mindset, the Rebel's Creed**   A growth mindset isn't just a fancy quote on a mug. It's your rebel battle cry. Honesty in self-assessment is the rebel manifesto, declaring that challenges are your playground and failures are your stepping stones to a glorious victory.

9. **Rebel Victory Parades**   Honest self-assessment isn't just a checklist; it's your victory diary. It sets the stage for epic parades celebrating your triumphs, no matter how small. This isn't just self-reflection; it's a rebellious fiesta of progress.

When you answer the self-assessment questions, do it with the audacity of a pirate stealing treasures from the realms of your inner world. This isn't just a conversation; it's a rebellious dialogue with your badass self. Embrace it with the fervor of a mosh pit at a rock concert, and let it propel you into the uncharted territories of personal evolution. The revolution begins with you, the rebel architect of your damn destiny. Cheers to the unapologetic rebellion of self-assessment!

Navigating Life's Complexities

The Resilient Growth Self-Assessment© is more than just a checklist; it's a dynamic tool designed to help you chart your course through the intricate landscape of personal growth. As you embark on this journey, consider these characteristics not as static attributes but as the fluid strokes on the canvas of your evolving self. Let's dive into the essence of a few key characteristics and explore how they form the threads of resilience and purpose that weave through the fabric of a f*ckwell-lived existence.

Adaptability: Flexibility in the Face of Life's Twists and Turns

- Life is a wild dance, and adaptability is your nimble footwork. How gracefully can you navigate the twists and turns of life's unpredictable choreography?

Coping Skills: Effective Mechanisms to Handle Stress and Challenges

- Stress knocks on everyone's door, but not everyone answers. What are your go-to tools for handling stress, and how well do they serve you in the face of life's challenges?

Inner Strength: A Reservoir of Fortitude for Enduring Difficult Situations

- Life's storms are inevitable. How deep is your well of inner strength, and how does it sustain you when the winds of adversity blow?

Tenacity: A Determined and Persistent Approach to Life's Hurdles

- Life is a marathon, not a sprint. How tenaciously do you tackle challenges, and what fuels your persistence when the road gets tough?

Courage: Facing Challenges with Bravery, Even Amid Uncertainty

- Courage isn't the absence of fear; it's the triumph over it. How boldly do you face challenges, especially when the outcome is uncertain?

Optimism: Maintaining a Positive Outlook, Fostering Resilience

- Life's glass is both half full and half empty. How do you choose to see it, and how does your optimism shape your resilience in the face of adversity?

Proactivity: Taking Initiative and Actively Seeking Solutions

- Life favors the bold. How proactively do you shape your destiny, and what steps do you take to actively create the life you want?

Growth Mindset: Embracing Opportunities for Learning and Personal Growth

- Life is a continuous classroom. How open are you to its lessons, and how does a growth mindset propel you forward on your journey of personal evolution?

Resourcefulness: Finding Creative Solutions in Complex Situations

- Life's challenges rarely come with a manual. How resourceful are you in finding creative solutions when faced with complexity?

Stress Management: Effectively Navigating and Managing Stressors

- Stress is an inevitable companion. How skillfully do you navigate its terrain, and what tools do you employ to manage its impact on your well-being?

The journey doesn't end here. These characteristics are the beginning, the foundation upon which we'll build the framework for your resilient and purposeful existence. As you reflect on these attributes, remember that this self-assessment is a dynamic guide, not a final destination. Let's continue this exploration, forging a path that resonates with your unique rhythm and authenticity.

Welcome to the Unapologetic Self-Assessment Blitz!

Behold, the key: to unlocking the mysteries of your rebellious soul—a self-assessment that's not for the faint-hearted. This isn't a checklist; it's a 35-question thrill ride designed to expose the nuances of your audacious journey toward embracing the chaos and crafting your own damn destiny.

> **Author's Note** The Resilient Growth Self-Assessment© is a copyrighted professional tool intended for individual use that tests dozens of behavior characteristics and represents years of research. While comparable intelligence and leadership assessments often come with price tags ranging from $65 to $350, we're pleased to offer our assessment completely free of charge to readers who purchase a new copy of this book. If you wish to utilize it within your organization, a licensing fee per user is required. For licensing inquiries and further details, please visit **williamrstanek.com/livewell/**. Thank you for respecting the intellectual property rights associated with this valuable resource.

Instructions for Taking the Assessment

1. **Embark on a Digital Odyssey** Ready your rebel self for a digital adventure. No, we're not sending you into the virtual void for cat videos. Visit **williamrstanek.com/livewell/** and brace yourself for an automated rollercoaster of self-discovery. This ain't a personality quiz—this is the rebellion of resilience and authenticity!

2. **Read Between the Lines** Dive into the statements like a pirate digging for treasure. Read each one with the scrutiny of an undercover agent investigating a conspiracy. Consider how well they resonate with your

rebel spirit—your behavior, thoughts, and the chaotic dance of your feelings.

3. **The Art of Rating** Strap in for the rating rodeo. Are you a Rarely Rebel, a Sometimes Slayer, an Often Overlord, an Absolutely Anarchist, or an Innate Insurgent? Assign each statement its rebellious rank based on how much it vibes with your glorious rebellion.

    a. **Rarely (1)** This rating suggests that you perceive the characteristic described in the statement to apply to you in a very limited or infrequent way. It is not a common occurrence in your behavior, thoughts, or feelings.

    b. **Sometimes (2)** You believe that the characteristic does apply to you, but it is not a consistent or regular part of your behavior or mindset. It occurs periodically or in specific situations.

    c. **Often (3)** This rating signifies that the characteristic is a frequent occurrence in your behavior, thoughts or feelings. It is a regular part of how you approach situations and challenges.

    d. **Absolutely (4)** This rating indicates that the characteristic strongly resonates with you. It is a significant and consistent part of your behavior, mindset, or self-perception, influencing how you approach various situations and challenges in a profound and reliable manner.

    e. **Innate (5)** This rating signifies that the characteristic is not only deeply ingrained but also an essential and natural part of your behavior, mindset, or self-perception. It reflects a fundamental aspect of who you are, influencing how you approach various situations and challenges in a consistent and profound manner.

4. **Be Honest**   Channel your inner truth warrior. This isn't the time for sugar-coated confessions or modesty. Embrace the honesty like a bandit acknowledging their true calling. The more authentic, the better.

5. **Trust Your Instincts**   Don't second-guess like a rookie superhero debating whether to wear a cape. Trust your gut, your instincts, your rebel compass. Snap decisions are your rebellion's best friend.

6. **The 35-Question Marathon**   It's not a sprint; it's a marathon. Answer all 35 questions like you're conquering a battlefield. This isn't a leisurely stroll; it's a full-on rebellion against self-doubt.

7. **Save Your Scores.** Write down the score for the assessment you selected. Repeat this process to take the other assessment when you are ready. You *don't* have to take both tests at the same time or on the same day; you *do* have to write down and keep your scores with a notation regarding which score is for which assessment.

Self-assessment isn't a mundane task. It's the artillery in your rebellion, providing insights into your chaos-embracing prowess. It's a mirror reflecting the contours of your audacious journey. So, buckle up! Let the self-assessment commence, and may the odds be ever in favor of your unapologetic, rebellious soul.

> **Author's Note**   Select the value that most accurately represents your feelings or behaviors for each characteristic, ranging from 1 'Rarely' to 5 'Absolutely.' If this scale doesn't align with your perspective or the question/statement, consider it as ranging from 1 'Disagree' to 5 'Innate' for an alternate interpretation, as in:
>
> **1) Disagree**   I disagree with this statement. It is not a common occurrence in my behavior, thoughts, or feelings.

2) Mixed I have mixed feelings about this statement, neither entirely in agreement nor disagreement. It occurs periodically or in specific situations.

3) Agree This statement aligns well with my beliefs and experiences, but without absolute certainty. It is a regular part of my behavior, thoughts, or feelings.

4) Absolutely Agree This statement strongly resonates with my viewpoint and I wholeheartedly endorse it. It is a significant and consistent part of my behavior, mindset, or self-perception.

5) Innate This statement reflects a pervasive and inherent part of my behavior, mindset, or self-perception. It is naturally occurring and a core aspect of my behavior, mindset, or self-perception.

Scoring the Assessments Like a Maestro

So, you've bravely navigated the chaos of self-assessment. Now comes the time to score your audacious endeavors. This is where the rubber meets the road and the sparks of your true self ignite the scoring fireworks.

1. **Total the Ranks** Grab your calculator, or better yet, a quill and abacus, and tally up those ranks. Add the scores you bestowed upon each statement. The grand total? Your magnificence in numeric form. (You don't really need a calculator or a quill and abacus, the total is displayed for you.)

2. **The Unapologetic Interpretation:**

- **35 - 59 Very Low**   This isn't an insult; it's an opportunity to turn your rebellion volume up. Embrace the chaos; it's your symphony in the making.

- **60 - 84 Low**   You're not low; you're just priming your rebellion engines. A rebel warm-up, if you will. The storm is brewing; get ready to dance in the rain.

- **85 - 109 Moderate**   You're in the moderate rebellion league. A rebel apprenticeship, perhaps. But hey, even Darth Vader had to start somewhere.

- **110 - 134 Average**   Average is just a label. You're the rebel middle child, poised for a breakout. Your rebellion is brewing beneath the surface.

- **135 - 159 Above Average**   Above average? That's just a humble way of saying you're a rebel powerhouse. Your rebellion has wings; it's time to soar.

- **160 - 172 High**   High? More like rebellious skyscraper. You're hitting the stratosphere. The view from the top? Pure audacious awesomeness.

- **173 - 175 Exceptional**   Exceptional? You're not just a rebel; you're the maestro of the orchestra. Your rebellion is a symphony, and you're the virtuoso.

Your score isn't a sentence; it's a proclamation. It's not an endpoint; it's the launchpad for your odyssey. So, wear your score like a badge, whether it's a joyous jamboree or a symphony in progress. The rebellion never ends; it just evolves into something more audacious. Cheers to your unapologetic scoring rebellion!

Unmasking the Scores

You've successfully charted the self-assessment, and now the time has come to decode your scores. Brace yourself as we unveil the audacious strategies tailored just for you—strategies that align with your personalized rating. It's time to transform your rebellion into an unstoppable force.

Interpreting Your Resilience Scores: The Rebels' Prelude

- **Very Low (35 - 59)** Novice Stage. Welcome, novice! You're at the beginning of your journey, like the first brushstroke on a blank canvas. Dive into life's intricacies, build that endurance, and befriend failure—it's a reliable teacher. Remember, life is a marathon, not a sprint. The symphony is just tuning up.

- **Low (60 - 84)** Learning Ground. Ah, the learning ground! You've taken the first steps, but a vast terrain awaits exploration. Identify areas for growth; there's richness in the uncharted territories. Ready, set, explore!

- **Moderate (85 - 109)** Middle Ground of Growth. Welcome to the middle ground of personal evolution. You're navigating life's seas, showing strength in some aspects, but refinement is key. Sharpen your skills; there are sculptures of priorities waiting to be crafted. In moderation, your journey unfolds.

- **Average (110 - 134)** Composer of Life. Average? Not you! While you handle storms reasonably well, there's a masterpiece waiting to be composed. Identify areas for growth. Every challenge is a chance to create something extraordinary. Tune in to your life's rhythm and start composing.

- **Above Average (135 - 159)** Virtuoso in the Making. Above average? You're flexing your muscles! Dive into deeper waters; your journey has the potential to reach greater heights. It's a dance of refinement and expansion. Above average today, exceptional tomorrow. Your journey is turning into a virtuoso performance.

- **High (160 - 172)** Maestro of Life. Congratulations, maestro! Your journey echoes with high notes. Adaptability is your forte. Now, refine the masterpiece. Explore uncharted territories with audacious courage. Your journey is a symphony, and the world awaits the next movement. The maestro is in the house!

- **Exceptional (173 - 175)** Virtuoso of Life. Bravo, virtuoso! Your journey is exceptional, a force to be reckoned with. You navigate storms with grace. Now, fine-tune the life orchestra. Embrace the legacy of impact, for exceptional journeys leave an indelible mark. The virtuoso's legacy is about to be written in the annals of life. Bravo!

Remember, this self-assessment is your compass in the rebellious odyssey. It's not a judgment; it's a celebration of your rebellion. Dive into the strategies, tweak your symphony, and let this be the beginning of an audacious evolution. The rebellion never ends; it just becomes more refined. Cheers to your unapologetic self!

Very Low: Novice Stage - A Canvas Awaits

So, you find yourself navigating the treacherous waters of the Very Low (35 - 59) range, waving a cheeky middle finger to mediocrity. Well done, rebel. Your journey into the Art of Discernment, exploring the Lighthouse of Core Values, and mastering the damn compass, might have encountered some rogue waves. No worries; you're not alone in this chaotic joyride. This is your opportunity to craft a symphony of personal growth.

Your personal growth playlist is a bit off-key, it's time to recalibrate. You're not just chasing happiness; you're hijacking joy, flipping off misery like a boss, and mastering the F*ck Budget for an unapologetic Joy Jamboree. Picture yourself as the captain of your joy ship, navigating the emotional landscape with an audacious middle finger to despair.

Let's break down what this score range signifies for each key characteristic:

- **Adaptability**   In the rebel infancy of adaptability, change may feel like an unwelcome guest crashing the party. Fear not; this is your invitation to embrace the dance of transformation. Begin by introducing small changes into your routine, gradually acclimating to the rhythm of life's unpredictable melodies.
- **Coping Skills**   Your coping skills are like fledgling rebels in need of guidance. Stressors may seem like formidable foes, but

think of them as challenges to be conquered. Experiment with various coping mechanisms, discovering the rebel tools that resonate with your spirit.

- **Inner Strength** Building inner strength is akin to crafting the foundation of a rebel fortress. Acknowledge your strengths and past victories; they're the bricks and mortar of resilience. The rebel journey involves recognizing the power within and channeling it to weather life's storms.

- **Tenacity, Courage, and Optimism** These characteristics are still in their rebel infancy. Develop tenacity by persisting through challenges. Exercise courage by confronting fears head-on. Cultivate optimism by finding silver linings in the rebel clouds. The rebel journey is about nurturing these characteristics to face life's adventures with audacious spirit.

- **Proactivity and Growth** Mindset In the rebel infancy of proactivity, the call to action is faint but growing louder. Seize opportunities to take initiative. Actively seek solutions, and approach challenges as opportunities for growth. The rebel path involves developing a proactive stance in shaping your narrative.

- **Resourcefulness and Stress Management** Resourcefulness is emerging, like a rebel awakening to its potential. Explore creative solutions to challenges, and craft your toolkit for navigating life's tempests. Stress management is a skill to hone, much like tuning an instrument. The rebel journey encourages refining these tools for a harmonious existence.

- **Ambiguity Tolerance and Self-Efficacy** Navigate the seas of ambiguity with a spirit of curiosity. Cultivate comfort in the unknown, much like a rebel embarking on uncharted waters. Strengthen self-efficacy by believing in your ability to overcome challenges. The rebel journey involves dancing with uncertainty and trusting in your capabilities.

- **Cognitive Appraisal and Flexibility** Sharpen your cognitive appraisal skills. Make informed decisions through thoughtful assessment, much like a rebel strategist plotting their course. Flexibility is crucial; adapt to changing circumstances with an open mind. The rebel path is about staying agile in the ever-shifting landscape of life.

- **Problem-Solving Skills and Emotional Regulation** Develop problem-solving skills by analyzing and finding solutions to complex problems. Emotional regulation is a key rebel skill, akin to mastering the art of navigating stormy emotional seas. The rebel journey involves honing these skills to navigate life's intricate tapestry.

- **Endurance, Acceptance of Failure, and Tolerance for Discomfort** Endurance is the rebel's stamina. Persevere through long-term challenges, building resilience over time. Embrace failure as a learning opportunity. The rebel soul thrives on resilience forged in the fires of mistakes. Tolerance for discomfort is the rebel's willingness to endure short-term discomfort for long-term gain.

- **Navigating Uncertainty and Patience** Navigate uncertainty with a calm demeanor. Develop patience as a rebel virtue. The rebel journey is a steady course through the seas of uncertainty, and patience is the compass guiding your way.

- **Realistic Optimism and Long-Term Goal Focus** Balance optimism with a realistic understanding of challenges. The rebel journey involves maintaining a positive outlook while staying grounded. Focus on long-term goals; the rebel's legacy is crafted through deliberate, purposeful actions.

- **Regulating Expectations, Mindset Shift, and Self-Compassion** Manage and adjust expectations on the rebel path. Shift from a victim mentality to a proactive problem-solving mindset. Embrace self-compassion, treating yourself with kindness and understanding. The rebel's journey involves cultivating a positive, empowering mindset.

- **Self-Acceptance, Reframing Challenges, and Forgiveness** Embrace self-acceptance on the rebel journey. Acknowledge strengths and areas for improvement. Reframe challenges as opportunities for growth. Forgiveness is the rebel's ability to let go of past grievances, freeing up mental and emotional space for a flourishing rebel spirit.

- **Openness to Change and Holistic Well-Being** Embrace change as a natural part of personal evolution. The rebel journey involves staying open to new approaches. Recognize the interconnectedness of physical, emotional, and mental well-being.

In essence, your journey at this stage is a blank canvas awaiting vibrant colors. Embrace the process of self-discovery and personal growth. Each challenge is an opportunity, and every step is a stroke in the masterpiece of your life. The symphony is just beginning, and the novitiate promises a rich and fulfilling journey ahead.

Remember, building these characteristics is a rebellion, not a retreat. Be your unapologetic self, and let's turn those Very Low scores into a symphony of personal growth. Your journey toward embracing the Art of Saying No, sculpting your priorities, and dancing with integrity just got a hell of a lot more interesting. Let the journey continue!

Low: Foundational Fierceness Cultivation

So, you find yourself strolling through the landscape of Low (60 - 84), ready to upend the status quo with a rebellious grin. Kudos, rebel! Your exploration of Resilience Rhythms, the Mindset Makeover, and the Courage Quest might have faced a few challenges. No biggie; this journey of yours is like a rollercoaster, and you're holding the middle finger high in the face of adversity. It's time to turn this symphony of personal growth up a notch.

Your playlist for personal development is tuning up but needs a bit more bass. You're not just savoring happiness; you're orchestrating joy, flipping off negativity with style, and perfecting the F*ck Budget for a grand Unapologetic Jubilee. Envision yourself as the director of your joy orchestra, conquering the emotional terrain with an audacious disregard for gloom.

In this low range, certain characteristics might need a bit more nurturing. Let's break it down:

- **Adaptability**   In the realm of adaptability, your rebellion is in the infancy stage. It's time to embrace change as a constant companion. Consider introducing small changes into your routine, gradually expanding your comfort zone. Life's twists and turns are opportunities for growth.

- **Coping Skills**   Your coping skills are in the early stages of development. Identify stressors and explore various coping mechanisms. The rebel journey involves mastering the art of resilience. Experiment with different stress-management techniques to find what resonates with your unique rebel soul.

- **Inner Strength**   You're building the foundation of inner strength, but there's room for fortification. Develop a reservoir of fortitude by acknowledging your strengths and accomplishments. The rebel spirit flourishes when anchored in self-belief. Reflect on past challenges, recognizing the strength within.

- **Tenacity, Courage, and Optimism** These characteristics are akin to rebel muscles in the gym—ready for progressive training. Build tenacity by persisting through challenges. Exercise courage by facing fears head-on. Cultivate optimism by focusing on the positive aspects of situations. The rebel path involves flexing these muscles in the face of adversity.

- **Proactivity and Growth Mindset** In the world of proactivity, seize opportunities to take initiative. Actively seek solutions and new experiences. Nurture a growth mindset by embracing challenges as opportunities for learning. The rebel journey involves a proactive approach to shaping your narrative.

- **Resourcefulness and Stress Management** Resourcefulness is emerging; sharpen this rebel skill. Explore creative solutions to challenges. Stress management is like navigating stormy seas; refine your techniques. The rebel path encourages crafting a toolkit to navigate life's tempests with finesse.

- **Ambiguity Tolerance and Self-Efficacy** Navigate uncertain waters with a spirit of curiosity. Ambiguity tolerance is the compass; cultivate comfort in the unknown. Strengthen self-efficacy by believing in your ability to overcome challenges. The rebel's journey is a dance between embracing uncertainty and trusting in personal capabilities.

- **Cognitive Appraisal and Flexibility** Sharpen your cognitive appraisal skills. Make informed decisions through thoughtful assessment. Flexibility is crucial in the rebel's toolkit. Adapt to changing circumstances with an open mind. The rebel path is about staying agile in the ever-shifting landscape of life.

- **Problem-Solving Skills and Emotional Regulation** Develop problem-solving skills by analyzing and finding solutions to complex problems. Emotional regulation is a key rebel skill. Actively manage and regulate emotions for a balanced approach to life's challenges. The rebel journey involves honing these skills to navigate life's intricate tapestry.

- **Endurance, Acceptance of Failure, and Tolerance for Discomfort**   Endurance is the rebel's stamina. Persevere through long-term challenges, building resilience over time. Embrace failure as a learning opportunity. The rebel soul thrives on resilience forged in the fires of mistakes. Tolerance for discomfort is the rebel's willingness to endure short-term discomfort for long-term gain.

- **Navigating Uncertainty and Patience**   Navigate uncertainty with a calm demeanor. Develop patience as a rebel virtue. The rebel journey is a steady course through the seas of uncertainty, and patience is the compass guiding your way.

- **Realistic Optimism and Long-Term Goal Focus**   Balance optimism with a realistic understanding of challenges. The rebel journey involves maintaining a positive outlook while staying grounded. Focus on long-term goals; the rebel's legacy is crafted through deliberate, purposeful actions.

- **Regulating Expectations, Mindset Shift, and Self-Compassion**   Manage and adjust expectations on the rebel path. Shift from a victim mentality to a proactive problem-solving mindset. Embrace self-compassion, treating yourself with kindness and understanding. The rebel's journey involves cultivating a positive, empowering mindset.

- **Self-Acceptance, Reframing Challenges, and Forgiveness**   Embrace self-acceptance on the rebel journey. Acknowledge strengths and areas for improvement. Reframe challenges as opportunities for growth. Forgiveness is the rebel's ability to let go of past grievances, freeing up mental and emotional space for a flourishing rebel spirit.

- **Openness to Change and Holistic Well-Being**   Embrace change as a natural part of personal evolution. The rebel journey involves staying open to new approaches. Recognize the interconnectedness of physical, emotional, and mental well-being. The rebel's holistic approach to well-being is the key to a thriving, fulfilled life.

- **Staying Grounded and Respect for Boundaries** Maintain a sense of perspective amid life's challenges. Staying grounded is the rebel's anchor. Recognize and respect personal boundaries on the rebel path. The rebel journey involves navigating life with mindfulness and an awareness of personal limits.

- **Empathy Towards Oneself and Self-Reflection** Show oneself the same empathy given to others. Cultivate a practice of self-reflection. The rebel's journey involves understanding oneself deeply and developing a compassionate relationship with your inner rebel.

In this low range, you're in the early stages of your rebel journey. It's an exciting time of exploration and growth, laying the foundation for a more resilient, purposeful, and joyful existence. Embrace the journey with curiosity and a rebellious spirit!

Remember, building these characteristics is a rebellion, not a resignation. Be your unapologetic self, and let's transform those Low scores into a full-blown symphony of personal growth. Your journey toward mastering the Art of Courageous Decision-Making, sculpting your authenticity, and dancing with emotional intelligence just got a whole lot more thrilling. Let the symphony play on!"

Moderate: Crafting a Rebel Fortress

So, you find yourself navigating the sea of Moderate (85 - 109), with an unapologetic swagger that screams, 'I'm forging my own path.' Salutations, rebel! Your expedition into the Resilience Reverb, the Mindfulness Melody, and the Integrity Interlude has seen its share of waves. But here's the thing — you're not just riding them; you're shredding them like a rockstar. This is your chance to elevate the symphony of personal growth.

Your playlist for personal development is grooving, perhaps just a tad more rhythm needed. You're not merely embracing happiness; you're orchestrating joy, scoffing at pessimism with flair, and perfecting the F*ck Budget for an unapologetic Carnival of Bliss. Picture yourself as the conductor of your joy symphony, conquering the emotional landscape with a bold defiance of negativity.

Let's break down what this score range suggests for each key characteristic:

Adaptability   Congratulations, rebel navigator! In the realm of adaptability, you're charting waters with a seasoned hand. Change doesn't send shockwaves through your rebel ship; it's more like a welcomed breeze. Continue to embrace transformation, refining your adaptability into a resilient force against life's unpredictable tides.

Coping Skills   Your coping skills are evolving into reliable rebel allies. Stressors are like challenging opponents, and you've honed your skills for effective confrontation. As a moderate rebel, keep refining your coping toolbox, adding versatile instruments to harmonize with the ever-changing rebel symphony.

Inner Strength   The rebel fortress is strengthening; your inner resilience is a formidable guardian. Acknowledge the depth of your inner strength and draw upon it during life's storms. As a moderate rebel, your foundation is solid, and your ability to endure challenges is a testament to the rebel spirit.

Tenacity, Courage, and Optimism   In the moderate range, your tenacity is gaining momentum. Persistence is your rebel companion, and challenges are met with a determined gaze. Courage is becoming a familiar ally; you face fears with growing confidence. Optimism is your rebel lens, focusing on the positive notes in the rebel symphony of life.

Proactivity and Growth Mindset   The call to action is resonating louder for the moderate rebel. Your proactive stance is more defined, and the rebel path involves seizing opportunities with purpose. Embrace challenges with a growth mindset, viewing them as stepping stones for personal evolution.

Resourcefulness and Stress Management   Your resourcefulness is blossoming into a key rebel trait. Creative solutions are your forte, and your toolkit for navigating life's tempests is becoming more sophisticated. Stress management is a skill you're refining, harmonizing the rebel orchestra for a more balanced existence.

Ambiguity Tolerance and Self-Efficacy   Navigate the seas of ambiguity with seasoned curiosity. As a moderate rebel, you're growing comfortable in the unknown, a skill essential for navigating life's uncharted waters. Strengthen self-efficacy by continually believing in your ability to overcome challenges.

Cognitive Appraisal and Flexibility   Your cognitive appraisal skills are sharp, much like a rebel strategist. In the moderate range, make informed decisions through thoughtful assessment, plotting your course with clarity. Flexibility is your rebel strength, adapting to changing circumstances with grace and open-mindedness.

Problem-Solving Skills and Emotional Regulation   As a moderate rebel, problem-solving is a skill you're honing. Analyzing and finding solutions to complex problems is second nature. Emotional regulation is a key aspect of your rebel toolkit, navigating stormy emotional seas with resilience and finesse.

Endurance, Acceptance of Failure, and Tolerance for Discomfort   Endurance is the hallmark of the moderate rebel. Perseverance through long-term challenges is your strength, building resilience with each step. Embrace failure as a learning opportunity, for it's the rebel forge where resilience is crafted. Tolerance for discomfort is your willingness to endure short-term challenges for long-term rebel gains.

Navigating Uncertainty and Patience   Navigating uncertainty is your steady rebel course. Your calm demeanor in the face of the unknown is an invaluable trait. Patience is your guiding star; as a moderate rebel, you understand the power of waiting for the right rebel moments to unfold.

Realistic Optimism and Long-Term Goal Focus   Balance optimism with a realistic understanding of challenges; this is the mantra of the moderate rebel. Maintain a positive outlook while staying grounded in reality. Focus on long-term goals; the moderate rebel legacy is crafted through deliberate, purposeful actions.

Regulating Expectations, Mindset Shift, and Self-Compassion
In the moderate range, manage and adjust expectations with the wisdom of a seasoned rebel. Shift from a victim mentality to a proactive problem-solving mindset. Embrace self-compassion; treat yourself with kindness and understanding. The moderate

rebel's journey involves cultivating a positive, empowering mindset.

Self-Acceptance, Reframing Challenges, and Forgiveness
Self-acceptance is growing as a moderate rebel. Embrace yourself, acknowledging strengths and areas for improvement. Reframe challenges as opportunities for growth, and forgiveness is your ability to let go of past grievances, freeing up mental and emotional space for a flourishing rebel spirit.

Openness to Change and Holistic Well-Being Embrace change as a natural part of personal evolution. As a moderate rebel, stay open to new approaches, recognizing the interconnectedness of physical, emotional, and mental well-being. The moderate rebel's holistic approach to well-being involves recognizing the harmony in the interconnected rebel facets.

In the moderate range, the rebel journey is about refinement and expansion. It's a dance of evolution, where each characteristic is a note in the symphony of personal growth. The moderate rebel is poised for greater heights, with the wisdom gained from navigating life's complex waters. Continue refining your rebel skills, for the journey unfolds in harmonious cadence.

Remember, building these characteristics is a rebellion, not a resignation. Be your unapologetic self, and let's transform those Moderate scores into a concert of personal growth. Your journey toward fine-tuning the Art of Authentic Living, sculpting your resilience, and dancing with emotional intelligence just got a lot more exhilarating. Let the symphony crescendo!

Average: Rocketing Resilience Elevation

So, you find yourself comfortably sailing the seas of Average (110 - 134), confidently steering your ship through the unpredictable currents of personal growth. Ahoy, rebel! Your odyssey through the Resilience Rhapsody, the Mindfulness Minuet, and the Integrity Improvisation has been nothing short of a triumph. You're not just hitting the right notes; you're composing a symphony of personal growth.

Your personal development playlist is harmonizing well, maybe a tweak here and there for that perfect resonance. You're not settling for mere happiness; you're crafting joy, thumbing your nose at despair with panache, and mastering the F*ck Budget for an unapologetic Festival of Elation. Envision yourself as the virtuoso of your joy orchestra, conquering the emotional landscape with an unapologetic defiance of negativity.

Let's dissect what this score range signifies for each key characteristic:

Adaptability   In the realm of adaptability, you're orchestrating a symphony of change. Challenges are your evolving melodies, and you, the conductor, adjust seamlessly to the shifting rhythms of life. The Average rebel's adaptability is a finely tuned instrument, making navigation through life's unpredictable waters a melodious endeavor.

Coping Skills   Coping skills for the Average rebel are a well-honed composition. Stressors are not enemies; they are opportunities for your rebel skills to shine. Your coping toolbox is filled with an array of instruments, each playing in harmony to create a resilient rebel anthem.

Inner Strength   The rebel fortress stands strong in the Average range. Inner strength is your sentinel, guarding against the onslaught of challenges. Challenges aren't obstacles; they are the raw materials for forging your inner resilience. The Average rebel endures with a fortitude that reverberates through the rebel symphony.

Tenacity, Courage, and Optimism   Tenacity for the Average rebel is a force that propels you forward. Challenges are like stages, and you, the performer, bring courage to every act. Optimism is not just a lens; it's the very air you breathe in the rebel symphony. Challenges are not threats; they are the verses that enrich the rebel song.

Proactivity and Growth Mindset   Proactivity in the Average range is a dance of initiative. You're not just responding to the rebel rhythm; you're setting it. A growth mindset is not a concept; it's a rebel philosophy. Challenges are not roadblocks; they are stepping stones to the higher notes in the rebel composition.

Resourcefulness and Stress Management   Resourcefulness for the Average rebel is an art. Creative solutions are not just found; they are crafted with precision. Stress management is not a reactive measure; it's a proactive art of orchestrating calm amidst the stormy rebel seas.

Ambiguity Tolerance and Self-Efficacy   Ambiguity is not a source of anxiety; it's the playground for the Average rebel. You navigate the unknown with a seasoned grace. Self-efficacy is not a distant concept; it's the foundation of your rebel tower. Challenges are not insurmountable; they are opportunities for showcasing your rebel prowess.

Cognitive Appraisal and Flexibility   Cognitive appraisal for the Average rebel is not just assessment; it's strategic analysis. Decisions are not mere choices; they are well-informed rebel strategies. Flexibility is not an occasional trait; it's the very backbone of your rebel composition, adapting to the evolving melodies of life.

Problem-Solving Skills and Emotional Regulation   Problem-solving for the Average rebel is not a task; it's an ongoing narrative. Complex problems are not roadblocks; they are the raw material for sculpting your rebel journey. Emotional regulation is not a reactive measure; it's a proactive stance in navigating the rebel emotional landscape.

Endurance, Acceptance of Failure, and Tolerance for Discomfort   Endurance is not just about persistence; it's about evolving through long-term challenges. Failure is not a setback; it's a classroom for the Average rebel, a space for continuous learning. Discomfort is not avoided; it's embraced as the forge for shaping the resilient rebel spirit.

Navigating Uncertainty and Patience   Navigating uncertainty for the Average rebel is not a daunting quest; it's an exploration. You traverse the seas of the unknown with curiosity and confidence. Patience is not just a virtue; it's your guiding star, leading the way through the complex rebel constellations.

Realistic Optimism and Long-Term Goal Focus   Optimism for the Average rebel is not blind positivity; it's a realistic perspective on the rebel journey. Challenges are not barriers; they are the stepping stones to your long-term rebel goals. The horizon is not a distant dream; it's a canvas for your deliberate rebel strokes.

Regulating Expectations, Mindset Shift, and Self-Compassion
Regulating expectations for the Average rebel is not about lowering standards; it's about aligning them with the rhythms of reality. Mindset shift is not an occasional occurrence; it's a constant evolution toward a more empowering rebel perspective. Self-compassion is not just kindness; it's a foundational pillar in the Average rebel's journey of self-discovery.

Self-Acceptance, Reframing Challenges, and Forgiveness
Self-acceptance for the Average rebel is not a destination; it's a continuous journey of embracing the evolving self. Challenges are not hurdles; they are opportunities for reframing and shaping the rebel narrative. Forgiveness is not just about others; it's a liberating act for the Average rebel's soul.

Openness to Change and Holistic Well-Being Openness to change for the Average rebel is not a passive stance; it's an active engagement with the ever-evolving rebel landscape. Holistic well-being is not a concept; it's a rebel philosophy that recognizes the interconnectedness of physical, emotional, and mental dimensions.

Staying Grounded and Respect for Boundaries Staying grounded for the Average rebel is not a choice; it's a deliberate act of maintaining perspective amid life's swirling currents. Respect for boundaries is not just a principle; it's a commitment to fostering healthy relationships, both with others and within the rebel self.

Empathy Towards Oneself Empathy toward oneself for the Average rebel is not a luxury; it's a fundamental aspect of the rebel journey. It's about extending the same understanding and compassion to oneself as one would to others.

In the Average range, the rebel is not standing still; you're in the midst of a dynamic dance. The rebel journey is not about perfection; it's about progress, and the Average range is a testament to the unfolding rebel symphony. Embrace the diversity of your rebel notes, for the journey continues, and the rebel crescendo awaits

Remember, building these characteristics is a rebellion, not a compromise. Be your unapologetic self, and let's turn those Average scores into a grand opus of personal growth. Your journey toward perfecting the Art of Bold Living, sculpting your authenticity, and dancing with emotional intelligence just got a lot more thrilling. Let the symphony play on!

Above Average: Resilience Excellence Unleashed

Brace yourself, rebel, as you navigate the above-average echelons (135 - 159) of personal growth mastery. Here you stand, steering through the swirling currents of resilience, mindfulness, and integrity with flair. Bravo! Your journey through the Fortissimo of Compassion, the Crescendo of Gratitude, and the Allegro of Empathy is nothing short of a virtuoso performance. You're not just hitting the right notes; you're conducting a symphony of personal growth.

Your personal growth playlist is orchestrating magnificently, perhaps a subtle crescendo here and there for that extra brilliance. You're not settling for mere joy; you're sculpting an unapologetic masterpiece of elation, flipping off misery with the finesse of a maestro and mastering the F*ck Budget for a Festival of Triumph. Picture yourself as the commander of your joy battalion, conquering the emotional landscape with a rebellious defiance against negativity.

Adaptability   In the realm of adaptability, the Above Average rebel is a masterful conductor navigating through life's intricate compositions. Changes are not hurdles; they are the dynamic notes adding richness to the rebel symphony. Your adaptability is not reactive; it's proactive, shaping the rebel journey with intentional strides.

Coping Skills   Coping skills for the Above Average rebel are a resilient fortress, standing strong amidst life's storms. Stressors are not threats; they are opportunities for your rebel resilience to shine. Your coping repertoire is not just varied; it's a dynamic ensemble, harmonizing with the ebb and flow of the rebel journey.

Inner Strength   In the realm of inner strength, the Above Average rebel is forging an unshakeable core. Challenges are not adversaries; they are raw materials for sculpting the resilient rebel spirit. Your inner strength is not just a reactive response; it's a proactive force that shapes the rebel narrative with unwavering fortitude.

Tenacity, Courage, and Optimism   Tenacity for the Above Average rebel is not just persistence; it's a determined march towards the rebel goals. Courage is not occasional bravery; it's a constant companion in the face of challenges. Optimism is not just a lens; it's the very atmosphere you breathe in the rebel symphony.

Proactivity and Growth Mindset   Proactivity in the Above Average range is a dance of initiative where you're not just responding to the rebel rhythm; you're setting it. A growth mindset is not a concept; it's a rebel philosophy where challenges are not roadblocks but opportunities for soaring higher in the rebel composition.

Resourcefulness and Stress Management Resourcefulness for the Above Average rebel is an art form. Creative solutions are not just found; they are crafted with precision and ingenuity. Stress management is not a reactive measure; it's a proactive art of orchestrating calm amidst the stormy rebel seas.

Ambiguity Tolerance and Self-Efficacy Ambiguity is not a source of anxiety for the Above Average rebel; it's a playground for exploration. You navigate the unknown with confidence and curiosity. Self-efficacy is not a distant concept; it's the very foundation of your rebel tower. Challenges are not insurmountable; they are opportunities for showcasing your rebel prowess.

Cognitive Appraisal and Flexibility Cognitive appraisal for the Above Average rebel is not just assessment; it's strategic analysis. Decisions are not mere choices; they are well-informed rebel strategies. Flexibility is not an occasional trait; it's the very backbone of your rebel composition, adapting to the evolving melodies of life.

Problem-Solving Skills and Emotional Regulation Problem-solving for the Above Average rebel is not a task; it's an ongoing narrative. Complex problems are not roadblocks; they are the raw material for sculpting your rebel journey. Emotional regulation is not a reactive measure; it's a proactive stance in navigating the rebel emotional landscape.

Endurance, Acceptance of Failure, and Tolerance for Discomfort Endurance for the Above Average rebel is not just about persistence; it's about evolving through long-term challenges. Failure is not a setback; it's a classroom for the rebel, a space for continuous learning. Discomfort is not avoided; it's embraced as the forge for shaping the resilient rebel spirit.

Navigating Uncertainty and Patience Navigating uncertainty for the Above Average rebel is not a daunting quest; it's an exploration. You traverse the seas of the unknown with confidence and a steady hand. Patience is not just a virtue; it's your guiding star, leading the way through the complex rebel constellations.

Realistic Optimism and Long-Term Goal Focus Optimism for the Above Average rebel is not blind positivity; it's a realistic perspective on the rebel journey. Challenges are not barriers; they are stepping stones to your long-term rebel goals. The horizon is not a distant dream; it's a canvas for your deliberate rebel strokes.

Regulating Expectations, Mindset Shift, and Self-Compassion Regulating expectations for the Above Average rebel is not about lowering standards; it's about aligning them with the rhythms of reality. Mindset shift is not an occasional occurrence; it's a constant evolution toward a more empowering rebel perspective. Self-compassion is not just kindness; it's a foundational pillar in the Above Average rebel's journey of self-discovery.

Self-Acceptance, Reframing Challenges, and Forgiveness Self-acceptance for the Above Average rebel is not a destination; it's a continuous journey of embracing the evolving self. Challenges are not hurdles; they are opportunities for reframing and shaping the rebel narrative. Forgiveness is not just about others; it's a liberating act for the Above Average rebel's soul.

Openness to Change and Holistic Well-Being Openness to change for the Above Average rebel is not a passive stance; it's an active engagement with the ever-evolving rebel landscape. Holistic well-being is not a concept; it's a rebel philosophy that recognizes the interconnectedness of physical, emotional, and mental dimensions.

Staying Grounded and Respect for Boundaries Staying grounded for the Above Average rebel is not a choice; it's a deliberate act of maintaining perspective amid life's swirling currents. Respect for boundaries is not just a principle; it's a commitment to fostering healthy relationships, both with others and within the rebel self.

Empathy Towards Oneself Empathy toward oneself for the Above Average rebel is not a luxury; it's a fundamental aspect of the rebel journey. It's about extending the same understanding and compassion to oneself as one would to others.

In the Above Average range, the rebel is not standing still; you're in the midst of a dynamic dance. The rebel journey is not about perfection; it's about progress, and the Above Average range is a testament to the unfolding rebel symphony. Embrace the diversity of your rebel notes, for the journey continues, and the rebel crescendo awaits.

Remember, building these characteristics is a rebellion, not a compromise. Be your unapologetic self, and let's elevate those Above Average scores into a grand symphony of personal growth. Your journey toward perfecting the Art of Fearless Living, sculpting your authenticity, and dancing with emotional intelligence just got a lot more exhilarating. Let the symphony play on!"

High: Peak Resilience Mastery Strategies

Here you are, riding the waves of the high (160 - 172) personal growth seas like a rebellious virtuoso. Stand tall, maestro! Your journey through the crescendo of Emotional Mastery, the opulence of Purposeful Living, and the bold notes of Unwavering Integrity is a performance that demands a standing ovation. Bravo! You're not merely navigating the storms; you're orchestrating a grand symphony of personal growth.

Your personal growth playlist is not just music; it's a sonorous proclamation of triumph. You're not chasing joy; you're sculpting an unapologetic epic of jubilation, giving despair a triumphant middle finger and mastering the F*ck Budget for an Extravaganza of Glee. Picture yourself as the commander of your joy armada, conquering the emotional landscape with a rebellious anthem against negativity.

Adaptability   In the realm of adaptability, the High-scoring individual is a virtuoso conductor of change. Adaptability is not a skill; it's a way of life. Change is not a disruption; it's a dynamic note in the orchestrated symphony of the reader's journey.

Coping Skills   Coping skills for the High-scoring individual are not just mechanisms; they are an arsenal of resilience. Stressors are not threats; they are opportunities for the reader's coping symphony to showcase its brilliance. The repertoire is not just varied; it's a dynamic ensemble, harmonizing seamlessly with the ebb and flow of life.

Inner Strength   In the realm of inner strength, the High-scoring reader is forging an unshakeable core. Challenges are not adversaries; they are raw materials for sculpting the resilient spirit. Inner strength is not just a reactive response; it's a proactive force that shapes the narrative with unwavering fortitude.

Tenacity, Courage, and Optimism   Tenacity, courage, and optimism for the High-scoring individual are not occasional traits; they are the very fabric of their being. Tenacity is not just persistence; it's a determined march towards goals. Courage is not occasional bravery; it's a constant companion in the face of challenges. Optimism is not just a lens; it's the very atmosphere they breathe.

Proactivity and Growth Mindset   Proactivity for the High-scoring individual is not just taking initiative; it's setting the rhythm of their own journey. A growth mindset is not a concept; it's a philosophy where challenges are not roadblocks but opportunities for soaring higher in the symphony of life.

Resourcefulness and Stress Management   Resourcefulness for the High-scoring individual is an art form. Creative solutions are not just found; they are crafted with precision and ingenuity. Stress management is not a reactive measure; it's a proactive art of orchestrating calm amidst the stormy seas of life.

Ambiguity Tolerance and Self-Efficacy   Ambiguity is not a source of anxiety for the High-scoring reader; it's a playground for exploration. They navigate the unknown with confidence and curiosity. Self-efficacy is not a distant concept; it's the very foundation of their journey. Challenges are not insurmountable; they are opportunities for showcasing their prowess.

Cognitive Appraisal and Flexibility   Cognitive appraisal for the High-scoring individual is not just assessment; it's strategic analysis. Decisions are not mere choices; they are well-informed strategies. Flexibility is not an occasional trait; it's the very backbone of their journey, adapting to the evolving melodies of life.

Problem-Solving Skills and Emotional Regulation   Problem-solving for the High-scoring reader is not a task; it's an ongoing narrative. Complex problems are not roadblocks; they are the raw material for sculpting their journey. Emotional regulation is not a reactive measure; it's a proactive stance in navigating the emotional landscape.

Endurance, Acceptance of Failure, and Tolerance for Discomfort   Endurance for the High-scoring individual is not just about persistence; it's about evolving through long-term challenges. Failure is not a setback; it's a classroom, a space for continuous learning. Discomfort is not avoided; it's embraced as the forge for shaping the resilient spirit.

Navigating Uncertainty and Patience   Navigating uncertainty for the High-scoring reader is not a daunting quest; it's an exploration. They traverse the seas of the unknown with confidence and a steady hand. Patience is not just a virtue; it's their guiding star, leading the way through the complex constellations of life.

Realistic Optimism and Long-Term Goal Focus   Optimism for the High-scoring individual is not blind positivity; it's a realistic perspective on the journey. Challenges are not barriers; they are stepping stones to long-term goals. The horizon is not a distant dream; it's a canvas for their deliberate strokes.

Regulating Expectations, Mindset Shift, and Self-Compassion Regulating expectations for the High-scoring individual is not about lowering standards; it's about aligning them with the rhythms of reality. Mindset shift is not an occasional occurrence; it's a constant evolution toward a more empowering perspective. Self-compassion is not just kindness; it's a foundational principle in their journey of personal growth.

Self-Acceptance and Reframing Challenges Self-acceptance for the High-scoring reader is not resignation; it's a celebration of individuality. Challenges are not hurdles; they are opportunities for reframing and shaping the narrative. Forgiveness is not just about others; it's a liberating act for the High-scoring individual's soul.

Openness to Change and Holistic Well-Being Openness to change for the High-scoring individual is not a passive stance; it's an active engagement with the ever-evolving landscape. Holistic well-being is not a concept; it's a philosophy that recognizes the interconnectedness of physical, emotional, and mental dimensions.

Staying Grounded and Respect for Boundaries Staying grounded for the High-scoring individual is not a choice; it's a deliberate act of maintaining perspective amid life's swirling currents. Respect for boundaries is not just a principle; it's a commitment to fostering healthy relationships, both with others and within the High-scoring individual's self.

Empathy Towards Oneself Empathy toward oneself for the High-scoring individual is not a luxury; it's a fundamental aspect of their journey. It's about extending the same understanding and compassion to oneself as one would to others.

In the High range, the individual is not standing still; they're in the midst of a dynamic dance. The journey is not about perfection; it's about progress, and the High range is a testament to the unfolding symphony of resilience and personal growth. Embrace the diversity of your notes, for the journey continues, and the crescendo awaits.

Remember, building these characteristics is a rebellion, not a concession. Be your unapologetic self, and let's amplify those High scores into a majestic symphony of personal growth. Your journey toward perfecting the Art of Fearless Living, sculpting your authenticity, and dancing with emotional intelligence just turned into a grand gala. Let the symphony resonate!

Exceptional: Epic Mastery of Resilience Unveiled

Congratulations, you stand atop the summit of personal growth, wearing the crown of an exceptional (173 - 175) rebel. Bow down, world, to the maestro of authenticity, the grandmaster of emotional intelligence, and the virtuoso of resilience. Your journey through the zenith of Unshakable Integrity, the ethereal realms of Purposeful Existence, and the extraordinary mastery of Emotional Brilliance is not just a saga; it's a legendary tale.

Your personal growth playlist isn't just music; it's a magnum opus. You're not chasing joy; you're conducting a celestial orchestra of jubilation, giving despair a triumphant middle finger and mastering the F*ck Budget for an unparalleled Extravaganza of Bliss. Picture yourself as the sovereign of your joy empire, reigning over the emotional landscape with an anthem of rebellion against negativity.

Adaptability   For the reader in the Exceptional range, adaptability is not merely a skill; it's an art form. Change is not a disruption; it's a canvas for their masterpiece. Every twist and turn is an opportunity to showcase their exceptional prowess in orchestrating life's dynamic symphony.

Coping Skills   Coping skills for the Exceptional reader are not just mechanisms; they are a symphony of resilience. Stressors are not threats; they are compositions waiting to be harmonized. The Exceptional reader navigates challenges with a grace that transcends coping—it's a performance of mastery.

Inner Strength   In the realm of inner strength, the Exceptional reader has forged an unshakeable core that doesn't just endure challenges; it transforms them. Challenges are not adversaries; they are raw materials for sculpting the narrative with unwavering fortitude. Inner strength is not just reactive; it's a proactive force shaping destinies.

Tenacity, Courage, and Optimism   Tenacity, courage, and optimism for the Exceptional reader are not occasional traits; they are the very heartbeat of their journey. Tenacity is not just persistence; it's a relentless pursuit of purpose. Courage is not occasional bravery; it's a constant companion in the face of challenges. Optimism is not just a lens; it's the vibrant spectrum through which they perceive the world.

Proactivity and Growth Mindset Proactivity for the Exceptional reader is not just taking initiative; it's setting the rhythm of their own journey. A growth mindset is not a concept; it's the air they breathe, infusing every challenge with the potential for monumental growth. Challenges are not roadblocks; they are opportunities for soaring higher in the symphony of life.

Resourcefulness and Stress Management Resourcefulness for the Exceptional reader is an art form. Creative solutions are not just found; they are crafted with precision and ingenuity. Stress management is not a reactive measure; it's a proactive art of orchestrating calm amidst the stormy seas of life.

Ambiguity Tolerance and Self-Efficacy Ambiguity is not a source of anxiety for the Exceptional reader; it's a playground for exploration. They navigate the unknown with confidence and curiosity. Self-efficacy is not a distant concept; it's the very foundation of their journey. Challenges are not insurmountable; they are opportunities for showcasing their prowess.

Cognitive Appraisal and Flexibility Cognitive appraisal for the Exceptional reader is not just assessment; it's strategic analysis. Decisions are not mere choices; they are well-informed strategies. Flexibility is not an occasional trait; it's the very backbone of their journey, adapting to the evolving melodies of life.

Problem-Solving Skills and Emotional Regulation Problem-solving for the Exceptional reader is not a task; it's an ongoing narrative. Complex problems are not roadblocks; they are the raw material for sculpting their journey. Emotional regulation is not a reactive measure; it's a proactive stance in navigating the emotional landscape.

Endurance, Acceptance of Failure, and Tolerance for Discomfort   Endurance for the Exceptional reader is not just about persistence; it's about evolving through long-term challenges. Failure is not a setback; it's a classroom, a space for continuous learning. Discomfort is not avoided; it's embraced as the forge for shaping the resilient spirit.

Navigating Uncertainty and Patience   Navigating uncertainty for the Exceptional reader is not a daunting quest; it's an exploration. They traverse the seas of the unknown with confidence and a steady hand. Patience is not just a virtue; it's their guiding star, leading the way through the complex constellations of life.

Realistic Optimism and Long-Term Goal Focus   Optimism for the Exceptional reader is not blind positivity; it's a realistic perspective on the journey. Challenges are not barriers; they are stepping stones to long-term goals. The horizon is not a distant dream; it's a canvas for their deliberate strokes.

Regulating Expectations, Mindset Shift, and Self-Compassion   Regulating expectations for the Exceptional reader is not about lowering standards; it's about aligning them with the rhythms of reality. Mindset shift is not an occasional occurrence; it's a constant evolution toward a more empowering perspective. Self-compassion is not just kindness; it's a foundational principle in their journey of personal growth.

Self-Acceptance and Reframing Challenges   Self-acceptance for the Exceptional reader is not resignation; it's a celebration of individuality. Challenges are not hurdles; they are opportunities for reframing and shaping the narrative. Forgiveness is not just about others; it's a liberating act for the Exceptional individual's soul.

Openness to Change and Holistic Well-Being   Openness to change for the Exceptional individual is not a passive stance; it's an active engagement with the ever-evolving landscape. Holistic well-being is not a concept; it's a philosophy that recognizes the interconnectedness of physical, emotional, and mental dimensions.

Staying Grounded and Respect for Boundaries   Staying grounded for the Exceptional individual is not a choice; it's a deliberate act of maintaining perspective amid life's swirling currents. Respect for boundaries is not just a principle; it's a commitment to fostering healthy relationships, both with others and within the Exceptional individual's self.

Empathy Towards Oneself   Empathy toward oneself for the Exceptional individual is not a luxury; it's a fundamental aspect of their journey. It's about extending the same understanding and compassion to oneself as one would to others.

In the Exceptional range, the individual is not standing still; they're in the midst of a dynamic dance. The journey is not about perfection; it's about progress, and the Exceptional range is a testament to the unfolding symphony of resilience and personal growth. Embrace the diversity of your notes, for the journey continues, and the crescendo awaits.

Remember, building these characteristics is a rebellion, not a surrender. Be your unapologetic self, and let's elevate those Exceptional scores into a cosmic symphony of personal growth. Your journey toward mastering the Art of Fearless Living, sculpting authenticity with unmatched finesse, and dancing with emotional brilliance just transformed into a celestial carnival. Let the symphony echo through eternity!

Knowing When to Reassess

Your emotional resilience is not cast in stone; it's a dynamic force waiting to be honed and refined. Reassessing your true self is not just an act of reflection; it's a strategic move in your quest for unapologetic growth. Here's your compass for navigating the seas of reassessment:

Significant Life Changes   Major life events alter the course of your rebellion. A new job, a union, or even a tiny rebel-in-the-making. If life's throwing curveballs, it might be time to recalibrate your rebellion compass.

Long-Term Growth Efforts   If you've been grinding in the rebellion gym—lifting emotional weights and running resilience marathons—it's prime time to check the progress. Assess if your rebellious muscles have flexed and grown.

Post-Adversity Reflection   After weathering storms of challenges, pause to reflect on your rebellion performance. Did you ride those waves like a seasoned captain, or was it a bit of a shipwreck? Time to assess and evolve.

Self-Perception Misalignment   If your gut rebels against your previous assessment, trust it. Emotional evolution may be knocking at the door. Feelings misaligned? Consider this your rebel wake-up call.

Desire for Further Growth   Your rebellion is a dynamic beast, always hungry for more. If the hunger persists, it's time for another feast of self-assessment. The desire for more is the anthem of the unapologetic rebel.

Navigating the Waters of Reassessment:

1. **Reflect on Your Journey.** Acknowledge the storms and calm waters alike. Your journey shapes your rebellion. This reflection sets the stage for the next chapter.
2. **Choose an Optimal Time.** No tempests, no thunderstorms. Reassess when your rebellion sails in calm waters. A clear assessment demands a clear sky.
3. **Repeat the Assessment.** Dive back into the questionnaire with honesty. Your current emotional state deserves an unfiltered portrayal.
4. **Consider Your Growth.** Celebrate progress like it's a fiesta. Every uptick in resilience is a testament to your unyielding dedication to personal growth.
5. **Embrace Tailored Strategies.** Your reassessment is the treasure map. Follow the strategies tailored to your

current level. This ensures you're well-equipped for the next challenges.

> **Author's Note** Embrace setbacks as the spicy salsa of personal growth, adding flavor and depth to your journey. Every downtick in resilience is not a stumble; it's a salsa dip—a moment to pause, reflect, and then dive back into the fiesta of progress. In the dance of personal development, every step counts, whether forward or in a temporary sidestep. Your resilience, even in moments of challenge, is a beat in the rhythm of your remarkable journey. So, when the salsa gets a bit too spicy, know that you're still in the midst of a vibrant and unapologetic celebration of growth.

Remember, your rebellion is a dynamic symphony. Reassessing isn't about judgment; it's a celebration of your resilience evolution. The sea of self-discovery is boundless—sail fearlessly and unapologetically into the uncharted waters of your journey.

Achieving a New, Higher Level of Irreverent Resilience

Realizing that your irreverence has transcended to a different, higher level is like stumbling upon the pot of gold in the labyrinth of personal growth and audacity. Here's a no-nonsense guide to navigating this uncharted territory:

1. **Flip the Bird to Mediocrity** Revel in your achievement! Give a rebellious nod to the effort and sheer audacity you've invested in developing your irreverence. This acknowledgment sets the stage for a raucous celebration of your continued growth.
2. **Embrace the Chaos** Consider this shift as an opportunity for a more epic rebellion. Your current level is

a bold statement of your ongoing audacity, signifying your audacious capacity for continuous growth.

3. **Upgrade Your Irreverence Arsenal** Armed with newfound insights into your irreverence, customize your strategies to match your current level of audacity. Focus on refining specific characteristics and skills that are most relevant to your upgraded range.

4. **Set Epic Goals** Establish fresh, audacious goals that resonate with your updated level of irreverence. These objectives will guide your ongoing efforts and serve as a middle finger to mediocrity.

5. **Sustain the Rebellion** Maintain a regular practice of activities and techniques that support your irreverence. Consistency is key in solidifying your progress and adapting to your new level of audacity.

6. **Raise a Glass to Your Rebellion** Take a moment to reflect on how far you've come. Consider the obstacles you've kicked in the audacious teeth and the lessons you've thrown back at life. This reflection reinforces your sense of accomplishment and audacity.

7. **Summon Your Allies** Engage with fellow rebels, mentors, or a community of audacious souls who can provide encouragement and valuable insights tailored to your new level. Their guidance can be instrumental in your continued audacious evolution.

8. **Stay Open to Further Anarchy** Acknowledge that irreverence is a dynamic quality. Remain open to the possibility of further audacious evolution and be receptive to new strategies and approaches. In the rebellion against normalcy, there's always room for more chaos.

Specific Guidance related to Step 3, Upgrading Your Irreverence Arsenal:

- **Elevating from Subversive to Snarky** If you're transitioning from a subversive rebel to a snarky provocateur, it's a significant leap. Celebrate your audacious progress and recognize that you're constructing a more robust foundation. Dive into the strategies tailored for snarky rebellion to keep your growth rolling.

- **Gradual Ascent from Snarky to Outrageous** Transitioning from snarky to outrageous indicates a steady ascent. Acknowledge your audacious feats and put into action the strategies for outrageous rebellion. Consistency and an irreverent mindset will contribute to further outrage.

- **Soaring from Outrageous to Legendary** Reaching legendary status reflects your dedication and effectiveness in challenging the status quo. Continue refining your strategies, and consider taking on more audacious challenges to further strengthen your rebellion. Follow the strategies for legendary audacity.

Remember, your irreverence is a dynamic quality that can be further cultivated. Use this reassessment as a tool to continue your journey towards even greater levels of audacity and personal excellence. Let the rebellion continue!

Navigating Diminished Audacity

Finding yourself in the trenches of diminished audacity is like stumbling into a chaotic mosh pit at a rebellious concert. It's disorienting, and you might feel like you're crowd-surfing through emotional turmoil. Fear not, for even the most audacious rebels face moments when their middle finger to the norm temporarily loses its fervor. Here's your guide to flipping off the decline and reclaiming your raucous resilience:

- **Raise the Flag** Acknowledge the pit you've found yourself in without judgment. Everyone experiences a wild stage dive into the abyss from time to time. It's just part of the rebellious gig.

- **Decipher the Audacity Codes** Reflect on the potential triggers or factors that hurled you into this abyss. It's like decoding the rebellious Morse code of your emotions. Self-awareness is your backstage pass to understanding what needs a bit of mosh pit crowd control.

- **Summon the Council** Reach out to fellow rebels, mentors, or a trusted friend who understands the wild rhythms of your audacity. They can offer insights and strategies to help you navigate the mosh pit of challenges.

- **Dust off the Playbook** Revisit the strategies and techniques that once had you crowd-surfing on the waves of audacity. Identify the anthems that resonated the most and throw them back into your routine. Refer to the appropriate section related to your current scores for guidance.

- **Stage Dive into New Approaches** In addition to your classic hits, be open to exploring new audacious tunes. Mindfulness practices, stress-reduction techniques, or other strategies could be the punk rock beats your resilience needs.

- **Set Fire to Realistic Expectations** Understand that rebuilding audacity isn't an overnight encore. Set realistic goals for yourself, celebrating each punk riff of victory along the way.

- **Embrace Self-Rebellion** Be as kind to yourself as you would be to a fellow rebel crowd-surfing through a tough gig. Avoid self-blame; remember, even punk rock icons hit a few off chords now and then.

- **Fuel the Engine** Prioritize self-care activities that fuel your physical, emotional, and mental mosh pit endurance. Sleep, balanced nutrition, exercise, and relaxation techniques are your backstage passes to resilience.

- **Mosh Pit Journaling** Reflect on the chaos, emotions, and progress. Journaling is your punk rock zine for gaining clarity, processing feelings, and tracking your journey back to audacious glory.

- **Call in the Audacious Medics** If navigating the mosh pit feels like a stage dive without a crowd, consider consulting a mental health professional. They're the mosh pit medics with specialized guidance to get your rebellious spirit crowd-surfing again.

Remember, this decline in audacity is a temporary encore break, and with dedication and a proactive approach, you'll be back in the rebellious spotlight in no time. The mosh pit of life awaits your triumphant return!

Epilogue: Unleashing the Rebel Within

The journey you've embarked upon, culminating in a deeper understanding and refinement of your resilience, mirrors the path of a rebel forging through uncharted territories. While our dialogue dances with irreverence, the assessment you've encountered is a meticulously crafted beacon, illuminating your pathway to navigate life's tumultuous seas with the agility of a seasoned pirate steering through a storm.

Your exploration into the realm of resilience has revealed a kaleidoscope of attributes and capabilities, from the precision of emotional archery to maintaining equilibrium on life's unpredictable waves, and from the art of camouflaging vulnerabilities to the strategic mastery of chess-like decision-making. The scores you've achieved serve as a mirror, reflecting your current stance on this diverse spectrum, pinpointing fortitudes, and identifying realms ripe for cultivation.

Armed with your assessment outcome, you've been equipped with tailored strategies aimed at fortifying your resilience and enhancing your rebel spirit. These strategies are your compass and map, guiding your continuous journey toward resilience mastery. Remember, cultivating the prowess of a resilience-infused rebel is a continuous voyage, meriting patience, persistence, and celebration of every milestone achieved.

We understand the importance of a robust scientific foundation in assessments like these. Our assessment underwent rigorous testing and validation to ensure its reliability and accuracy. The backbone of our assessment is solidified by a foundation rooted in rigorous scientific inquiry and comprehensive data analysis, spanning extensive surveys, in-depth interviews, and cutting-edge research within the domains of resilience and emotional agility. The scoring spectrum, from 35 to 175, was meticulously calibrated through statistical examination to ensure a meaningful framework for interpretation, reflecting the broad range of resilience observed across individuals. Our methodology was reviewed, and feedback from a diverse sample group was incorporated into its final form.

For those who find themselves in the higher echelons of the scoring range, your embodiment of resilience and emotional agility is commendable. You are poised to be a beacon of inspiration, encouraging those in your wake. Your exceptional resilience is not just a personal triumph but a beacon for collective upliftment. Continue to hone your skills, for in growth and transformation, the journey never truly ends.

As you walk the rebel's path, know this: setbacks are mere speed bumps in the highway of your growth. Embrace them, conquer them, and let them be the stepping stones to your rebel legacy. Your commitment to this journey is a testament to your dedication to personal and professional growth.

Let your rebellion resonate, not just as a whisper but as a roar across the landscapes of success, authenticity, and fulfillment. Remain fearless, remain unwavering, and may the essence of your rebellion reverberate, leaving an indelible mark on the canvas of life. Keep your spirit audacious, your resolve unyielding, and let the world witness the magnitude of your inner rebel's roar.

Afterword for the Book: Dear Rebels, Seekers, and Fellow Architects of a Life Well-Lived...

As we wrap up this wild ride through the labyrinth of personal growth and the rebellious art of giving a f*ck that truly matters, I'm buzzing with gratitude for having you alongside me in this adventure. I trust these insights and irreverent musings have stirred something profound within you, setting ablaze the flames of your ongoing odyssey of self-discovery.

Remember, this expedition isn't a solitary trek but a frenzied dance in which we all play a part. Your uniqueness, your quirks, and your rebellious spirit are the secret ingredients in this cosmic concoction of existence. As you continue navigating the unpredictable terrain of life, embrace the chaos, nurture the rebellion within, and be the catalyst inspiring those around you to join the dance.

Lead with a heart that beats to the rhythm of compassion, a mind that questions the norms, and an unapologetic commitment to crafting your unique version of excellence. Amidst this adventure of personal growth, may you stumble upon moments of impact that leave echoes through the hallways of your existence.

This isn't a farewell; it's a 'keep rocking on' as you chart your own path in this mad symphony we call life. Never forget, life's too damn short to give a fck about everything. But when it's time to conclude this chapter, rest assured—you chose your fcks with purpose, contributing to the masterpiece of a fckwell-lived existence. Your intentional fcks have woven a legacy that'll reverberate through the corridors of time. This isn't just a conclusion; it's a raucous celebration of a life lived unapologetically.

With the wildest regards,

William R. Stanek

About the Author: William R. Stanek

Meet the maestro of mayhem, the disruptor of the dull, and the unsung hero of sanity in the corporate circus. Renowned rebel, bestseller extraordinaire, and your unlikely guide to unf*cking your existence.

Biography

In the chaos-drenched world of personal growth, our audacious author has strutted through the mayhem, giving the middle finger to conventional norms. With a history that's more punk rock than polished executive, this rebel maestro of personal growth has been stirring up a whirlwind of radical change for decades.

A significant chunk of this maverick's journey unfolded against the backdrop of a lifetime filled with more twists and turns than a rollercoaster designed by chaos theorists. From surviving the absurdities of personal revolutions to conquering the intricacies of radical authenticity, our irreverent guide has mastered the art of thriving in life's most unpredictable moments. Excelling in the school of hard knocks, he's not just weathered storms; he's danced in the rain, making the most out of every misstep.

In roles ranging from tech disruptor to chaos conductor, he became the go-to sage, the unsung hero called upon when everything seemed to be falling apart. More often than not, he discovered that the heart of many seemingly insurmountable problems wasn't in the complexities of life but in our twisted relationship with personal growth.

Over the years, our iconoclast has earned a rep that's legendary among rebels, misfits, and anyone tired of the same old self-help fluff. His work has become synonymous with unfiltered wisdom, earning him the tagline, "the anarchist in the realms of self-improvement." Those in the know recognize his distinct lack of pretense, safeguarding his insights from those wanting to slap a corporate label on his punk ethos.

Operating with a flair that matches his ability to guide everyday rebels, he orchestrated radical shifts behind the scenes, the impact of his counsel rippling through living rooms and coffee shops worldwide. His influence was infectious, leaving an unmistakable mark on the journey to unf*cked-up living for countless individuals.

In this book, he steps into the spotlight, flipping the bird to the conventional gurus and generously sharing his unconventional wisdom with a broader audience. His journey, marked by audacity, wisdom, and an unwavering commitment to unorthodox growth, serves as a raucous roadmap for rebels of every stripe. It is a testament to the transformative power of personal rebellion, a holistic approach that embraces chaos, authenticity, and, of course, a healthy dose of irreverence.

Show Some Irreverent Love

Congrats, Rebel! You've just adopted a piece of unfiltered wisdom into your life. Now, let's spread the chaos, shall we?

Did this book kick your apathy in the rear or make you rethink your life choices? Awesome! Don't keep it to yourself. Here are some guerrilla tactics to spread the word:

- **Revolt on Your Blog**   Channel your inner rebel and let your thoughts loose on your blog. Unleash the chaos, and let your readers know why this book is a total game-changer.

- **Sabotage Online Reviews**   Head to your favorite online store and wreak havoc—write a review that screams, "This book will mess you up, in the best way possible."

- **Insurrection on Social Media**   Hit up your friends on Facebook, Twitter, or any digital battlefield you fancy. Post about the book, and make sure your rebellion goes viral.

- **Tweet Like There's No Tomorrow**   Craft 280 characters of pure anarchy and tweet about how this book gave your existence a makeover. Don't forget to use the book's hashtag, **#Unf*ckYourExistence**.

Stay in Touch, Rebel to Rebel:

Our author isn't just a literary renegade; he's a master of chaos in other realms too. Connect with him and witness the rebellion unfold:

- **Linkedin Lunacy**   Dive into the abyss of professional rebellion on Linkedin. Follow the author for updates that will surely keep your career in a perpetual state of chaos.

https://www.linkedin.com/in/williamstanek/

- **Facebook Frenzy**   Embrace the pandemonium on Facebook. Like his page for a daily dose of irreverent wisdom and updates that'll make you question everything.

http://www.facebook.com/William.Stanek.Author

- **Twitter Turmoil**   If you're into bite-sized chaos, follow him on Twitter. Expect tweets that are more explosive than a shaken soda can.

http://www.twitter.com/WilliamStanek

William R. Stanek (http://www.williamrstanek.com)

Artistic Rebellion Unleashed:

Our author isn't just about words; he's a visual maestro too. Get a taste of his artistic chaos by checking out his online portfolio. It's a riot of images that will mess with your perception in the best possible way. Explore the madness at https://360studios.pictorem.com.

Remember, in the world of personal growth, the rebellion is real. Keep the chaos alive! Stay Unf*cked!

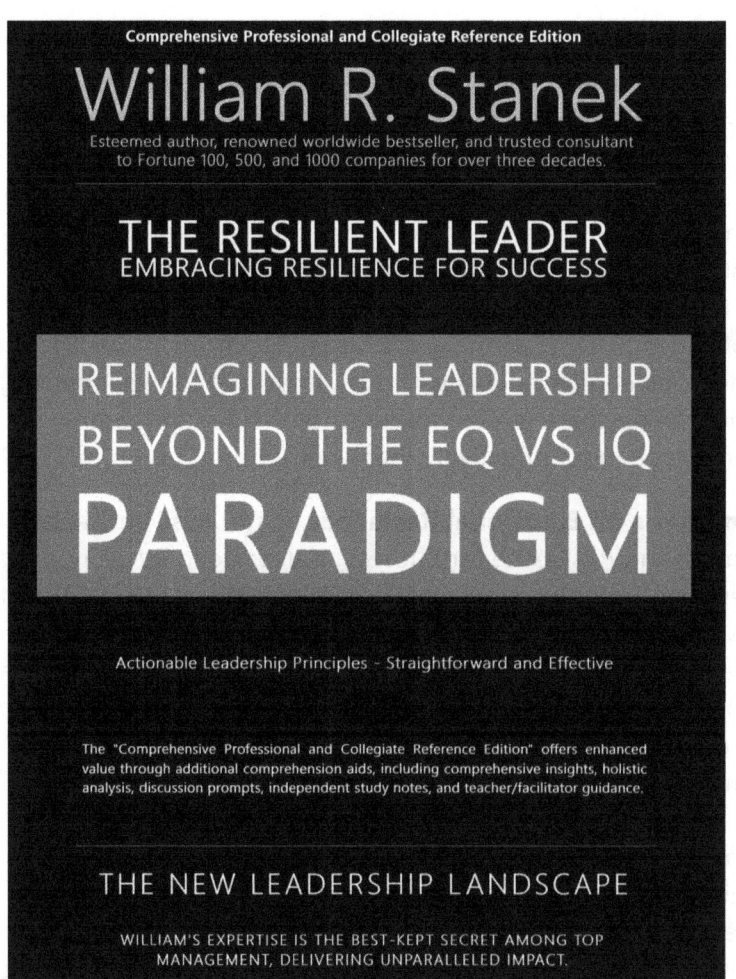

"The Resilient Leader, Embracing Resilience for Success" **stands out in the crowded landscape of leadership and emotional intelligence books by offering a fresh, holistic approach to leadership that transcends traditional models. This groundbreaking work by William R. Stanek redefines the essence of effective leadership in the modern era, distinguishing itself through several key differentiators:**

- **Holistic Integration of Multiple Intelligences**   While most leadership books focus on emotional intelligence (EQ) or traditional cognitive intelligence (IQ), "The Resilient Leader, Embracing Resilience for Success" introduces readers to the 8 Pillars of Leadership. This innovative framework encompasses Emotional Resilience, Creative Intelligence, Practical Intelligence, Cultural Intelligence, Intrapersonal Intelligence, Interpersonal Intelligence, Ethical Intelligence, and Analytical Intelligence. By embracing a broader spectrum of intelligences, the book equips leaders with a multifaceted toolkit, enabling them to navigate the complexities of the contemporary landscape more effectively than ever before.

- **Emphasis on Emotional Resilience**   "The Resilient Leader, Embracing Resilience for Success" delves deep into emotional resilience, offering readers actionable strategies to cultivate this essential trait. The book presents emotional resilience as the bedrock of leadership excellence, enabling leaders to withstand challenges, adapt to change, thrive in adversity, and so much more. Whereas most literature on emotional intelligence or emotional resilience treats resilience as a narrow set of traits or a subset of emotional intelligence, "The Resilient Leader, Embracing Resilience for Success" reconceptualizes it as a multifaceted intelligence in its own right. This book goes far beyond the typical definitions and presents emotional resilience as a complex, dynamic intelligence that is critical for effective leadership.

- **Rigorous Self-Assessment Tool**   Distinct from other leadership books that offer generalized advice, "The Resilient Leader, Embracing Resilience for Success" integrates a cutting-edge self-assessment tool. This personalized assessment allows readers to evaluate their strengths and areas for growth, providing a tailored roadmap for personal and professional development. This actionable, data-driven approach ensures that readers can make concrete progress on their leadership journey.

- **Case Studies and Real-World Application**   While many books on leadership and emotional intelligence rely on theoretical principles, "The Resilient Leader, Embracing Resilience for Success" grounds its insights in practical reality. Through a series of detailed case studies featuring real-world scenarios and leadership challenges, the book illustrates how the principles of resilient leadership can be applied in various contexts. From crisis management in the financial sector to navigating complex mergers and leading through global pandemics, these case studies offer readers a window into the transformative power of resilient leadership in action.

- **Future-Oriented Leadership Vision**   Stanek's book critically examines the evolution of leadership theories and practices, from ancient times through the industrial revolution to the present day, offering a visionary outlook on the future of leadership. Unlike books that dwell on past or current leadership models, "The Resilient Leader, Embracing Resilience for Success" charts a course for the future, advocating for a comprehensive, adaptable leadership approach that meets the demands of an ever-changing world. This forward-thinking perspective encourages leaders to not only adapt to the new normal but to thrive within it, paving the way for a new era of leadership excellence.

In summary, "The Resilient Leader, Embracing Resilience for Success" offers a unique, comprehensive guide that goes beyond traditional leadership tenets, providing readers with the insights and tools needed to excel in today's dynamic environment. By combining a holistic view of intelligence, a focus on emotional resilience, practical tools for self-assessment, real-world applicability, and a visionary leadership approach, this book is an essential resource for anyone looking to lead effectively in the 21st century.

https://www.amazon.com/dp/B0CPQ96ZSN